LET THEM EAT GRASS
THE 1862 SIOUX UPRISING IN MINNESOTA

Volume One

SMOKE

Other John Koblas titles from North Star Press:

F. Scott Fitzgerald in Minnesota: Toward the Summit (1996)
The Jesse James Northfield Raid: Confessions of the Ninth Man (1999)
J.J. Dickison: Swamp Fox of the Confederacy (2000)
Willow River: A Father Copes with Divorce and Nature (2000)
Jesse James Ate Here (2001)
When the Heavens Fell: The Youngers in Stillwater Prison (2002)
The Great Cole Younger & Frank James Historical Wild West Show (2002)
Robbers of the Rails: The Sontag Boys of Minnesota (2003)
The Swamp Fox and the Columbine (2003)
H.V. Jones: A Newspaperman's Imprint on Minneapolis History (2003)
Bushwhacker!: Cole Younger & the Kansas-Missouri Border War (2004)
The Last Outlaw: The Life of Pat Crowe (2005)
Minnesota Grit: The Men Who Defeated the James-Younger Gang (2005)
Jesse James in Iowa (2006)

Coming Soon:
Let Them Eat Grass, Volume II: Fire (2007)
Let Them Eat Grass, Volume III: Ashes (2007)
"Ma":The Life and Times of "Ma" Barker and Her Boys (2007)
The Kidder Massacre: Prelude to the Little Big Horn (2007)

In the Doc and Tweed History Mystery series for middle readers:

Peril at Pig's-Eye Cave (2004)
The Return of Jesse James (2005)
The F. Scott Fitzgerald Caper (2005)

Coming Soon:
The Benedict Arnold Cipher (2006)
Mayhem on the Mississippi Mile (2007)
The Phantom of the North Shore (2007)

Let Them Eat Grass

The 1862 Sioux Uprising in Minnesota

Volume One

Smoke

John Koblas

NORTH STAR PRESS OF ST. CLOUD, INC.
St. Cloud, Minnesota

Cover Art: Jon Arfstrom

Copyright © 2006 John Koblas

ISBN: 0-87839-238-6

First Edition, October 2006

Printed in the United States of America by Versa Press, Inc.,
East Peoria, Illinois

Published by
North Star Press of St. Cloud, Inc.
P.O. Box 451
St. Cloud, Minnesota 56302

northstarpress.com

Dedication

For Wally Baardson
Heart and Soul of the Magpies

Acknowledgments

The author wishes to thank the following persons and organizations, who took the time and energy to share research materials for inclusion in this volume. Without their valuable assistance, this project could not have come to fruition: Bob Burgess, Darla Gebhard, and Mary Murphy, Brown County Historical Society, New Ulm, Minnesota; Caryl Busman, Murray County Historical Society, Slayton, Minnesota; Jim Davis, North Dakota Historical Society, Bismarck, North Dakota; Alice Dewitz, Kidder County Historical Society, Steele, North Dakota; Dan Fjeld, Lower Sioux Agency Historic Site, Morton, Minnesota; Evan Kelley, Dakota County Library, Eagan, Minnesota; Randy Kvam and Carl Nelson, Fort Ridgely State Historic Site, Fairfax, Minnesota; Deborah Nelson and Sara Syverson, Biebl, Ranweiler, Christiansen, Meyer, Thompson & Co. Chtd, (Erd Building), New Ulm, Minnesota; ; Barbara Peterson, Howard Lake Public Library, Howard Lake, Minnesota; Reference Librarians, Spirit Lake Public Library, Spirit Lake, Iowa; Researchers, Jackson County Historical Society, Lakefield, Minnesota; Roseann Schauer, Lake Shetek State Park, Currie, Minnesota; June Slinger, Fort Abercrombie Historic Site, Abercrombie, North Dakota; Don Smith, Bismarck-Mandan Historical & Genealogical Society, Bismarck, North Dakota.

SMOKE

My humble gratitude also goes out to Ron Affolter, Jeff Amland, Tammy Amland, Jon Arfstrom, Roger Brezina, Dale Berven, Jamie Lee Foot, Emmett Hoctor, John LaBatte, Perry LeClaire. Karen Mariluch, Wade Olson, Chuck Parsons, Diana Pierce, ·Deann Reynolds, Corky Reynolds, David Skare, and Rob Utz, for their help above and beyond the call of duty.

Contents

SWINDLED INTO DEBT,
SWINDLED INTO DEATH

Injustice doesn't justify injustice.

In 1862, thirty-eight Dakota Sioux
Dropped in unison into the hand of God—
The red man's God, the white man's God, the God of all of us—
And shamed Mankato, Minnesota, by the noose.

The Indians, defeated by the white ascendancy,
Were cheated out of their own independency
And forced into accepting a dependency
Upon corrupted men within the Indian agency.

Mistrusted and misled to live imprisoned on their reservation,
This people, treated less than persons and suffering starvation
Arose to fight the undue deeds in blind retaliation:
Marauding, massacring and maiming with inhuman mutilation.

The frontier flowed crimson with the blood of a thousand settlers
With butcherings and outrages so horrid and appalling
That history was glossed and left to shadows whispering
Of badges, rights and mindless ironies befalling.

In 1862, December 26th,
While many Christmas trees again were gaily lit
And standing over opened precious Christmas gifts,
Thirty-eight men were hanging—dying—opposite
The law of God and the law of man,
The law of the river and the law of the land,
Handed over to the law and then to the Almighty's hand.

Injustice never justifies injustices by either side.

—Roger G. Brezina

Chapter One

Beginning of the End

"It gives me great pleasure to announce to Congress that the benevolent policy of the government, steady pursued for nearly thirty years, in relation with the removal of the Indians beyond the white settlements is approaching to a happy consummation. The consequences of a speedy [removal] will be important to the United States, to individual states, and to the Indians themselves. It puts an end to all possible danger of a collision between the authorities of the general and state governments, and of the account of the Indians. It will place a dense population in large tracts of country now occupied by a few savaged hunters. By opening the whole territory between Tennessee on the north and Louisiana on the south to the settlement of the whites it will incalculably strengthen the Southwestern frontier and render the adjacent states strong enough to repel future invasion without remote aid. It will separate the Indians from immediate contact with settlements of whites; enable them to pursue happiness in their own way and under their own rude institutions; will retard the progress of decay, which is lessening their numbers, and perhaps cause them gradually, under the protection of the government and through the influences of good counsels, to cast off their savage habits and become an interesting, civilized, and Christian community."

—Andrew Jackson

"Am I a negro, a slave? My skin is dark but not black. I am an Indian—a Seminole. The white man shall not make me black. I will make the white man red with blood; and then blacken him in the sun and rain, where the wolf shall smell of his bones, and the buzzard live upon his flesh."

—Osceola[1]

1

HE TERMINATION OF THE AMERICAN INDIAN way of life commenced, not during the nineteenth-century confrontations with United States soldiers, but on the very first day whites set foot upon North American soil. The following report describing the white man's first exposure to the natives of the West Indies is extracted from the 1492 diary of Christopher Columbus upon setting foot in the New World:

> As I saw that they were very friendly to us, and perceived that they could be much more easily converted to our holy faith by gentle means than by force, I presented them with some red caps, and strings of beads to wear upon the neck, and many other trifles of small value, wherewith they were much delighted, and became wonderfully attached to us. Afterwards they came swimming to the boats, bringing parrots, balls of cotton thread, javelins, and many other things which they exchanged for articles we gave them, such as glass beads, and hawk's bells; which trade was carried on with the utmost good will. But they seemed on the whole to me, to be a very poor people. They all go completely naked, even the women, though I saw but one girl. All whom I saw were young, not above thirty years of age, well made, with fine shapes and faces; their hair short, and coarse like that of a horse's tail, combed toward the forehead, except a small portion which they suffer to hang down behind, and never cut. Some paint themselves with black, which makes them appear like those of the Canaries, neither black nor white; others with white, others with red, and others with such colors as they can find. Some paint the face, and some the whole body; others only the eyes, and others the nose. Weapons they have none, nor are acquainted with them, for I showed them swords which they grasped by the blades, and cut themselves through ignorance. They have no iron, their javelins being without it, and nothing more than sticks, though some have fish-bones or other things at the ends. They are all of a good size and stature, and handsomely formed. I saw some with scars of wounds upon their bodies, and demanded by signs the [nature] of them; they answered me in the same way, that there came people from the other islands in the neighborhood who endeavored to make prisoners of them, and they defended themselves. I thought then, and still believe, that these were from the continent. It appears to me, that the people are ingenious, and would be good servants and I am of opinion that they would very readily become Christians, as they appear to have no religion. They very quickly learn such words as are spoken to them. If it please our Lord, I intend at my return to carry home six of them to your Highnesses, that they may learn our language. I saw no beasts in the island, nor any sort of animals except parrots.
>
> These are the words of the Admiral.

Saturday, 13 October. At daybreak great multitudes of men came to the shore, all young and of fine shapes, very handsome; their hair not curled but straight and coarse like horse-hair, and all with foreheads and heads much broader than any people I had hitherto seen; their eyes were large and very beautiful; they were not black, but the color of the inhabitants of the Canaries, which is a very natural circumstance, they being in the same latitude with the island of Ferro in the Canaries. They were straight-limbed without exception, and not with prominent bellies but handsomely shaped. They came to the ship in canoes, made of a single trunk of a tree, wrought in a wonderful manner considering the country; some of them large enough to contain forty or forty-five men, others of different sizes down to those fitted to hold but a single person. They rowed with an oar like a baker's peel, and wonderfully swift. If they happen to upset, they all jump into the sea, and swim till they have righted their canoe and emptied it with the calabashes they carry with them. They came loaded with balls of cotton, parrots, javelins, and other things too numerous to mention; these they exchanged for whatever we chose to give them. I was very attentive to them, and strove to learn if they had any gold. Seeing some of them with little bits of this metal hanging at their noses, I gathered from them by signs that by going southward or steering round the island in that direction, there would be found a king who possessed large vessels of gold, and in great quantities. I endeavored to procure them to lead the way thither, but found they were unacquainted with the route. I determined to stay here till the evening of the next day, and then sail for the southwest; for according to what I could learn from them, there was land at the south as well as at the southwest and northwest and those from the northwest came many times and fought with them and proceeded on to the southwest in search of gold and precious stones. This is a large and level island, with trees extremely flourishing, and streams of water; there is a large lake in the middle of the island, but no mountains: the whole is completely covered with verdure and delightful to behold. The natives are an inoffensive people, and so desirous to possess any thing they saw with us, that they kept swimming off to the ships with whatever they could find, and readily bartered for any article we saw fit to give them in return, even such as broken platters and fragments of glass. I saw in this manner sixteen balls of cotton thread which weighed above twenty-five pounds, given for three Portuguese *ceutis*. This traffic I forbade, and suffered no one to take their cotton from them, unless I should order it to be procured for your Highnesses, if proper quantities could be met with. It grows in this island, but from my short stay here I could not satisfy myself fully concerning it; the gold, also, which they wear in their noses, is found here, but not to lose time, I am determined to proceed onward and ascertain whether I can reach Cipango. At night they all went on shore with their canoes.[2]

The meaning of this voyage is highly contested. On the one hand, it is witness to the tremendous vitality and verve of late medieval and early modern Europe—which was on the verge of acquiring a world hegemony. On the other hand, the direct result of this and later voyages was the virtual extermination, by ill-treatment and disease, of the vast majority of the native inhabitants, and the enormous growth of the transatlantic slave trade.

The first British Colony of Roanoke, originally consisting of 100 householders, was founded in 1585, twenty-two years before Jamestown and thirty-seven years before the Pilgrims landed in Massachusetts, under the ultimate authority of Sir Walter Raleigh. In 1584 Raleigh had been granted a patent by Queen Elizabeth I to colonize America.[3]

The first and second expeditions took place from 1584 to 1586. The goals of these expeditions were to make contact and establish friendly relations with a native tribe called the Croatoan, fortify the island, and search for an appropriate place for the permanent settlement. The colony was run by Ralph Lane after Sir Richard Grenville, who had transported the colonists to Virginia, returned to Britain for supplies.

In 1586, Lane dispatched his report to Sir Walter Raleigh. The following excerpt from "The Colony of Roanoke," detailed the arrival of the first expedition:

> To the Northwest the farthest place of our discovery was to Chawanook distant from Roanoak about 130 miles. Our passage thither lies through a broad sound, but all fresh water, and the channel of a great depth, navigable for good shipping, but out of the channel full of shoals. Chawanook itself is the greatest province and Seigniorie lying upon that river, and that the town itself is able to put 700 fighting men into the field, besides the force of the province itself.
>
> The king of the said province is called Menatonon, a man impotent in his limbs, but otherwise for a savage, a very grave and wise man, and of a very singular good discourse in matters concerning the state, not only of his own country, and the disposition of his own men, but also of his neighbors round about him as well far as near, and of the commodities that each country yields.
>
> When I had him prisoner with me, for two days that we were together, he gave me more understanding and light of the country than I had received by all the searches and savages that before I or any of my company had had conference with: it was in March last past 1586. Among

other things he told me, that going three days' journey in a canoe up his river of Chawanook, and then descending to the land, you are within four days' journey to pass over land Northeast to a certain king's country, whose province lies upon the Sea, but his place of greatest strength is an island situated, as he described unto me, in a bay, the water round about the island very deep.

Out of this bay he signified unto me, that this King had so great quantity of pearls, and does so ordinarily take the same, as that not only his own skins that he wears, and the better sort of his gentlemen and followers are full set with the said pearls, but also his beds, and houses are garnished with them, and that he has such quantity of them, that it is a wonder to see...

The king of Chawanook promised to give me guides to go overland into that king's country whensoever I would: but he advised me to take good store of men with me, and good store of victual, for he said, that the king would be loth to suffer any strangers to enter into his country, and especially to meddle with the fishing for any pearls there, and that he was able to make a great many of men in to the field, which he said would fight very well . . .

And for that not only Menatonon, but also the savages of Moratoc themselves do report strange things of the head of that river, it is thirty days, as some of them say, and some say forty days' voyage to the head thereof, which head they say springs out of a main rock in that abundance, that forthwith it makes a most violent stream: and further, that this huge rock stands so near unto a Sea, that many times in storms (the wind coming outwardly from the sea) the waves thereof are beaten into the said fresh stream, so that the fresh water for a certain space, grows salt and brackish: I took a resolution with myself, having dismissed Menatonon upon a ransom agreed for, and sent his son into the pinnace to Roanoak, to enter presently so far into that river with two double whirries, and forty persons one or other, as I could have victual to carry us, until we could meet with more either of the Moraroks, or of the Mangoaks, which is another kind of savages, dwelling more to the westward of the said river: but the hope of recovering more victual from the savages made me and my company as narrowly to escape starving in that discovery before our return, as ever men did, that missed the same . . .

And that which made me most desirous to have some doings with the Mangoaks either in friendship or otherwise to have had one or two of them prisoners, was, for that it is a thing most notorious to all the country, that there is a province to the which the said Mangoaks have resource and traffic up that river of Moratoc, which has a marvelous and most strange mineral. This mine is so notorious among them, as not only to the savages dwelling up the said river, and also to the savages of Chawanook, and all them to the westward, but also to all them of the main: the country's name is of fame, and is called Chaunis Temoatan.

The mineral they say is Wassador, which is copper, but they call by the name of Wassador every metal whatsoever: they say it is of the color of our copper, but our copper is better than theirs: and the reason is for that it is redder and harder, whereas that of Chaunis Temoatan is very soft, and pale: they say that they take the said metal out of a river that falls very swift from high rocks and hills, and they take it in shallow water: the manner is this. They take a great bowl by their description as great as one of our targets, and wrap a skin over the hollow part thereof, leaving one part open to receive in the mineral: that done, they watch the coming down of the current, and the change of the color of the water, and then suddenly chop down the said bowl with the skin, and receive into the same as much ore as will come in, which is ever as much as their bowl will hold, which presently they cast into a fire, and forthwith it melts, and does yield in five parts at the first melting, two parts of metal for three parts of ore.

Of this metal the Mangoaks have so great store, by report of all the savages adjoining, that they beautify their houses with great plates of the same: and this to be true, I received by report of all the country, and particularly by young Skiko, the King of Chawanooks son of my prisoner, who also himself had been prisoner with the Mangoaks, and set down all the particulars to me before mentioned: but he had not been at Chaunis Temoatan himself: for he said it was twenty days' journey overland from the Mangoaks, to the said mineral country, and that they passed through certain other territories between them and the Mangoaks, before they came to the said country.

Upon report of the premises, which I was very inquisitive in all places where I came to take very particular information of by all the savages that dwelt towards these parts, and especially of Menatonon himself, who in everything did very particularly inform me, and promised me guides of his own men, who should pass over with me, even to the said country of Chaunis Temoatan, for overland from Chawanook to the Mangoaks is but one day's journey from sun rising to sun setting, whereas by water it is seven days with the soonest: These things, I say, made me very desirous by all means possible to recover the Mangoaks, and to get some of their copper for an assay, and therefore I willingly yielded to their resolution: But it fell out very contrary to all expectation, and likelihood: for after two days' travel, and our whole victual spent, lying on shore all night, we could never see man, only fires we might perceive made along the shore where we were to pass, and up into the country, until the very last day.

In the evening whereof, about three of the clock we heard certain savages call as we thought, Manteo, who was also at that time with me in the boat, whereof we all being very glad, hoping of some friendly conference with them, and making him to answer them, they presently began a song, as we thought, in token of our welcome to them: but

Manteo presently betook him to his piece, and told me that they meant to fight with us: which word was not so soon spoken by him, and the light horseman ready to put to shore, but there lighted a volley of their arrows among them in the boat, but did no hurt to any man . . .

Choosing a convenient ground in safety to lodge in for the night, making a strong corps of guard, and putting out good sentinels, I determined the next morning before the rising of the sun to be going back again, if possibly we might recover the mouth of the river, into the broad sound, which at my first motion I found my whole company ready to assent unto: for they were now come to their dog's porridge, that they had bespoken for themselves if that befell them which did, and I before did mistrust we should hardly escape.

The end was, we came the next day by night to the river's mouth within four or five miles of the same, having rowed in one day down the current, much as in four days we had done against the same: we lodged upon an island, where we had nothing in the world to eat but pottage of sassafras leaves, the like whereof for a meat was never used before as I think. The broad sound we had to pass the next day all fresh and fasting: that day the wind blew so strongly and the billow so great, that there was no possibility of passage without sinking of our boats. This was upon Easter eve, which was fasted very truly. Upon Easter day in the morning the wind coming very calm, we entered the sound, and by four of the clock we were at Chipanum, whence all the savages that we had left there were left, but their wares did yield us some fish, as God was pleased not utterly to suffer us to be lost: for some of our company of the light horsemen were far spent. The next morning we arrived at our home Roanoak . . .[4]

These colonists were ill-prepared and not particularly clever, because, although they depended upon the local Indians for food, they also antagonized the Indians by such tactics as kidnapping them and holding them hostage in exchange for information. Unfortunately for the colonists, who were desperately in need of supplies, Grenville's return was delayed.

It is during the second expedition that there was an attempt to leave a small force of men behind, while the ships returned to England for supplies. They left a few more than one hundred men, which were needed to finish fortifying the island, to continue the search for a permanent settlement sight, and to keep an English hold on the island. The effort failed due to the lack of supplies, weather conditions, and the strained relations with the Croatoans and other more violent native tribes. The situation became extremely desperate for the men when they were forced to resort to their dogs as a source of food. Luckily for the colonists, Sir Francis Drake put in at Roanoke after destroying the Spanish colony of St. Augustine, and brought all but fifteen men back to England.

The third expedition of almost one hundred twenty people (men, women, and children) ready for colonization arrived on the island in the spring of 1587. Their intent was to locate the fifteen men who were left behind in the second expedition, and then find a new settlement sight. It was discovered that the fortifications built by the colonists the year before had been abandoned, and there were no clues as to the fate of the fifteen men. The newly arriving colonists needed to find a new site for settlement, but political arguments back in England, prohibited any such action. Therefore, the colonists were forced to settle in the area of the abandoned fortifications for the time being.

While the colonists were assembling their homes, contact with the Croatoans was re-established. During their conversations as to the fate of the fifteen men left behind in the previous expedition, the Croatoans told how an enemy tribe had attacked the fort and killed some of the men, but how many was not known.

John White, upset with the news of the dead men and the recent discovery of a dead colonist, decided to launch an attack against the enemy, the Powhatans. Instead of attacking the enemy, however, John White's men attacked their friends, the Croatoans. With this violation of trust, the relations between the Croatoans and the colonists deteriorated. The Croatoans refused to supply the colonists with food, and the supplies brought with the colonists had commenced to spoil. With the shortage of supplies and winter soon approaching, the colonists decided that someone must return to England with the ships in order to relieve them of their supply shortage. John White was sent for the supplies in the late summer of 1587. He left approximately one hundred sixteen men, women, and children on Roanoke Island.

John White did not return with the requested supplies until 1590, and he found the colony abandoned. This three-year delay was caused by a war between England and Spain. Discovering the word Croatoan carved into a tree, White reasoned that the colonists had moved near or with the Croatoans. Before White could make any more progress, the captain and his crew, having no interest in the colonists' fate, chose to return to England. This fourth expedition returned to England not knowing the fate of the Roanoke Colonists.

In June 1606, King James I granted a charter to a group of London entrepreneurs, the Virginia Company, to establish an English colony in the Chesapeake Bay region of North America. By December, 108 settlers sailed from London instructed to settle Virginia, find gold and a water route to the Orient.[5]

On May 14, 1607, the Virginia Company party landed on Jamestown Island, sixty miles from the mouth of Chesapeake Bay. This site was selected because the deep water channel permitted their ships to ride close to shore, close enough, to moor them to the trees. Almost immediately upon landing, the colonists were under attack from Algonquian natives. As a result, the settlers constructed a wooden fort with palisade walls forming a protective triangle around a storehouse, church, and a number of houses.

The relationship between the Jamestown settlers and the Indians of Virginia was strained from the start. On one occasion, Captain John Smith was bartering for corn with Powhatan's half-brother Opechancanough when he discovered that he and his party were surrounded by a large party of Indians. Smith seized the chief by his scalplock, dug his pistol into his ribs, and announced: "Here I stand, shoot he that dare. You promised to freight my ship ere I departed, and so you shall; or I mean to load her with dead carcasses. Yet as if friends you will come and trade, I once more promise not to trouble you, except you give me the first occasion. And your King shall be free and be my friend, for I have not come to hurt him or any of you."[6]

Much of the initial ill will was rooted in the colonists' belief that the Indians would welcome them and willingly supply food. From the white perspective, it seemed that a mutually beneficial arrangement could be made by exchanging European tools and Christianity for sustenance. That bargain made little sense to the natives, however. The settlers failed to realize that the Indians lived very close to the subsistence level by hunting and gathering little more than their immediate needs required. Additional pressure on their food supply raised the real possibility of starvation.

Tensions were heightened when the colonists allowed their livestock to wander into Indian cornfields, and especially when the whites used their superior firepower to extort food contributions from the tribes.

The primary native leader in the area was known to the settlers as Powhatan, but properly as Wahunsonacook. He headed a loose confederation of about thirty Algonquian tribes from a village north of Jamestown on the York River. Powhatan was at first fascinated by English tools, but that interest was soon dampened by threats to native lands and food supplies.

While disease, famine, and continuing attacks of neighboring Algonquians took a tremendous toll on the population, there were times when the Powhatan Indian trade revived the colony with food for copper and iron implements. Captain John Smith kept the colony from dissolving, but following his departure in 1609, the majority of the settlers starved to death. Only sixty of the original 214 settlers at Jamestown survived.

That June, the survivors decided to bury cannon and armor and abandon the settlement, but the new governor, Lord De La Ware, and his supply ships arrived and brought the colonists back to the fort and put the colony back on its feet. Although the suffering did not totally end at Jamestown for decades, some years of peace and prosperity followed the wedding of Pocahontas, the favored daughter of the Algonquian chief Powhatan, to tobacco entrepreneur John Rolfe.

Relations improved for a number of years, but the death of Pocahontas in 1617 and Powhatan's own demise the following year enabled the more aggressive Opechancanough to exert control over the confederacy. The new chief feigned an interest in Christianity and issued invitations to settlers to move farther onto native lands.

In March 1622, the Indians launched a surprise attack on the dispersed white settlements. Nearly 350 whites were killed—nearly one-third of the population. Livestock was slaughtered, and crops were burned. The Indian uprising of 1622 rang the death knell for the Virginia Company. With the colony in total disarray, the company declared bankruptcy. A number of tobacco planters had become wealthy, but the Virginia Company itself was never profitable. In 1624, Virginia was made a royal colony and would remain so until independence.

Warfare between the races continued for another decade, but no decisive battle was won by either side. The settlers gave up any pretense of coexisting with the Indians and embarked upon a policy of extermination. In 1632, the tribes were forced to make major land concessions in the western Chesapeake Bay area. Resistance flared again in 1644, when more than 400 settlers were killed. That conflict, however, was not a threat to the greatly enlarged colony's existence. The nearly 100-year-old Opechancanough was captured in 1646 and died, probably a victim of murder, in Jamestown.

Then followed the Pilgrims. . . . Although they had first sighted land off Cape Cod, they did not settle until they arrived at Plymouth, which had been named by Captain John Smith in 1614. Plymouth offered an excellent harbor, and a large brook provided a resource for fish. The Pilgrims' biggest concern was the threat of attack by the local Native American Indians. But the Patuxets were a peaceful group and did not prove to be a threat.

The first winter was devastating to the Pilgrims. The cold, snow, and sleet wreaked havoc and crippled the efforts of the workers as they tried to construct their settlement. March brought warmer weather and the health of the Pilgrims improved, but many had died during the long winter. Of the 110 Pilgrims and crew who left England, less that fifty survived the first winter.

On March 16, 1621, an Indian brave walked into the Plymouth settlement. The Pilgrims were frightened until the Indian called out, "Welcome," in the English language. His name was Samoset, an Abnaki, who had learned English from the captains of fishing boats that had sailed off the coast. After staying the night, Samoset left the next day. He soon returned with another Indian named Squanto, who spoke even better English than Samoset. Squanto told the Pilgrims of his voyages across the ocean and his visits to England and Spain. It was in England where he had learned English.

Without Squanto's guidance, the settlers would not have survived. He taught the Pilgrims how to tap the maple trees for sap and which plants were poisonous and which had medicinal powers. He taught them how to plant

Indian corn by heaping the earth into low mounds with several seeds and fish in each mound. The decaying fish fertilized the corn. He also taught them to plant other crops with the corn. (Developed in Middle America, corn was one of the "three sisters." The other two companion plants often planted with corn were beans and squash.)

The harvest in October was very successful, and the Pilgrims found themselves with enough food to put away for the winter. There was corn, fruits and vegetables, fish to be packed in salt, and meat to be cured over smoky fires. Pilgrim Governor William Bradford proclaimed a day of thanksgiving to be shared by all the colonists along with their neighboring Native Americans. They invited Squanto and the other Indians to join them in their feast. Their chief, Massasoit, and ninety braves attended the celebration, which lasted for three days. They played games, ran races, marched and played drums. The Indians demonstrated their skills with the bow and arrow, and the Pilgrims demonstrated their musket skills.

In the seventeenth century the Pequot tribe, rival of the Narragansett, was centered along the Thames River in southeastern Connecticut. As the colonists expanded westward, friction began to develop. Points of tension included unfair trading, the sale of alcohol, the destruction of Pequot crops by colonial cattle, and competition over hunting grounds. Also working against an amicable relationship was the disdain with which the Indians were held by the colonists; many felt no qualms about dispossessing or killing those whom they regarded as "ungodly savages."

In 1634, a disreputable trader named Captain John Stone was banished from the colony. While his ship was anchored in the mouth of a Connecticut river, he and two of his crew were murdered during an Indian raid. According to the Pequots, Stone had kidnapped a party of Indians whom he took aboard his ship and later held for ransom.[7]

In July 1636, John Oldham, another dishonest trader, was killed by the Pequot off Block Island. The incident led Governor John Endicott to call up the militia. What followed was the first significant clash between English colonists and North American natives. Allying themselves with the Mohegan and Narragansett, the colonists attacked a Pequot village on the Mystic

River in May 1637. Surrounding their enemies under the cover of night, the colonists set the Indian dwellings ablaze, then shot the natives as they fled from their homes. From 400 to 700 Indian men, women, and children were killed; many of the survivors were sold into slavery in Bermuda. The Pequot chieftain Sassacus was captured by the Mohawks and executed. His tribe was virtually exterminated.

During this same period, Massasoit, was *sachem* (chief) of the Wampanoag. The tribe occupied lands from the eastern side of Narragansett Bay to Cape Cod, including Martha's Vineyard and Nantucket. Massasoit had cultivated harmonious relations with the colonists, being especially helpful to the pilgrims in their early travails, but tribal lands diminished sharply as the colonists expanded. In 1662, Metacom, a son of Massasoit and known to the colonists as King Philip, became *sachem*. The Wampanoags' dependence upon English manufactured goods compelled them to sell off much of their land, resulting in further resentment and tension.

In 1675, three tribal members were tried and executed by the English for the murder of a converted Wampanoag, touching off more than a year of hostilities known as King Philip's War. Beginning in June 1675, the Wampanoag, outfitted with rifles and armor, attacked numerous settlements and took the lives of dozens of colonial men, women, and children. English forces retaliated by destroying native villages and slaughtering the inhabitants. Soon, other tribes, including the Narragansett, joined the fray, and the entire region fell into conflict.[8]

The tide turned in April 1676, when the Narragansett were decisively defeated and their chief killed. Hostilities ground to a halt a few months later when Philip was betrayed, captured and killed. His corpse was drawn and quartered, and his severed head placed on a stake to be paraded through Plymouth Colony. Philip's son was sold into slavery in Bermuda, and many other captives were forced into servitude in homes throughout New England.

The colonists prevailed in King Philip's War, but the cost was tremendous. It would be more than two decades before all of the devastated frontier settlements could be reoccupied, and longer still before they began further expansion in the West. The New England Native Americans had been decimated to the extent that their impact on future events would be almost nonexistent.

Difficulties between Native Americans and whites were not confined only to the East and South during this period. Spain had begun its expansion into New Mexico and Arizona as early as 1540 and seized more than 100 Indian *pueblos* (villages). Spanish soldiers and priests imposed a forced-labor system—*encomienda*—which resembled slavery, and prevented the Pueblo Indians from communing with their gods.

Nearly a century and a half later, the Indians retaliated. Led by charismatic shaman Popé from Taos pueblo, they assaulted several Spanish settlements in August 1680 and achieved overwhelming success due to superior numbers—more than 8,000 warriors against fewer than 200 armed settlers. Despite different dialects, the Indians coordinated their attacks to occur everywhere at once. They killed twenty-one Franciscan friars and more than 400 Spaniards. One thousand survivors fled to the governor's palace in Sante Fe, where the Indians laid siege. Deprived of water for several days, the Spaniards managed to escape to El Paso del Norte (El Paso, Texas). Popé became the ruler of New Mexico.

The Pueblo leader had engineered the most successful Indian uprising in the history of the West up to that time. The Pueblo Indians remained independent for a dozen years, and during that time, Popé ordered the eradication of almost every vestige of the Roman Catholic Church. He also penalized Spanish language use and discouraged surnames—and even preached against using the plow, a Spanish tool. Less than a year after Popé's death in 1692, however, troops under Diego de Vargas easily re-conquered New Mexico for Spain.

In 1710, a group of Germans and Swiss established a settlement on the Neuse River in an ancestral area of the Tuscarora people in North Carolina. New Bern rapidly became a prosperous community, but the natives became enraged by encroachment on their lands as well as continuing unfair trading practices. On September 22, 1711, the Tuscarora under Chief Hancock attacked New Bern and other settlements in northern Carolina. Hundreds of settlers were killed and their homes and crops destroyed. It was not until

1713 that the settlers regained control, when Captain James Moore, supplemented by Yamasee warriors, defeated the Tuscarora at their village of Neoheroka. Some of the captured Tuscarora were sold into slavery to help defray war costs, while the remainder was forced out of Carolina. Eventually the Tuscarora ended up in New York and later became the sixth nation in the Iroquois Confederation.

The Yamasee Indians, meanwhile, were part of the Muskhogean language group. Their traditional homelands lay in present-day northern Florida and southern Georgia. The advent of the Spanish in the late sixteenth century forced the Yamasee to migrate north into what would become South Carolina. Relations between the tribe and English settlers in that region were generally positive during the latter half of the seventeenth century.

Not surprisingly, problems between the races eventually developed. The continuing influx of white settlers put pressure on Indian agricultural and hunting lands. The relationship was further complicated in that the tribe had become dependent on English firearms and other manufactured items and had incurred a large debt, typically payable in deerskins. White fur traders acted on their displeasure by enslaving a number of Yamasee women and children to cover portions of the outstanding debt.

In the spring of 1715, the Yamasee formed a confederation with other tribes and struck at the white settlements in South Carolina. Several hundred settlers were killed, homes burned and livestock slaughtered. The frontier regions were emptied; some fled to the relative safety of North Carolina and others pushed on to even more secure Virginia. Charleston also received large numbers of frightened settlers.

At the height of the fighting, it appeared that the tribal confederation's overwhelming numerical superiority would end in the white settlements' complete destruction in the region. But the Cherokee gave in to the lure of English weapons and other goods, and chose to aid the Carolinians. In a further stroke of good fortune, the besieged settlers also managed to gain support from Virginia.

The tide turned against the Yamasee, who were slowly pushed south through Georgia back into their ancestral lands in northern Florida. There, the tribe was virtually annihilated by protracted warfare with the Creeks, but some members were absorbed by the Seminole. The Yamasee War took a heavy toll in South Carolina. Such terror had been instilled in the minds of the frontiersmen that it would take nearly ten years for resettlement to occur in many areas.

NATIVE AMERICAN CULTURE revolved around the creation of the world, humanity, and the hunting and gathering of food. Although not all the tribes cultivated crops, those that did depended on clement weather. The gods of sky, sun, and rain were importuned with song, ritual, and, of course, tobacco. Rituals were frequently conducted to assist in the growing of maize, beans, and other valuable crops and certain plants were cultivated for medicinal purposes. Animals provided food, clothing, and lodge covering, and were essential to the survival of the various tribes.[9]

But each European colony had different and varying relations with the numerous Indian tribes, many of whom led a migratory existence. The most cordial and lasting relationship was established by William Penn in his pacts with the Lenni-Lenape (Delaware) tribes in New Jersey, Delaware, and Pennsylvania. During a period of some fifty years (1682 to 1730), the English, Welsh and German settlers (Quakers and Mennonites) in these areas did not invade or take over the lands reserved for the Indians. Whites and Indians lived, traded and moved freely throughout this territory.[10]

All that changed, however, when two white men, John Cartlidge and his brother Edmund, got in serious trouble in the spring of 1722. They had killed a Seneca Indian in the woods after making him drunk with rum in a fur trade. It was the first Indian killed in the province by an Englishman (not a Quaker) since the coming of William Penn.

After the expulsion of the Delaware by the Iroquois, clashes occurred on the border areas of William Penn's land. The situation was aggravated by the French and Indian wars, which started in 1745; the attempted settlement of the tribal areas by mostly Scotch-Irish and run-away indentured servants; unscrupulous traders (guns and whiskey); and by the savage massacre, in 1763, of peaceful Indians. Indian men, women, and children were killed and scalped by white men known as the Paxton Boys. Quakers were expelled from the Society of Friends for "marrying out" and for joining the militias needed to control not only the Indians, but the invasion of property by the new and unruly immigrants. Due to these pressures, many of the earlier colonists (mostly Quakers and German Mennonites) left Pennsylvania, moved to Virginia (some to Loudoun County) about 1750, where land was cheap and not so crowded.[11]

Following King George's War, 1740 to 1748, French authorities in North America began to establish a string of forts in the Ohio country west of the Allegheny Mountains. Their intent was to keep fur-trapping and trading activities in the hands of French citizens and to deny the area to land-hungry American colonists, especially a group of Virginians who had received from the English crown a massive land grant for lands in the Ohio valley. The subsequent Ohio Company was established for the purpose of investing in western lands and, secondarily, for engaging in the fur trade. Understandably, tensions between the contending powers mounted rapidly.

The picture was further complicated by the allegiances of the area's natives. As a rule, most of the tribes tended to favor the French, who enjoyed a reputation for conducting business more fairly than the British. Furthermore, the French trappers and traders did not threaten to inundate the region with settlers, unlike the British colonists.

In 1753, George Washington and a small party of men were dispatched into the disputed territory by Virginia Lieutenant Governor Robert Dinwiddie, himself a member of the Ohio Company, as were Washington and his brother Lawrence. The intent was to deliver a letter of protest to French officials, who summarily refused the request to vacate. During this journey, Washington noted a strategically located site at the confluence of the Allegheny and Monongahela rivers, where the Ohio River is formed and is the location of present-day Pittsburgh. Acting later on Washington's intelligence report, British officials sent a small force to the area where they began to construct a fort. Their labors were interrupted by a much larger French contingent, which chased off the British and completed the fortification, naming it Fort Duquesne.

In 1754, Governor Dinwiddie sought, but failed to secure, assistance from other colonies in a proposed effort to expel the French. He turned again to Washington, then twenty-two years old, who led his men westward into the disputed area. On May 28, Washington's forces surprised a group of French and Indians, inflicted heavy casualties and took a number of captives. The colonial forces then hastily constructed the aptly named Fort Necessity, in the Great Meadows, not far from Fort Duquesne. On July 3rd, the French forces struck back. After a day-long battle—the first of the French and Indian War—Washington signed terms of surrender and returned with his defeated men to Virginia. The French commander treated his opponents leniently in the hope of avoiding a broader conflict. Nevertheless, the opening shots of the French and Indian War had been fired, and that war would culminate in a British victory.

The Indian tribes of the Ohio Valley were surprised and angered by the defeat of their French allies, and when word arrived in the Ohio Valley that the tribes were expected to turn their loyalty to a new European monarch, George III of Britain, they were outraged. A native visionary, who was known simply as the Delaware Prophet preached ardently for a return to traditional ways and for the rejection of contact with the British. This policy was soon adopted by Ottawa chieftain, Pontiac, whose message found sympathetic ears among the Delaware, Seneca, Chippewa, Miami, Potawotomi and Huron, among others. The resulting conflict in the Ohio Valley has been labeled Pontiac's Rebellion.

The chief held a war council with like-minded tribes in April 1763. A plot to take over Fort Detroit by subterfuge was foiled, but Pontiac led an attack against the fortress in May and organized a siege. Later during the summer, a British force attempted to free the fort by launching a surprise attack against Pontiac's village. The plan was discovered and the attacking British troops suffered heavy casualties in the Battle of Bloody Run on July 31, 1763. Pontiac continued his unsuccessful efforts at Detroit into November.

To the east, another British bastion, Fort Pitt, was also the target of allied Indians. British relief forces under Colonel Henry Bouquet were en route to the besieged fort when they encountered a large Indian force. The resulting Battle of Bushy Run, August 5-6, 1763, was costly to the British, but they successfully preserved the fort. Despite these two defeats, the allied tribes were highly successful during much of 1763. Eight British forts fell, which included major installations at Presque Isle, Sandusky, and Michilimackinac. Fort Niagara saw no action during the uprising.

After 1764, Pontiac's influence among the tribes waned rapidly. He made recruiting trips into the south and west but found few interested parties. In 1766, a general peace treaty was signed in which Pontiac received a pardon. He lived quietly for several more years before being killed by a fellow Indian.

White settlers, many from Virginia, ignored the treaties right from the beginning. Thousands crossed the Appalachians and lesser numbers pushed beyond the Ohio. Clashes between the races became increasingly frequent. In May 1774, eleven Mingos were killed in a confrontation near Steubenville, Ohio; included among the dead were the father, brother, and sister of Logan, a Mingo chief. Many natives in the area wanted full-scale war against the white intruders, but the Shawnee chieftain Cornstalk resisted.

Logan sought out the perpetrators of the killings and led an attack into western Pennsylvania. Thirteen whites were killed during the foray, prompting the British commander at Fort Pitt to stage counterattacks against a series of Mingo villages.

Virginia governor, John Murray, the fourth Earl of Dunmore, prepared a two-pronged offensive—one directed against the natives in the Kentucky (present-day West Virginia) area, the other, led by Dunmore himself—marched toward Fort Pitt in Pennsylvania. But when Andrew Lewis led his force into the Little Kanawha Valley, this presence of a British force in native lands convinced Cornstalk that he should discard his moderation and form a large war party. In the Battle of Point Pleasant on October 10, 1774, the Shawnee were defeated and forced northward to the villages across the Ohio River. The Shawnee, Mingo, and Delaware later signed the Treaty of Camp Charlotte (near present-day Chillicothe, Ohio), in which they pledged to allow free navigation on the Ohio River, to return all captives and release their claims to the lands south and east of the Ohio.

In 1811 General William Henry Harrison led an army in the Battle of Tippecanoe against Prophet's Town on the Tippecanoe River in Indiana. Prophet's Town was the home of Tecumseh and his brother Tenskwatawa, the Prophet, and since 1808, was the center of Tecumseh's Confederacy. Harrison wanted to defeat the Indians before Tecumseh succeeded in uniting the Indians into an unbeatable force.[12]

Harrison marched against Prophet's Town while Tecumseh was away trying to recruit more Indians for his confederacy. The Prophet told his followers they were invincible. The camping ground was a spot of high oak land rising several feet above a marshy prairie fronting it on the southeast, and extending to the Indian town. The height at the west bank of this tract was much greater and overlooked a small prairie, through the edge of which, near the border of the camping ground, ran a small stream known as Burnett's Creek. This stream was skirted on either side by a dense growth of willow and other shrubs. The place was an admirable camping ground, but it afforded every facility for a night surprise, which was just the kind of an attack meditated by the Indians. General Harrison, familiar with the methods of Indian warfare, was ever ready for emergencies.[13]

To offset this danger, he ordered his army to encamp in readiness for battle, the men sleeping upon their arms. The front, or southeast, and rear lines along the creek were guarded by columns of infantry, separated on the north, or left flank, by about 159 yards, but at the right, or south end, where the ground approached an abrupt point, the front and rear lines were but about eighty yards distant. This flank occupied a line about 150 yards north of the point, and was composed of Captain Spencer's company of eighty mounted riflemen. This company was known as the Yellow-jackets, because of the color of their uniform. The left flank was more exposed and consisted of 120 mounted riflemen, under command of Major-general Wells, of the Kentucky volunteers. The front line, facing the marshy prairie to the southeast, was composed of Major Floyd's battalion of United States infantry, flanked on the left and right by two companies.

The rear line, facing Burnett's Creek, was occupied by Major Baen's battalion of United States infantry, and four companies of militia infantry, commanded by Lieutenant-Colonel Decker. Two companies of dragoons, consisting of sixty men, under command of Major Joseph H. Daveiss, occupied a position in the rear of the left flank, while Captain Parke, with a larger force, was placed to the rear of the front. In case a night attack was made, the dragoons were instructed to parade dismount, with pistols in belt, as a reserve corps.

An Indian army of about 450 warriors attacked Harrison's army at 4:30 in the morning of November 7, 1811. Harrison's army, comprised of about a thousand troops, included infantry and cavalry. The American army defeated the Indians but suffered heavy losses. Sixty-two men were killed or died later from their wounds. One hundred and twenty six men were wounded. The Indian's losses are impossible to record because they carried off most of their dead and wounded. Harrison guessed that at least forty Indians were killed. The American army drove off the Indians and burned Prophet's Town to the ground. The Indians no longer believed in the Prophet, and Tecumseh's dreams of an Indian confederacy ended in the ashes of Tippecanoe.[14]

The following account of the battle of Tippecanoe is taken from the official dispatch sent by General Harrison to the secretary of war, on the eighteenth of November, eleven days after the battle:

> I had risen at a quarter after four o'clock, and the signal for calling out the men would have been given in two minutes, when the attack commenced. It began on the left flank; but a single gun was fired by the sentinels, or by the guard in that direction, which made not the least resistance, but abandoned their officer and fled into camp; and the first notice which the troops of that flank had of the danger, was from the yells of the savages a short distance from the line; but, even under these circumstances, the men were not wanting to themselves or to the occasion. Such of them as were awake, or were easily awakened, seized their arms and took their stations; others, which were more tardy, had to contend with the enemy in the doors of their tents. The storm first fell upon Captain Barton's company, of the Fourth United States Regiment, and Captain Guiger's company of mounted riflemen, which formed the left angle of the rear line. The fire upon these was excessively severe, and they suffered considerably before relief could be brought to them. Some few Indians passed into the encampment near the angle, and one or two penetrated to some distance before they were killed. I believe all the other companies were under arms,

and tolerably formed, before they were fired on. The morning was dark and cloudy. Our fires afforded a partial light, which, if it gave us some opportunity of taking our position, was still more advantageous to the enemy, affording them the means of taking a surer aim. They were, therefore, extinguished as soon as possible.

Under these discouraging circumstances, the troops (nineteen-twentieths of whom had never been in an action before) behaved in a manner that can never be too much applauded. They took their places without noise, and with less confusion than could have been expected from veterans placed in a similar situation. As soon as I could mount my horse, I rode to the angle that was attacked. I found that Barton's company had suffered severely, and the left of Guiger's entirely broken. I immediately ordered Cook's company, and the late Captain Wentworth's, under Lieutenant Peters, to be brought up from the center of the rear line, where the ground was much more defensible, and formed across the angle, in support of Barton's and Guiger's. My attention was then engaged by a heavy firing upon the left of the front line, where were stationed the small company of United States riflemen (then, however, armed with muskets), and the companies of Baen, Snelling, and Prescott, of the Forth Regiment.

I found Major Daveiss forming the dragoons in the rear of those companies, and understanding that the heaviest part of the enemy's fire proceeded from some trees about fifteen or twenty paces in front of those companies, I directed the major to dislodge them with a part of the dragoons. Unfortunately, the major's gallantry determined him to execute the order with a smaller force than was sufficient, which enabled the enemy to avoid him in the front and attack his flanks. The major was mortally wounded, and his party driven back. The Indians were, however, immediately and gallantly dislodged from their advantageous position, by Captain Snelling, at the head of his company.

In the course of a few minutes after the commencement of the attack, the fire extended along the left flank, the whole of the front, the right flank and part of the rear line. Upon Spencer's mounted riflemen, and the right of Warrick's company, which was posted on the right of the rear line, it was excessively severe. Captain Spencer, and his first and second lieutenants were killed, and Captain Warrick mortally wounded. Those companies, however, still bravely maintained their posts; but Spencer's having suffered so severely, and having originally too much ground to occupy, I reinforced them with Robb's company of riflemen, which had been driven, or, by mistake, ordered from their position in the left flank, toward the center of the camp, and filled the vacancy that had been occupied by Robb with Prescott's company of the Fourth United States Regiment. My great object was to keep the lines entire—to prevent the enemy from breaking into the camp, until daylight should enable me to make a general and effectual charge. With this view I had reinforced every part of the line that had suffered much; and as soon as the approach of morning discovered itself, I withdrew from the front line Snelling's, Posey's (under Lieutenant Allbright) and Scott's, and from the rear line Wilson's companies, and drew them up upon the left flank; and, at the same time, I ordered Cook's and Baen's companies—the former from the rear, and the latter from the front line—to reinforce the right flank, forseeing [sic] that, at these points, the enemy would make their last efforts. Major Wells, who commanded on the left flank, not knowing my intentions precisely, had taken the command of these companies—had charged the enemy before I had formed the body of dragoons with which I meant to support the infantry; a small detachment of these were, however, ready, and proved amply sufficient, for the purpose. The Indians were driven by the infantry at the point of the bayonet, and the dragoons pursued and forced them into a marsh, where they could not be followed. Captain Cook and Lieutenant Larrabee had, agreeably to my order, marched their companies to the right flank and formed them under fire of the enemy; and, being then joined by the riflemen of that flank, had charged the Indians, killed a number, and put the rest to precipitate flight.

The whole of the infantry formed a brigade, under the immediate orders of Colonel Boyd. The colonel, throughout the action, manifested equal zeal and bravery in carrying into execution my orders—in keeping the men to their posts, and exhorting them to fight with valor. His brigade-major, Clarke, and his aide-de-camp, George Croghan, Esq., were also very serviceably employed. Colonel Joseph Bartholomew, a very valuable officer, commanded, under Colonel Boyd, the militia infantry. He was wounded early in the action, and his services lost to me. Major G.R.C. Floyd, the senior officer, of the Fourth United States Regiment, commanded immediately the battalion of that regiment, which was in the front line. His conduct, during the action, was entirely to my satisfaction. Lieutenant-colonel Decker, who commanded the battalion of militia on the right of the rear line, preserved his command in good order. He was however, but partially attacked. I have before mentioned to you that Major-general Wells, of the Fourth Division of Kentucky Militia, acted, under my command, as a major, at the head of two companies of mounted volunteers. The general retained the fame which he had already acquired in almost every campaign, and in almost every battle which has been fought with the Indians since the settlement of Kentucky. Of the several corps, the Fourth United States Regiment, and the two small companies attached to it, were certainly the most conspicuous for undaunted valor. The companies commanded by Captains Cook, Snelling, and Barton; Lieutenants Larrabee, Peters, and Hawkins, were placed in situations where they could render most service, and encounter most danger; and those officers eminently distinguished themselves. Captains Prescott and Brown performed their duty, also, entirely to my satisfaction, as did Posey's company of the Seventh

Regiment, headed by Lieutenant Allbright. In short, sir, they supported the fame of American regulars; and I have never heard that a single individual was found out of line of his duty.

Several of the militia companies were in no wise inferior to the regulars. Spencer's, Guiger's and Warrick's maintained their posts amid a monstrous carnage—as, indeed, did Robb's, after it was posted on the right flank. Its loss of men (seventeen killed and wounded), and keeping its ground, is sufficient evidence of its firmness. Wilson's and Scott's companies charged with the regular troops, and proved themselves worthy of doing so. Norris' company also behaved well. Hargrove's and Wilkin's companies were placed in a situation where they had no opportunity of distinguishing themselves, or, I am satisfied, they would have done it. This was the case with the squadron of dragoons also. After Major Daveiss received his wound, knowing it to be mortal, I promoted Captain Parke to the majority, than whom there is no better officer. My two aides-de-camp, Majors Hurst and Taylor, with Lieutenant Adams, of the Fourth Regiment, the adjutant of the troops, afforded me the most essential aid, as well in the action as throughout the campaign.

The arrangements of Captain Piatt, in the quartermaster's department, were highly judicious; and his exertions on all occasions—particularly in bringing off the wounded—deserve my warmest thanks. But, in giving merited praise to the living, let me not forget the gallant dead. Colonel Abraham Owen, commandant of the Eighteenth Kentucky Regiment, joined me, a few days before the action, as a private in Captain Guiger's company. He accepted the appointment of volunteer aide-de-camp to me. He fell early in the action. The Representative of his State will inform you that she possessed not a better citizen, nor a braver man. Major J.H. Daveiss was known as an able lawyer and a great orator. He joined me as a private volunteer; and, on the recommendations of the officers of that corps, was appointed to command the three troops of dragoons. His conduct, in that capacity, justified their choice. Never was there an officer possessed of more ardor and zeal to discharge his duties with propriety, and never one who would have encountered greater danger to purchase military fame. Captain Baen, of the Fourth United States Regiment, was killed early in the action. He was unquestionably a good officer and a valiant soldier. Captains Spencer and Warrick, and Lieutenants McMahan and Berry, were all my particular friends. I have ever had the utmost confidence in their valor, and I was not deceived. Spencer was wounded in the head. He exhorted his men to fight valiantly. He was shot through both thighs and fell; still continuing to encourage them, he was raised up, and received a ball through his body, which put an immediate end to his existence. Warrick was shot immediately through the body. Being taken to the surgery to be dressed, as soon as it was over (being a man of great bodily vigor and able to walk) he insisted on going back to the head of his company, although it was evident that he had but few hours to live.[15]

In the early 1800s, the Upper Creek Indians (Red Sticks) in Georgia and Alabama were deeply troubled by the continuing encroachment of white settlers onto their lands. Tribal leaders counseled restraint and also urged neutrality in the developing rift between the United States and Britain. In 1811, however, the great Shawnee leader Tecumseh visited the southern tribes and urged formation of the confederation to end the diminishment of Indian lands and ways of life. He won many ardent supporters among the younger warriors.

When war erupted in 1812, the Creek sided with the British because they presented less of an immediate threat to occupy tribal lands. A series of raids was launched against frontier farms and settlements, and losses were heavy. The Creek War (1813 to 1814), reached crisis proportions in August 1813. Fort Mims, a small outpost north of Mobile, Alabama, was overrun; warriors ignored pleas for restraint from their leader Red Eagle (also known as William Weatherford) and slaughtered more than 500 white men, women, and children.

Word of the massacre reached Andrew Jackson, who was in Nashville recuperating from a gunshot wound suffered in a brawl with Thomas Hart Benton. Jackson organized a Tennessee militia force of more than 2,000 men and supplemented it with another 1,000 Lower Creek and Cherokee warriors. Beginning in the fall of 1813, Jackson's ill-trained force engaged the enemy in a series of indecisive battles.

The Battle of Horseshoe Bend was fought on March 27, 1814, near an Upper Creek village on a horseshoe-shaped bend in the Tallapoosa River near present-day Alexander City, Alabama. Jackson permitted the native women and children to cross the river to safety before he attacked. Then his men nearly wiped out the enemy force. Jackson wrote later that the carnage was "dreadful." The Upper Creek lost more than 550 killed, while Jackson's combined forces lost only forty-nine.

In the early eighteenth century, bands of Muskogean-speaking Lower Creek, known as the Seminole (separatists) migrated to Florida from Georgia. The Spanish permitted the Seminole to settle there in order to create a buffer zone between their sphere of influence and that of the British. The natives occupied rich lands in northern Florida that were hungrily eyed by American settlers in adjacent Georgia, although Florida still belonged to Spain at the beginning of the nineteenth century. Another cause of potential conflict was the Seminole tendency to provide refuge to runaway slaves. While the United States was fighting the War of 1812 with Britain, a series of violent incidents aggravated hostility between the United States. and the Seminole.

The First Seminole War, 1817 to 1818, erupted over forays staged by United States authorities to recapture runaway black slaves living among Seminole bands, who stiffly resisted. In 1818, Major-general Andrew Jackson was sent with an army of more than 3,000 troops to Florida to punish the Seminole. After liquidating several native settlements, and executing two British traders held for reportedly encouraging Seminole resolve, General Jackson captured the Spanish fort of Pensacola in May 1818 and deposed the government. However, he failed to eliminate Seminole opposition.

THE EARLIEST WRITTEN RECORD of the Sioux peoples dates from the 1640s when French priests encountered them in what is now Wisconsin. The people fished and hunted in deep forests and lived in houses made of bark and wood. Within a few years, they began to move west toward South Dakota. Three groups came to the Great Plains, each with its own customs and languages. They quickly learned to ride horses and hunt buffalo and lived as nomads on the prairie. Soon, the Dakotas, Lakotas, and Nakotas pushed the Arikaras north and the Mandans, Cheyennes, and Crows farther north and west.

The word "Sioux" is the shortened version of Nadouessioux, the Plains Indian peoples of Siouan linguistic stock. Sioux warriors assisted the British during the War for Independence as well as the in the War of 1812. Nevertheless, in 1815, the bands in the East inked peace treaties with the new United States. An additional agreement in 1825 assured the Sioux control of a vast region that encompassed much of what is today Missouri, Iowa, Wyoming, the Dakotas, Minnesota, and Wisconsin. In 1837, the United States purchased from the Sioux all their possessions east of the Mississippi River, followed by more land acquisition in 1851.

26

But the whites were pushing too as the Sioux watched the settlers moving onto their hunting lands and their food and game rapidly disappearing. Following many border skirmishes of the Sioux and their allies against the Sauk and the Fox, the commissioners again assembled the tribal leaders in Prairie du Chien. If a single invisible line across the grasslands, unmarked by a fence post or border stone and existing only on the white man's map, would not be recognized by the Indians, then a wider mark on another map, cutting a swath twenty miles wide on each side of the old diagonal line would, perhaps, be more effective.[16]

This treaty of 1830, on which the representatives of the Sioux, the Sauk, and the Fox made their marks with the goose quill, was part of the general Indian policy of Andrew Jackson, who sat comfortably in Washington as the Great White Father. Drive all the eastern Indians west across the Mississippi into the grasslands and high plains, leaving the lakes, forests, and prairies of trans-Appalachia to the ever moving, restless farmer. Let the Mississippi be the perpetual boundary between two cultures that were irreconcilable. Surely there was enough land on either side of the river to satisfy both peoples.

Neither side was, in fact, satisfied for very long. Jackson's prognostication was as cloudy as Jefferson's had been in 1783 when he had hailed the Paris Peace Treaty, ceding to the United States all territory of the Old Northwest, as providing enough land for white Americans for a thousand generations. Jefferson's three millennia allotment had been nearly consumed in forty years. Jackson's perpetual boundary was to last less than two.

The Indians, however, made the first move. The proud Sauk peoples of Illinois were not reconciled to giving up their lands and their great, hundred-lodge village of Saukenuk, the largest Indian village in the West, located at the juncture of the Rock River with the Mississippi, where the rivers teemed with fish, and the flat lands grew good ears of corn and round, sweet melons. Saukenuk, the capital and pantheon of the Sauk nation, could not be given away by a simple mark on a piece of the white man's paper.

The Sauks and their Fox allies, refusing to give up their homes and ancestral graves, had an wise, old leader to turn to in their moment of anger and despair. Chief Black Hawk, having fought in 1812 alongside the Shawnee Chief Tecumseh and the British at the battles of Frenchtown and Fort Meigs, had lived on through middle age waiting for the Great Spirit to send another leader with a prophet to drive back the white devils who kept coming across the mountains closer to his people's lands. Now in his sixty-fifth year, Black Hawk was still ready to fight rather than surrender his lands to the white invaders. He was not impressed by all those pieces of paper that the white men held, going back in time to the Treaty of 1804, which the white men claimed gave them the right to take the lands of the Sauk and the Fox whenever they wished. Indian delegates, drunk with white man's whiskey, could not, by a simple X mark, give up that which did not belong to them, but belonged to the Great Spirit who watched over them. Black Hawk, backed by his old companions who had fought with him as allies of the British nearly twenty years before, announced that, in spite of the treaty of 1830, he and his people would return to Saukenuk in the early spring. Their women would plant their fields, and the men would fish and hunt and tend the graves of their ancestors as they had done each spring since the Great Spirit had made them stewards of this land.

Black Hawk was elderly and still cherished the ancient hopes that had died with Tecumseh and his mystic brother the Prophet. The young men of his nation could see the present and the future as it was and would be, not as it should have been. They turned to a young leader, Keokuk, who counseled caution and collaboration with the white men across the river. After all, the land given them along the Iowa River was good land. The corn grew as well here as it did in the fields of Saukenuk. Only by accepting the inevitable could the Sauk and the Fox expect the white men to send soldiers to help them hold their present lands against the Sioux and the Chippewas.

So Black Hawk crossed the Mississippi in the spring of 1831 with but a part of his people—and those mainly women who wanted to return to their old lodges and till familiar soil again. They found that white settlers had already moved in, and the army was there too, under the command of General Edmund P. Gaines. There were enough troops to drive Black Hawk and his band back across the Mississippi. Keokuk came over to Saukenuk to

persuade Black Hawk's followers that resistance was useless and his concil-
iatory talk carried the day. The young chief persuaded Gaines to call one
more meeting to reason with Black Hawk and his intransigent British Band,
so-called because it consisted largely of veterans, like Black Hawk, of the
War of 1812.

On June 30, 1831, Keokuk and Black Hawk, with their respective followers, met with Gaines and his troops at the council house on Rock Island.
Gaines again went over the old familiar ground, the treaties which had ceded
all of Illinois to the white men. Then Gaines's aide, Lieutenant George
McCall, read the prepared Articles of Agreement and Capitulation. By the
terms of this new treaty, Black Hawk and his supporters were to recognize
Keokuk's leadership of the Sauk nation, were to move out of Illinois forever,
and were to abandon any further communication with the British in Canada.
In return, the United States would guarantee forever the Sauk and Fox lands
west of the Mississippi, and in addition, although not a formal part of the
treaty, Gaines would recognize the existence of the women's cornfields
already planted and would give to Black Hawk and his women, corn from the
army's stores equal to what the squaws could have expected to reap had they
stayed for the fall harvest. Because of this codicil, given orally, the agreement
of 1831 has been known through history as the Corn Treaty.

The reading being completed and the promise given, Gaines began to
call the names of the Indians present, for them to come forward to make
their mark. First read was the name of Quashquame, Black Hawk's old ally
and friend, followed by the name of Black Hawk himself. The old warrior
arose slowly, all the pain and humiliation of lost hopes written in his face. He
came forward to the table, grabbed the goose quill pen, and fiercely drew his
X on the hated paper. "With a force which rendered that pen forever unfit
for further use . . . I touched the goose-quill pen to this treaty, and was determined to live in peace," Black Hawk later wrote.

The old chief returned to the new lands across the river, acknowledged
the leadership of the young Chief Keokuk, and looked forward only to a sad
peace and an early death. One of the few young men who supported Black
Hawk's old dream was a Sauk brave named Neapope. While Black Hawk was

in Rock Island signing the Corn Treaty, Neapope was in Canada talking with the British. He returned to say that the British would come down from Canada to help if Black Hawk would rally his people and take to the warpath again. Neapope brought the exciting news to the Winnebagoes of the north that the Great Spirit had given a new Prophet, a Prophet who looked to Black Hawk for leadership as the man of destiny. The old man aroused himself from the torpor of defeat and began to make new plans.

The Black Hawk War was not really a war, but a pathetic final act of defiance against reality. Nevertheless, it was to be of major consequence for all the Indians of the Middle West and for the grasslands that lay between the two great rivers. Crossing the Mississippi a few miles below the old village of Saukenuk during the first week in April 1832, Black Hawk and his band headed north to follow the Rock River up to the Prophet's village in Illinois, where he expected to be joined by the Winnebagoes. From there, the plan was to follow the Rock River to its source in Wisconsin Territory, then to join forces with the British. There they would make their stand against the expected attack of the United States Army, drive it back, and reclaim all the lands of Illinois and Wisconsin for the triumphant Indians. General Henry Atkinson, commander of American troops in the western district, upon receiving word of Black Hawk's move into Illinois, immediately called out the militia to pursue the old chief up the Rock River. It soon became clear that the British were not coming, indeed never had any intention of coming. The Winnebagoes quickly retreated into a neutrality that would soon become open aid to the American army.

What followed was a long chase after Black Hawk through northern Illinois and southern Wisconsin Territory, during which neither the American militia nor the pursued Indians distinguished themselves with glory. Brief skirmishes, in which the militiamen were occasionally routed in panic, marked Black Hawk's slow movement north to a rendezvous with allies who never materialized. By the time Black Hawk's band reached Wisconsin, it was clear even to the old chief that the impossible dream was now finished. In a last desperate effort to escape the trap, Black Hawk swung his small, diminishing company westward, hoping to reach and cross the Mississippi, but at the mouth of the appropriately named Bad Axe River north of Prairie du Chien, the war came to its inevitable conclusion. The trap was closed. Black Hawk's hiding place was revealed by the Winnebagoes, and he was sent in irons down the Mississippi to Jefferson Barracks in St. Louis, Missouri.

All the Indians of the region were to pay a price for Black Hawk's last venture. General Winfield Scott, representing the Great White Father, met with representatives of the Sauk and Fox at Fort Armstrong in Rock Island on September 21, 1832, and terms were dictated. Keokuk was treated as summarily as if he had been the enemy rather than the great counselor of peace and conciliation. The Sauk and Fox were to give up their newly acquired lands along the Iowa and were to move farther west into the grasslands. In return for the eastern segment of the grasslands that only two years before had been given in perpetuity to the Indians, the American government would make thirty annual payments of $20,000 and assume existing Indian debts to the white traders of $40,000. The door had at last been opened to white settlement.

On May 26, 1830, the Indian Removal Act of 1830 was passed by the Twenty-first Congress of the United States of America. After four months of strong debate, Andrew Jackson signed the bill into law. Land greed was a big reason for the federal government's position on Indian removal. This desire for Indian lands was also fueled by the hatred of Indians by some American frontiersmen.

This period of forcible removal commenced with the Cherokee Indians in the state of Georgia. In 1802, the Georgia legislature signed a compact giving the federal government all of her claims to western lands in exchange for the government's pledge to extinguish all Indian titles to land within the state. By the mid-1820's, however, Georgians began to doubt that the government would uphold its part of the bargain. The Cherokee Indian tribes had lived for many generations upon a large tract of land in Georgia. They were worried about losing their land, so they forced the issue by adopting a written constitution proclaiming that the Cherokee Nation had complete jurisdiction over its own territory. When the Cherokees sought help from newly elected president Andrew Jackson, he informed them that he would

not interfere with the Georgia law system. He suggested that laws be enacted so that the Indians would have to move west of the Mississippi River.[17]

But the Cherokees were not the only civilized tribe to be exploited by
the white man during this period. The Seminoles had endured similar land
disputes with the state of Florida. The Creek Indians fought many battles
against the federal army so they could keep their land in the states of
Alabama and Georgia. The Chickasaw and Choctaw had disputes with the
state of Mississippi. To ensure peace, the government forced these tribes,
dubbed the Five Civilized Tribes, to move off their lands where they had
lived for generations to land given to them in parts of Oklahoma. Andrew
Jackson was quoted as saying that this was a way of protecting them and
allowing them time to adjust to the white culture. This land in Oklahoma
was thinly settled and was thought to have little value. Within ten years of
the Indian Removal Act, more than 70,000 Indians had moved across the
Mississippi, many of whom died on this journey.

Over this ten-year period, known as the "Trails of Tears," the tribes
were given a right to all of Oklahoma except the Panhandle. The government promised this land to them "as long as grass shall grow and rivers run,"
but they were later forced to move to other reservations.

The Trails of Tears was comprised of several trails that the tribes traveled on their way to their new lands. Many Indians died because of famine
or disease. Sometimes a person would die because of the harsh living conditions. The Indians had to walk all day and were given very little rest. At that
time there was reported to be sightings of gold in the Cherokee territory in
Georgia, which caused prospectors to rush in, tearing down fences and
destroying crops.

The 19,525,966 acres in the new Indian Territory were divided among
the the five tribes. The Choctaws received 6,953,048 acres in the southeast
part of Oklahoma; the Chickasaw over 4,707,903 acres west of the Choctaws
reservation; the Cherokees 4,420,068 acres in the northeast; the Creek
received 3,079,095 acres southwest of the Cherokees; and the Seminoles
purchased 365,852 acres from the Creeks. The Chickasaw and the Choctaw
owned their lands jointly because they were so closely related.

The Trade and Intercourse Act of 1834, passed by Congress on June 30, 1834, reorganized the Indian offices, creating the United States Department of Indian Affairs. This single piece of legislation redefined the Indian Territory and permanent Indian frontier, and gave the army the right to quarantine Indians. Among other provisions of this act were those concerning the licensing (for a period no longer than three years) of all persons engaged in trade in the Indian country, and the regulation of intercourse with the Indians, including fine and removal of all persons unauthorized to reside in the country. No hunting, trapping or grazing of cattle, nor settlement of any white persons should be permitted. Liquor traffic within the Indian country was prohibited in all forms.

For legal purposes the Indian country was attached to Missouri and Arkansas. Section 24 reads: "That for the sole purpose of carrying this act into effect, all that part of the Indian country west of the Mississippi River, that is bounded north by the north line of lands assigned to the Osage tribe of Indians, produced east to the state of Missouri; west by the Mexican possession; south, by Red River; and east, by the west line of the territory of Arkansas and the state of Missouri, shall be, and hereby is, annexed to the territory of Arkansas," . . . . the Indian country to the north being annexed to the judicial district of Missouri. The criminal laws of the United States were declared in force in the Indian country, but not to apply to crimes committed by one Indian against another and a superintendent of Indian affairs for the Indian country west of the Mississippi was created with residence at St. Louis.

President Jackson and his associates of the time were clearly sincere in their belief that the Indian country, as formed by the act of 1834, was forever dedicated to the home and uses of the Indian, and that in thus raising a barrier against the intrusion of white settlement, they had taken measures to guard the Indians from the evils which had brought them to their miserable condition. The arguments by which the president justifies his actions are presented in his message of December 1835, and the message also recites something of what the government did for the Indians in reward for the peaceable emigration:

The plan of removing the aboriginal people who yet remained within the settled portion of the United States, to the country west of the Mississippi River, approaches its consummation. It was adopted on the most mature consideration of the condition of this race, and ought to be persisted in till the object is accomplished, and prosecuted with as much vigor as a just regard to their circumstances will permit, and as fast as their consent can be obtained. All preceding experiments for the improvement of the Indians have failed. It seems now to be an established fact that they cannot live in contact with a civilized community and prosper. Ages of fruitless endeavors have, at length, brought us to a knowledge of this principle of intercommunication with them. The past we cannot recall, but the future we can provide for. Independently of the treaty stipulations into which we have entered with the various tribes for the usufructuary rights they have ceded to us, no one can doubt the moral duty of the government of the United States to protect, and, if possible, to preserve and perpetuate the scattered remnants of this race, which are left within our borders. In the discharge of this duty, an extensive region in the west has been assigned for their permanent residence. It has been divided into districts, and allotted among them. Many have already removed, and others are preparing to go; and with the exception of two small bands, living in Ohio and Indiana, not exceeding fifteen hundred persons, and of the Cherokees, all the tribes on the east side of the Mississippi, and extending from Lake Michigan to Florida, have entered into engagements which will lead to their transplantation.

The plan for their removal and re-establishment is founded upon the knowledge we have gained of their character and habits, and has been dictated by a spirit of enlarged liberality. A territory exceeding in extent that relinquished, has been granted each tribe. Of its climate, fertility and capacity to support an Indian population, the representations are highly favorable. To these districts the Indians are removed at the expense of the United States; and, with certain supplies of clothing, arms, ammunition, and other indispensable articles, they are also furnished gratuitously with provisions for the period of a year after their arrival at their new homes.

In that time, from the nature of the country, and of the products raised by them, they can subsist themselves by agricultural labor, if they choose to resort to that mode of life; if they do not, they are upon the skirts of the great prairies, where countless herds of buffalo roam, and a short time suffices to adapt their own habits to the changes which a change of the animals, destined for their food, may require. Ample arrangements have also been made for the support of schools; in some instances council houses and churches are to be erected, dwellings constructed for the chiefs, and mills for common use. Funds have been set apart for the maintenance of the poor, the most necessary mechanical arts have been introduced, and blacksmiths, gunsmiths, wheelwrights, millwrights, etc., are supported among them. Steel and iron, and sometimes salt, are purchased for them; and ploughs, and other farming utensils, domestic animals, looms, spinning wheels, cards, etc., are presented to them. And besides these beneficial arrangements, annuities are, in all cases, paid, amounting, in some instances, to more than thirty dollars for each individual of the tribe; and in all cases sufficiently great, if justly divided and prudently expended, to enable them, in addition to their own exertions, to live comfortably. And, as a stimulus for exertion, it is now provided by law that in all cases of the appointment of interpreters, or other persons employed for the benefit of the Indians, a preference shall be given to persons of Indian descent, if such can be found who are properly qualified for the discharge of the duties.

Such are the arrangements for the physical comfort, and for the moral improvement, of the Indians. The necessary measures for their political advancement, and for their separation from our citizens, have not been neglected. The pledge of the United States has been given by Congress that the country destined for the residence of this people, shall be forever "secured and guaranteed to them." A country, west of Missouri and Arkansas, has been assigned them, into which the white settlement are not to be pushed. No political communities can be formed in that extensive region, except those which are established by the Indians themselves or by the United States for them, and with their concurrence. A barrier has thus been raised, for their protection against the encroachments of our citizens, and guarding the Indians, as far as possible, from those evils which have brought them to their present condition. Summary authority has been given by law, to destroy all ardent spirits found in their country, without waiting the doubtful result and slow process of a legal seizure. I consider the absolute and unconditional interdiction of this article, among these people, as the first and great step in their amelioration. Half-way measures will answer no purpose. These cannot successfully contend against the cupidity of the seller, and the overpowering appetite of the buyer. And the destructive effects of the traffic are marked in every page of the history of our Indian intercourse.

ANDREW JACKSON'S CAMPAIGN in the First Seminole War did not succeed in subduing the Floridian natives. The United States government decided that removal of all Indians of Florida to the Indian Territory in the West was the best solution for persistent conflict between the Seminole and encroaching white settlers.

By the terms of the Treaty of Paynes Landing (1832), the Seminole were supposed to migrate west of the Mississippi River within thirty-six months. By 1834, 3,824 Indians had made the journey. The largest faction of Seminole, led by their chief Osceola (1804? to 1838), refused to go. Osceola, whose father was not Indian, vowed "to fight till the last drop of Seminole blood has moistened the dust of his hunting ground." In response to his resistance, Osceola was briefly imprisoned. A few months following his release, he commenced attacks on the Americans. In November the Second Seminole War (1835 to 1842) erupted. Federal troops were sent to Florida but had little success against the Indians, whose raiding parties struck quickly and then vanished.[18]

On Christmas Day, Chief Philip led his Miccosukee warriors in an attack on five plantations south of St. Augustine. The population of St. Augustine swelled as white refugees and their slaves flocked into the town for safety. Soldiers also filled the streets of St. Augustine, some on leave, others on duty, many recovering from wounds, but most recovering from malaria and various fevers.[19]

On December 28, 1835, Osceola murdered Indian agent Wiley Thompson. When Osceola had verbally opposed the removal of the Seminole by becoming abusive, making threats and insulting remarks, he was placed in chains and irons and dragged into a jail cell by soldiers. His frenzied cries went unheeded, and Thompson was told the threats were aimed at him. "The sun is high," shouted Osceola. "I will remember the hour. The agent has had his day. I will have mine."[20]

General Wiley Thompson was dining at Mr. Erastus Rogers's (the sutler at Fort King) house with nine other persons, just outside the gates to Fort King. The fort's garrison had just left with Brigadier General Duncan Lamont Clinch, for his plantation "Auld Lang Syne," because of a lack of food and supplies. Before leaving, General Clinch sent a dispatch to Fort Brooke for troops to relieve the garrison. After the soldiers departed, Osceola and a band of supporters, who were lying in wait until the column was gone, came up on the cabin and fired a volley towards the front door of the house. The door was soon kicked open by the Seminoles, and the members of the dinner party that were not killed in the first volley scrambled for the windows. Several men made it out of the window and ran for the woods, only to be killed by their pursuers. Five of the dinner party survived the ambush and got away to tell their story. General Thompson was found with a total of fifteen musket balls in him. According to reports one of the rounds came from a silver-plated rifle that he had given to Osceola in lieu of his help in keeping peace on the reservation.

The same day, Major Francis Langhorne Dade and his U.S. troops were ambushed by 300 Seminole warriors near Fort King (Ocala). Dade had written his mother a week earlier that, "We are every day expecting an attack," but "all the Indians in Florida could not do us the slightest injury."[21] The column included a detachment of Company "B," Fourth Infantry, Company "C," detachments from Companies "B" and "H" of the Second Regiment of Artillery, and Company "B" of the Third Regiment of Artillery, along with a guide, surgeon, and teamsters; the force totaling approximately 100 men and eight officers bound for Fort King from Fort Brooke. Dade's force was told upon leaving Fort Brooke to be ready for any hostilities. There had been reports of recent uprisings north of the reservation and their route would take them into the heart of Seminole country. The messages sent by General Clinch from Fort King were vague in the description of the current situation. In his dispatches, he had just stated that he needed troops at Fort King immediately, never stating why. The commanding officer at Fort Brooke took this as meaning the fort was under siege and needed help immediately. He frantically mustered the force and sent them on their way hoping to send re-enforcements as soon as they arrived by ship at Fort Brooke, which was reported to him as any day.[22]

Once Dade reached the pine barrens, he believed that there would be little to no trouble on his way to Fort King. Near Wahoo Swamp, however, Chiefs Micanopy, Alligator, and Jumper laid in ambush for the column. Their initial musket volley at point-blank range killed or wounded half the command. Major Dade and Captain Upton S. Fraser were the first to be killed. Three of the six surviving officers were wounded. Captain George W. Gardiner rallied the men and returned fire with the six-pound cannon.

As the Seminoles withdrew a short distance, the soldiers hastily built a small breastwork made out of logs in a triangle. They then cared for the wounded and collected ammunition from the fallen. The Indians' second attack lasted until about 2:00 P.M., when all the firing from the breastwork ceased. Most of the command was dead. The Seminoles, followed by their black allies, closed in. Three wounded soldiers, Edwin DeCourcey, Joseph Sprague, and Ransom Clark made it to Fort Brooke alive. Dade's black interpreter, Louis Pacheco, was taken captive. The Seminoles, with only three warriors killed and five wounded, retired to Wahoo Swamp to celebrate.

These events led to the Second Seminole War. The natives retreated into the Everglades, began guerilla tactics against United States forces and fought desperately for more than seven years. By 1837, the Seminole apparently had managed to force a truce. During negotiations, however, Oceola was arrested while negotiating under a flag of truce. He was confined first at Saint Augustine, then Fort Moultrie at Charleston, South Carolina, where he died on January 30, 1838.[23]

His followers fought on, but, by 1842, they were nearly exterminated. Some 4,420 Seminoles surrendered and were deported to Oklahoma. A few hundred managed to remain in the Everglades under the leadership of Billy Bowlegs, their principal chief. The American forces did not overcome the Seminole resistance until 1842. The cost for the United States was 1,500 dead and $20,000,000.

In 1837, A SMALLPOX EPIDEMIC erupted among the Mandan, Hidatsa, and Arikara tribes of the upper Missouri. From 1837 to 1870, at least four different smallpox epidemics ravaged western tribes. The disease came to the Upper Missouri aboard the American Fur Company steamboat, *St. Peter*. On its supply voyage north to Fort Clark and Fort Union in the spring of 1837, smallpox broke out among the ship's crew. By the time the *St. Peter* reached the government's agency for the Sioux near Fort Pierre in early June, three Arikaras passengers traveling north to Fort Clark were in the advanced stages of the disease. Though they had recovered before disembarking at Fort Clark on June 19, the Arikaras remained infectious and introduced the disease to the villages near the post. Meanwhile, Jacob Halsey had boarded the steamboat at Fort Pierre to make the journey to Fort Union, after leaving Fort Clark. Halsey came down with smallpox. His case, however, was not of a serious nature, for he was recovering by the time the St. Peter reached Fort Union on June 24. Nevertheless, Halsey remained infectious, thereby bringing the virus to the Northern post.[24]

But the diseases of the white man were not confined to the Upper Missouri. By November 1847, an outbreak of measles spread through the Cayuse Indian tribes in Oregon. The Cayuse felt they had suffered long enough from new diseases and the failed ministrations of Dr. Marcus Whitman. In their culture, a shaman or curer who failed was subject to death. This doctor, a strapping, determined white man had come into their lands uninvited. The mission he and his wife established worked like a magnet to draw immigrants. Each year the wagon trains descended the Blue Mountains and, like the grasshoppers that swept across the countryside, they heralded discomforting changes. Smallpox, measles, fevers, death, and mourning came in their wake.[25]

On November 29, 1847, a band of Cayuse men, fed by fear and resentment, fell upon the missionary station. In a matter of hours, they killed Marcus and Narcissa Whitman and a dozen others. Two more died subsequently of exposure and forty-seven, many orphaned children of immigrants, were taken captive. The Spaldings fled Lapwai and skirted the Cayuse homeland in their dash to safety. Panic swept through the Willamette settlements. Initially the settlers thought the tribes of the Columbia Plateau might drive through the Gorge and attempt to murder them, too.

The Provisional Legislature faced its greatest test. While Peter Skene Ogden of the Hudson's Bay Company was rushing east with sixteen men to try to ransom the hostages, Governor Abernathy called for "immediate and prompt action." The legislature authorized raising companies of volunteers to go to war against the Cayuse Tribe. It entrusted command to Colonel Cornelius Gilliam and named a committee to negotiate with the Hudson's Bay Company for loans of arms, ammunition, and supplies to mount the campaign. The government wrestled with two approaches: one, to send peace commissioners to try to persuade the Cayuse to turn over the perpetrators, and, two, to wage a war of retribution. In short order it did both. Governor Abernethy appointed a peace commission—Joel Palmer, Henry A.G. Lee, and Robert Newell. Gilliam, who did not approve of the commission, set out in January 1848 with more than 500 volunteers.

The Cayuse War became, at times, a war of nerves. The peace commissioners and friendly Indians tried to end hostilities and get the Cayuse to turn over the killers of those at the Whitman station. Gilliam and his forces, eager for action, provoked conflicts with both friendly and hostile Indians. In March, having persuaded the Cayuse to surrender five men, the military brought them to Oregon City. They were charged, tried, and hanged in 1850. The guilt of the five Indians and the jurisdiction of the court were not fully established. Controversy swirled for decades after this trial—the first culminating in capital punishment following legal proceedings in the Oregon Territory.

In THE SEVENTEENTH CENTURY, the Navajo lived in the area between the Little Colorado and San Juan rivers in northeast Arizona, but they ranged well beyond that region. The Navajo were a predacious tribe of some fifty clans who, frequently with their Apache allies, regularly pillaged the Pueblo and later the Spanish and Mexican settlements in New Mexico, principally for livestock.

Suddenly the Americans arrived in Santa Fe in August 1846 with the intent to make the territory home. Navajo leaders met with American soldiers that November and concluded the Bear Springs Treaty. However, persistent quarrels with American soldiers provoked organized hostilities. Punitive expeditions against the Navajo were only temporarily successful. Meanwhile, Mexico and the United States signed the Treaty of Guadalupe Hidalgo on February 2, 1848, which concluded the Mexican War. Having lost, Mexico was compelled to relinquish half of its territory, including Texas, New Mexico, Colorado, Arizona, Utah, Nevada, and California. The Navajo homeland was part of this vast cession of land. Navajos now existed within the formal jurisdiction of the United States government. In 1851, Fort Defiance was erected in Navajo country. The first United States fort built in what would become Arizona Territory (1863), Fort Defiance's purposes were to thwart the Navajo, labeled as one of the "wild tribes," and encourage Anglo-American settlement. The Americans also attempted to assign the Navajo to a reservation, but they refused. In 1858, Manuelito, a Navajo chief, discovered sixty head of his livestock shot by U.S. soldiers. Outraged, he confronted the commander at Fort Defiance and told him the land belonged to him and his people, not to the soldiers. Troops from the fort, augmented by 160 paid Zuni warriors, torched Manuelito's fields and village. The chief then resolved to drive the soldiers off the land and commenced to rally other Navajo leaders for war. In 1860, more than 1,000 Navajos attacked Fort Defiance. They nearly overran it, but superior gunfire forced a retreat. This would lead to the army's policy of "total war" against the Navajos.

IN 1849, CONGRESS TRANSFERRED the Bureau of Indian Affairs from the War Department to the newly created Department of the Interior. With this transfer came a change in policy and responsibilities. The removal of tribes to reservations had brought about disease and starvation, which forced the government to begin providing tribes with food and other supplies. Administering the distribution of this aid became a responsibility of the Bureau of Indian Affairs.[26]

DURING THE 1850S, there was an immense immigration from the eastern and southern states to the new states and territories. These new settlers moved into the State of Iowa and the Territories of Kansas, Nebraska, and Minnesota. These immigrants into the new settlements were confined to narrow belts along the streams and lakes where large groves of timber were in abundance.

Further west, the Indian, with no friend or law to protect him, was often wantonly shot down by the white man. These outrages culminated in the Mariposa War, 1850 to 1851, in California. During this war, hundreds of

Indians were killed and thousands of dollars looted from the state treasury. The first attack occurred at Volcano where a party of Indians was digging for gold. A party of miners came along and began digging. Soon after this, a miner lost his pick and accused an Indian of stealing it. The Indian chief then started on the run for the rancheria to make inquiry about the pick. The miner, believing him guilty, raised his rifle and shot him dead. The Indians raised the war cry and began arming for a fight. The miners then aroused the white men of the vicinity by circulating the report that the chief had killed a white man. The whites then drove the savages from the place, killing a large number of them.[27]

In the south, in Fresno County, the Indians launched the first attack. They accused the whites of driving off the game from their hunting ground, poisoning the streams and killing the fish, and they said they would starve if action was not taken. In January 1850, the Indians threatened to exterminate the whites if they did not leave the country. Soon after this threat, they swooped down upon the miners and drove off all of their horses, mules, and cattle to their mountain rancherias. Detached companies of whites were organized, and the armed miners pursued the Indians. In one skirmish, two members of the company from Big Oak Flat were killed.

At this time, James A. Savage was conducting two stores, one on the Fresno River and the other at Agua Fria. Late in December 1850, the Indians made an attack upon the stores and killed three whites. The Indians stripped the dead of all their clothing, broke open the safe and took all of the gold dust and hastened away, driving with them all of the horses and cattle of that vicinity. About the same time, Savage's Agua Fria store was also attacked, two men were killed, and Savage's wife was taken prisoner. Cassiday, a rival storekeeper, was also killed, as well as four miners working upon Four Creeks.

One soldier, who was engaged in the fracas with the Indians, later wrote:

> At this point, engaged in gold mining, [Savage] had employed a party of native Indians. Early in the season of 1850 his trading post and mining camp were attacked by a band of the Yosemite Indians. This tribe, or band, claimed the territory in that vicinity, and attempted to drive

42

Savage off. Their real object, however, was plunder. They were considered treacherous and dangerous, and were very troublesome to the miners generally.

Savage and his Indian miners repulsed the attack and drove off the marauders, but from this occurrence he no longer deemed this location desirable. Being fully aware of the murderous propensities of his assailants, he removed to Mariposa Creek, not far from the junction of the Aqua Fria, and near to the site of the old stone fort. Soon after, he established a branch post on the Fresno, where the mining prospects became most encouraging, as the high water subsided in that stream. This branch station was placed in charge of a man by the name of Greeley.

At these establishments Savage soon built up a prosperous business. He exchanged his goods at enormous profits for the gold obtained from his Indian miners. The white miners and prospecting parties also submitted to his demands rather than lose time by going to Mariposa village. The value of his patrons' time was thus made a source of revenue. As the season advanced, this hardy pioneer of commerce rapidly increased his wealth, but in the midst of renewed prosperity he learned that another cloud was gathering over him. One of his five squaws assured him that a combination was maturing among the mountain Indians, to kill or drive all the white men from the country, and plunder them of their property. To strengthen his influence over the principal tribes, Savage had, according to the custom of many mountain men, taken wives from among them, supposing his personal safety would be somewhat improved by so doing. This is the old story of the prosperous Indian trader. Rumor also came from his Indian miners, that the Yosemites threatened to come down on him again for the purpose of plunder, and that they were urging other tribes to join them. These reports he affected to disregard, but quietly cautioned the miners to guard against marauders.[28]

Governor McDougal authorized the sheriff of Mariposa County to enlist 250 men for duty. The Indian peace commissioners also visited Mariposa to see if they could not arrange terms of peace, as it was well known that the Indians had been abused and unjustly treated by the settlers. Indians friendly to the whites were sent to all the surrounding tribes, inviting them to come in and meet the commissioners. Some of the tribes sent their agents. The majority failed to respond; they feared the treachery of the whites. Among the latter was the Yosemite tribe. Their chief, Ten-ie-ya, told the messenger, Pon-wat-chee, that they would remain in the mountains.

This settled the question with the Yosemite tribe, and it was finally resolved to drive them out of their secret fortress, then unknown to the whites.[29]

Major Savage sent a special message to Ten-ie-ya to come and see him. The old chief came and said the tribe would come the next day, but they failed to appear. Then the Mariposa battalion of forty picked men was organized to march in and drive out the Yosemite tribe. The company was under the command of Major Savage and Captain Boling, and they compelled the old chief to lead the way to the Sierra fortress. Some fifteen miles from their starting point the company met a number of the tribe coming from the valley. They were loaded down with Indian goods and slowly floundering through the snow. The old chief now declared that there were no more Indians in the mountains. As there were no warriors among the Indians, Savage knew that some two hundred braves had been left behind. The old chief was permitted to return to Savage's camp. A young Indian was compelled to act as guide, and the company pushed on through the snow, from three to five feet in depth. Traveling on, they reached a high cliff. The battalion began its descent, and traveling five miles along a deep and narrow pathway, on the night of May 5, 1851, they camped in the Yosemite Valley. The following morning they began hunting for the braves. All that they found was the smouldering campfires of the Indians. They had retreated far back in the mountains. Remaining two days in the valley, the company returned to Savage's camp.

The Indians who had come to the upper valley were now permitted to return to their Yosemite home, as it was believed that they would give no further trouble. Immediately they began to make hostile demonstrations. A second expedition consisting in part of United States troops was organized, and they took several prisoners, among them Ten-ie-ya's three sons. The next year, the Indians killed five miners at work in Coarse Gold Gulch. The alarmed settlers sent word to Fort Miller, and a detachment of regulars under the command of Lieutenant Moore started in pursuit. Upon finding the Indians, five of them were dressed in the dead miners' clothing; as this was considered positive proof of their guilt, they were shot. The balance of the tribe fled far back into the mountains. Expecting that if they would push on they would find the old Chief Ten-ie-ya, the troops kept in pursuit but failed to find any Indians and returned to Fort Miller. In 1853 a fight took place between the Yosemite and Mono tribes. The Yosemite tribe was completely destroyed and the Monos, on catching old Ten-ie-ya, stoned him to death.

Dr. Lafayette Houghton Bunnell, who served with the Thirty-sixth Regiment of Wisconsin Volunteers, later wrote: "During 1850, the Indians in Mariposa County, which at that date included all the territory south of the divide of the Tuolumne and Merced rivers within the valley proper of the San Joaquin, became very troublesome to the miners and settlers. Their depredations and murderous assaults were continued until the arrival of the United States Indian commissioners, in 1851, when the general government assumed control over them. Through the management of the commissioners, treaties were made, and many of these Indians were transferred to locations reserved for their special occupancy."[30]

That same year, angered by the ever-encroaching of whites, the Yuma and Mojave Indians went on the warpath. The Yumans had prospered in the area, eventually helping white settlers and gold seekers across the Colorado River into California and making a profit at it. Although they resented the sheer number of whites who were entering the area, they still maintained benefits from their journeys. However, whites soon became jealous of their monopoly on the river crossings. Scalp-hunter John Joel Glanton led a group that tried to kill off the Yuman and monopolize the river crossings. Their attempts failed, and most of the scalp-hunters were killed. Eventually, Fort Yuma was reestablished in the area by Major Samuel Heintzelman in February 1852, which took away the river crossing business from the Yuma. The Fort helped establish the Colorado Ferry Company as it began operation there soon after the reestablishment of the fort. The last battle the Yumans fought was in 1857. They, along with their allies the Mohaves, attacked the Maricopa Indians on the other side of the river. The Maricopas, counterattacking on horseback, killed over 100 Yumans, thus weakening their immediate threat in the area.

At the time of the Indian uprising, late in 1851 and early in 1852, considerable anxiety was felt for the safety of the government stores at new San

Diego, it being suggested that the depot would be a natural point of attack for the "loot-loving savages," and the number of regular troops being small. Several whites were killed by the Indians in a massacre at Warner's ranch.[31]

ATROCITIES SUCH AS THESE caused the government to reexamine their Indian policy and make some concessions to the various tribes. The Treaty of Fort Laramie was signed on September 17, 1851, between the federal government and chiefs of several different Indian nations in an effort to placate the insurgent Indians for losses of game and grass caused by white invasion. The safety of immigrant trains and the maintenance of peace were at stake. The treaty read:

> Articles of a treaty made and concluded at Fort Laramie, in the Indian Territory, between D.D. Mitchell, superintendent of Indian affairs, and Thomas Fitzpatrick, Indian agent, commissioners specially appointed and authorized by the President of the United States, of the first part, and the chiefs, headmen, and braves of the following Indian nations, residing south of the Missouri River, east of the Rocky Mountains, and north of the lines of Texas and New Mexico, viz, the Sioux or Dahcotahs, Cheyennes, Arrapahoes, Crows, Assinaboines, Gros-Ventre Mandans, and Arrickaras, parties of the second part, on the seventeenth day of September, A.D. one thousand eight hundred and fifty-one. (a)
>
> ARTICLE 1. The aforesaid nations, parties to this treaty, having assembled for the purpose of establishing and confirming peaceful relations amongst themselves, do hereby covenant and agree to abstain in future from all hostilities whatever against each other, to maintain good faith and friendship in all their mutual intercourse, and to make an effective and lasting peace.
>
> ARTICLE 2. The aforesaid nations do hereby recognize the right of the United States Government to establish roads, military and other posts, within their respective territories.
>
> ARTICLE 3. In consideration of the rights and privileges acknowledged in the preceding article, the United States bind themselves to protect the aforesaid Indian nations against the commission of all depredations by the people of the said United States, after the ratification of this treaty.
>
> ARTICLE 4. The aforesaid Indian nations do hereby agree and bind themselves to make restitution or satisfaction for any wrongs committed, after the ratification of this treaty, by any band or individual of their people, on the people of the United States, whilst lawfully residing in or passing through their respective territories.

ARTICLE 5. The aforesaid Indian nations do hereby recognize and acknowledge the following tracts of country, included within the metes and boundaries hereinafter designated, as their respective territories, viz; The territory of the Sioux or Dahcotah Nation, commencing the mouth of the White Earth River, on the Missouri River; thence in a southwesterly direction to the forks of the Platte River; thence up the north fork of the Platte River to a point known as the Red Buts, or where the road leaves the river; thence along the range of mountains known as the Black Hills, to the head-waters of Heart River; thence down Heart River to its mouth; and thence down the Missouri River to the place of beginning. The territory of the Gros Ventre, Mandans, and Arrickaras Nations, commencing at the month of Heart River; thence up the Missouri River to the mouth of the Yellowstone River; thence up the Yellowstone River to the mouth of Powder River in a southeasterly direction, to the head-waters of the Little Missouri River; thence along the Black Hills to the head of Heart River, and thence down Heart River to the place of beginning. The territory of the Assinaboin Nation, commencing at the mouth of Yellowstone River; thence up the Missouri River to the mouth of the Muscle-shell River; thence from the mouth of the Muscle-shell River in a southeasterly direction until it strikes the head-waters of Big Dry Creek; thence down that creek to where it empties into the Yellowstone River, nearly opposite the mouth of Powder River, and thence down the Yellowstone River to the place of beginning. The territory of the Blackfoot Nation, commencing at the mouth of Muscle-shell River; thence up the Missouri River to its source; thence along the main range of the Rocky Mountains, in a southerly direction, to the head-waters of the northern source of the Yellowstone River; thence down the Yellowstone River to the mouth of Twenty-five Yard Creek; thence across to the head-waters of the Muscle-shell River, and thence down the Muscle-shell River to the place of beginning. The territory of the Crow Nation, commencing at the mouth of Powder River on the Yellowstone; thence up Powder River to its source; thence along the main range of the Black Hills and Wind River Mountains to the head-waters of the Yellowstone River; thence down the Yellowstone River to the mouth of Twenty-five Yard Creek; thence to the head waters of the Muscle-shell River; thence down the Muscle-shell River to its mouth; thence to the head-waters of Big Dry Creek, and thence to its mouth. The territory of the Cheyennes and Arrapahoes, commencing at the Red Bute, or the place where the road leaves the north fork of the Platte River; thence up the north fork of the Platte River to its source; thence along the main range of the Rocky Mountains to the head-waters of the Arkansas River; thence down the Arkansas River to the crossing of the Santa Fe' road; thence in a northwesterly direction to the forks of the Platte River, and thence up the Platte River to the place of beginning. It is, however, understood that, in making this recognition and acknowledgement, the aforesaid Indian nations do not hereby abandon or prejudice any rights or claims they may have to other lands; and further, that they do not surrender the privilege of hunting, fishing, or passing over any of the tracts of country heretofore described.

ARTICLE 6. The parties to the second part of this treaty having selected principals or head-chiefs for their respective nations, through whom all national business will hereafter be conducted, do hereby bind themselves to sustain said chiefs and their successors during good behavior.

ARTICLE 7. In consideration of the treaty stipulations, and for the damages which have or may occur by reason thereof to the Indian nations, parties hereto, and for their maintenance and the improvement of their moral and social customs, the United States bind themselves to deliver to the said Indian nations the sum of fifty thousand dollars per annum for the term of ten years, with the right to continue the same at the discretion of the President of the United States for a period not exceeding five years thereafter, in provisions merchandise, domestic animals, and agricultural implements, in such proportions as may be deemed best adapted to their condition by the President of the United States, to be distributed in proportion to the population of the aforesaid Indian nations.

ARTICLE 8. It is understood and agreed that should any of the Indian nations, parties to this treaty, violate any of the provisions thereof, the United States may withhold the whole or a portion of the annuities mentioned in the preceding article from the nation so offending, until, in the opinion of the President of the United States, proper satisfaction shall have been made.[32]

The primary purpose of the Fort Laramie Treaty of 1851 had been to assure safe passage for whites along the Oregon Trail. During the late summer of 1854, about 4,000 Brule and Ogallala Sioux had camped near Fort Laramie to receive their annual distribution of goods provided under the terms of the treaty. On August 18th, a party of Danish immigrants, who had been converted to the Mormon faith, headed through a valley on their way to settlements in Utah. A cow belonging to the Hans Peter Olsen Company broke away, strayed into the Brules' camp and was killed by High Forehead, a visiting Miniconjou Sioux. The animal's owner reported the incident to authorities at Fort Laramie and demanded that the responsible Indian be punished.[33]

Realizing the seriousness of the incident, Conquering Bear hurried to Fort Laramie to pay for the cow. Lieutenant Hugh B. Fleming, commander

Fort Laramie, 1849. (Author's collection)

of the post, considered the killing a trivial matter and took no action, even though Conquering Bear offered to trade a horse for the dead cow. The following morning, the respected Ogalala Chief Man-Afraid-of-His-Horses, went to the fort and conferred with the commander, but he was treated as "just another Indian" and possibly a spy.[34]

Lieutenant John L. Grattan, fresh from West Point, insisted on the arrest of High Forehead. Accompanied by an inebriated interpreter, twenty-eight troops, and two twelve-pounder howitzers, Grattan rode toward the Brules' camp looking for trouble. Man-Afraid-of-His-Horses later stated:

> I was encamped at Bissonette's at the time of the first occurrence, heard of the close proximity of the Agent, and moved down to the Ogallala camp. They and the Brule were encamped close together. When I got there they told me that a Minniconjou had killed an emigrant's cow. I went to Bordeau's with a Crow Indian. The clerk gave a paper to the Crow to go to the fort. I [went to the] fort with the Crow. We came to the fort and the commanding officer was asleep. We sat in the store some time when he came in and the Crow gave him the paper. He then gave the Crow some provisions and gave me some also. The officer then took out a large paper and was looking at it a long time and mentioned my name and the interpreter who was there pointed me out to him. He then turned to me and asked why I had not told my name when I came in, for had he known me he would have given me more provisions. He told me to look for the arrival of the agent, as he was close. After he said this to me he looked at the paper the Crow had given him and while looking at it two men came in a great hurry and

gave him another paper. He read it and I heard him say "Minniconjou." The interpreter asked me if I knew of a cow being killed. At first I said no but then recollected that a cow had been killed. I then said, "Yes, I have heard of a cow having been killed by a Minniconjou Indian." The officer went out and I saw him go to the big house. He then came back from the store and talked very loud. I do not understand English and do not know what he said.

The young officer [John L. Grattan] then went to the Soldier's House and the next thing I saw was a wagon go over to the Adobe Fort and next saw the soldiers draw a cannon out of the fort. I went out of the store and stood by the cannon and saw the soldiers taking a great many things out of the house. Then I saw them clean out the cannon preparing to load it. The officer then went to the store and talked very loud.

The interpreter said to me, "It is my place to do as the captain tells me and I suppose the Sioux will want to kill me or think hard of me that they were going to get the Indian who had killed the cow." The officer then said to me, "I will give the Bear forty soldiers today. [He said] that the Bear had been chief of the Sioux for three years and had always done something foolish. I then told the commanding officer I would go, but he said to me, "No, do not go. If you get there and tell the news, the Indian who killed the cow will run off" and to let the soldiers go first and then for me to go afterward. The two officers talked a great deal together. The wind was blowing very hard at this time. The interpreter said to me that he believed that he had to die. At this time the young officer was playfully sticking at the interpreter with his sword, telling him to make haste. The interpreter said to me, "I am ready but must have something to drink before I die." They gave him a bottle and he drank.

By this time the horse was saddled for him. The horse belonged to the storekeeper. I said to the officer, "You had better not go tonight, that there are a great many Sioux." The officer said to me, "Yes, that is good." The wagons and cannons by this time had crossed the river. I started to go to the river and the interpreter called me. The officer, interpreter, and one white man who was not a soldier and myself started together and went ahead. When we got on the hill, I told the officer that there was a heap of lodges, but he said it was good as he was going to war [with] them. He told me if any other Indians wanted to interfere to tell them to stay to one side. We then got in sight of the lodges. I told him again, "Look, my friend, you not see a heap of lodges?" By this time the interpreter was drunk and was talking a great deal. He said the soldiers had killed three Minniconjous last summer, and that all the Sioux were women. He was drinking all along the road. The soldiers in the wagon were drinking out of the bottle. By this time they were in a fullness. . . . We got to Gratiot's houses and all the soldiers went in. Some whites who were in the house came out and asked me what was the matter. I said to them that they were white and for them to ask the soldiers. The soldiers came out of the house and some loaded their guns and fixed bayonets. I went into a lodge. Interpreter and the officer called me out and said that the Ogallalas had nothing to do with this business. "We are going to the Bear's camp as the Minniconjous are camped with him, and we will ask the Bear for the Indian and we will get him. . . ."[35]

Grattan and his party rode into the Sioux encampment. Chief Conquering Bear, the spokesman for all the Sioux, tried to defuse the situation by offering another horse in return for the dead cow, but Grattan refused the offer. When Conquering Bear turned to walk away, a soldier immediately shot him. Both sides then opened fire. Within moments all the white soldiers were dead except for one. He had his tongue cut out and later died at Ft. Laramie.

When news of the Grattan Massacre reached the War Department, plans were immediately formulated to punish the Sioux. General William Selby Harney, fifty-three years of age and a veteran of thirty-six years in the military, was in Paris on what was supposed to be a two-year leave of absence from the Army to spend time with his wife and children, who made their residence there. In late October he received orders to return to St. Louis to take command of a punitive expedition to begin the following year against the Sioux Indians.

General Harney journeyed from Fort Leavenworth to Fort Laramie with 1,200 men. The expedition consisted of two companies of the Second

South view of Fort Leavenworth. (Author's collection)

General John Buford. (Author's collection)

Dragoons with future general, John Buford, five companies of the Sixth Infantry, one of the Tenth Infantry, and a battery of the Fourth U.S. Artillery. The purpose of the expedition was to enforce order, provide security for travelers on the Overland Trail and impress the Indians with a show of the army's power. Harney and many of his men, however, had orders to avenge the 1,854 deaths of Lt. John Grattan and his men, who had been massacred a few miles east of Fort Laramie.[36]

Because of its rich grasslands, this area was the grazing land of thousands of buffalo. These beasts, in turn, attracted Indians, and among the most powerful was the Sioux nation. Red Cloud, chief of the Oglala Sioux, was born in Garden County in 1821, and became a leader early in life. Ash Hollow, bounded on the north by the North Platte River, was the converging point of the Mormon Trail and two branches of the Oregon Trail. The general course of this latter trail was along the South Platte to a point near Big Spring. There the South Platte was crossed, and the trail led northward to Ash Hollow, where the travelers rested before continuing westward. Another trail crossed the South Platte at Hershey, in Lincoln County, following the river's north branch from there to Ash Hollow. This was the same path that had been followed by most of the Mormons in 1846.

At Ash Hollow, General Harney's army attacked a band of Brule Oglala and Minneconjoe Sioux and a party of Northern Cheyenne, all under the command of Little Thunder. General Harney's force of dragoons, artillery, and six infantry regiments had assembled at Fort Kearny and moved up the Platte River. Upon reaching Ash Hollow, they discovered the Indians had left a day or two before. Continuing up the North Platte, scouts soon found the Indians camped at the mouth of a Platte tributary. When the Indian camp was first sighted on September 2, 1855, arrangements were made to attack at dawn on the following morning at Ash Hollow on Blue Water Creek, and at ten o'clock that night the stream was forded. Harney planned to hem the Indians between

American Horse (wearing Western clothing) and Red Cloud (wearing native headdress) shaking hands near Pine Ridge Reservation, 1891. (Author's collection)

the cavalry at their rear, and the infantry, who would approach from the front. But while Harney's men were quietly assuming their positions during the night, they were sighted by an Indian woman and her two children, who spread the alarm. The Indians prepared for battle by donning war bonnets and shouting challenges from the opposite river bank.[37]

Harney's 600 soldiers came eye to eye with 250 Sioux men, women, and children under the leadership of Little Thunder, who had succeeded Conquering Bear as the chief of the Brules. Harney, who only days earlier had declared, "By God, I'm for battle—not peace," ordered his men to open fire.

In the ensuing battle, the Indians were routed. Most of them retreated to the north, but a small force hid on the slopes of the hills. They were driven out by the infantry while the cavalry pursued those who retreated. An officer reported hearing shots from a hill fronting the river, and a force was organized to drive them out. This hill was composed of rotten limestone, filled with tiny caves and covered with underbrush. When the piercing cry of a child indicated women and children were hidden in these caves, the troops retired. General Richard S. Drum later told of finding an Indian child abandoned in some thick grass after the battle. When a sergeant attempted to pick up the baby, it scratched and bit him and refused to be quiet. General Drum then gave the sergeant his canteen, which contained lemonade with a fair amount of whisky. This soon quieted the baby, and she was taken to the prisoners' camp. When all the smoke cleared, eighty-five Brules had been killed.

After the Ash Hollow battle, General Harney erected a small field works there. He wanted to establish a post for the support of immigrant trains and to furnish escorts for the monthly mail passing between Forts Kearny and Laramie. A small garrison was stationed there but for only a month. Harney then led his men on a march through Sioux country to demonstrate the army's strength to other Sioux bands, but they encountered no further resistance.

In 1856, General Harney held a council with the Sioux at Fort Pierre. He was still searching for the man who had killed the cow. The Sioux agreed to deliver the man and to make restitution for property destroyed. They did so, making a settlement they would have been glad to make before or during the battle.[38]

For his handling of Ash Hollow, Harney was forever afterwards known among the Sioux as "the Butcher." However, for United States military officials and the ever-increasing numbers of immigrants traveling the Oregon and Mormon Trails, Harney's execution of the affair bought them ten more years of relative peace. One young Oglala Teton who had been in the camp the night Conquering Bear received his fatal blow would especially be remembered. His name was Crazy Horse, and, in a vision soon after the incident, he would discover his purpose and destiny as a war chief in battles to come.[39]

In 1864, as soldiers searched the plains for any hostile Sioux, they came upon some ruins on the prairie. Captain Eugene Ware penned the following in his diary: "The ruins, first and second, were ruins of stone stations which had been put up by ranchmen for the overland express company running through to Salt Lake; but the express company, for the time being, was knocked out of existence, so that there was at the time of which I speak no mail, stage, or express carried over the road except by soldiers. There was also a pile of stone about two feet high and ten feet square, where the celebrated Gratton massacre had taken place. This has been written of so often that I will not refer to it except to say that a lieutenant with a few men was sent to deal with some Indians, several years before, and make them surrender some property, and having a piece of artillery, the Indians being obstinate, he fired over the heads of the Indians to scare them, and the Indians immediately massacred the whole detachment."[40]

W HILE HOSTILITIES CONTINUED IN THE WEST, a third clash between the government and the Seminoles erupted in Florida. The Third Seminole War, 1855 to 1858, also known as the Billy Bowlegs War, was the final clash of an intermittent guerrilla conflict between the Seminole Indians of Florida and the United States. By the mid-1850s, more than 3,000 Seminole had been deported. The Seminole leader at this point was Billy Bowlegs (Olactomico), a chief who was part of a ruling family. In the 1850s, while he and fellow Seminole were still subsisting quietly on their own lands in south Florida, the chief was sorely provoked by a United States surveying corps under a Colonel Harney. Under cover of darkness, Harney and his surveyors sneaked into Bowlegs's flourishing banana plantation and thrashed the crop. When faced by the stunned chief, the surveyors bluntly claimed responsibility because they wanted "to see old Billy cut up." Thus began the Third Seminole War.

Relentless United States military incursions, complete with bloodhounds, reduced the Seminole population to between 200 and 300 individuals. The war ended with Bowlegs's surrender on May 7, 1858. He had only forty warriors with him. Shortly afterwards, Colonel Loomis, commander of the forces in Florida, announced an end to all hostilities. In effect, the

United States government had abandoned efforts to remove all Seminoles. In exchange for small cash outlays, Bowlegs agreed to leave Florida with about 165 members of his tribe and travel to Oklahoma, but the old chief died shortly thereafter. Two organized bands and several families stayed behind in Big Cypress and other secluded parts of Florida, living in "unwalled, palm-thatched chickees set in trackless swamps." The tiny remnant that hung on had never surrendered.[41]

A TREATY NEGOTIATED WITH GREAT BRITAIN in 1846 and the Whitman incident, spurred efforts to establish the American presence more firmly in the lands of Oregon. In 1849 the United States Army established outposts to protect settlers along the Oregon Trail. The 1850 Land Claim Donation Act allowed couples to claim up to 640 acres. All that blocked northwest settlement was Indian title to the lands.

In 1855, Governor and Superintendent of Indian Affairs for Washington Territory Isaac Ingalls Stevens, and Joel Palmer, superintendent for the State of Oregon, organized the Walla Walla Council with regional Indians in the Walla Walla Valley. Altogether, approximately 5,000 Indians from the east side of the Cascades, including Umatillas, Cayuses, and Walla Wallas attended the late May through early June 1855 meetings.

As Governor Stevens traveled to the Walla Walla Council in May 1855, he stopped at Fort Dalles asking for a small body of troops to escort the commissioners to the meetings. The troops were also needed to guard the presents, which would be distributed among the Indians. Lieutenant Lawrence Kip, among the recruits who joined the governor at Fort Dalles, traveling with him to the council, recorded his experiences:

> Wednesday, May 23d. At two o'clock P.M. we arrived at the ground selected for the council, having made the march in six days. It was in one of the most beautiful spots of the Walla Walla Valley, well wooded and with plenty of water. Ten miles distant is seen the range of the Blue Mountains, forming the southeast boundary of the Great Plains along the Columbia, whose waters it divides from those of the Lewis River. It stretches away along the horizon until it is lost in the dim distance where the chain unites with the Snake River Mountains. Here we found

General Palmer, the Superintendent of Indian Affairs, and Governor Stevens, with their party, who had already pitched their tents.[42]

Lieutenant Kip also penned:

When about a mile distant they halted, and half a dozen chiefs rode forward and were introduced to Governor Stevens and General Palmer, in order of their rank. Then on came the rest of the wild horseman in single file clashing their shields, singing and beating their drums as they marched past us. Then they formed a circle and dashed around us, while our little group stood there, the center of their wild evolutions. They would gallop us as if about to make a charge, then wheel round and round, sounding their loud whoops until they had apparently worked themselves up into an intense excitement. Then some score or two dismounted, and forming a ring danced for about twenty minutes, while those surrounding them beat time on their drums. After these performances, more than twenty of the chiefs when over to the tent of Governor Stevens, where they sat for some time, smoking the "pipe of peace," in token of good fellowship, and then returned to their camping ground. . . .[43]

For days Stevens and Palmer tried to convince the Indians that it was in their best interest to cede land to the United States. Said Stevens: "What shall we do at this council? We want you and ourselves to agree upon tracts of lands where you shall live; in those tracts of land we want each man who will work to have his own land, his own horses, his own cattle, and his home for himself and his children."

Tauitua, the young chief of the Umatilla Valley, however, declared, ". . . the land where my forefathers are buried should be mine. That is the place that I am speaking for. We shall talk about it . . . we shall then know, my brothers, that is what I have to show you, that is what I love—the place we get our roots to live upon—the salmon comes up the stream."[44]

An irritated Cayuse leader named Young Chief stated: "I wonder if the ground is listening to what is said. . . . The ground says, it is the Great Spirit that placed me here. . . . The Great Spirit directs me, feed the Indians well. The grass says the same thing, feed the horses and cattle. . . . The ground says, the Great Spirit has placed me here to produce all that grows on me, trees and fruit."

Chief Owhi of the Yakimas added: "Shall I give the land which is part of my body and leave myself poor and destitute? . . . I cannot say so."[45]

Joel Palmer did not give up and told them that white men would be coming to the region "like grasshoppers on the plains," and no one would be able to stop them. Palmer promised that entering into a treaty would allow the Indians to choose their lands. At the same time, the Indian agents tried to convince the Cayuse, Walla Walla, and Umatilla to move to Nez Perce Country.

After much wrangling, the commissioners changed their tactics, promising the Cayuse, Walla Walla, and Umatilla a reservation in the Umatilla Valley. On June 9, 1855, two Umatilla leaders, Weyatenatemany and Wenap-snoot, signed the Walla Walla, Cayuse, and Umatilla Treaty. More than 6.4 million acres of land was ceded in northeastern Oregon and southeastern Washington. By June 11, all the tribes present signed over their lands in exchange for reservations, cash, schools, mills, carpenter shops, and blacksmith shops. The Nez Perces, Cayuses, and Yakamas each got $200,000 cash. The Walla Wallas and Umatillas would share a reservation and $150,000. Schools, housing, health care, and education were promised, and the tribes reserved rights to fish, hunt, and gather traditional foods on the ceded lands.[46]

Shortly after the treaties were signed, Stevens learned of a plot to murder him and his escort. The element of surprise was lost, and Stevens and his party moved on to councils in the north. Word of the Puget Sound treaties and increased pressure by settlers created an ugly mood among the Native Americans. Almost 5,000 Indians were present.

Fayette McMullen (who later became governor of the Washington Territory) wrote:

> . . . The Indian tribes within our own territory living west of the Cascade Mountains, numbering some twelve thousand, are showing many signs of discontent, being unquestionable stimulated and encouraged to acts of outrage and violence by the tribes east of the mountains. They . . . could annihilate our settlements, with perhaps the exception of the more considerable villages, in a single night. They complain that the government of the United States has been giving away and is still selling their lands to settlers, without making them any sort of compensation—that they have in good

faith made treaties with the Agent of the United States, whereby they were to receive compensation for their lands, and that these treaties have not been carried out in good faith by our government.

They also say they are put off with promises by the Indian Agents, with the sole purpose keeping them quiet until the white population becomes strong enough to drive them off entirely. . . . They do not understand by what right these things are done, and upon what principals of justice, the government refuses to ratify the treaties and pay them for the land, while it yet passes laws giving away and selling their homes, their hunting grounds and their graves. Reasoning thus, they regard the settlers as trespassers upon their domain, and consequently view them with extreme jealousy.[47]

The actual war began in mid-September 1855 when Charles H Mason, acting governor of the territory, was informed that Indians killed a number of men traveling into eastern Washington. He hurriedly sought aid from Fort Steilacoom and dispatched Lieutenant William A. Slaughter and his men to Naches Pass and east of the Cascades. A large party of Yakima Indians were gathering, however, so they moved back to the western side of the pass.

At the end of October, Captain Maloney went to reinforce Slaughter's troops. He had received orders to take the pass and continue into Eastern Washington, but he decided to stop near the pass and contact his superiors. He became worried about a possible outbreak in the Puget Sound with no military to stop it.

Maloney's suspicions were well founded. A few days later, local Indians struck at the White River settlement and killed several people. Later, two men were killed. Then, in October, Andrew J. Bolon, the first Indian agent for tribes east of the Cascades, was returning to Fort Dalles on horseback, after visiting at the lodge of Chief Kamiakin on the Yakima River. He went there to Investigate the reported murder of two mining prospectors from Seattle, Jameison and Charles Walker. He was assassinated by a band of Indians on the old Wishram Indian trail near a large spring at the head of Bowman Creek in the Simeoe Mountains. The Army responded, and war resulted. The bloody battle of the Yakima Indian War, Pisco Meadows, occurred soon afterward.[48]

In writing of Captain Maurice Maloney, William P. Bonney recorded: "Perhaps at no time in the history of this territory and state has the young military officer been placed in the responsible and delicate position as was

Captain Maloney during the latter part of October 1855—had he not exercised the sound judgment which he displayed . . . when he stopped to consider the situation, the history of the Indian War of 1855-1856 would be written entirely differently than we find it."[49]

Abraham Salatat, an Indian, rode through the Puyallup Valley warning settlers of impending attacks. More than eighty settlers fled their homes and went to Fort Steilacoom. During the war, Ezra Meeker commented about the conditions at the fort: "A sorry mess . . . of women and children crying; some brutes of men cursing and swearing; oxen and cows bellowing, sheep bleating; dogs howling; children lost from their parents; wives from husbands; no order, in a word, the utmost disorder."[50]

Although there were many skirmishes and clashes, the decisive battle of the war west of the mountains was fought in March of 1856 near Connell's Prairie on the main trail to Naches Pass. Lieutenant Gilmore Hays reported that one hundred fifty warriors attacked the one hundred ten men of his command. The battle lasted most of the day before the Indians were routed, put to flight and pursued for a mile or more along the trail. On May 19, 1856, Lieutenant Colonel Silas Casey, commander of the troops at Fort Steilacoom, reported to his superiors that the war west of the Cascade Mountains was at an end.

But war with the Indians was anything but over in the Northwest. Frederick M. Smith, sub-Indian agent at Port Orford, in 1854 addressed the attacks on the Indians in his district. They were ravaged by hunger, dispossession of their villages, suffering the onset of new and fatal diseases, and fearing overt murders. Reporting the massacre of the Lower Coquille Indians, he wrote: "Bold, brave, courageous men! to attack a friendly and defenseless tribe of Indians; to burn, roast, and shoot sixteen of their number, and all on suspicion that they were about to rise and drive from their country three hundred white men!" Smith's lament, the mourning cries of the Indian women, the death rituals of rubbing the hair with pitch, and the inexorable course of hunger, attack, and death precipitated the conflicts known as the Rogue River Wars. The troubles seethed between 1852 and 1856. Finally the United States Army had sufficient forces to mount a campaign in 1855-1856 to destroy the Indians' ability to resist.[51]

It was largely the white man's fault for trading the Indian guns and ammunition for gold and favors from their women. Within a year's time, after the 1855 attacks, the Indians had thrown away their bows and arrows and armed themselves with guns and pistols, and all knew how to use them. After a hard-fought final battle was ended at Big Bend on the lower Rogue River, peace was declared. The Rogue, Illinois River, and Applegate Indians were removed to the Siletz Reservation on the northern Oregon coast during July of 1856.[52]

Forced marches through winter snows or over the rocky headlands and through the sand dunes of coastal Oregon became trails of tears for the hundreds of people driven to the distant reservations. Other survivors were herded aboard the *Columbia*, a side-wheel steamer, which removed them from Port Orford to the Columbia and lower Willamette River area. Then they had to walk the muddy trail to the reservations.[53]

DURING THE SUMMER OF 1857, the United States government decided to make an example of the Cheyenne Indians who had conducted raids in an area west of the forts in the fall of 1856. A campaign was launched to find and fight the Cheyenne—the first true campaign against the Plains Indians that would last nearly forty years. Two widely-spaced columns under Colonel Edwin Sumner, left the forts in eastern Kansas, met near the Colorado border, then joined up and started heading back east. They saw little on the ride out, but as they were riding back directly through the known Indian hunting grounds they expected to draw the Cheyenne into a fight.[54]

The Cheyenne, however, were prepared for a fight against the soldiers. Two medicine men had concocted a medicine they believed would make the warriors bullet-proof. All the Cheyenne warriors would have to do when the white soldiers fired would be to hold up their hands and the bullets would drop harmlessly to the ground.

On July 29, 1857, the Indians organized themselves along the banks of the South Fork of the Solomon River west of what is now Morland, a rural area of northwestern Kansas marked by hills and gullies of sometimes dry creek beds. The Indians were unconcerned as the United States Army troops approached and drew their carbines. Then, unexpectedly, Sumner ordered his men to holster their carbines and draw their sabers.

The Indians panicked, for they had no medicine against "the long knives." They turned and ran, heading east and south. The excited cavalrymen, ignoring their officers' orders, rushed after them. The disciplined attack plan crumbled as the Cheyenne scattered. Only two soldiers were killed in this incident and no more than eight Indians. Militarily, the Battle of South Solomon Fork was insignificant, but what happened on this featureless field is historic. The battle was the first time the United States government targeted the Plains Indians.

BUT MORE WHITE INTRUDERS came with the gold discovery in the northern Columbia River Valley. The Indians became even more alarmed when forts were built at Yakima and Walla Walla. This was not a sign of peace. Then they learned of Lieutenant Colonel Edward J. Steptoe, who was bringing 158 men to Spokane country. Steptoe set out from Fort Walla Walla on May 6, 1858. Soon they were engaged in war, with Steptoe taking most of the casualties. More troops were sent to Forts Vancouver, the Dalles, and Walla Walla. In the meantime, Indians took U.S. branded horses and mules from the battlefield and traded them.

On August 3, Colonel George Wright set out with a full contingent of men and animals to take revenge on the northern tribes. It wasn't long before they engaged the Indians in war. Armed with a new rifle, the white men were able to fight from a much greater distance. Casualties for the Indians were high. On the first of September they engaged again at what would later be called the Battle of Spokane Plains. Wright had 680 men and the Indians had somewhere between 500 and 1,000. These were tribes from the Spokane, Yakima, Nez Perce, Pend Oreille, Palouse, and Coeur d'Alene. Though the Indians fought well, they still had to retreat. On September 7, the Indians sent a contingent to talk peace with Wright, who demanded unconditional surrender by all parties involved in the war and threatened total extermination for those who refused. These were harsh terms, but eventually the natives agreed. Some 800 horses were killed by the Army to prevent the Indians from using them against them. The party also destroyed native beef cattle and graineries.

On September 11th, Wright met with the Indians, with Jesuit father Joseph Joset representing them. Wright demanded that the Indians surrender the men who attacked Colonel Steptoe, give back all federal government property, allow white people to pass through unharmed, and surrender one chief and four men and their families to be taken as hostages back to Walla Walla. The Indians complied. Shortly afterward, forts were built at Boise and Colville to protect white settlers and deal with the conquered Indians. Father Pierre DeSmet was brought in to tend to the spiritual needs of the tribe and act as a liaison between them and the government. DeSmet also brought back the hostages from Fort Walla Walla.

Superintendent of Indian Affairs J.W. Nesmith stated in an 1858 report: "The effort of raising a savage to a state even approaching civilization is met by a thousand obstacles, and not the least among their number is their prejudice to any change from the life pursued by their ancestors. Ignorance and superstition must be constantly combated; arguments are useless. . . ."[55]

Nesmith, however, closed his eyes to the stubbornness of his own government in its refusal to allow the natives to live the only way they knew how, and the "thousand" obstacles he projected fell far short of the true number which would follow. In the end, the Native American would suffer the most, but thousands of lives, innocent and guilty, on both sides would be sacrificed, as the newly created state of Minnesota would soon find out.

Notes

[1] John T. Sprague, *The Origin, Progress, and Conclusion of the Florida War*, New York, Appleton, 1948, p. 86.

[2] Christopher Columbus: Extracts from a Journal, 1492. A Treasury of Primary Documents.

[3] Ralph Lane report entitled "The Colony at Roanoke" sent to Sir Walter Raleigh in 1586. The American Colonist's Library, A Treasury of Primary Documents.

[4] Ibid.

[5]The Association for the Preservation of Virginia Antiquities, Internet.

[6]Alan Axelrod, *Chronicle of the Indian Wars from Colonial Times to Wounded Knee*, New York, Prentice Hall General Reference, 1993, p. 10.

[7]Ibid, p. 23.

[8]Ibid, pp. 24-37.

[9]Terri Hardin, editor, *Legends & Lore of the American Indians*, New York, Barnes & Noble, 1993, p. xvii.

[10]Lancaster (Pennsylvania) County Historical Society, Volume 57, p. 117.

[11]*History of Franklin County, Pennsylvania*, Early settlers and Indian Wars, 1887.

[12]Ohio Historical Society Archives.

[13]Reed Beard, *The Battle of Tippecanoe Historical Sketches of the Famous Field Upon Which General William Henry Harrison Won Renown That Aided Him in Reaching the Presidency Lives of the Prophet and Tecumseh with Many Interesting Incidents of their Rise and Overthrow the Campaign of 1888 and the Election of General Benjamin Harrison*, Chicago, Hammond Press, W.B. Conkey Company, 1911.

[14]Ohio Historical Society Archives.

[15]Reed Beard, *The Battle of Tippecanoe Historical Sketches of the Famous Field Upon Which General William Henry Harrison Won Renown That Aided Him in Reaching the Presidency Lives of the Prophet and Tecumseh with Many Interesting Incidents of their Rise and Overthrow the Campaign of 1888 and the Election of General Benjamin Harrison*.

[16]Joseph Frazier Wall, *Iowa: A Bicentennial History*, 1978.

[17]Alan Axelrod, *Chronicle of the Indian Wars from Colonial Times to Wounded Knee*, pp. 141-142.

[18]Gorton Carruth, *The Encyclopedia of American Facts and Dates*, 10th Ed. New York: Harper Collins Publishers, 1997.

[19]Jean Parker Waterbury, *The Oldest City St. Augustine Saga of Survival*, St. Augustine, St. Augustine Historical Society, 1983, p. 164.

[20]W.W. Smith, *Sketch of the Seminole War, and Sketches During a Campaign*, Charleston, South Carolina, Dan J. Dowling, 1836, p. 10; Mark F. Boyd, "The Complete Story of Osceola," Reprinted in *Florida Historical Quarterly*, 33, numbers 3 & 4, January-April 1955, pp. 274-275; John Lee Williams, *The Territory of Florida*, New York, Goodrich, 1837, p. 216; M.M. Cohen, *Notices of Florida and the Campaign*, Gainesville, University of Florida Press, 1964, Reprint of 1836 Edition, p. 56; Woodburne Potter, *The War in Florida*, Baltimore, Lewis & Coleman, 1836, p. 80; Frank Laumer, *Dade's Last Command*, Gainesville, University Press of Florida, 1995, pp. 121-124; Irvin M. Peithmann, *The Unconquered Seminole Indians*, St. Petersburg, Great Outdoors Association, 1957, p. 27.

[21]*Columbus* (Georgia) *Inquirer*, February 10, 1835.

[22]Frank Laumer, *Dade's Last Command*, pp. 176-190.

[23]Gorton Carruth, *The Encyclopedia of American Facts and Dates*, 10th Ed. New York: Harper Collins Publishers, 1997.

[24]David L. Ferch, "Fighting the Smallpox Epidemic of 1837-38," *Museum of the Fur Trade Quarterly*, Volume 20, Number 1, Spring 1984, p. 4-9.

[25]The Oregon Blue Book, Oregon History, Cayuse Indian War, Internet.

[26]C.L. Henson, "From War to Self-Determination, A History of the Bureau of Indian Affairs," American Studies Today Online.

[27]George H. Tinkham, *California Men and Events*, Panama-Pacific Exposition Edition, 1915.

[28]Lafayette Houghton Bunnell, *Discovery of the Yosemite and the Indian War of 1851, Which Led to that Event*.

[29]George H. Tinkham, *California Men and Events, Panama-Pacific*, Exposition Edition, 1915.

[30]Lafayette Houghton Bunnell, *Discovery of the Yosemite and the Indian War of 1851, Which Led to that Event*.

[31]William E. Smythe, *History of San Diego 1542-1908, An Account of the Rise and Progress of the Pioneer Settlement on the Pacific Coast of the United States*, San Diego, San Diego Historical Society, 1907.

[32]LeRoy R. Hafen and Francis Marion Young, *Fort Laramie and the Pageant of the West*, Lincoln and London, University of Nebraska Press, 1938, pp. 177-196.

[33]Mormon Trails Association; Lloyd E. McCann, "The Grattan Massacre," *Nebraska History*, Volume XXXVII, Number 1, March 1956, pp. 4-6.

[34]Lloyd E. McCann, "The Grattan Massacre," *Nebraska History*, Volume XXXVII, Number 1, March 1956, pp. 6-7; Richard J. Stachurski, "Harney's Fight at Blue Water Creek," *Wild West*, April 2003, pp. 28-30.

[35]National Archives, accessioned in the Department of the West, February 13, 1855.

[36]R.A. Quelle, Garden County, *Who's Who in Nebraska*, 1940.

[37]Richard J. Stachurski, "Harney's Fight at Blue Water Creek," *Wild West*, April 2003, pp. 28-30.

[38]Lewis F. Crawford, *The Exploits of Ben Arnold, Indian Fighter, Gold Miner, Cowboy, Hunter, & Army Scout*, Norman, University of Oklahoma Press, 1926, pp. 58-59.

[39]R.A. Quelle, Garden County, *Who's Who in Nebraska*, 1940.

[40]Captain Eugene F. Ware, *The Indian War of 1864*, Lincoln, University of Nebraska Press, 1965.

[41]Angie Debo, *A History of the Indians of the United States*, Norman, University of Oklahoma Press, 1970, p. 126.

[42]Lt. Lawrence Kip, "The Indian Council at Walla Walla, May and June of 1855," *Army Life on the Pacific: a Journal*.

[43]Ibid.

[44]Washington State Historical Society Archives.

[45]Angie Debo, A History of the Indians of the United States, Norman, University of Oklahoma Press, 1970, p. 126.

[46]George W. Fuller, A History of the Pacific Northwest (New York: Alfred A. Knopf, 1948), pp. 220-228.

[47]Daffodil Valley Times, Internet.

[48]Robert Ballou, "The Indian War in the Klickitat Valley," Early Klickitat Valley Days. Goldendale: The Goldendale Sentinel, 1938, p. 329-333.

[49]Daffodil Valley Times, Internet.

[50]Ibid.

[51]Oregon Blue Book, Internet.

[52]Josephine County (Oregon) Historical Society Archives.

[53]Oregon Blue Book, Internet.

[54]Clint Johnson, In the Footsteps of J.E.B. Stuart, Winston-Salem, John F. Blair, Publisher, Inc., 2003. The third volume of the trilogy of In The Footsteps of Robert E. Lee (2001) and In The Footsteps of Stonewall Jackson (2002).

[55]Washington University Library Archives.

Chapter Two

Spirit Lake Massacre

Kolapila takuyakapi—lo!
Maka kin mitawa yelo!
Epinahan blehemicive—lo!

(Comrades, kinsmen,
Now have ye spoken thus,
The earth is mine,
Tis my domain,
Tis said, and now anew I exert me.)

—Sioux War Song[1]

"It is no easy matter for us who have never seen death in his most savage forms, never lived in scenes of bloodshed, never suffered from privation and want, never braved the rough-and-tumble life of the prairie, or dared the war-hoop or scalping-knife, to realize fully the horror described in the following pages." —Abigail Gardner[2]

MINNESOTA'S BOLD SIOUX uprising had its beginnings not in 1862 Minnesota but in 1846 Iowa when Henry Lott and his family settled near the confluence of the Boone and Des Moines rivers in Webster County. Lott, a bootlegger and common thief, was able to ply his trade in the Iowa Territory without interference from the law. He was reputed to be the leader of a horse-stealing enterprise that shuttled horses into Wisconsin and Missouri.[3]

Lott was able to break the law because none existed in that part of Iowa during the time of his nefarious dealings. During the late 1840s and early 1850s, several pioneer families, like that of Lott's, settled in northwest Iowa beyond Fort Dodge; areas that were without organized law and that were unprotected by the military. This infringement upon the lands of the Wapekutah Sioux and subsequent killing of the buffalo by the white man became the spark that ignited the flame of the uprising.

Since the earliest days of the fur trade, alcohol had become an indispensable commodity for trading with the Indians. The Indians' fatal weakness for the white man's firewater made it impossible for any trader to do without it. In the United States and its territories, it was illegal to give or sell alcohol to the Indians, but the law was nearly impossible to enforce. Large quantities of whiskey were brought into Indian country every year for "medicinal purposes" until a July 1832 Congressional ruling declared the importation of alcohol for any purposes illegal.[4]

But men like Lott were numerous. On February 24, 1843, John Chambers, territorial governor of Iowa and ex-officio superintendent of Indian affairs for Iowa, wrote a letter to the commissioner of Indian affairs in Washington stating:

> Mr. Ewing describes very correctly, I have no doubt, some of the many infamous practices resorted to by unprincipled men to cheat and abuse the Indians, and he might with great propriety have extended his representations to some of those he calls "regular traders" whose dealing with them are characterized by the vilest extortion. . . . With all your experience . . . you cannot, I apprehend, have more than a very imperfect idea of the "regular" Indian trade. If the vengeance of Heaven is ever inflicted upon man in this life, it seems to me we must see some signal evidence of it among these "regular traders." It would be worthy the labors of a casuist to determine whether the wretch who sells a diseased or stolen horse to a poor Indian, or the "regular trader" who sells him goods of no intrinsic value to him at nine hundred percent advance on the cost, is the greater rascal.
>
> It makes me heart sick to dwell upon the injuries and injustice to which the Indian race is subjected by the injudicious system by which our intercourse with them is governed.[5]

But despite treaties, laws, and proclamations, many whites were not concerned with the pledges of their government or for the welfare of the Indians. Without regard to law, order, or fair play, these men moved onto Indian lands. The military was in constant fear that hostilities would ensue between these men and the Indians. At least half the blame for the bloodshed, which occurred on a bloody Sunday in March 1857, in Iowa, can be attributed to the whites, who by incessant greed placed themselves and their families in peril. Men such as Lott regularly violated treaties prohibiting their entrance upon the hunting grounds of the Sioux.

Before 1842, the Fox and Sac tribes of Indians dwelled in Iowa, but on October 11, these Indians ceded all their lands west of the Mississippi River to the United States Government. They reserved the right of occupancy for three years to all ceded lands, which ran west of a line running due north and south from the painted rocks on the White Breast fork of the Des Moines River.[6]

Lands north of Iowa and west of the Mississippi as far as Little Rapids on the Minnesota River, were occupied by Mdewakanton and Wakpekute bands of Sioux, who were at war with the Sacs and Foxes. The Wakpekute band was led by two principal chiefs—Wamdisapa (Black Eagle) and Tasagi (His Cane). The lawless and predatory campaign of Wamdisapa prolonged the war and created problems with the other Wakpekutes, who separated their band from his. Wamdisapa and his band moved to the west near the Missouri and Vermillion rivers. When the Wakpekutes and Mdewakantons ceded away their lands in the Treaty of 1851, Wamdisapa's people were not regarded as part of the tribes and took no part in the treaty negotiations. By 1857, all that remained of Wamdisapa's struggling band was ten or fifteen lodges under the chieftainship of Inkpaduta or Scarlet Point. He and his band of vagabonds ranged the country from Spirit Lake to the Missouri River.

While many of the Sioux did not fully understand the treaties they made with the whites, settlers moved onto the lands ceded by the Indians in the 1851 treaty. According to the treaty, the Sioux gave up all claims to land in Iowa, and most of the Indians moved across the Big Sioux River into the

Dakota Territory. Not all the Sioux had departed, however, and those who remained confined their hunting and trapping activities to the border areas, well away from the settlers. Iowa appeared to be secure from any chance of Indian uprising, and so sure was the federal government of this that they abandoned Fort Dodge as a military installation in March 1853 and moved its troops farther north to Fort Ridgely in Minnesota.[7]

One band of Sioux, consisting of outcasts from numerous other tribes, frequently hunted along the Des Moines River in north central Iowa. In 1848, their leader, Sidominadotah (Two Fingers), reputed to be the brother of Inkpaduta, traced some stolen horses to the cabin of Henry Lott. Because of Lott's practice of selling bad liquor to the Indians, he was well known to Sidominadotah, chief of a tribe Lott with whom did business.[8]

Sidominadotah, who had lost three fingers in battle, stood about five feet ten inches tall, with high cheek bones and penetrating black eyes. He was easily recognizable since he boasted double rows of teeth in both jaws. Upon discovering that six of his horses were missing, he approached Lott and ordered him to leave the country. Lott refused.[9]

When the Wapekutahs under Sidominadotah raided Lott's cabin, he and his stepson escaped and hid in the brush. Lott and his boy fled downriver leaving his wife and younger children to the mercy of the Sioux. The Indians ripped apart the inside of his cabin, destroyed Lott's beehives and livestock, and mistreated his family.

Lott's twelve-year-old son, Milton, took off to search for his father. At a point about three miles from the town of Boone, and about twenty miles downstream from the Lott cabin, he froze to death. His body was found a few days later by a relief party from Peas Point (now Boone).

Although the rest of the family survived the ordeal, Mrs. Lott eventually died from her cruel treatment by the Indians. She became the first woman to die in Webster County and was buried in the Vegors Cemetery, a few miles down the Des Moines River from the town community of Lehigh.

Lott vowed he would get even with the Indians. During the autumn of 1853, Lott and his stepson passed through Fort Dodge with three barrels of whiskey for "trading purposes." He constructed a new cabin at what was later dubbed Lott's Creek, which emptied into the Des Moines River in Humboldt County. Sidominadotah and his family of nine were camped a short distant up the creek.

Lott and his stepson visited the camp and told Sidominadotah that a large herd of elk had been seen in the river bottoms and suggested the chief accompany him to hunt the animals. The chief and his family were badly in need of food, and he readily accepted the white man's offer.

Deep in the thicket, Sidominadotah stood to shoot the first elk, and when he did, the two white men shot him. They then decapitated his body and returned to the campsite and murdered the remainder of his family, including the chief's elderly mother.[10] Two of Sidominadotah's children—a ten-year-old girl and her older brother, although wounded, escaped. Following the mass killings, Lott and his stepson pushed the bodies of the chief's family under the ice of the creek and took flight down the Des Moines River. Because the creek ran red with blood, it gained the name "Bloody Run."[11]

A party of Sioux discovered Sidominadotah's body two weeks later and reported the murder to Major William Williams at Fort Dodge, demanding immediate action. Major Williams dispatched a party of whites and Indians to arrest, capture, or kill Lott, but the group returned empty-handed.

A coroner's jury met in the county seat of Homer, and Lott was found guilty of the murder of the chief and his family. Sidominadotah's body was brought to the inquest without its head. Two brothers, Asa and Ambrose Call, had stumbled upon a pole leaning against a cabin bearing the chief's decapitated head. The bloody face was propped towards the road with the chief's long matted hair dangling in the wind two feet below it. Although a grand jury in Des Moines indicted Lott and his stepson, the Sioux were enraged over the murders and the white man's lack of duty. And, of course, Lott and his stepson could not be found.

Lott had, in fact, loaded his few household possessions and set off for parts unknown. He stopped in Fort Dodge and gave his little girl to a family named White. Lott had known White, a former soldier stationed at Fort Dodge, for several years. He also stopped at the home of L. Wares, who lived on the river below Boonsborough. That was the last ever seen or heard of him in Iowa.[12]

Revenge was imminent. According to one source, "The Indian lived in his memories. His wrongs held his mind and heart in thrall. Fear might hold back his hand in revenge but charity seldom did. The invasion of the hunting grounds by either enemy tribes or by the heedless or the unscrupulous whites incited him to an inside rage relentless and ruthless in character."[13]

The strained relationship between the whites and the Sioux worsened following the slaying of Sidominadotah. When Inkpaduta heard of the crime, he was infuriated, even though authorities promised that they would hastily round up and punish the murderers, even suggesting they would turn them over to the Indian people for punishment. Unfortunately, the resulting investigation was "turned into a farce and a joke," as the prosecuting attorney, Granville Berkley, of Hamilton County, Iowa, not only failed to return Sidominadotah's remains to the Indians, but nailed the slain man's skull to a pole over his house. No further attempt was made to apprehend the murderers.[14]

The hungry and embittered Indians took a liking in 1854 to settler James Dickerson's prize rooster. Dickerson and his family had settled at Clear Lake in Cerro Gordo County. A young Indian man approached the property and stole the rooster. During his flight, he knocked over Dickerson's grindstone, which broke into many pieces. Dickerson took off after the brave, caught up with him and smashed the side of the Indian's head with a fragment of the grindstone. This incident became known as the "Grindstone War."[15]

The angry Sioux demanded a settlement from Dickerson for the brave's injury. When they asked for Dickerson's best horse or one-hundred dollars, Mrs. Dickerson stepped forward and gave them six dollars and several blankets. The Sioux left the area, but they did so reluctantly and retained a dislike of Dickerson. Although incidents such as the Dickerson affair caused fear among the white settlers, it did not hamper the influx of more white immigrants into northern Iowa.

"I came west in the spring of 1854 and spent most of the time till the fall of 1857, at or near Webster City, Iowa," recalled Captain Jareb Palmer. "During that time there were several Indian scares but no one had been killed so far as I knew, and we were not much afraid of them. So it was that in the summer of 1856 several from the aforesaid place started out to hunt claims and eventually reached what is now Jackson County, then a part of Brown County, Minnesota, which was still at that time a territory. There they took claims along the Des Moines River."[16]

During the spring of 1856, William Freeborn established a settlement at Spirit Lake, Iowa, with six or seven families. Sixteen miles north, a settlement was organized at Springfield, Minnesota, by three brothers—George, William, and Alexander Wood.[17] Though these pioneer settlements were on government land, they were in the heart of Indian country, unprotected and defenseless.[18]

"The settlement at the time of the trouble . . . contained two trading houses, and several families; this was the nearest settlement on the north, there being no habitation nearer than the Watonwan River," wrote Charles E. Flandrau. "There is no settlement on the west of it. The nearest settlement on the south is reported to be about forty miles down the river, which takes its source in Spring Lake, known among the Indians as Inyanyan Key, or Rock River. It will be seen that this locality is isolated and on the extreme verge of civilization, and without it possessed the means of defence [sic] within itself, would be unprotected in case of danger from an enemy. The settlers' houses are always a considerable distance apart, and generally not within sight of each other, and would fall an easy prey to half a dozen men acting in concert."[19]

The winter of 1856-1857 was one of the worst on record with temperatures dropping beyond twenty-five degrees below zero and snow drifting several feet deep. Game was scarce, and the few buffalo that roamed Iowa had moved westward into Nebraska and the Dakotas with the coming of the white man. The Sioux faced famine, and their huts offered little protection against the elements. The whites, meanwhile, lived in warm, comfortable cabins with plenty of food to eat—or so the Indians perceived them. Most settlers, at least, were better off than they. Many of the Sioux, threatened with extinction, considered killing the whites and taking their food.[20]

Surviving that terrible winter at Spirit Lake and on the banks of West Okoboji Lake, on land belonging to the Sioux, were the squatter families of Rowland Gardner, Harvey Luce, J.M. Thatcher, Dr. Isaac H. Herriott, Alvin M. Noble, and William Marble. These hardy pioneer families totaled thirty persons and lived scattered over a six-mile area.[21]

Rowland Gardner was born in New Haven, Connecticut, in 1815 and moved to New York as a young man. He married Frances M. Smith in 1836. Gardner had always wanted to travel west, and in 1853, he and his family—including children Abigail, Eliza, and Rowland—journeyed to Iowa in a wagon. With them came their married daughter Mary, her husband Harvey Luce, and the young couple's little son, Albert. After spending a year at Clear Lake, the family, now having added a daughter Amanda, took to the road again, this time with several yoke of oxen and a herd of young cattle. They arrived on the shores of the Okoboji lakes, the largest of which was Spirit Lake, on July 16, 1856.[22]

Spirit Lake was known to the Sioux as Minnewaukon and to the French as Lac d'Esprit. The lake was sacred to the Sioux, who believed it was under the guardianship of the Great Spirit. To the Indians, the waters were haunted by spirits, and no member of any tribe dared cross it in a canoe.

Explorer Joseph Nicollet described the Spirit Lake region during his 1838-1839 expeditions:

> Lac d'Esprit of the voyageurs comprises a large group of lakes of different sizes. The most extensive is about seven miles from N.W. to S.E. and four miles from E. to W.—it is for its h[e]ight very well timbered though only interruptedly. The lakes are alternately Sand beeches or fortified with im[m]ense ac[c]umulations of granit[e] & grauwake [greywacke] boulders—these boulders are beautifully dressed with different beautiful plants, as they contain in their intervalles a rich Soil & composition of Loam—Gravel—Sand—Rotten Shell from the Lakes—Weed thrown out by the waves. The Sandy Beech is however very naked, generally an undulated bank [forty to fifty] yard from the Water edge [and six to eight] feet deep...["][23]

74

Lake Okoboji. (Author's collection)

The second largest lake in the chain, West Okoboji, the Sioux called Okoboozhy, meaning Place-of-Rest. Spirit Lake was initially called Minnetonka, but when it was discovered that a lake in Minnesota bore that name, the title was abandoned.

The Gardners and Luces decided to build their cabins on West Okoboki and selected a site one mile south of a strait known as Pillsbury Point. The Gardner cabin was the first one constructed at West Okoboji. Because it was too late in the year to plant crops, the men busied themselves with getting the ground ready for crops to be grown the following spring and constructing a shelter for their cattle.

North of the strait were four young men from Red Wing, Minnesota, all of whom were single men with the exception of William Granger. South of the strait dwelt James and Mary Mattock with their five children—Alice, Daniel, Agnes, Jacob, and Jackson. Another Mr. Mattock and his eighteen-year-old son, Robert, stayed with the family. On the east side of East Okoboji lived Joel and Mille Howe and their six children, who like the Gardiners, had just constructed their cabin.

The leader of the Sioux, who also lived in the area, was Inkapaduta, a brother of the murdered Sidominadotah.[24] Inkpaduta, well over six feet tall, had a pockmarked face characterized by tiny holes, the result of smallpox. Somewhere between fifty and sixty years old, the chief possessed a burning hatred of all whites.[25]

An Indian recollection of Inkpaduta, however, described him as "tall and slender, gentle and kind to his family. He was industrious, there was not a summer but he and his band planted a garden at some place . . . he seemed like a pitiful man with a soft voice. . . . Among the Indians, the more a man loved his family, kindred and tribe, the braver he was to defend them."[26]

Inkpaduta was a chief of the Wahpekute Dakota Indian tribe, which roamed the prairies of South Dakota, Iowa, and Minnesota. The Wahpekute Indians were widely known as a group of outlaws. Inkpaduta's father's name was Black Eagle, and he was also a chief of the Wahpekute Dakota Indian tribe. Black Eagle had at least two wives, one from the Mdewakanton tribe and another from the Sisseton tribe. Inkpaduta also had two brothers, Sintominidotah, and Napenomnana. He had one sister. Inkpaduta lived from 1815 to 1882

The Wahpekutes was the smallest of the Dakota tribes with about 550 people. They were closely related to many other Indian tribes, including the Mdewakantons by the Mississippi River, the Sissetons, and the Wahpetons on the Minnesota River.

Inkpaduta and his Wahpekutes were regarded as outcasts by the Sioux. They belonged to a band that had been headed by Wamdisapa in the 1840s when they killed Tasagye and had fled west into the Missouri River Valley. Under Inkpaduta's leadership, they showed up at Redwood in Minnesota to benefit from the annuity distribution. The main body of reservation Wahpekutes, however, demanded that Inkpaduta and band be denied any such benefits, and the government agency refused to grant formal recognition to them.[27]

Inkpaduta's renegades were as heartily hated by the Sioux as they were by the whites. In 1849 Wa-wandi-a-akapi, chief of the Wapekuta band, and his followers were encamped in a clearing near Lowville Township in western Minnesota after the American Fur Company had abandoned its fur trading post. The band little expected an attack, especially from its fellow Sioux. As the village slept, Inkpaduta and his renegade band slipped into the timber and pounced upon the sleeping Wapekutas. Before an alarm aroused the village, Wa-wandi-a-akapi and seventeen of his braves had been stabbed to death. Inkpaduta withdrew without the loss of a single man. The father of Inkpaduta had been a co-chief of the Wapekutas. Those murdered in the Bear Lake clearing were Inkpaduta's tribal brothers.[28]

By 1856, it was apparent to Inkpaduta that the promises to investigate the killing of Sidominadotah would not be carried out because the whites never intended to apprehend the murderers. A massacre of white settlers was discussed in the fall and winter of 1856, and war dances were held to "work up the courage to the proper pitch."

The white settlers had hints something bad was going to happen.[29]

Joshpatuda, the orphan son of Sidominadotah, had been raised by a white family since the murder of his parents, and he made frequent visits to see Inkpaduta. During one of these visits, he learned of the murderous intent of his uncle and tried to warn his white benefactors. The whites however, paid little heed to reports of danger the youth brought them, and eventually, fearing retribution from his own people, the boy fled and was never heard from again.

Inkpaduta's band commenced its reign of plunder on February 21, 1857, at the home of Almer Bell, where they killed some cattle and plundered the home of provisions. At another nearby residence, they knocked down the wife of A.S. Mead and kidnapped two women. They later released them.

The roving band of Indians appeared at the Smithland settlement southwest of Sioux City, Iowa. Here was hope of good hunting, for though the elk had been driven from the prairie by the bitter winds, they had taken shelter in a nearby grove of trees. Local whites, however, were alarmed that the Dakotas were so near, even though one local family was sharing a well with them without any trouble. Soon, suspicion arose that the hungry Dakotas were stealing corn from the settlers' cribs.[30]

Trouble began brewing when some of the braves were whipped by whites. A show of force by the whites caused the wanderers to move south to the valley of the Little Sioux River. The braves stole food and ammunition at Correctionville and one settler claimed he had been beaten by them.[31]

On the heels of this trouble came a heated dispute over an elk hunt. Finally, a group of armed settlers marched into Inkpaduta's camp and ordered him to leave the area. Inkpaduta said he would depart the next day, promising to go downriver to the Omaha Indians. But the settlers feared a night ambush, and took away the Sioux's guns, telling Inkpaduta he could retrieve them on his way out of town. The guns were never redeemed.[32]

Instead of heading south, Inkpaduta immediately headed north up the Little Sioux. Perhaps he feared that the whites were planning an ambush or he was just enraged. Passing through the settlements of Pilot Rock, Cherokee, and Peterson, his people stole weapons and killed cattle as they went. Word spread—breathless tales of rape and plunder—and the frightened settlers let the angry Dakotas do as they pleased. None of the settlers were killed.

The Sioux continued up the river to the Milford settlement, where they killed more livestock and destroyed property. They frightened white settlers at Milford by slamming their tomahawks to the cabin floors and brandishing scalping knives, but they did no killing. At Gillett's Grove, one of the Indians was killed for allegedly making advances to Mrs. Gillett. The following day, a pair of settlers found the corpse and beheaded it. The Indians threatened revenge, and the white settlers fled to Sauk Rapids.[33]

On February 13, 1857, Inkpaduta and his braves visited Clay County, some fifty miles south of Lake Okoboji. In the tiny town of Peterson, where some white settlers had staked out claims, the Indians went to the Bicknell house and demanded food. After taking all the flour and cornmeal they could find in the house, they slit the comforters and pillows on the bed and scattered the goose feathers on the ground. A young family member, Jane Bicknell, later recorded in her diary the terror she experienced during the ordeal.[34]

In March 1857, Inkpaduta and his followers were hunting elk in an area near the Rock River settlement when they encountered some whites. The Indians claimed the whites had intercepted their hunt. During the interchange, one of the Indian hunters was bitten by a mongrel dog belonging to one of the settlers. The Indian immediately killed the dog, and then its owner administered a severe beating to the brave. Inkpaduta's party took umbrage, also claiming that the whites had beaten their women whom they had caught stealing hay and corn. Before a major confrontation could ensue, a party of whites entered the Indian village and disarmed the braves, although they later regained their arms.[35]

When the Indians arrived at Spirit Lake, they were given food by the settlers. Inkpaduta arrived with twelve men, two boys, and some women, and they, too, demanded food from the same settlers. When they were told there was none to give, Inkpaduta took his eldest son aside and told him it was a disgrace to ask for food from the whites when they ought to take it for themselves instead of having it thrown to them like dogs.

". . . A growing interest is evident among us in the social, intellectual and moral state of the Indians," wrote Abigail Gardiner, who was kidnapped by the Sioux in 1857. "Many among the red denizens of our western prairies, after having been driven to their present territories, and suffered everything from the hands of the whites that a strong and proud race ever inflicted on weak neighbors, are naturally exasperated, and like old King Philip, of New England, and Opechanchanough of Virginia, long to become the perpetrators instead of the victims of extermination."[36]

On Sunday, March 8, 1857, the Rowland Gardner family was about to leave for Fort Dodge to pick up supplies. As the family and guests sat down to breakfast, the door opened and a Sioux brave entered. He pretended to be a friend and sat down with the family to eat. Soon, Inkapaduta, his fourteen warriors, women and children came into the cabin and began eating.[37]

The Indians quickly became sullen, and one of the braves lunged for Mr. Gardner's powder horn, which was hanging on the wall. Luce restrained the man and the Indians departed for the Mattock cabin situated between the two Okobojis. As they stumbled through the snow, they began shooting the Gardner livestock. Two Gardner guests—Harvey Luce and Robert Clark—attempted to get around the southern end of East Okojobi and warn the other families, but the two men were killed by the Sioux.

The Gardner family hovered in silence, waiting for an expected Indian attack. About 5:00 P.M., Gardner decided to walk out into the fields and investigate the situation. He returned to the cabin and reported that nine Indians were coming back. Gardner quickly barricaded the door and commenced loading his rifle, but Mrs. Gardner intervened, stating, "If we have to die, let us die innocent of shedding blood."[38]

When the Sioux entered the cabin, thirteen-year-old Abbie was rocking the baby, Amanda, with four-year-old Albert and six-year-old Rowland standing on either side of her. The Indians demanded flour and as Gardner turned to get them some, the braves shot him in the heart. Mrs. Gardner and Mrs. Luce attempted to grab the gun stock from the Indians but they were dragged outside and brutally murdered. The Indians grabbed the small children and beat them to death with sticks of fire wood.

"The infant, however, was not long left an orphan," recalled Abigail Gardner. "The fatal war club dashed out his little brains, as also those of its brother and young uncle, Rowland Gardiner. Struck dumb with inexpressible fright, overwhelmed and paralized [sic] with the suddenness and horror of the bloody attack, all the unfortunate victims perished in breathless silence and without one effort of resistance."[39]

While the braves scalped their victims, Abbie was taken away as a prisoner. As the Sioux and their captive passed the Mattock's burning cabin, a horrified Abigail saw the bodies of five men, two women, and four children scattered in the snow. Passing north to the Granger cabin, Abigail saw the headless body of Carl Granger, his head chopped off above the mouth by a blow from an axe.[40]

As the sun went down on this, the first day of vengeance, twenty bodies lay scattered in the snow. The Indians conducted a scalp dance, which lasted late into the night. Forced to watch the spectacle, young Abbie nearly passed out when her eyes encountered a dancing brave whose belt was adorned with the still-dripping scalp of her mother.

The members of the four remaining white families had no knowledge of the slayings. The braves, meanwhile, rubbed charcoal from the fires on their faces, black being the traditional war color of the Sioux, and moved out along the east shore of Lake Okoboji. Joel Howe was also walking along the shore; his family had run out of flour, and he was on his way to visit a neighbor to borrow some.

Howe was slain, his head thrown into the ice of Lake Okoboji, and the Indians descended upon the Howe cabin. Mrs. Millie Howe, seventeen-year-old Jonathan, a teenager daughter, Sardis, and three smaller children were all killed, their bodies left lying in the yard.

Proceeding to the Thatcher cabin, Inkpaduta and the Sioux warriors again feigned friendship. Mr. Thatcher was away at Shippey's Point, where his oxen had become embedded in the snow. Inside the cabin were Mrs. Elizabeth Thatcher, nineteen, John Noble and his twenty-year-old wife, Lydia, Enoch Ryan, and two small children. Ryan and Noble were shot, the young children, two-year-old John Noble and a seven-month-old baby Dora Thatcher, were snatched from their mothers' arms and taken outside where the marauders dashed their brains out against an oak tree. Mrs. Noble and Mrs. Thatcher were taken captive.

En route to camp, the Indians and their captives paid another visit to the Howe cabin to make sure no one had survived the slaughter. The terrified women saw the mutilated bodies of the Howe family. Mrs. Noble saw the body of her mother, Mrs. Howe, beneath a bed, where she had crawled to hide after being beaten with a flatiron. In the yard, Mrs. Noble encountered her thirteen-year-old brother Jacob, brutally beaten but still alive. As he stood and propped himself against a tree, she urged him to crawl into the cabin and hide beneath the bed covers, but he was seen by a brave and killed.

The Indians returned to camp with their three female captives. The women discussed the horrors they had witnessed and were then taken to separate lodges where they were ordered to paint their faces and braid their hair so they would resemble Indian women.

The Sioux broke camp and crossed West Okoboji on the ice on Tuesday morning, March 10th. The following day they moved north to the west shore of Spirit Lake. While hunting on the shores of the lake, a group of Sioux discovered the cabin of Mr. and Mrs. William Marble. Instead of attacking, they returned to camp and reported their find to Inkapaduta.

Friday morning, March 13th, the Indians removed the charcoal from their faces so Marble would not be suspicious when they reached his cabin. Once more the braves pretended to come in friendship, and when they asked for food, they were given some. One of the braves asked Marble to trade guns with him, and the settler agreed. Following their meal, the brave who had traded guns suggested they partake in a shooting contest so they could both test the weapons they had exchanged. A wooden slab was placed against a tree to serve as the target.

As the men took aim, the Sioux surrounded them, pretending to be having a good time as spectators. After one of their shots hit the slab, it fell to the ground, and Marble went to pick it up and put it back in place. As he did so, his spine was shattered from a barrage of Sioux bullets, his own gun that he had traded away aimed against him. He was the thirty-second person killed in the Spirit Lake Massacre. His wife, Margaret Ann Marble, had seen the killing of her husband from the window, and she quickly rushed for the door, but she was immediately captured before she could make her passage outside.

"It was then that the fearful work began, for while putting up the target the fiendish savage leveled his gun and shot my noble husband through the heart," wrote Margaret Ann Marble in an 1885 letter. "With a scream, I rushed for the door to go to him, but two brawny savages barred my passage and held fast the door. But love and agony were stronger than brute force, and with frantic energy I burst the door open, and was soon kneeling by the side of him who a few minutes before was my loving and beloved husband. But before I reached him a merciful God had released his spirit from mortal agony. He wore a belt around his waist containing a thousand dollars in gold. This belt was soaked with his precious blood. The Indians immediately took possession of the money, and, entering the house, they began searching for valuables."[41]

Inkpaduta and his band of renegade Sioux left Spirit Lake, taking with them the leather belt containing a thousand dollars in gold pieces from the Marble cabin. In addition to the gold, the Indians carried away several other commodities they didn't know what to do with or how to use. Among the assortment of stolen goods were baking soda and cream of tartar.

Abigail Gardiner later wrote, "After having spilled out on the weird shores of Spirit Lake, more than forty human souls in all, and left their mangled and slaughtered bodies gory in their blood, exposed to the ravages of weather and wild beasts, the barbarians started on their homeward journey on the morning of the fourteenth of March, 1857."[42]

The grisly situation at the Okobojis was discovered by a trapper, Morris Markham, who lived with the Thatcher family. He had been absent during the murders because he had been away tracking down some cattle that had strayed. On his way back to the Thatcher cabin, he became lost in a fierce snowstorm, which delayed his getting back and undoubtedly saved his life.[43]

Upon witnessing the carnage at the Gardner place, he set out for the Marble cabin. In doing so, he walked right into the midst of the Sioux camp. The Indians were asleep, and although a dog barked to announce his coming, he slipped away undetected into the darkness. Markham found the same hideous scene at the Mattock and Thatcher cabins.

H.W. Granger later penned: "Having formerly boarded at Howes, and his trunk being there, [Markham] went in, found his trunk rifled, feathers strewn over the floor, and a pile of hay in the corner; did not discover the bodies under it. He left . . . and hid in a snow bank all night."[44]

The following morning, the 10th, he set off along the Des Moines River and made it safely to a cabin belonging to George Granger. He told his story to two trappers, who immediately set off for Fort Dodge to bring back help. The *Minnesota Pioneer & Democrat*, St. Paul, published an account of the massacre:

> According to the report of Mr. Markham, of Spirit Lake, in this Territory, a shocking affair took place there on the 9th of this month— Spirit Lake is about [fifteen] miles from Springfield, on the Des Moines River, in a south-westerly course, and near the Iowa line. Mr. Markham had been to the Des Moines River to see after his oxen, which were there feeding upon rushes, and in going home got bewildered and hungry, and started for the nearest house. Upon reaching it, he found the door and windows broken open, and on the inside, upon the floor, laid the body of an old lady. A short distance from the house, upon the snow, he found a boy about twelve years of age, who was also dead. A short distance from the

other houses where families had been living, but no person was there; everything in the houses was thrown over the floors. He started for the sixth house, expecting to stay all night, but found several Indian tents pitched before the door, and the house filled with Indians. He being fatigued, crept into a snow bank and laid until morning, when he started for the settlement at Springfield. They finding that he was in earnest about his story, and swearing to its correctness, immediately dispatched two men for Fort Ridgely, who succeeded in raising fifty soldiers to come to their assistance. The men are in this place this evening, and will start for the Des Moines River in the morning. The soldiers will camp for the night at South Bend.—We have heard Indian stories before, but we are inclined, from the source, to believe this to be true.[45]

Markham hurried to Springfield (now Jackson), Minnesota, to warn people there of an imminent attack, although he was not the first to do so. Captain Jareb Palmer recalled:

The first intimation we had of any hostile feeling on the part of the Indians, was about the first of March. I was then at work for the Woods; George being the only one at home at the time. One day an Indian came there from the direction of Spirit Lake. Mr. Woods recognized him as a member of Inkpaduta's band. He said the band was at that time camped at Spirit Lake. This could not have been true . . . but they were very likely on the Little Sioux, not far distant.

[Black Buffalo] remained over night, and while there he and Wood did considerable talking in the Sioux language. Before leaving he begged a few potatoes, and borrowed a sack to carry them in, promising to return it full of feathers. After he was gone Mr. Wood informed me that the Indian had told him that war had been declared against the whites. Mr. Wood seemed to take the matter as a joke or matter of no consequence; and for my own part, I scarcely gave the report a second thought, as all the Indians we had seen during the winter had appeared so very friendly, and we were entirely ignorant of the feeling entertained by Inkpaduta's band toward the whites.[46]

Markham arrived in Springfield bearing the same news as Black Buffalo. His warning, however, fell upon dead ears. Under Inkapudata's son, the Indians pretended to be friendly and even purchased ammunition from storekeeper William Wood. Wood had refused to believe Markham's story of the massacre.

One night, after two strange Indians had visited Wood's store, an Indian band led by Umpashota moved their camp upriver near that of

Caboo. William Wood went up to see them a few times, and Umpashota also visited the store. He admitted that the two Indians were members of Inkpaduta's band, and that they had boasted of killing all the whites at Spirit Lake. They even claimed Inkpaduta's fourteen-year-old son had personally killed eight persons in a fair fight.[47]

Nothing more was heard about Inkpaduta, and a band of settlers prepared to leave for Spirit Lake accompanied by Umpashota to bury the dead. Wood intervened and told them that Umpashota had changed his mind, believing Inkpaduta and his band were still at Spirit Lake drying beef from all the cattle they had stolen. The expedition was canceled.

The Indians struck unexpectedly, but the attack was not an all-out assault. Mr. Wood met with them at their camp, and, after transacting his business, he was shot and killed while returning home. His brother, George Wood, had started to give the alarm from the opposite side of the river when he, too, was shot and killed.[48] The Sioux plundered the store and piled brush over the mutilated bodies of their victims.

The settlers of Springfield quickly gathered at the home of a Mr. Thomas and discussed measures of defense. Thomas lived in a double log house, a large structure at the edge of an oak grove, near the west branch of the Des Moines River. Two men were dispatched to walk the seventy-five miles to Fort Ridgely to bring back help. They were well armed and well provisioned.[49]

A week later, nine-year-old Willie Thomas scampered into the house full of excitement, declaring that the two men were coming back. The two men dressed like whites, however, were both Indians wearing the clothes of men killed at Spirit Lake. The outlaw chief had declared war on all whites, and on March 26th, as predicted by Markham, Inkpaduta and his band attacked the village of Springfield.

The main party of Dakota warriors, who were approaching from another direction, opened fire on the party of men, women, and children. Little Willie Thomas was shot through the head and fell to the ground mortally wounded. Miss Swanger was shot through the shoulder, suffering a severe flesh wound, while Mr. Thomas took a hit through the left arm and

Carver in the stomach area. All the settlers, except for little Willie Thomas, rushed into the cabin and bolted the door.

"We immediately retreated into the house and commenced a lively fusillade from the only porthole we had on the side from which the attack had come; but we soon made other port holes, by knocking out chinking from between the logs," recalled Captain Palmer. "It was now impossible for them to approach the house, without facing a loaded gun with somebody behind it."[50]

The firing became intense on both sides and continued for two to three hours. The Indians charged the house several times, hoping to set it on fire but were driven back each time. The women loaded the guns for the men, and Mrs. Church stuffed her handkerchief under Miss Swanger's dress to control the bleeding from her shoulder. Mrs. Thomas wrapped her husband's injured arm and stopped the bleeding. Mrs. Church and Miss Gardner stepped into an adjacent room, and spotting an Indian outside behind a tree, Mrs. Church grabbed a shotgun. Mrs. Church later stated:

"I plainly saw a large dark object by the side of the tree, which I knew to be the head of an Indian, and at this I discharged the gun. I was terribly excited and fell back, and cannot tell you whether I hit him or not! I certainly wanted to kill him!"[51]

H.W. Granger later wrote: "In the attack on Church and Thomas the Indians did not succeed very well after the first onslaught. The inhabitants rushed into the houses. Some of the men tore up puncheons and barred the doors and window—Mrs. Church and sister loading guns, Mr. Bradshaw and others firing whenever a chance offered. In one case two shots were required before a 'big Indian' was laid out. Mrs. Church did absolutely shoot one herself, and evinced a courage well worthy the imitation of the sterner sex."[52]

One of the women in the Thomas house—a Mrs. Stewart—became hysterical over her fear of the Indians. Believing the Indians had gone, her husband decided to bring her home. Upon reaching their home, Stewart was called to the door, and upon opening it, was shot in the face by the same Indians that had assaulted the Thomas place. The warriors then murdered his hysterical wife and their two children. A young son, Johnny, hid behind a log, and after the Indians plundered the cabin and departed, rushed back to the Thomas house.

The home of the Churches was also pillaged and all their household goods stolen. Several horses from the Thomas barn were also taken. As darkness descended upon the village, the settlers started south with an ox team and sled towards the nearest village. After a two-day march through deep snows, they encountered a party of men whom they mistook for Indians. As the women and children began to scream, John Bradshaw stacked their eight loaded guns, prepared to make a fight out of it. But the men signaled him, and Bradshaw knew the rescue party had finally come for them.

Because of Markham's warning, however, seven of Inkpaduta's warriors were slain. The Indians hastily marched away with their captives and returned to camp. The Sioux had been pushed back from Springfield by the settlers all the way to Heron Lake. Seventeen whites, however, perished in the Springfield battle

The Sioux brought back to camp several bolts of calico and red flannel and decorated themselves with the goods. Many of them wore red leggings, shirts, and blankets, while their women tried on the white women's dresses. The Indian women discovered that the dresses did not fit them well so they cut off the top halves and wore them as skirts.[53]

As soon as the Springfield settlers were certain the Indians had left the area in the direction of the Dakota Territory, they started on a 130-mile walk to Fort Dodge. Captain Palmer later wrote:

> The weather, which had been fine in the fore part of the day, had towards night become foggy and cloudy, though not cold. We made very slow progress, as we had often to beat a path in front of the oxen before they could proceed. In this way, we traveled till about midnight, when being uncertain what course to pursue, as there was neither sun, moon nor stars by which to guide our course, we decided to wait where we were till morning.
>
> When morning came we found we were only about three miles from the Thomas cabin, which was still in plain sight. We hastened on our way, fearing the savages would get sight of us and pursue and again attack us. We kept our guns always ready for use and also kept a sharp lookout for pursuing savages. But as we had only one yoke of oxen to haul five women,

two wounded men and half a dozen children, they gave out entirely before noon and it was agreed that one of us should go on to George Granger's and get him to come to our assistance with his oxen.[54]

After a long, hazardous journey, they reached Fort Dodge safely. Although the two trappers had gone before them with the news of the uprising, the authorities in Fort Dodge did not take their story seriously and did nothing about it. So many conflicting reports reached the city involving reputed Indian troubles that the people of Fort Dodge were more or less dubious or hesitant about accepting them as the truth.[55]

It was not until a party of land hunters and trappers from Newton in Jasper County stumbled upon the mutilated bodies near Lake Okoboji and brought the news to Fort Dodge on March 21st that the tragedy was given credibility. The three men—Orlando C. Howe, Cyrus Snyder, and Robert M. Wheelock—signed an affidavit which stated:

"On the evening of Monday, March 16th, 1857, we in company with B.F. Parmenter arrived at the house of Joel Howe in the vicinity of Spirit Lakes, Dickinson County, Iowa. We noticed that the house had apparently been broken into. And articles of furniture Books . . . thrown out and scattered around. Two of us (Howe and Wheelock) then went to the house of Milton Thatcher, about a mile and a half beyond and found that in a similar condition and then first expected the affair to be the work of Indians. On returning to Mr. Howe, Snyder and Parmenter had noticed within the house a dead body, there was on the floor a quantity of clothing and bedding and nearly covered by it lay a dead body. We had noticed moccasin tracks several days old about the houses, and from some indications suspected that there were yet Indians in the Groves." The affidavit went on to describe in gory detail the finding of the other bodies.[56]

H.W. Granger gave March 15th as the date of the grisly discovery. The men "knocked, received no answer, went in, built a fire and commenced getting their supper; the fire burning lightly, enabled them to see into the corner of the room; one seeing a boot lying on the edge of a hay pile, went up and took hold of it, and discovered to his infinite horror and alarm, a man's foot and limb in it. Further examination disclosed five dead bodies under the hay. They immediately hauled their load of provisions into the prairie—turned their team loose, and reached the Irish Colony next morning; they went thence to Fort Dodge. . . ."[57]

Fort Dodge was no longer a military post in 1857, but several discharged soldiers were living in the area. Upon hearing the news, Major William Williams, the founder of Fort Dodge, called a meeting at the schoolhouse and an expedition to bury the survivors and catch up with the Sioux was organized. Messengers carried news of the massacre to Homer, Border Plains, and Webster City, and these shocked communities sent men to join the expedition. The party made the trek from Webster city to Fort Dodge in eight hours over nearly impassable roads. About seventy men volunteered in Fort Dodge, and they were placed in two companies.[58]

The 240-mile expedition under Major Williams left Fort Dodge on Tuesday, March 24th, but made only six or seven miles the first day. Snow was nearly four feet deep on the ground and oxen wallowed in ravines and creek beds that were covered with fifteen feet of snow. They camped the first night along the Des Moines River, the second in Dakota City and got only as far as McKnight's Point, twelve miles northwest of Dakota City, by the fourth night. The men were exhausted and several suffered from frostbite.

"We took up our line of march on the 25th of March, and proceeded up the west branch of the Des Moines River to intercept the savages, who, reports said, were about to sweep all the settlements on that river," recalled Major William Williams. "By forced marches through snow banks from fifteen to twenty feet deep, and swollen streams, we forced our way up to the state line, where we learned the Indians embodied 200 or 300 strong at Spirit Lake and Big Island Groves. Never was harder service rendered by any body of men than by those 110 men under my command. We had to ford streams breast deep every few miles, and at all snow-banks or drifts, had to shovel roads or draw wagons through by hand with tug ropes, also the oxen and horses. All were wet all day up to the middle at least, and lay out upon the open prairies at night, without tents, or other covering, than a blanket or buffalo-robe."[59]

A discussion was held to ascertain whether the expedition should continue. The men agreed to go on after being told by Major Williams: "You now understand that is not to be a holiday campaign, and any man in the battalion who feels that he has gone far enough is at liberty to return."

After spending the next night at Shippey's Point, they left the Des Moines River and followed the Dragon Trail to the Irish Colony (now Emmetsburg) on the shores of Medium Lake. "The morning after arriving at the Irish Colony," recalled Frank E. Mason, "Maj. Williams selected ten of the strongest men from the company to scout the country north, northeast and northwest for Indians and Indian signs. Our week of provisions consisted of about forty pounds of coarse corn meal and twenty pounds of flour. I was one of the ten men selected."[60]

Several Irishmen from the colony joined their ranks and the rescue party swelled to 125 able-bodied men. They spent the seventh night at Mud Lake, and on the eighth, met refugees from Springfield.

"About eighty miles up we met those who had escaped the massacre at Springfield, composed of three men unhurt, and two wounded, and several women and children, in all numbering some [fifteen to twenty] persons," recalled Williams. "They escaped in the night, carrying nothing with them but what they had on when the were attacked—had nothing to eat for two days and one night. They were about exhausted and the Indians on their trail pursuing them. Had not our scouts discovered them and reported, there can be no doubt that they would have been murdered that night."[61]

Upon reaching Grangers Point, southeast of the lakes, on the eighth night, they were met by a cavalry officer, who informed them a force from Fort Ridgely had gone to Spirit Lake to bury bodies as well. The party was informed that Inkpaduta had heard of their advance and fled, so it was useless to continue their pursuance and attempt to overtake him. The men were suffering from snow blindness. On the open prairies there was no wood for fires, and the men had to huddle together to keep from freezing. All they had to eat were dry crackers and raw ham.[62]

Williams split his force, sending half the men back to the Irish Colony, the others to Spirit Lake to aid in the burials of the victims. The burials took two full days and the party, split into two groups, left for home along different routes.

They were caught in a blizzard that afternoon and the main group became scattered due to lack of visibility. Three men—Captain Johnson, William Burkholder, and a man named Smith—were so exhausted they sat down in the snow to rest. Johnson and Burkholder began taking off their boots to massage their frozen feet, but Smith warned them they would not be able to get their boots back on once removed. Neither man heeded his warning, and Smith, realizing he had to keep moving to survive, went on without them.

The bodies of Captain Johnson and Burkholder were not found until eleven years later at the place where they were left by Smith. Their powder flasks and rifles were lying near their skeletons. The remainder of the party made it back safely although exhausted and frostbitten. One of the men, Cyrus Carpenter, later governor of Iowa, said in recounting the experience:

"I have marched with armies engaged in actual war from Cairo to Chattanooga, but I have never experienced a conflict with the elements that could be compared with those two nights and one day on Cylinder Creek."[63] Carpenter also wrote: "We marched over a route along which no team had been able to pass for weeks. Every foot of the way was covered with snow, and in places, where there was a depression in the surface of the prairie, or an elevation like a bluff or knoll, were drifts which seemed absolutely fathomless."[64]

The troops from Fort Ridgely had been dispatched by Colonel Alexander, commander of the fort. Leading the expedition were Captain Bee and Lieutenant Murray. "These troops encountered all the difficulties and obstacles incident to marching over prairies covered with deep snow," wrote Charles Flandrau, "and just at the transition stage between winter and spring, but persevered day after day, until they reached the lake. Here they ascertained that the Indians were two days in advance of them on the retreat, having been apprized by one of the traders of the approach of the troops; after which information they murdered him, plundered his establishment, and made good their retreat into a country which made capture improbable, with their small force, and pursuit unavailing. Had it not been for this untoward circumstance, the troops would have taken them on the spot."[65]

Captain Bee later wrote in a letter to a St. Paul newspaper:

On Saturday evening, March 30th, I arrived with my company at Caboo's Grove, several miles above Springfield, on the Des Moines, having made for that point with the expectation of finding a large band of Indians encamped there. While scouting through the grove, I encountered Coursall, or "Caboo," who had come from his camp, some distance off, to notify me that the Indians, fourteen in number, had attacked the settlement Thursday evening, and were then encamped at Heron Lake, some twenty-five miles off. My guide at that moment was absent, and I asked "Caboo" to lead me to this lake in the morning, provided that my guide could not do so. He consented and in the morning joined me in my pursuit of the Indians.

When we neared Heron Lake, there was so much probability of the Indians being there that I displayed my company and surrounded the groove in which they were supposed to be encamped; "Caboo" was in front of my men, his double-barreled gun loaded with ball, in his hand. His whole demeanor convinced me that he had come there to fight, his life, he told me, having been threatened by the Indians. The camp, however, had evidently been abandoned on Friday night, and as this was Sunday evening, I came to the conclusion that pursuit after mounted Indians was useless, with jaded foot troops, and made a forced march back to camp.[66]

Captain Bee gave up the chase and returned to Fort Ridgely, leaving Lieutenant Murray at the lake with twenty-four men. His report divulged that the Sioux had constructed fourteen large teepees, and he believed some 200 warriors had gathered in southern Minnesota with every intention of attacking settlements on the Des Moines River all the way south to Fort Dodge.[67]

The trek through those same snows was no better for the four female captives, and perhaps worse. As they trudged through the snow, they were forced to carry heavy packs on their backs for several days and even weeks. Abigail Gardiner carried eight bars of lead, one pint of leaden balls for shooting buffalo, one tent cover made of heavy cloth, one bed comforter, one Indian blanket, one iron bar about four feet long and an inch thick, a stick of wood, a very heavy gun, and a flat piece of wood about four feet long, which kept her back straight.[68]

Elizabeth Thatcher caught cold and developed a high fever. One of her breasts "gathered and broke" and one of her legs swelled to nearly twice its normal size. Although the medicine man did his best to treat her, she was still forced to tramp through the snow drifts and wade through icy water waist-deep in this condition.[69]

While crossing a deep river on a log, Mrs. Thatcher, began to falter because of her swollen limbs. One of the braves came up to her and pushed her into the icy river. Facing death, the unfortunate woman miraculously reached shore, and in an effort to stay afloat, she grasped roots along the bank. Another of her tormentors beat her with a club, and as she bobbed away in the stream, they shot and killed her.[70]

Abigail Gardiner later recalled: "Pursuing their journey still westward, the barbarian horde with their three remaining victims [Miss A. Gardiner, Mrs. Noble and Mrs. Marble] reached a small sheet of water called Skunk Lake. Here they paused for a short time and pitched their camp and were visited by two Indians of the Lac-qui-parle tribe, who entered their camp with some interesting proposals. They treated earnestly during two days with the Inkpaduta band, offering to purchase Mrs. Marble, that they might return her to the whites and claim the ransom which had been offered for her. After protracted deliberations, they bought her, giving in return several horses, quantities of powder, [and] lead . . ."[71]

Miss Gardiner was compelled to haul water, cut wood, help pitch tents at night, and bake bread. Mrs. Noble, a woman of "unyielding temper and high spirit," refused to do what she was told. Inkpaduta's son grew impatient with her, pulled her outside his tent, and beat her to death. The following morning as they started their march, one of the braves went over to the corpse and discharged his Colt into her face.

On Saturday, May 23rd, three Indians—Mazakutemani (The-Man-Who-Shoots-Metal-as-He-Walks), Hotonwashte (Beautiful Voice), and Chetanmaza (Iron Hawk) were sent by State Agent Charles E. Flandrau to collect a ransom for Miss Gardiner. The St. Paul Pioneer Press reported:

> On the 29th, following up the same trail, they arrived at a recently deserted camp, where they found the dead body of Mrs. Noble. The body was terribly mutilated; it was apparent that she had been most cruelly outraged, not only before but after death. Three bullet wounds were discovered in her head, and on her limbs and arms, the traces of brutal cruelties were visible.[72]

Miss Gardiner and her captors walked 150 miles to a Yankton camp on the Jaques River. The Yanktons professed to be friendly with the whites, but according to Miss Gardiner, "did not in the least ameliorate the condition, or lighten the burdens . . ." During the parley between the two factions, Inkpaduta sold Miss Gardiner to the Yanktons where "she continued to endure the same slavery until her final ransom by the whites."

In late June, word reached Fort Ridgely that Inkpaduta's son, Roaring Cloud, was visiting a woman at Yellow Medicine and a small detachment of soldiers was dispatched to the agency. Roaring Cloud was killed and the woman taken prisoner. Many of the annuity Indians became angry over the incident since they were on good terms with Roaring Cloud and the woman. The Indians became so unruly that Flandrau and the soldiers had to take refuge in a log cabin until reinforcements arrived in the area.[73]

Newspaper editors were frustrated over all the discrepancies coming in through unverified reports. These editors wondered if they should publish these reports at all since they discouraged immigration. The *St. Paul Daily Times* got out an extra on the massacre and subsequent events on April 15 and was denounced by competing newspapers as did the *Pioneer and Democrat*.[74]

The *Times* article was shocking and triggered pandemonium on the frontier. Under a sensationalistic heading, "SAVAGES ON OUR FRONTIER! SETTLERS MURDERED!!!" Based on a false rumor, the synthetic story startled Minnesotans, who pictured painted savages at every turn:

> We lose no time in laying before our readers in an Extra, the following startling information just received from a gentleman who came through from St. Peter, and who assures us that the information is reliable. Our informant is H. B. NELSON, who states that the citizens of St. Peter were startled by the rumor that the Sioux Indians had been murdering the whites at Blue Earth, and pillaging and burning the dwellings, and were moving down upon Mankato with the determination of destroying the lives of the whites.[75]

The *Henderson Democrat* proclaimed on April 16th:

> About a fortnight since, our community was startled with the report that several families had been massacred in southern Minnesota, by a

band of Missouri Sioux. That report has been confirmed. A letter to this paper upon the subject, from an officer in the United States army, will be found underneath this article. A report of a much more alarming character has just been received, which has caused the most intense excitement in this community—not only an account of the great number reported killed, but also because the place where the massacre took place is so near home.

The stage driver from St. Peter to this place, was in Mankato on Sunday night, and he reports that, a day previous, 500 Missouri Sioux slaughtered over [fifty] white persons, residing [fifteen] miles south of that place. They stripped the women naked, took their scalps, and cut out their breasts. Some escaped, and fled to Mankato, where [sixty] men were immediately raised, and at once started for the place where the wholesale murder had taken place. The Indians surrounded them, and the latter sought security in a large log house, which they used as a fort, and, at the last account, had sent [fourteen] of the redskins to their last account. One of the men in the house managed to escape and reach St. Peter, where, upon hearing the intelligence, 100 men at once enrolled themselves, under command of General Dodd, and started for the scene of action, well equipped, and with loads of provisions. We understand that companies have also been formed in Traverse des Sioux and LeSueur. Nothing has been heard concerning the fate of the Mankato volunteers.

The above report may be an exaggeration. We simply state the matter as it was stated to us by Mr. Wagner, the stage driver. He also informs us that the women and children for miles around St. Peter had fled to that place for protection. If the report proves correct, 100 men from Henderson will readily enlist to assist in teaching the Indians a lesson which they will not soon forget.[76]

Two days later the *St. Paul Minnesota Pioneer and Democrat* ran another story on the attacks:

As the difficulties between the settlers and the Indians originated at Spirit Lake, Iowa, a brief account of the settlement there, and at Springfield, will prove of interest at the present juncture, and will enable the public to judge correctly as to the truthfulness of the numberless rumors afloat.

In May last, Messrs. Freeborn, Lauver, Granger, Sweeny, Harriett, and Snyder, formed a company at Red Wing, in the Territory, for the purpose of laying out a town, farming, and erecting mills, on Spirit Lake, in Dickinson County, Iowa. In July, they dispatched several teams for the lake, containing supplies for the settlers, and Messrs. Granger, Harriett, and Snyder accompanied them. During the summer, several families from Iowa moved to the neighborhood of the lake; and in December last, when Mr. Granger returned to Red Wing, there were thirty-nine persons residing at Spirit Lake.

The Lake is not correctly set down on the maps. It is generally represented as being on the line between Iowa and Minnesota; it is situated, however, ten miles South of the line; the Little Sioux River being its outlet. The settlement at the lake, is about forty miles from Fort Dodge, Iowa, eighty miles from Sioux City, and one hundred miles from Mankato.

The attack on the settlers at Spirit Lake, was made on the 9th of March. It is feared all the settlers, thirty-eight in number, were killed by the savages. The only persons from this vicinity, residing at Spirit Lake, were Messrs. Harriett and Snyder of Red Wing. Among the names of those who bodies have been found, are those of Messrs. Howe, Gardiner [Gardner], Lucas [Luce], Mattocks, Stewart and their families. These were probably the only married men at the settlement.

Parties from Boonsboro, and Ft. Dodge, Iowa, proceeded to Spirit Lake as soon as the intelligence reached them, and buried all the dead bodies of the murdered settlers, that could be discovered.

On the 5th of April, Messrs. Freeborn, Lauver and other associates of Red Wing, dispatched five men, well supplied with provisions, arms, ammunition, . . . to Spirit Lake. This party is composed of the following persons: Messrs. Granger, Decay [DeKay], Lauver, Patten and Huntington. They started by way of Owatonna and Blue Earth city, as soon as possible after the news of the massacre reached Red Wing.

The Red Wing Company had expended at Spirit Lake, upwards of $3,000. At the time of the attack, there was a large supply of provisions on hand, fifty head of cattle, and eight or ten horses and mules.

Springfield, the scene of the second massacre, is in Brown county, fifteen or twenty miles north of Spirit Lake. The town was laid out by William Wood, a well known trader, and until lately a resident of Mankato. This place was attacked on the second day of April, and seven men killed, seven wounded, and four women carried off as prisoners. Those persons, in town, who were so fortunate as to be able to fortify their houses, escaped uninjured. The names of those murdered at Springfield, know to us, are William and George M. Wood, brothers, and Messrs. Church and Stewart.[77]

The *Henderson Democrat* attempted to explain what occurred at Spirit Lake by interviewing an Indian who had witnessed the murders and had spoken with some of Inkpaduta's band:

The difficulties first originated at a place the Indians call the "Grass Lodge," somewhere east of Spirit Lake, between Indians of the Scarlet

Point band of renegade Warpetkootys and some five or six settlers at that place, in which three of the settlers were severely wounded, and the white men all killed. This was the only resemblance to a fight that took place.

The men being killed, the women and children were also immediately murdered by the infuriated savages, who took the provisions and others articles belonging to the settlers, and proceeded toward Spirit Lake, determined to destroy all the whites they should encounter.

The settlers at Spirit Lake, wholly unaware of any difficulties with the Indians, were easily surprised. The buildings were set on fire, and as the men came out, they were successively stricken down by the Indians. All the men were killed in this manner, and the slaughter of the women and children followed. None were spared but four females, who are now prisoners with the Indians, enduring the torments of a thousand deaths in every hour of their lives. The Indians count over thirty whites (men, women and children) that were killed.

The Indians took with them every article they deemed of value, and proceeded leisurely toward the Sioux River, which they probably crossed at the mouth of the Rock River, where some four or five settlers were located, who, have doubtless also been massacred. The Indians are expected to cross the Missouri, and join either the Tetons or Yanktons west of the river.[78]

Settlers in Blue Earth County, Minnesota, believed the Indians were going to attack their settlements, as evidenced by an early county history:

The excitement now was at its height. The settlers in the extreme southwestern part of the county gathered into Shelbyville. Those living a little further down on the Blue Earth fortified themselves in Mr. Reed's house, near the present village of Vernon Center. Those along Perch Creek and along the Watonwan, below the Slocum neighborhood fled to Garden City, where two forts were built, one about Folsom's log house north of the village and the other on the south side of the river by Edson Gerry's house. Gerry had moved his first claim shanty from the village and put it near his other house. The space between the two houses was now closed in by log walls and port holes made in them and in the roofs of the houses.

Here an amusing incident occurred, though at the time it seemed serious enough to the persons involved. Two or three miles below the present village of Vernon Center, on the Blue Earth River, lived Dr. [Lemuel Harvey] Arledge. Just below the house on the river bottom were camped a few Indians making maple sugar. When the doctor heard of the massacres, he and his family were greatly agitated and imagined

97

they saw signs of mischief in the Indian camp. They wished to flee to Garden City, but did not dare to expose themselves outside the cabin for fear of inviting an attack. The son, Alexander, a grown up young man, finally dressed himself in a blanket and, thus disguised, mounted on a pony and armed with a rifle, he hoped to pass the Indian camp without their knowing he was a white man.

The previous fall Joseph McClanahan had located a claim in Shelby Township and then had gone back to Indiana. On this particular day he was returning to his claim and had reached Garden City. They told him of the Indian massacres and urged him to stay there as there were Indians all about. He pretended to disbelieve the whole story and thought he could get to his claim without trouble. The snow was still deep and melting, making walking very hard. He had gone about two miles and a half, when lo! and behold, coming down the road toward him full tilt was a blanketed Indian, on a pony and waving a gun. It did not take McClanahan but a very small fraction of a second to wheel about and take to his heels. It was a fearful race. Young Arledge (for it was he) hallooed to try and stop him, but all McClanahan heard were blood curdling war hoops, and he ran all the faster. For two miles he sped like a deer over that terrible road of half melted snow and then fell in a faint completely exhausted. Young Arledge jumped from his horse and rubbed his forehead and face with snow to restore him to consciousness. In his semi-delirious condition, McClanahan imagined the cold steel of the scalping knife pass around his head. The men building the fort by Gerry's were horror stricken to witness such a bold, shocking murder committed before their eyes, seizing their guns rushed up the road to the rescue. Fortunately Arledge managed to disclose his identity before they fired. McClanahan was so overcome by the fright and exhaustion that he was confined to his bed for many days.[79]

Edward A. Washburn, a settler from Vermont, wrote his father on April 21st:

I suppose you are feeling very anxious about us as you have probably heard greatly exaggerated accounts concerning the Indian War. I should not be much surprised if you have seen accounts something like this in the papers: The Indian War! Terrible Slaughter! All the Settlers on the Watonwan and Blue Earth Rivers have been murdered and scalped! The Indians in force one thousand strong are burning the houses! And marching upon Mankato! Later news: We have just learned from authentic sources that every settler in Minnesota Territory except one has been killed! And he escaped with so great difficulty that the Indian Bullets tore off his clothes and left him entirely naked![80]

Although Washburn was poking fun at the newspaper accounts, others studied the situation more seriously. The *Fort Dodge Sentinel* concluded on September 10th:

> The records of Indian warfare, though at all times marked with deeds of violence, nowhere present such atrocious acts as have recently been enacted by the Sioux, in the northwestern portion of our State and southern Minnesota; and rarely, if ever, have we witnessed such patient endurance, such courage and noble daring, as were shown by the sufferers. In times of profound peace, the Indians kindly received the hunting grounds laid open to them, with no cause of provocation, no treats to excite, no wrongs to avenge, in the depths of winter, among a thinly settled and defenseless people, they commence their fiendish work, each the preclude to greater acts of violence, desisting only when nothing remained to be accomplished.[81]

As alarming stories of Indian attacks, many of them fabricated, spread across the Minnesota frontier, Inkpaduta and his ruthless band went unpunished. The government had ordered the Sioux in Minnesota to deliver Inkpaduta or it would withhold their annuities. This was a terrible hardship for the Sioux, for whom Inkpaduta was already an outcast and only drew part of their annuities through fear. Mazakutemani, their speaker, said at a council meeting held at Yellow Medicine August 10, 1857, that the Indians who had killed the whites did not belong to them, and they should not be penalized for the actions of others outside their band.[82]

Stories circulated, too, as to the whereabouts of Inkpaduta, many of which were grossly exaggerated. Many settlers lived in constant fear of his return. In June 1858, it was falsely reported that he had been captured near St. Peter, and later that same month, another misstatement surfaced that he had been taken on the Yellow Medicine River. In April 1860, the death of a white man on the Cottonwood River was attributed to Inkpaduta, as were some stolen horses in Minnesota the following year.[83]

The following piece appeared in a Mankato newspaper in October 1858:

"TIME EXTENDED.—Superintendent Cullen requests us to state that the time for receiving applications for remuneration for expenses incurred and services rendered by individuals in the several expeditions against Inkpadutah's band of Indians, in the year, 1857, has been extended until the first day of November 1858, up to which time claims will be received."[84]

So many exaggerated stories about difficulties appeared in Iowa newspapers that newspapers in southern Minnesota were cautious about printing them. One story, however, published in the *Jasper County Free Press*, was given some credence and reprinted in the *Mankato Independent* on April 7, 1859:

"We learn from our townsman Judge A.A. Kellogg, who has just returned from Spirit Lake, that great excite prevails at that place, arising from fear of Indians, numbers of who are reported to be lurking in that vicinity."[85]

According to the report, two Indians and a half-Indian, with their women and children came into Spirit Lake and claimed that they were part of a group of ninety Indians under a white colonel, marching against Inkpaduta, and that they had been sent out to procure cattle. Their story was not believed by the whites, and the two Indians were taken into custody. They were later transported to Fort Dodge under an escort of soldiers but managed to escape during the trek. They were both recognized as having taken part in the 1857 massacre.

Only a few days later, fourteen Indians were arrested and charged with having taken part in the 1857 killings. One of the prisoners was identified as the brother-in-law of Inkpaduta. Meanwhile, several trappers arrived in the settlement and reported that between 100 and 150 Indians were "lurking" in the vicinity of Heron Lake. A party of scouts was dispatched to check out the rumor as great alarm prevailed at the lake and sentinels were posted day and night. One frontier family became so frightened, they left the settlement. A man from the settlement came into Fort Dodge, however, and reported that while the two Indians arrested had indeed escaped, the rumors of other Indians in the vicinity were false.

Judge of the Supreme Court and former Indian agent for the Sioux Charles E. Flandrau later said during his dedication speech for the erection of a monument at Spirit Lake:

"It has often been asked why the government never did anything to punish these marauding savages. The answer is plain. Colonel Alexander and myself had a well-matured plan to attack Inkpaduta the instant we learned of the fate of the captive women. We had five companies of the Tenth Infantry at our disposal, and could easily have destroyed his entire band, but, unfortunately, just before we were ready to move on the enemy, the whole regiment was ordered to Fort Bridger, in Utah, to aid General Albert Sidney Johnson's command in the suppression of the anticipated Mormon outbreak, and before any available troops came to our frontier to replace them, Inkpaduta and his people had passed out of recollection."[86]

To Inkpaduta and his followers, the failure of the whites to pursue them was construed as a sign of weakness and was bound to terminate in disastrous results for the exposed settlements on the frontier. They renegade band became more insolent and bolder than ever and harassed government employees in Minnesota.[87]

The *Mankato Independent* reported on October 27, 1857:

> Mr. Milton Thatcher, whose wife was taken prisoner at Spirit Lake and subsequently murdered by the Indians last spring, arrived in this place on Thursday last. From him we learn that the fiendish cruelties attending the atrocious butchery of the inhabitants of that settlement, have never been over-rated; in fact the half has not been told.
> He informs us that Miss Gardner, one of the rescued prisoners, was married in August last. She resides in the neighborhood of Fort Dodge, Iowa.[88]

Abbie Gardner did in fact marry Cosville Sharpe of Hampton and wrote an account of her experiences as a captive of the Sioux. She acquired thirteen acres of her father's land near Arnold's Park where the family settled in 1891. She lived there until her death in 1921, the last survivor of the Spirit Lake Massacre.[89]

State monument, Arnolds Park. (Author's collection)

Notes

[1] *Annals of Iowa*, Vol. XVIII, No. 5, Des Moines, Iowa, July 1932, Third Series, F.L. Herriott, "The Origins of the Indian Massacre Between the Okobojis, March 8, 1857," p. 323.

[2] Abigail Gardiner, *History of the Spirit Lake Massacre! 8th March 1857, and of Miss Abigail Gardiner's Three Months Captivity Among the Indians*, New Britain, CT., L.P. Lee, Publisher, 1857, p. 5.

[3] Bob Brown, *Northwest Iowa's Greatest Tragedy: The Spirit Lake Massacre* (Reprint of a Series of Six Articles on the March, 1857, Spirit Lake Massacre, Written by Bob Brown and Published in the Fort Dodge, *Iowa Messenger*, February 18-25, 1957, p. 1; *Lakefield Standard*, February 8, 1896.

[4] Davis Thomas and Karin Ronnefeldt, editors, *People of the First Man: Life Among the Plains Indians in Their Final Days of Glory*, New York, Promontory Press, 1982, p. 21; Marilyn Ziebarth and Alan Ominsky, *Fort Snelling: Anchor Post of the Northwest*, St. Paul, Minnesota Historical Society Press, 1979, p. 21.

[5] *Annals of Iowa*, Vol. XVIII, No. 5, Des Moines, Iowa, July 1932, Third Series, F.L. Herriott, "The Origins of the Indian Massacre Between the Okobojis, March 8, 1857," pp. 331-332.

[6] Mary Hawker Bakeman, *Legends, Letters and Lies: Readings about Inkpaduta and the Spirit Lake Massacre*, Roseville, Park Genealogical Books, 2001, p. 11.

[7] Joseph Frazier Wall, *Iowa: A History*, New York, W.W. Norton & Company, Inc., 1978, p. 61.

[8]Dr. William Houlette, *Iowa: The Pioneer Heritage*, Des Moines, Wallace-Homestead Book Company, 1970, p. 158.

[9]Bob Brown, *Northwest Iowa's Greatest Tragedy: The Spirit Lake Massacre*, p. 1; Paul N. Beck, *Soldier, Settler, and Sioux Fort Ridgely and the Minnesota River Valley 1853-1867*, Sioux Falls, The Center for Western Studies, Augustana College, 2000, pp. 42-43; *Lakefield Standard*, February 8, 1896.

[10]*Pipestone County Star*, April 10, 1997. Article by Mark Fode.

[11]Lott was allegedly killed during a brawl in California.

[12]*Lakefield Standard*, February 15, 1896.

[13]*Annals of Iowa*, Vol. XVIII, No. 5, Des Moines, Iowa, July 1932, Third Series, F.L. Herriott, "The Origins of the Indian Massacre Between the Okojobis, March 8, 1857" p. 337.

[14]*Pipestone County Star*, April 10, 1997. Article by Mark Fode.

[15]*Annals of Iowa*, Vol. XVIII, No. 5, Des Moines, Iowa, July 1932, Third Series, F.L. Herriott, "The Origins of the Indian Massacre Between the Okojobis, March 8, 1857" p. 337.

[16]*Lakefield Standard*, December 7, 1895.

[17]The name Springfield was later changed to Jackson.

[18]Daniel Buck, *Indian Outbreaks*, Minneapolis, Ross & Haines, Inc., 1965, p. 32.

[19]*Minnesota Pioneer and Democrat*, April 11, 1857.

[20]William J. Petersen, *The Story of Iowa: The Progress of an American State*, Volume I, New York, Lewis Historical Publishing Company, Inc., 1952, p. 139; Joseph Frazier Wall, *Iowa: A History*, p. 62; Peggy Rodina Larson, "A New Look at the Elusive Inkpaduta," *Minnesota History*, 48/1, Spring 1982, p. 24.

[21]Leland L. Sage, *A History of Iowa*, Ames, The Iowa State University Press, 1974, p. 107.

[22]Bea McNamara, *The Okoboji and Spirit Lake Massacre and Kidnapping Story*, Arnolds Park, Iowa, 1957, pp. 3-7; Joseph Frazier Wall, *Iowa: A History*, p. 62.

[23]Edmund C. Bray and Martha Coleman Bray, *Joseph N. Nicollet on the Plains and Prairies*, St. Paul, Minnesota Historical Society Press, 1976, p. 129.

[24]Inkpaduta, although blind and helpless, took part in the 1876 Custer massacre at the Little Bighorn. He was removed from the battlefield and taken to Canada where he died in the company of Sitting Bull.

[25]Bob Brown, *Northwest Iowa's Greatest Tragedy: The Spirit Lake Massacre*, p. 3.

[26]Peggy Rodina Larson, "A New Look at the Elusive Inkpaduta," *Minnesota History*, 48/1, Spring 1982, p. 27.

[27]Daniel Clayton Anderson, *Little Crow: Spokesman for the Sioux*, St. Paul, Minnesota Historical Society Press, 1986, p. 83; Daniel Buck, *Indian Outbreaks*, pp. 22-23.

[28]Robert B. Forrest, *A History of Western Murray County*, Murray Co., Minnesota, 1947, p. 67.

[29]*Pipestone County Star*, April 10, 1997. Article by Mark Fode.

[30]David L. Bristow, "Inkpaduta's Revenge: The True Story of the Spirit Lake Massacre," *The Iowan Magazine*, January-February 1999.

[31]Dr. William Houlette, *Iowa: The Pioneer Heritage*, pp. 1601-1610; Bea McNamara, *The Okoboji and Spirit Lake Massacre and Kidnapping Story*, p. 9.

[32]David L. Bristow, "Inkpaduta's Revenge: The True Story of the Spirit Lake Massacre," *The Iowan Magazine*, January-February 1999.

[33]Dr. William Houlette, *Iowa: The Pioneer Heritage*, pp. 1601-161; Bea McNamara, *The Okoboji and Spirit Lake Massacre and Kidnapping Story*, p. 9.

[34]Joseph Frazier Wall, *Iowa: A History*, p. 63.

[35]Arthur Francis Allen, *Northwestern Iowa, Its History and Traditions 1804-1926*, Chicago, S. J. Clarke Publishing Company, 1927, p. 583.

[36]Abigail Gardiner, *Spirit Lake Massacre*, p. 13.

[37]Bob Brown, *Northwest Iowa's Greatest Tragedy: The Spirit Lake Massacre*, pp. 4-6; Herb Lake, *Iowa Inside Out*, Ames, Iowa State University Press, 1968, p. 137.

[38]Bea McNamara, *The Okoboji and Spirit Lake Massacre and Kidnapping*, pp. 10-11; William J. Petersen, *The Story of Iowa: The Progress of an American State*, p. 140.

[39]Abigail Gardiner, *Spirit Lake Massacre*, p. 17.

[40]Bea McNamara, *The Okoboji and Spirit Lake Massacre and Kidnapping*, pp. 10-11.

[41]Mary Hawker Bakeman, *Legends, Letters and Lies*, pp. 107-108.

[42]Abigail Gardiner, *Spirit Lake Massacre*, p. 19.

[43]Bob Brown, *Northwest Iowa's Greatest Tragedy: The Spirit Lake Massacre*, pp. 7-8.

[44]*Minnesota Pioneer and Democrat*, April 24, 1857.

[45]*Minnesota Pioneer and Democrat*, March 26, 1857.

[46]*Lakefield Standard*, December 14, 1895.

[47]*Lakefield Standard*, January 4, 1896.

[48]Daniel Buck, *Indian Outbreaks*, pp. 33-34; Dr. William Houlette, *Iowa: The Pioneer Heritage*, p. 161; Arthur P. Rose, *An Illustrated History of Yellow Medicine County*, Marshall, Northern Historical Publishing Company, 1914, p. 36.

[49]Charles Aldrich, *Annals of Iowa*, 3rd Series, Volume III, Number 7, pp. 546-548.

[50]*Lakefield Standard*, January 11, 1896.

[51]Charles Aldrich, *Annals of Iowa*, 3rd Series, Volume III, Number 7, pp. 546-548.

[52]*Minnesota Pioneer and Democrat*, April 24, 1857.

[53]Bea McNamara, *The Okoboji and Spirit Lake Massacre and Kidnapping Story*, p. 13.

[54]*Lakefield Standard*, January 18, 1896.

[55]Bob Brown, *Northwest Iowa's Greatest Tragedy: The Spirit Lake Massacre*, pp. 8-11.

[56]*Annals of Iowa*, Vol. XVIII, No. 5, October 1932, F.I. Herriott, "The Aftermath of the Spirit Lake Massacre March 8-15, 1857," pp. 439-440.

[57]*Minnesota Pioneer and Democrat*, April 24, 1857.

[58]Bob Brown, *Northwest Iowa's Greatest Tragedy: The Spirit Lake Massacre*, pp. 8-11.

[59]Mary Hawker Bakeman, *Legends, Letters and Lies*, p. 79.

[60]*Annals of Iowa*, 3rd Series, Volume III, Number 7, pp. 532-533.

[61]Mary Hawker Bakeman, *Legends, Letters and Lies*, p. 81.

[62]Bob Brown, *Northwest Iowa's Greatest Tragedy: The Spirit Lake Massacre*, pp. 8-11; William J. Petersen, *The Story of Iowa: The Progress of An American State*, p. 141.

[63]Bob Brown, *Northwest Iowa's Greatest Tragedy: The Spirit Lake Massacre*, p. 11.

[64]*Annals of Iowa*, 3rd Series, Volume III, Number 7, p. 482.

[65]*Minnesota Pioneer and Democrat*, April 21, 1857.

[66]*Minnesota Pioneer and Democrat*, May 16, 1857.

[67]*Fort Dodge Sentinel*, September 10, 1857.

[68]Abigail Gardiner, *Spirit Lake Massacre*, pp. 21-30.

[69]Bea McNamara, *The Okoboji and Spirit Lake Massacre and Kidnapping Story*, p. 13.

[70]Abigail Gardiner, *Spirit Lake Massacre*, pp. 8-11.

[71]Ibid., p. 27; William J. Petersen, *The Story of Iowa: The Progress of An American State*, p. 142.

[72]*St. Paul Pioneer Press*, June 25, 1857.

[73]Peggy Rodina Larson, "A New Look at the Elusive Inkpaduta," *Minnesota History*, 48/1, Spring 1982, p. 32.

[74]George S. Hage, *Newspapers on the Minnesota Frontier 1849-1860*, St. Paul, Minnesota Historical Society Press, 1967, p. 112.

[75]*Minneapolis Times*, April 13, 1857.

[76]*Henderson Democrat*, April 16, 1857.

[77]*The Minnesota Pioneer and Democrat*, April 18, 1857.

[78]*Henderson Democrat*, May 7, 1857.

[79]Thomas Hughes, *History of Blue Earth County and Biographies of Its Leading Citizens*, Chicago, Middle West Publishing Company, p. 86.

[80]Edward A. Washburn letter to his father dated April 21, 1857. Edward and William Washburn Papers, Minnesota Historical Society.

[81]*Fort Dodge Sentinel*, September 10, 1857.

[82]Daniel Buck, *Indian Outbreaks*, p. 38.

[83]Peggy Rodina Larson, "A New Look at the Elusive Inkpaduta," *Minnesota History*, 48/1, Spring 1982, p. 33.

[64]*Mankato Independent*, October 21, 1858.

[85]*Mankato Independent*, April 7, 1859.

[86]*Annals of Iowa*, Vol. XVIII, No. 5, October 1932, F.I. Herriott, "The Aftermath of the Spirit Lake Massacre March 8-15, 1857," p. 469.

[87]Arthur P. Rose, *An Illustrated History of Yellow Medicine County*, p. 38.

[88]*Mankato Independent*, October 27, 1857.

[89]Dr. William Houlette, *Iowa: The Pioneer Heritage*, p. 163.

Chapter Three

Causes of the Dakota Conflict

"We have waited a long time. The money is ours, but we cannot get it. We have no food, but here are these stores, filled with food. We ask that you, the agent, make some arrangements by which we can get food from the stores, or else we make take our own way to keep ourselves from starving. When men are hungry they help themselves."   —Little Crow[1]

"So far as I am concerned, if they are hungry, let them eat grass or their own dung."
                                                                —Andrew Myrick

ENDOTA, MEANING "meeting of the waters" in the Dakota language is the oldest permanent white settlement in Minnesota. Traders and trappers flooded the area long before Fort Snelling was built in 1820. Mendota was the site of military encampments that preceded construction of the fort and was an integral part of life at the old fort.

The first white men to encounter the Santee Sioux in Minnesota were explorer-traders Medart Chouart, Sieur de Groseilliers, and Pierre Esprit Radisson, who were guests in the spring Feast of the Dead. The Santee, still armed with spears and bows and arrows, were eager to develop a trade with the French. For many years, tribes to the northeast had been receiving French goods and weapons, giving them battlefield superiority.[2]

But little was known about the Sioux people in the late eighteenth and early nineteenth centuries. During the winter of 1766-1767, Jonathan Carver reached a site, which later became Mankato, where the Blue Earth River runs into the Minnesota River. Carver wintered at nearby Swan Lake in Nicollet County, and, in April 1767, he invited both the plains and river bands of Sioux to trade with Major Robert Rogers, in an attempt to open trade negotiations. His men gave away most of the trade good as gifts, and the United States Government accused Carver of stirring up the Indians and creating unfair competition for the traders.[3]

The Dakota (Lakota) had lived in the Minnesota region for a long time; however, no one knows their relationship to the primitive peoples of the postglacial era. The Dakota are members of the Siouan linguistic family and part of a confederacy of seven tribes. The largest of the seven tribes was the Tetons, who, along with the Yankton and Yanktonai, were people of the plains area that stretched out to the Missouri River and beyond. The Santee were a group of four tribes that were primarily Minnesotan: Mdewakanton, Wahpekute, Wahpeton, and Sisseton. Of these, the Mdewakanton—meaning the "People of the Spirit or Holy Lake"—occupied the place of central importance in Minnesota.

Dakota Indians. [Author's collection]

The Dakota, tall, robust people, valued the skills of hunting and fishing and thrived on the rigors of warfare. Using no metals, they relied on stone, wood, and bone to fashion their tools and weapons. These nomadic people followed the plentiful buffalo herds, lived in skin-stitched tepees in winter and bark lodges in summer. They traveled on foot and in wooden dugouts or buffalo-skin boats, and later earned a reputation as the finest horsemen of the American plains. The Dakota culture remains rich in religion, music, and storytelling.

The title "Sioux" is at once a powerful and an ambiguous appellation. It is powerful because it evokes in the minds of most Americans an accurate image of a proud and courageous American Indian tribe. It is ambiguous because, to different disciplines, it means different things. To the modern archaeologist and anthropologist, it encompasses all the tribes that eventually evolved their own dialects from an ancient common Siouan language. This incorporates tribes across the northern and Midwestern United States and southern Canada.[4]

The Santee Sioux had once occupied the southern two-thirds of Minnesota and parts of the Dakotas and Iowa. They lived in an area of lakes and forests interspersed with prairies. But the white migration had pushed other tribes westward, and the Chippewa, armed with British trade muskets, forced the Sioux southward, isolating them on the prairie west of the Mississippi River in the eighteenth century. Although the two tribes fought each other for another century, the Sioux were unable to regain lost ground. The Sioux thus became displaced persons, woodland Indians forced to live on the great prairies.[5]

Like other Dakota bands, the Santees' inclusive kinship structure formed the basis of their economic, social and political life. The family comprised their basic social unit, and groups of families united by blood or marriage constituted a clan. The various clans made the individual bands of the Dakota tribe.

The Sioux men fought enemy tribes and did the hunting and fishing. The women carried water and wood, gathered and cooked food, put up the tents, tended the gardens, and raised the family's children. Visiting relatives were never turned away, and close relatives lived within the same lodge. Each family was characterized by numerous relatives:

> The sisters of his mother were his mothers. The brothers of his father were his fathers. The brothers of his mother and the sisters of his father were uncle and aunts, respectively. Children who are cousins according to the white tradition were his brothers and sisters. A child, then, could inherit many relatives of varying degrees from his parents.[6]

On September 23, 1805, Lieutenant Zebulon Pike negotiated a treaty with the Sioux in Minnesota, which became the beginning of the end for the Indian way of life in that state. Pike's mission was to prepare the way for the abolishing of British traders operating on American lands. His mission was not well organized, and his reports were inaccurate, but the encroachment by Americans opened the door to dishonesty, greed, and persecution.[7]

In Pike's speech to the Indians he spoke for the Great White Father:

> Brothers—I am happy to meet you here at this council fire which your father has sent me to kindle and to take you by the hands as our children.
> Brothers—I expect that you will all give orders to all your young warriors to respect my flag and protection, for was a dog to run to my lodge for safety, his enemy must walk over me to hurt him.
> Brothers—It is the wish of our government to establish military posts on the upper Mississippi at such places as might be thought expedient. I have, therefore, examined the country and have pitched on the mouth of the river St. Croix, this place and the falls of St. Anthony. I therefore wish you to grant to the United States nine miles square, of St. Croix, and at this place, from a league below the confluence of the St. Peter and Mississippi, to a league above St. Anthony, extending three leagues on each side of the river; and as we are a people who are accustomed to have all of our acts written down, in order to have them handed to our children, I have drawn up a form of an agreement which we will both sign in the presence of the traders.
> Brothers—I am told that hitherto the traders have made a practice of selling rum to you. All of you, to your right senses, must know that it is injurious; and occasions quarrels and murders amongst yourselves. For this reason, your father has thought proper to prohibit the traders from selling you any rum.
> Brothers—I now present you with some of your father's tobacco, and some other trifling things, as a memorandum of my good will, and before my departure I will give you some liquor to clear your throats.[8]

Of course, the Indians did not understand a treaty and they knew nothing of the white man's money. The treaty read:

> Whereas at a conference held between the United States of America and the Sioux nation of Indians: Lieutenant Z. M. Pike, of the army of the United States, and the chiefs and the warriors of said tribe, have agreed to the following articles, which, when ratified and approved of by the proper authority, shall be binding on both parties.
> Article 1. That the Sioux nation grant unto the United States for the purpose of establishment of military posts, nine miles square at the mouth of the St. Croix, also from the Mississippi to include the falls of St. Anthony, extending nine miles on each side of the river, that the Sioux nation grants to the United States the full sovereignty and power over said district for ever.
> Article 2. That, in consideration of the above grants, the United States shall pay (filled up by the senate with 2,000 dollars).
> Article 3. The United States promise, on their part, to permit the Sioux to pass and repass, hunt, or make use of the said districts as they have formerly done without any other exception than those specified in article first.[9]

Pike later wrote about the treaty he made with the Sioux:

> Prepared for the council, which we commenced about twelve o'clock. I had a bower or shade, made of my sails, on the beach, into which only my gentleman . . . and the chiefs entered. I then addressed them in a speech, which, though long and touching on many points, had for its principal object the granting of land at this place . . . and making peace with the Chipeways. . . . They gave me the land required . . . but spoke doubtfully with respect to the peace. I gave them presents to the amount of about $200, and as soon as the council was over, I allowed the traders to present them with some liquor, which, with what I myself gave, was equal to 60 gallons. In one half-hour they were all embarked for their respective villages.[10]

In 1817, Stephen H. Long made the first of two "northern" expeditions, and he visited the villages of the more commonly known Winnebago, some of whom had fought on the British side during the War of 1812 and turned against the Americans in other confrontations.[11]

North of the Winnebago were the villages of the Mdewakanton Sioux; their past too had been linked with the British. Long paid close attention to the Dakotas, who had no resident Indian agent and were little known to whites other than fur traders and the occasional travelers. Long was assisted by Augustin Rocque, a longtime trader on the upper Mississippi and a blood relative of Chief Wabasha. Long recommended a site at the mouth of the Minnesota River for the erection of a fort, which may or may not have been the decisive factor in the building of Fort Snelling. Artist George Catlin described the Indians in the area as "a sorry lot." Liquor, disease, and diminishing game had undermined their native way of life.[12]

George W. Featherstonhaugh, who made two trips up the Minnesota River in 1835 and 1837, was in awe of the Sioux but was also cautioned to be careful around them:

> Minor had warned me against extending my walks too far, observing that wandering bands of Sissetons were sometimes prowling about, who did not hesitate to scalp anyone they met, who was unarmed and without assistance. I was, therefore, habitually cautious, and, as I could command the whole country from around my position, felt very secure.[13]

Thomas Forsyth, the first government Indian agent to visit Minnesota, accompanied Henry Leavenworth and his troops of the Fifth Infantry up the Mississippi River in 1819. Leavenworth negotiated a treaty with the Sioux at Cantonment New Hope on August 9, 1820. Three reservations were created from the tract: a square mile fronting the Minnesota River, including the site of the American Fur Company's Mendota office for Duncan Campbell; another square mile for Campbell's sister, Peggy; and Pike Island for Mrs. Jean B. Faribault.[14]

In 1825, a multinational peace treaty signed at Prairie du Chien, Wisconsin, created a border line between the Chippewa and the Sioux. This treaty was not a land cession treaty, but a necessary predecessor. It sought to place all tribes in the Great Lakes region within boundaries that would then be considered "their land" temporarily. The ostensible reason for the treaty was a peace treaty primarily between the Ojibwe and Dakota (though other tribes also signed). In actuality it was to introduce the tribes to the concept of bounded regions of territory. The main content of the treaty was to draw a line dividing Minnesota, Wisconsin, and Michigan roughly in half, with Ojibwe territory north of the line, Dakota south of it. Once the concept of "this is your territory, inside the line" had been accepted, the land cessions commenced.[15]

An attempt to Christianize the Sioux was made when Joseph Renville, an explorer and fur trader whose mother was Dakota and father French, established a trading post at Lac Qui Parle in 1826. Renville invited missionaries to come out, and a mission was established where the Wahpeton Dakota had their village along the Minnesota River:

The valley site was located "where the Inkpa, or Lac Qui Parle River, joined with the Minnesota about a mile from the lake. Virgin prairie bluffs towered to a hundred feet above the valley floor to the east. The west side was covered with a good stand of timber. The sheltered valley between possessed rich soil and was covered with vegetation and Indian fields on both sides of the river. This had been a favorite Indian camp site from time immemorial. In addition to the river, there was a line of springs south of the lake which provided excellent water."[16] The missionaries were later forced out by the Sioux, most of whom opposed the spreading of Christianity among its peoples.

"I was also told by my father that a Catholic priest and other Indians of the Sioux tribe, and these Indians were scouts, went west, getting as far west as to where neb called Powder River, and this priest went up to make peace with the Indians, which he did," recalled Henry Has Holy. "And I was also told by my father that another Catholic priest went east to make peace with Sitting Bull's band. Now I do not know if they made peace or not but the Catholic priest has always worked among the Indians as far back as I can remember."[17]

On May 30, 1835, Reverend Jedediah Dwight Stevens, a Presbyterian minister, arrived at Fort Snelling with his family to establish a formal mission among the Sioux with the support of the American Board of Commissioners for Foreign Missions. When Dr. Thomas Williamson arrived to organize a mission at Lake Calhoun, Reverend Stevens insisted that only he should be the one to Christianize the Dakota in the area, as he had been planning the mission since 1829. Dr. Williamson thus moved on to Lac Qui Parle.[18]

The majority of the Dakota, however, retained their ancient customs, wandering about hunting and fishing through the great forests and plains. They paid little attention to the perimeter of their reservations, but roamed at will over their ancient hunting grounds as freely as though the same had never been ceded, and mingled with fullest freedom among the few scattered settlers, who from daily associations had come to look upon them without the least fear or suspicion.[19]

On September 29, 1837, Sioux chiefs taken to Washington by Major Lawrence Taliaferro, ceded away all their lands east of the Mississippi River—lands between the Black and Mississippi Rivers as far north as the Sioux-Chippewa boundary. The Sioux were given "various considerations" amounting to nearly one million dollars. The government, having conducted a similar treaty with the Chippewas, opened up the lands east of Fort Snelling to settlement and commercial exploitation.[20]

"The history of our first negotiations with the Sioux for the purchase of their lands, which included all of southern Minnesota, I do not know; but white men as well as Indians say that there was much deception connected with it," wrote Bishop Henry B. Whipple.[21]

Further trouble came when the Wisconsin Winnebagoes were forced to move to the western side of the Mississippi and in 1846 forced to move again, this time up river to a new reservation north of St. Cloud. Much resistance took place but eventually they began moving. Those traveling by water stopped at Wapasha's Prairie (now Winona). When joined by the land travelers, they decided to make camp along the slough now known as Lake Winona. As many whites were, the Winnebagoes were taken with the beauty of the area; they decided they wanted to settle on the prairie and offered to purchase it from Chief Wapasha III. The agents, backed by the soldiers, ordered them to move on. They paid no heed. The Winnebago, the Sioux and the soldiers all prepared for battle. The Indians danced a war dance the second night of the confrontation, but armed conflict did not come. Disillusioned, the Winnebagoes headed up river. For his part in the events, Wapasha was arrested and sent to the prison at Fort. Snelling. He was soon released, however.[22]

113

When Minnesota became a territory in 1849, its future growth and prosperity were linked to Indian issues. Indian contracts and annuity payments garnered huge sums of revenue, and the Indian trade, including sales of illicit liquor, provided enormous profits to anyone willing to risk such a venture. The prospects of acquiring valuable Indian lands by any means possible attracted many white settlers in and out of the government.[23]

The Chippewa, at this time, controlled most of the northern part of the territory while the Sioux possessed the southern part. The Mdewakanton or eastern bands of Sioux inhabited southeastern Minnesota along the Mississippi and Minnesota Rivers. The Mississippi bands of Ojibway lived along the rivers and lakes of northern and north-central portions of the new territory. The Chippewa villages closest to St. Paul were located at Mille Lacs Lake, the Snake River, Gull Lake, and the Crow Wing River.[24]

When the reluctant Sioux ceded away their vast hunting lands in 1851, the land speculators and settlers watched the negotiations with a heavy interest. Already thinking in terms of statehood, these men believed the only way to civilize the Indian was to take from them their old way of living. But it was the traders who watched most closely the negotiations with the Sioux. The Sioux already owed them tens of thousands of dollars through manipulation, to which the unwitting Indians had easily fallen prey, and the only way they could pay their debts was to sell their lands at a steal.[25]

This afforded the widest chance for frauds, as the Indians had no opportunity to dispute any of the claims. About $400,000 of the money due to the Indians under the treaties of 1851 and 1852 were thus paid for the first year to traders and agents on old debts, which roused great indignation among the Indians, who claimed they did not owe these parties a cent. One Hugh Miller was paid $55,000 for pretended services in helping to negotiate the treaties.

Heading the negotiations for the whites was Territorial Congressman Henry H. Sibley, who was also an acknowledged representative of the traders. Through Sibley, Governor Alexander Ramsey and Luke Lea, commissioner of Indian affairs, were appointed treaty commissioners. The treaty was to be conducted in two segments: a meeting with the Sissetons and the

Wahpetons at Traverse des Sioux in July, and another with the Mdewakantons and Wahpekutes at Mendota in August.

The chiefs, however, were not willing to give up their lands as the traders had speculated. The Sioux knew the land was valuable by white man's standing, and to them the prairies served as their sustenance and way of life. The Sioux were used to roaming the land, hunting the buffalo, and fighting their enemies. Life was carefree with few if any restrictions, with the old teaching the young the ways of the tribe.

> This happened at a place the Indians called Maka-Tan-onse [related Thomas Sees the Bear.] Now this was only a buffalo calf I shot as the older Indians taught me how to use the bow and arrow and run my two-year-old pony alongside the calf and shot the calf right behind the front leg and the calf was killed. This was great for a boy of my age to do. After this a war party . . . were getting ready to travel west from where we camped. We camped on the Missouri near now called Poplar, Montana. We traveled few nights and days until the scouts returned who usually go ahead to scout for the enemy. They returned one afternoon and they seen a great war party of Crow Indians on their way to battle the Sioux tribe, and we were going. The following evening we met and the fight began, shooting and war yells began and the enemies were shot down, horses running everywhere, their masters being killed, and our Indians were just the same.[26]

The plains Indians lived on buffalo meat although the earth-lodge tribes planted corn, squash, beans, and a few other vegetables. They gathered small seasonal amounts of wild berries, chokeberries, and turnips and fashioned animal skins into clothing. While many Sioux did not care for fish, they frequently ate what they caught. Their village sites offered a good water supply, plenty of wood, grazing and forage for horses, protection from the wind and enemies. They sought level, wooded bottom lands beneath bluffs and ridges, but at tribal assemblies, they camped on high, flat ground, pitching their tents in great circles with the main entrance facing the east.[27]

Victims of a culture clash, none of the Indians knew how much a million dollars comprised, and while Reverend Stephen R. Riggs and Alexander Faribault described the treaty provisions, the questions always related to the amount of money they would receive.

115

The first day of negotiations with the Wahkeputes and Mdewakan-tons between the Lower Sioux and the United States government took place in a warehouse in Mendota; the remaining sessions were held at Pilot Knob. The significant Treaty of Mendota opened the southern Minnesota lands of the Lower Sioux to settlement.[28]

These Sioux were to receive $1,410,000, but, of this, they would see only $250,000, and, by the white man's plan, that would pass them before they could even touch it. The only money other than the $250,000 to be given the two tribes was the five-percent interest on the principal, to be paid them yearly. This meant that the two tribes would only receive annually $30,000 cash and another $10,000 worth of provisions. The remainder of the money would go into what the whites called a "civilization fund," which would go towards their education and farming aids.

Of the quarter million cash settlement, $30,000 would be used towards the expenses of removing the Indians to the reservations, and $180,000 more of Indian monies was to be awarded to the traders, although the Sioux were not told this. The Sioux were to be given a reservation, a ten-mile piece of land on either side of the Minnesota River between the Yellow Medicine River and Little Rock Creek. Liquor would be prohibited on the reservation.

The chiefs wanted no part of the white man's "kindness," for their ancestors had been buried in their lands, and they knew nothing of the land the whites promised. Wabasha and his band had always lived in the woods and did not want to give up the rich timber, while Little Crow and Wacouta protested for similar reasons. Wabasha told the negotiators that he would not accept a civilization fund as they did not want to become farmers.

One unhappy chief remarked, "There is one thing more that our Great Father can do, that is, gather us all together on the prairie and surround us with soldiers and shoot us down." Reverend Stephen Riggs of Lac Qui Parle added, "This is an index of the state of feeling which seems to prevail."[29]

The chiefs agreed to sign only after Ramsey and Lea promised to pay money due the Indians from the Treaty of 1837. The government included a generous portion of provisions, for they knew that it was late in the year and too late for an extended hunt typically made by the Indians. Like the others, Little Crow knew they were facing a losing battle, and at one point during the negotiations he insisted, "We will talk about nothing but that money even if it takes until spring."

By Treaty of Washington in 1837, the Dakota had relinquished all their lands east of the Mississippi, and the islands therein, so a Wabasha County island and the lands across the river in Wisconsin passed from the Indians to the whites. All the land in this part of Minnesota was relinquished by the Dakota Indians as a result of the treaty made with the upper bands, signed at Traverse des Sioux, July 22, 1851, and which the lower bands signed at Mendota, August 5, 1851. At both places a feature of the gathering was a large brush arbor erected by Alexis Bailly, an early Wabasha trader.[30]

Chief Wabasha, from whom the county is named, opposed the Treaty of Mendota, but seeing the futility of opposition and realizing that the Indians, by refusing to give up their land, would subject themselves to extermination by the whites, was the second to sign.

The written copies of the Traverse des Sioux and the Mendota treaties, duly signed and attested, were forwarded to Washington to be acted upon by the Senate at the ensuing session of congress. An unreasonably long delay resulted. Final action was not taken until the following summer, when, on July 23, 1852, the Senate ratified both treaties with important amendments. The provisions for reservations on the upper Minnesota for both the upper and lower bands were stricken out and substitutes adopted, agreeing to pay ten cents an acre for both reservations, and authorizing the president, with the assent of the Indians, to cause to be set apart other reservations, which were to be within the limits of the original great cession. The provision to pay $150,000 to the half-bloods of the lower bands was also stricken. The treaties, with the changes, came back to the Indians for final ratification and agreement to the alterations.

The chiefs of the lower bands at first objected very strenuously, but finally, on Saturday, September 4, 1852, at Governor Alexander Ramsey's residence in St. Paul, they signed the amended articles, and the following Monday the chiefs and head men of the upper bands affixed their marks. As amended, the treaties were proclaimed by President Millard Fillmore, February 24, 1853. The Indians were allowed to remain in their old villages, or, if they preferred, to occupy their reservations as originally designated until the president selected their new homes. That selection was never made, and, the original reservations were finally allowed them. Congress, on July 31, 1854, passed an act by which the original reservation provisions remained in force. The removal of the lower Indians to their designated reservation above Redwood Falls on the Minnesota River began in 1853, but was intermittent, interrupted, and extended over a period of several years. The Indians went up in detachments, as they felt inclined. After living on the reservation for some time, some of them returned to their old hunting grounds, where they lived continuously for some time, visiting their reservation and agency only at the time of the payment of their annuities. Finally, by the offer of cabins to live in, or other substantial inducements, nearly all of them were induced to settle on the Redwood Reserve, so that, in 1862, at the time of the outbreak, less than twenty families of the Medawakantons and Wahpakootas were living off their reservation.

The Prairie du Chien Treaty of 1830 had also set aside the following Half-Breed Tract:

> The Sioux bands in council have earnestly solicited that they might have permission to bestow upon the half-breeds of their nation the tract of land within the following limits, to wit: Beginning at the place called the Barn, below and near the village of the Red Wing chief, and running back fifteen miles; thence, in a parallel line with Lake Pepin and the Mississippi, about [thirty-two] miles, to a point opposite the river aforesaid; the United States agree to suffer said half-breeds to occupy said tract of country; they holding by the same title, and in the same manner that other Indian titles are held.

This Half-Breed Tract, the reservation of which was doubtless made through the influence of the Indian traders and those in their employ who had married Indian women, subsequently was the cause of much trouble, which delayed the permanent settlement of the lands involved. A provision was made in the treaty of August 5, 1851, arranging for the purchase of the tract by the government for $150,000. This clause, however, was stricken out by the United

States Senate. Later a list of the half-breeds, mostly the children of the traders, was made out, and script issued, entitling each to a certain number of acres, the location within the tract to be chosen by the holder.

When General Shields brought the script to Minnesota for distribution, a great portion of it passed into the hands of parents or guardians of children, and from them it passed into the hands of speculators. There were about two hundred families of whites settled upon the agricultural portions of this tract, some in what is now Goodhue County and some in what is now Wabasha County. Some of these people had settled in the tract in ignorance of its limits, or of the fact that its status was different from that of the other government lands. Others knew of the provision of the 1851 treaty, purchasing the lands without knowing the further fact that the clause had been rejected by the Senate; others were adventurous and were willing to take their chances even though they knew their settlement was illegal; still more cautious ones secured quit-claim deeds from individual half-breeds or permission from the Indian relatives of the half-breeds. These quit claims and these permissions were, of course, valueless, as the half-breeds had no right except that which was embodied in the scrip and could transfer such rights only by transferring the actual possession of the script. Nothing but this scrip would avail in filing on any portion of the land.

The actual settlers—squatters—had naturally taken up the choicest portions, and in many cases had made somewhat extensive improvements. The soil had been broken, crops raised, and buildings and fences erected by people who were, in reality, only squatters without legal rights. When people who had purchased script from the speculators attempted to take up these improved claims and oust the squatters, the trouble began, and those who were in possession of the land, though illegally, effected an organization and resorted to extreme measures to avoid being dispossessed. These squatters had the sympathy of all the surrounding population, but holders of the scrip had the legal advantage of the situation, and commenced to obtain titles to farms already improved.

Red Wing, where the land office was located, at once became a scene of excitement. Meetings were held by the squatters, and counsel taken as to methods of procedure. They assessed upon themselves a tax, and sent one man to Washington to demand justice, as they called it, in their behalf. They secured from the land office correct copies of plats of all the townships and fractional townships included with the tract, and every quarter-section upon which a settler had made improvements was definitely marked. Holders of scrip were publicly warned against filing upon such land.

At a meeting of those interested in the cause of the squatters, which was held at the Kelly House in Red Wing, March 17, 1856, a vigilance committee of twenty-one members was chosen to prevent any more scrip being laid upon the land already occupied. This committee was empowered to demand that, in every case where scrip had been laid on the land already settled, said script should immediately be raised.

The members of the committee were men of dauntless courage and muscular power and devoted their whole time and energy to the work until it was accomplished. Two of them stood as sentinels at the land office armed with loaded revolvers, constantly watching every transaction therein, being relieved by another two at stated times.

In the meanwhile the majority of the committee were acting as detectives, arresting and bringing to trial those who had offended their self-made rules, the trial not being before a court of justice, but before the committee. There was at that time no courthouse and no jail, and the lawyers knew that the scrip holders were acting within their legal rights. The holders, however, were threatened and intimidated by the committee and fear compelled them to raise the scrip, though there was no record of any personal injury being inflicted on anyone. That such would have been inflicted in case of continued resistance, there is little doubt, as one man was led to a hole cut through the ice in the river, and given his choice either to raise his entry of scrip or be put through the hole, and though he was a man of strength and courage, he found it prudent to submit.

There were other cases of the same kind. The excuse for these extreme measures was soon after removed by a decision from the land office at Washington, whereby those who had settled on a tract of this land and made improvements thereon had the pre-emption and homestead rights the same as on other government lands. The same decision granted to the holders of half-breed script the privilege of laying the same upon any other government land not previously claimed by an actual settler.

All the vacant land on the half-breed tract was taken very soon after this decision, the situation near the river enhancing its value. The disadvantage of a few miles from market was considered a great drawback in those days, before the advent of railroads. Few or none of the mixed-bloods ever cared to settle on the agricultural land thus set apart for them. Occasionally, a decade or two afterward, there was an echo of the half-breed affair, when some half-breed, whose guardian had sold his (the half-breed's) scrip rights, would, upon attaining his majority, demand of the settler on the property that he, too, be paid. In most cases, these demands were complied with, the farmers, whose lands had greatly enhanced in value, deeming it wiser to pay a small sum than to undergo the expense of a lawsuit. Thus, passed the last vestige of Indian title to the rich valleys and plains of Minnesota, which was once, and for countless generations, a camping and hunting ground of the Indians.

Born in 1820, Little Crow descended from a long line of prominent chieftains. His name may have been derived by the Chippewa, who gave such names to his band because of their custom of carrying the dried skin of a crow as a charm to ward off evil spirits.[31] He was the eldest son of Cetanwakuwa (Charging Hawk). It was on account of his father's name, mistranslated "Crow," that he was called by the whites "Little Crow." His real name was Taoyateduta (His Red People).[32]

For as far back as anyone could remember a band of Sioux called Kaposia ("Light Weight" because they were said to travel light) inhabited the Mille Lacs region. Later they lived by St. Croix Falls, and eventually near St. Paul. In 1840, Cetanwakuwa was still living in what is now West St. Paul, but shortly after he was killed by the accidental discharge of his gun.

It was during a period of demoralization for the Kaposias that Little Crow became the leader of his people. His father, a well-known chief, had three wives, all from different bands of the Sioux. Little Crow was the only son of the first wife, A Leaf Dweller. There were two sons of the second wife and two of the third, and the second set of brothers conspired to kill their elder half-brother in order to keep the chieftainship in the family.

Two kegs of whisky were bought, and all the men of the tribe invited to a feast. It was planned to pick some sort of quarrel when all were drunk, and in the confusion Little Crow was to be murdered. The plot went smoothly until the last instant, when a young brave saved the intended victim by knocking the gun aside with his hatchet, so that the shot went wild. However, it broke Little Crow's right arm, which remained crooked all his life. The friends of the young chieftain hastily withdrew, avoiding a general fight, and later the council of the Kaposias condemned the two brothers, both of whom were executed, leaving Little Crow in undisputed possession of leadership.

Little Crow's mother had been a chief's daughter, celebrated for her beauty and spirit, and it was said that she used to plunge him into the lake through a hole in the ice, rubbing him afterward with snow. She believed this would strengthen his nerves, and that she would remain with him alone in the deep woods for days at a time, so that he might know that solitude was good and not be afaid to be alone with nature.

When Little Crow was very young, his mother made a feast for her boy and announced that he would fast two days. This was what might be called a formal presentation to the Spirit or God. She greatly desired that he become a worthy leader according to the ideas of her people. It appeared that she left her husband when he took his second wife and lived with her own band until her death. She did not marry again.

Little Crow was an intensely ambitious man without physical fear. He was always in perfect training shape and learned early the art of warfare. When he was about ten years old, he engaged with other boys in a sham battle on the shore of a lake near St. Paul. Both sides were encamped a little distance from one another, and the rule was that the enemy must be surprised; otherwise the attack would be considered a failure. One must come within so many paces undiscovered in order to be counted successful. Little Crow had a favorite dog which, at his earnest request, was allowed to take part in the game, and as a scout he entered the enemy camp unseen, by the help of his dog.

When he was twelve, he saved the life of a companion who had broken through the ice by tying the end of a pack line to a log and carrying it to the edge of the hole where his friend went down. He jumped in, but both boys saved themselves by means of the line.

As a young man, Little Crow was always ready to serve his people as a messenger to other tribes, a duty involving much danger and hardship. He was also known as one of the best hunters in his band. Although still young, he already had a war record when he became chief of the Kaposias, and this was a time when the Sioux were facing the greatest and most far-reaching changes that had ever come to them.

At this juncture in the history of the northwest and its native inhabitants, the various fur companies had paramount influence. They did not hesitate to impress the Indians with the idea that they were the authorized representatives of the white races or peoples, and they were quick to realize the desirability of controlling the natives through their most influential chiefs. Little Crow became quite popular with the post traders. He was an orator as well as a diplomat, and one of the first of his nation to indulge in politics and promote unstable schemes to the detriment of his people.

When the United States government commenced acquiring territory from the Indians so that the flood of western settlement might not be checked, commissions were sent out to negotiate treaties, and in case of failure it often happened that a delegation of leading men of the tribe were invited to Washington. At that period, these visiting chiefs, attired in all the splendor of their costumes of ceremony, were treated like ambassadors from foreign countries.

One winter in the late eighteen-fifties, a major general of the army gave a dinner for the Indian chiefs then in the city, and on this occasion Little Crow was appointed toastmaster. There were present a number of Senators and members of Congress, as well as judges of the Supreme Court, cabinet officers, and other distinguished citizens. When all the guests were seated, Little Crow rose and addressed them with much dignity:

> Warriors and friends: I am informed that the great white war chief who of his generosity and comradeship has given us this feast, has

expressed the wish that we may follow to-night the usages and customs of my people. In other words, this is a warriors' feast, a braves' meal. I call upon the Ojibway chief, the Hole-in-the-Day, to give the lone wolf's hunger call, after which we will join him in our usual manner.

The tall and handsome Ojibway stood and straightened his superb form to utter one of the clearest and longest wolf howls that was ever heard in Washington, and, at its close, came a tremendous burst of war whoops that fairly rent the air, and no doubt electrified the officials.

On one occasion Little Crow was invited by the commander of Fort Ridgely, Minnesota, to call at the fort. On his way back, in company with a half-breed named Ross and the interpreter Mitchell, he was ambushed by a party of Ojibways, and again wounded in the same arm that had been broken in the first attempted assassination. His companion, Ross, was killed, but Little Crow managed to hold the war party at bay until help came and thus saved his life.

As time passed, Little Crow fell prey to the selfish interests of the traders and politicians. The immediate causes of the Sioux outbreak of 1862 came in quick succession to inflame an outraged people to desperate action. The two bands on the so-called lower reservations in Minnesota were Indians for whom nature had provided most abundantly in their free existence. After one hundred and fifty years of friendly intercourse, first with the French, then the English, and finally the Americans, they found themselves cut off from every natural resource, on a tract of land twenty miles by thirty, which to them was virtual imprisonment. By treaty stipulation with the government, they were to be fed and clothed, houses were to be built for them, the men taught agriculture, and schools provided for the children. In addition to this, a trust fund of a million and a half dollars was to be set aside for them, at five per cent interest, the interest to be paid annually per capita. They had signed the treaty under pressure, believing in these promises on the faith of a great nation.

However, on entering the new life, the resources described to them failed to materialize. They suffered from crop failure, were hemmed in by German and Scandinavian immigrants on a narrow tract of land, and fell prey to a corrupt Indian-agency system that diverted funds and supplies guaranteed them by the treaty. Many families faced starvation every winter, their only support the store of the Indian trader, who was baiting his trap for their destruction. Very gradually they awoke to these facts.[33]

When an agreement was reached with the whites, one that most of the chiefs did not understand, Little Crow signed the treaty, followed by Wabasha, Wacouta, Cloud Man, Gray Iron, Good Road, and Shakopee. Forty sub-chiefs and braves signed the treaty with their "X." Representing the Wahpekutes, the treaty was signed by Red Legs and eight warriors.[34] Little Crow made the greatest mistake of his life when he signed this agreement.

Once the Indians had signed the treaty, the merchants tricked the Sioux into signing the "traders' paper." Each chief signed a government agreement with no indication of the amount of money involved and was given a "second" copy of the transaction to sign. This document was an agreement that the Indians owed certain debts to the traders and constituted their pledge to repay them. In addition to the Sioux representatives, Reverend Riggs and Sioux Agent Nathaniel McLean declared they knew nothing about the paper until after it had been signed.

A Wahpeton, Big Curly Head, reacting to the white man's skullduggery, snapped, "You have our land, and soon you will have all our money also."

Meanwhile, to make matters worse, the cash annuities were not paid for nearly two years. The Civil War had begun and funds had been siphoned into that. When it was learned that the traders had taken all of the ninety-eight thousand dollars "on account," there were very bitter feelings. In fact, the heads of the leading stores were afraid to go about as usual, and most of them stayed in St. Paul. Little Crow was justly held as partly responsible for the deceit, and his life was not safe.

The Upper Sioux reservation extended from Lake Traverse to the Yellow Medicine River. Congress did not ratify the treaty until the spring of 1852. By then the government had deleted the section that stated that the Sioux had a permanent home on the Minnesota River. Instead, it substituted a clause about paying ten cents an acre for the land originally set aside and gave the president power to move the Indians whenever and wherever he chose.

The Mdewakantons then refused to sign the new treaty until the trader's paper was deleted. Ramsey threatened to return their first annuity payment, which he had brought with him from Washington if the Dakota did not sign. Wabasha shouted angrily, "Take back the money, then we can take back our land." The Dakota chiefs finally signed when the money was placed in their hands.

During another meeting at Traverse Des Sioux with the Upper Bands, Red Iron, a powerful Wahpeton, protested so violently that Governor Ramsey called out soldiers from Fort Snelling, and the chief was locked up. The other Dakotas fell into line but mostly because it was November and the Sioux needed money. Governor Ramsey was investigated by Congress, but it was found that, as a commissioner, he had no control over the trader's paper incident.

According to one Dakota man, Chaskee, Red Iron was drunk when he signed the treaty. Chaskee did not know the name of the agent who gave Red Iron the liquor, but it was maintained among the Sioux nation that some government representatives did give the Indians liquor. Chaskee also said the council did not know when they signed the treaty that they had relinquished their right to hunt and fish. They had understood that they were not selling any islands in the river or any hunting or gaming privileges.[35]

"We think something was wrong with the interpreter because our people knew nothing of what the treaty meant," stated Chaskee, in a later interview. "We were made to believe that we would keep [ten] miles on each side of the Minnesota River from Sleepy Eye to Big Stone Lake. Instead we were sent to Red Wood where we have been ever since."[36]

President Millard Fillmore extended his permission to allow the Dakotas to live on their new reservation for five years, but in 1853, the great migration began. The move was a simple one for the Wahpetons and Sissetons, who lived near by, but for others, such as Wabasha's Lake Pepin band, it involved a major effort. Richard G. Murphy became Sioux agent on May 28, 1853.

The government moved quickly onto its new lands. After the proclamation February 24, 1853, of the Sioux treaties, a great tide of immigration began to flow into the southwestern part of the Territory. Steamboats on the Mississippi, the Minnesota, and the St. Croix were crowded with passengers and cargo; all the river landings bustled with colorful activity. With every boat, new arrivals disembarked and departed on stagecoaches over the newly constructed government roads.[37]

Many boarded boats at Galena, Dunleith, or St. Louis. Others made the tedious journey overland in prairie schooners, driving their cattle, fording streams, and camping by the way. A few hoped to make their fortunes in commercial or professional fields, but the majority were eager for lands offered by the government at a cost of $1.25 an acre, plus proof of occupancy and cultivation.

Pioneer homes began to dot the wilderness, at first chiefly in the hardwood country nearest the watercourses. Breaking and clearing the land was a laborious task with the limited facilities at hand, and comparatively little was initially cultivated. But by the close of 1854, about 500,000 acres had been sold in Minnesota; in 1856 more than 1,000,000 acres were transferred to settlers, and in 1858 nearly 2,500,000 more.

Villages sprang up almost overnight. The clatter of grist mills was heard on a dozen streams. Merchant milling had its first substantial beginnings in the St. Anthony vicinity in 1854, and soon Mississippi River traffic began to swell with shipments of wheat and flour to eastern and southern markets.

Painter/lithographer Henry Lewis made trips up the Upper Mississippi in 1846, 1847, and 1848. He later described the new lands opened up to the U. S. government:

> The whole of the region west and north of the fort [Snelling] has, by a treaty signed in 1851 by the Sioux Indians, come into possession of the government and is now rapidly filling up with an adventurous population. A small Indian trading post, called St. Paul's, which . . . contained only forty or fifty families, has now a population of more than 5,000. St. Paul's has become the capital of the new territory called Menesotah, formed out of part of the purchase and partly out of the state of Wisconsin.[38]

In April, three steamboats chugged up the Minnesota River from Fort Snelling to the reservation. The first boat was loaded with soldiers, whose mission it was to construct Fort Ridgely in Nicollet County. Two other boats continued on to the mouth of the Redwood River where other soldiers were to erect the agency.

Indians began arriving before the camp was set up. A letter in the *Redwood Gazette*, described the Indians as "semi-starved and begged that we issued first something they could cook quickly. We gave them shelled corn which they boiled, but not waiting for it to be thoroughly swelled, gorged themselves on it, and we soon had scores of sick Indians to look after."[39]

A young girl later recalled a steamboat ride up the Minnesota River and her meeting Dakota Indians:

> The Indians were friendly. On our way from St. Paul on the steamboat we saw them in great numbers at Traverse des Sioux. Twenty-five came to our house one day on a begging dance. They all sat on the floor until the room was cleared.
> The chief motioned for a pail of water and sugar to sweeten it like sap. Then he took a loaf of bread and broke it into small pieces and gave each one a piece. They formed a circle and sang, "Ho Wo Wo, Ho Wo Wo," moving their feet, heel toe, heel toe, until the house shook. They drank the sweetened water, ate the bread and went on to the next house.[40]

In 1855, THE FIRST OF TWO WINNEBAGO (Ho-Chunk) Treaties was signed between the tribes and the United States government in which the Winnebagoes ceded all their lands in the state of Minnesota. Although no Ho-Chunk reservations remain in Minnesota, in years before the 1800s considerable numbers of the people lived here. For some years, a very small Winnebago reservation had been maintained in the southeast corner of the state. The treaty was ratified March 3, 1855:

> Articles of agreement and convention, made and concluded at Washington City on the twenty-seventh day of February, eighteen hundred and fifty-five, between George W. Manypenny, commissioner on the part of the United States, and the following-named chiefs and delegates representing the Winnebago tribe of Indians, viz: Waw-kon-chaw-

koo-kaw, The Coming Thunder, or Kinnoshik; Sho-go-nik-kaw, or Little Hill; Maw-he-coo-shah-naw-zhe-kaw, One that Stands and Reaches the Skies, or Little Decorie; Waw-kon-chaw-hoo-no-kaw, or Little Thunder; Hoonk-hoo-no-kaw, Little Chief, or Little Priest; Honch-hutta-kaw, or Big Bear; Wach-ha-ta-kaw, or Big Canoe; Ha-zum-kee-kaw, or One Horn; Ha-zee-kaw, or Yellow Bank; and Baptiste Lassallier, they being thereto duly authorized by said tribe:

ARTICLE 1. The Winnebago Indians hereby cede, sell, and convey to the United States all their right, title, and interest in, and to, the tract of land granted to them pursuant to the third article of the treaty concluded with said tribe, at Washington City, on the thirteenth day of October, one thousand eight hundred and forty-six, lying north of St. Peter's River and west of the Mississippi River, in the Territory of Minnesota, and estimated to contain about eight hundred and ninety-seven thousand and nine hundred (897,900) acres; the boundary-lines of which are thus described, in the second article of the treaty concluded between the United States and the Chippewa Indians of the Mississippi and Lake Superior, on the second day of August, one thousand eight hundred and forty seven, viz: "Beginning at the junction of the Crow Wing and Mississippi Rivers; thence, up the Crow Wing River, to the junction of that river with the Long Prairie River; thence, up the Long Prairie River, to the boundary line between the Sioux and Chippewa Indians; thence, southerly, along the said boundary-line, to a lake at the head of Long Prairie River; thence, in a direct line, to the sources of the Watab River; thence, down the Watab to the Mississippi River; thence, up the Mississippi, to the place of beginning:" Provided, however, That the portions of said tract embracing the improved lands of the Indians, the grist and saw mill, and all other improvements made for or by them, shall be specially reserved from pre-emption, sale, or settlement until the said mills and improvements, including the improvements to the land, shall have been appraised and sold, at public sale, to the highest bidder, for the benefit of the Indians, but no sale thereof shall be made for less than the appraised value. And the President may prescribe such rules and regulations in relation to said sale as he may deem proper; and the person or persons purchasing said mills and improvements, shall have the right, when the land is surveyed, to enter the legal subdivisions thereof, including the improvements purchased by them, at one dollar and twenty-five cents per acre.

ARTICLE 2. In consideration of the cessions aforesaid, and in full compensation therefore, the United States agree to pay to the said Indians, the sum of seventy thousand dollars, ($70,000,) and to grant them, as a permanent home, a tract of land equal to eighteen miles square, on the Blue Earth River, in the Territory of Minnesota, which shall be selected and located by the agent of the Government and a delegation of the Winnebagoes, immediately after the ratification of this instrument, and after the necessary appropriations to carry it into effect shall have been made; and a report of such selection and location, shall be made in writing, to the superintendent of Indian affairs for the Territory of Minnesota, who shall attach his official signature to the same, and forward it to the Commissioner of Indian Affairs; and the country thus selected shall be the permanent home of the said Indians; Provided, Said tract shall not approach nearer the Minnesota River than the mouth of the La Serrer fork of the Blue Earth River.

ARTICLE 3. It is agreed, that the moneys received form the sale of the Indian improvements, as provided for in the first article, and the sum stipulated to be paid by the second article of this instrument, shall be expended under the direction of the President, in removing the Indians to their new homes, including those who are now severed from the main body of the tribe, living in Kansas Territory, Wisconsin, or elsewhere; in subsisting them a reasonable time after their removal; in making improvements, such as breaking and fencing land, and building houses; in purchasing stock, agricultural implements and household furniture, and for such other objects as may tend to promote their prosperity and advancement in civilization. And the said Winnebago Indians agree to remove to their new homes immediately after the selection of the tract hereinbefore provided for, is made.

ARTICLE 4. In order to encourage the Winnebago Indians to engage in agriculture, and such other pursuits as will conduce to their well-being and improvement, it is agreed: that, at such time or times as the President may deem advisable, the land herein provided to be selected as their future home, or such portions thereof as may be necessary, shall be surveyed; and the President shall, from time to time, as the Indians may desire it, assign to each head of a family, or single persons over twenty-one years of age, a reasonable quantity of land, in one body, not to exceed eighty acres in any case, for their separate use; and he may, at his discretion, as the occupants thereof become capable of managing their business and affairs, issue patents to them for the tract so assigned to them, respectively; said tracts to be exempt from taxation, levy, sale, or forfeiture, until otherwise provided by the legislature of the State in which they may be situated, with the assent of Congress; nor shall they be sold or alienated, in fee, within fifteen years after the date of the patents, and not then, without the assent of the President of the United States being first obtained. Prior to the patents being issued, the President shall make such rules and regulations as he may deem necessary and expedient, respecting the disposition of any of said tracts, in case of the death of the person or persons to whom they may be assigned, so that the same shall be secured to the families of such deceased person; and should any of the Indians to whom tracts may be assigned, thereafter abandon them, the President may take such action in relation to such abandoned tracts, as in his judgment may be necessary and proper.

ARTICLE 5. All unexpended balances now in the hands of the agent of the tribe, arising under former treaties, for schools, pay of interpreter therefor, support of blacksmiths and assistants; and also of the sum of ten thousand dollars set apart by the treaty of October thirteenth eighteen hundred and forty-six, for manual-labor schools, shall be expended and applied, in the opening of farms, building and furnishing of houses, and the purchase of stock for said Indians. And the stipulations in former treaties providing for the application or expenditure of particular sums of money for specific purposes, are hereby so far modified and changed, as to confer upon the President the power, in his discretion, to cause such sums of money, in whole or in part, to be expended for, or applied to such other objects and purposes and in such manner as he shall deem best calculated to promote the welfare and improvement of said Indians.

ARTICLE 6. No part of the moneys stipulated to be paid to the Winnebago Indians by these articles of agreement and convention, nor any of the future installments due and payable under former treaties between them and the United States, shall ever be taken, by direction of the chiefs, to pay the debts of individual Indians, contracted in their private dealings, known as national or tribal debts.

ARTICLE 7. The missionaries, or other persons who are, by authority of law, now residing on the lands ceded by the first article of this agreement, shall each have the privilege of entering one hundred and sixty acres of the said ceded lands, to include any improvements they may have, at one dollar and twenty-five cents per acre: and such of the mixed-bloods, as are heads of families, and now have actual residences and improvements of their own, in the ceded country, shall each have granted to them, in fee, eighty acres of land, to include their improvements: Provided, however That said entries and grants shall in no case be upon, or in any manner interfere with, any of the lands improved by the Government, or by or for the Indians, or on which the agency building, saw and grist mill, or other public or Indian improvements have been erected or made.

ARTICLE 8. The laws which have been or may be enacted by Congress, regulating trade and intercourse with the Indian tribes, shall continue and be in force within the country herein provided to be selected as the future permanent home of the Winnebago Indians; and those portions of said laws which prohibit the introduction, manufacture, use of, and traffic in, ardent spirits in the Indian country, shall continue and be in force within the country herein ceded to the United States, until otherwise provided by Congress.

ARTICLE 9. All roads and highways authorized by law, the lines of which may be required to be laid through any part of the country herein provided as the future permanent home of the Winnebago Indians, shall have right of way through the same; a fair and just value of such right being paid to the Indians, in money, to be assessed and determined according to the laws in force for the appropriation of land for such purposes.

ARTICLE 10. The said tribe of Indians, jointly and severally, obligate and bind themselves, not to commit any depredation or wrong upon other Indians, or upon citizens of the United States; to conduct themselves at all times in a peaceable and orderly manner; to submit all difficulties between them and other Indians to the President, and to abide by his decision; to respect and observe the laws of the United States, so far as the same are to them applicable; to settle down in the peaceful pursuits of life; to commence the cultivation of the soil; to educate their children, and to abstain from the use of intoxicating drinks and other vices to which many of them have been addicted. And the President may withhold from such of the Winnebagoes as abandon their homes, and refuse to labor, and from the idle, intemperate, and vicious, the benefits they may be entitled to under these articles of agreement and convention, or under articles of former treaties, until they give evidences of amendment and become settled, and conform to, and comply, with the stipulations herein provided; or, should they be heads of families, the same may be appropriated, under the direction of the President, to the use and enjoyment of their families.

ARTICLE 11. These articles of agreement and convention, shall be in lieu of the "Articles of a convention made and concluded between Willis A. Gorman and Jonathan E. Fletcher, on the part of the United States, and the chiefs and head-men of the Winnebago tribe of Indians, on the 6th day of August, A.D. 1853," and the amendments of the Senate thereto, as expressed in its resolution of July twenty-first eighteen hundred and fifty-four; to which amendments the said Winnebago Indians refused to give their assent, which refusal was communicated to the Commissioner of Indian Affairs, by the governor of Minnesota Territory, on the twenty-fourth of January, eighteen hundred and fifty-five.

ARTICLE 12. The United States will pay the necessary expenses incurred by the Winnebago delegates in making their present visit to Washington, while here, and in returning to their homes.

ARTICLE 13. This instrument shall be obligatory on the contracting parties as soon as the same shall be ratified by the President and the Senate of the United States.

In testimony whereof the said George W. Manypenny, commissioner as aforesaid, and the said chiefs and delegates of the Winnebago tribe of Indians, have hereunto set their hands and seals, at the place and on the day and year hereinbefore written.

George W. Manypenny, commissioner, [L. S.]

Waw-kon-chaw-koo-haw, the Coming Thunder, or Win-no-shik, his x mark [L. S.]

Sho-go-nik-kaw, or Little Hill his x mark [L. S.]

Maw-he-coo-shaw-naw-zhe-kaw, One that Stands and Reaches the Skies, or Little Decorie, his x mark [L. S.]

Waw-kon-chaw-hoo-no-kaw, or Little Thunder, his x mark [L. S].

Hoonk-hoo-no-kaw, Little Chief or Little Priest his x mark [L. S.]

Honch-hutta-kaw, or Big Bear, his x mark [L. S.]

Watch-ha-ta-kaw, or Big Canoe, his x mark [L. S.]

Ha-zhun-kee-kaw, or One Horn, his x mark [L. S.]

Ha-zee-kaw, or Yellow Bank, His x mark, [L. S.]

Baptiste Lasallier.

In presence of—
George Culver,
Asa White,
John Dowling,
J.E. Fletcher,
Peter Manaiy, United States interpreter.[41]

Patricipants in the 1858 treaty signed in Washington, D.C., that ceded half of the reservation to the government. Left to right: standing: Joseph R. Brown, Sioux agent; Antoine J. Campbell; Has a War Club; Andrew Robertson, builder of Upper Agency and head of reservation schools; Red Owl; Thomas Robertson, Andrew's son and a courier between Little Crow and General Sibley during the uprising; Nathaniel Brown, Joseph's brother and a trader; seated: Mankato, second to Little Crow in the Dakotah war command, killed in the Wood Lake battle; Wabasha, nominal head of the Minnesota Sioux who remained friendly during the war; and Henry Belland, trader killed at Lower Agency. (Courtesy Minnesota Historical Society)

In 1858, THE SIOUX WERE COERCED into selling all their lands in South Dakota to the United States government. The April 1858 treaty culminated in the negotiation of a treaty in which the Sioux ceded every square acre of their land, except the Yankton reservation. Even before the 1858 treaty, whites had attempted to settle on the Sioux lands but were promptly driven off by the hostile Indians. A group of prominent Minnesotans from St. Paul, formed "The Dakota Land Company," and established towns along the Big Sioux River and in a valley named "Medary," after Minnesota's governor, and "Flandrau," after the St. Paul judge.[42]

Flandrau wrote of the Indian treaties:

> In consideration of the cession to the United States of the lands of these Indians, they were to receive annuities in Money, goods of all kinds, payable semi-annually a civilization and an educational fund, Doctors, Blacksmiths, Farmers and many other benefits which were intended to make them Self sustaining at the expiration of the fifty years the treaties were to run.
>
> The Indians were at the time of the making of the treaties in their natural state of barbarism. All the country to the west and northwest of their reservation was in a state of nature, there being no white inhabitants between them and the Rocky Mountains. The country abounded with buffalo and all kinds of wild animals, and the Indians spent most of their time away from their reservations, gaining their subsistence by the chase.
>
> Farms were opened for them on the reservations. Houses built for them, Traders opened Stores to supply them with articles of all kinds, trusting to the annuity money, and their catch of furs for payment.
>
> Everything went along harmoniously at the agencies except on occasional misunderstanding, which usually arose from the delays in the arrival of the government funds, which gave rise to discontent and grumbling among the Indians, but no one anticipated any serious trouble.[43]

In MINNESOTA, JOSEPH RENSHAW BROWN became Indian Agent in 1857 and was confronted by Little Crow over broken promises and unfulfilled treaties. Little Crow was agitated over a clause that permitted reservation Indians the right to leave the reservation and live like white men, providing they gave up their treaty rights. According to Little Crow, they should not be allowed to do so, for once away from the reservation, "they become corrupted, drink liquor and act badly . . ."[44]

134

In order to relieve tensions between frightened white settlers and angry Sioux, the federal government invited several Indian chiefs to Washington so they would return with a "wholesome impression of the resources and power of the U.S. government." United States Interpreter A.J. Campbell and two or three assistants brought the Sioux leaders to the nation's capitol, while Agent Joseph Renshaw Brown journeyed to New York where he picked up $25,000 in presents for distribution to the Sioux as partial consideration for the land they had just ceded to the government.[45]

The twenty-seven chiefs and head braves; all members of the "Medaywakontwaun, Waukpaykoota, Waukpaytwaun, and Sissetwaun," spent four months in Washington. They departed for home June 22, 1858, on the steamer *Jeanette Roberts* by way of New York and Niagara Falls.

The fear of Indian attack, however, ran rampant through southern Minnesota, and Inkapaduta was suspected of being everywhere. One Minnesota newspaper published a letter written by Henry Sibley on June 26, 1858:

> I have requested the acting Superintendent of Indiana Affairs to dispatch a special messenger to these savages, to inform them that the Superintendent will soon visit them, and distribute among them a certain amount of money, or of goods and provisions, in accordance with an appropriation made by Congress for this purpose. This will, no doubt, tend much to restrain these Indians, but our citizens are entitled to full protection from the State authorities, and inasmuch as the garrison of U.S. troops at Fort Ridgely is much reduced in numbers, too much to allow of any considerable numbers being sent on detached service. I recommend that the Governor be authorized by law to call out volunteers, mounted or unmounted, and in case of necessity to furnish them with State arms, and of appropriating a sum not exceeding ten thousand dollars, to defray necessary expenses. This authority is required to enable the Governor to protect the people of the state in case of actual invasion by the Indians, or of a continuance of their depredations.[46]

The same newspaper proclaimed on July 3rd:

TROUBLE AT THE SIOUX AGENCIES.—We understand that a band of the Lower Sioux have broken open and plundered the Government warehouses at both the Upper and Lower Agencies. The delay in the distribution of the provisions and the payment of the other annuities is their excuse. There is but a mere handful of troops at Fort Ridgely—

a force utterly inadequate or overawe or check the marauding proclivities of these Indians. Unless the fort can be manned by a sufficient force to be effective for the purposes for which it is maintained, it had just as well be abandoned at once. At no time within a year past has there been a garrison of sufficient strength to afford protection to the fort itself. It may become necessary yet to act upon Mrs. Swisshelm's suggestion to the residents about Fort Ripley, during the Chippewa disturbances last year, to wit: To go down South and steal a nigger, and run him off into Minnesota, and thus secure the immediate presence of the whole effective force of the U.S. Army and Navy. That would fetch 'em.[47]

This ugly brand of racism and total disregard for the well being of Native Americans continued to flourish in both the cities and prairie settlements as evidenced by yet another newspaper article:

GAME—We noticed an Indian in town yesterday, with the carcasses of five deer. The rascals are thinning out the game in this county. We would like to hear of some attempt being made to enforce the law looking to their confinement to their respective Reservations, the material portions of which we published some weeks since.[48]

The *Mankato Independent* declared in January 1859:

The Iowa papers are again excited over the prospects for Indian disturbances at Spirit Lake. A late number of the *McGregor Times* announced that Governor Love has dispatched a company of troops to that point for the protection of the settlers.
We receive reports from that vicinity almost daily, and are advised that no Indians have been seen in that region for some months and that no wars whatever, are entertained of disturbances from that source. The worst apprehensions of the settlers is from fear of troops being quartered upon them—provisions being scarce and high. The mail has been carried from this place to Sioux City, semi-monthly during the winter, by way of Spirit Lake, and the carrier has yet to meet the first red-skin.
Editors will confer a favor upon the settlers in the Spirit Lake region by discountenancing these periodical sensation paragraphs. Rumors of disturbances there are all fabrications.[49]

On July 5th, the steamer *Frank Steele* arrived in Mankato from the Upper Minnesota. She had sustained considerable damage on her trip—her left wheel house was partially carried away, her railings and guards damaged, and she had suffered leakage. Her officers reported that Major William Cullen with a party of teamsters and government supplies for the Yankton Indians in Dakota Territory had passed Yellow Medicine about fifteen miles when they were confronted by 200 Sisseton warriors, who refused to let them pass. The Sioux were angry at having not received their promised annuities at the last payment of the Lower Sioux, and while the superintendent had offered to pay them when he returned, they refused to allow his party to proceed without an immediate compliance with their demands.[50]

Major Cullen immediately returned to Fort Ridgely for reinforcements and was promised about 400 fully armed troops. He reiterated his determination to force his way through to his destination. Cullen wrote Governor Sibley, telling him he expected a fight and asked that a volunteer force be placed on alert in case he needed assistance.

Charles Flandrau wrote:

> In the year 1860 [sic] the civil war broke out, and men in great numbers from Minnesota and the adjacent States were sent to the South. Of course the Indians were fully informed as to what was going on in this direction, and began to discuss among themselves the question as to whether they might not take advantage of the situation and recover their lost country. It must always be remembered that when a tribe of North American Indians cede to the United States a splendid empire of land, filled with everything that tends to their welfare and happiness, and are pushed on westward, they comprehend perfectly that they are compelled to yield to the demands of a more powerful nation, and bad blood is engendered, which only needs an opportunity to seek revenge. Ambitious men among them took advantage of the situation and pushed them on to rebellion.[51]

With a change of administration in 1861 came a change of agents and a change of policy. Instead of paying the annuities in money they were paid in goods, which afforded greater opportunity for fraud, if anything, than before, and caused greater dissatisfaction to the Indians. There were also vexatious delays in the payment of these annuities. Settlers, also, were pouring into the country more and more every year, and the land was fast being taken by them. The game, which had been the hunters' sustenance, was fast disappearing, and the Sioux were beginning to realize what they had done in ceding their land to the whites, and how soon they would be driven out of the home of their fathers.

On May 9, 1861, a report circulated that a trapper had been murdered by Indians on the Des Moines River. "We have been unable to trace it to any reliable source," proclaimed a Mankato newspaper, "and presume it originated in the vague fears and anticipations of Indian troubles, consequent of the distracted state of the country and the removal of the garrison from Fort Ridgely. All such apprehensions will be quieted now, since the re-garrisoning of the fort."[52]

Later that same month, the steamboat *Jeanette Roberts* journeyed up the Minnesota River heavy laden with goods for the Sioux tribes. She also discharged a considerable amount of freight for the Winnebagoes. Major Galbraith was aboard the steamer, having just recovered from an illness he had suffered in Washington.[53]

The following month, this same steamer traveled up the Minnesota "loaded to the guards" with stores and agricultural implements for the Sioux. Superintendent Clark W. Thompson and Major Thomas Galbraith were on board "fully prepared to make the annual money payment to the Indians."[54]

Hunger was wide spread on the reservations during the spring and summer of 1862. This was not the first spring the Indians had known hunger, but in the past, they had always been saved by the government's timely annuity payments. These poor economic prisoners were led to believe by the whites that they had only to hold out until late June when the annuities and provisions were distributed on the reservations. But this year the annuity payments were late, and rumors circulated that they might not be coming at all.

The buffalo hunt had been bad, so the Indians had no choice but to buy their supplies from the traders on credit. The trader, of course, knew how much money each Indian was entitled to and was careful not to allow too much credit. When payday came, which was usually in June of each year, a large party of annuity Sioux assembled at the agency, waiting for the arrival of the paymaster.[55]

"The paymaster did not come," recalled Big Eagle, "and week after week went by and still he did not come. The payment was to be in gold.

Somebody told the Indians that the payment would never be made. The government was in a great war, and gold was scarce, and paper money had taken its place . . ."[56]

The white traders and mixed-bloods were worried too, for their livelihood depended on the annuities. The Sioux depended on them for their food and supplies, but the worried traders cut off their credit. The traders sold their goods almost entirely to the Indians and maintained accurate records of each and every transaction. By selling inferior goods at inflated prices, the traders accumulated great profits, and each year they claimed nearly the entire annuity amounts. The Indians purchased their goods on credit, but, not knowing what they were signing for, did not understand the white man's accounting.

George W. Crooks, a Dakota Indian who lived near Redwood Falls, later explained:

> When the Indians would go to the trading post for their supplies, the white people that owned the store, knowing that the Indians were entirely ignorant of the value of the new paper money, saw the opportunity to make a fortune for themselves. When an Indian would take a twenty-dollar bill to the post for five dollars worth of supplies, the post owners would keep the change for they knew the Indians would not know the true value of the paper money that they had given them.
>
> When they were using their gold coin, their money from the government would last them from one payment to the next, but after the change of money, it was not long until the money was gone and they had no food.[57]

Most of the annuity Indians had been through the same scenario many times. The paymaster, his assistant, and the Indian traders sat around a table, surrounded by a squad of soldiers from Fort Ridgely, for the purpose of maintaining order and preventing any disturbances. The Indians were called in one man at a time. The agent would count the sum he was entitled to, and as the man was about to receive it, the trader or storekeeper stepped in and presented a bill to the agent against that man. Most, if not all, the money was handed instead to the trader without any further conversation, and the Indian was dismissed to make room for another.[58]

Since the Sioux could neither read nor write, he could not challenge the figures presented by the trader. The Indian lost as well on the issue of the fur trade. The most valuable furs were sold by the Indians, but they had no concept of the true value of this merchandize. The traders provided them with cheap goods in exchange for far less than half the valuation. The traders made excessive profits, while the trusting Sioux had little to show for it. Plus, unscrupulous whites and half-breeds resorted to the illegal sale of bad liquor, and, as a rule, the Indian would be cleaned out of every cent he had in a very short time.

When at last the Sioux sobered up and realized how badly they had been taken, their resentment of the whites increased, and they were led to believe that all whites were thieves and scoundrels. They waited patiently for the day when they could get even. Whites in the 1860s considered the nature of the Indian to be savage, cruel, and brutal, believing the "proverbial imps of hell" could not outdue him in cruelty.

While the Sioux were cruel by white standards, they were perhaps no more so than other savage nations. If we judge the Dakota with fairness, we must not compare him with nations that have enjoyed the benefits of civilization and Christianity for over thirty or forty generations, but with other savages such as white Anglo-Saxon Britons, Gauls, and Germans, who lived two thousand years ago. They were certainly in no way more barbaric than our ancestors, and we need only look back half a century to see the atrocities of Nazi Germany in their extermination of millions of Jews.[59]

"The Sioux were a warlike people; [but] they had been our friends," wrote Bishop Henry B. Whipple. "General Sibley, who was chief factor thirty years for the Northwest Fur Company, said: 'It was the boast of the Sioux that they had never taken the life of a white man. In the earlier days of my residence amongst them I never locked the door of my trading-post, and when I rose in the morning I often found Indians camped on the floor. The only thing which I have ever had stolen was a curious pipe, which was returned by the mischievous boy who took it, after I had told the Indians that if the pipe were not returned I should keep the door locked.'"[60]

Of course, there is no atonement for the atrocious massacre of white settlers in 1862. Hochokaduta, Little Crow, and others had been fed and clothed by government annuities for more than twenty years. They had been provided with tobacco to smoke, and money to purchase whiskey; and with all their needs supplied, they spent a great portion of their time in idleness. In this state of demoralization, they were thrown together on their little reservation where all the worst characters in the tribe could act on concert.[61]

But not more than one Indian in ten entertained the idea of an assault on the whites and perhaps not as many as ten men on the entire reservation would have favored an attack. It became the work of a mob, commencing with a very few disgruntled warriors, and spreading throughout the tribe. Many joined because of their clannish ties; others because they feared the victors would not discriminate between the innocent and the guilty.

One defender of New Ulm during the uprising, who was associated with the Sioux as a government official blamed the outbreak on the federal government:

> [I] found [the Sioux] possessed of many of the virtues common to the human family, and that socially and morally their lives were of a standard quite as high as among civilized races. The outbreak was induced by long-continued violation of treaty obligations on the part of the government, inflicting upon these unfortunate wards untold want and suffering. Like violent acts of mobs among civilized communities, the massacre was a barbarous and unreasoning protest against injustice. Had the government faithfully carried out the treaty obligations and dealt with the Sioux justly and humanely, the outbreak would not have occurred.[62]

Because of the bad buffalo hunt in 1861-1862, the Indians were in dire need of dried buffalo meat, especially for their infants, who faced starvation. The government at both agencies had allowed some land to be plowed, and corn and potatoes were planted for the benefit of the Sioux, but this did little to diminish in any way the dire need for nourishment. Stories circulated among the Dakota people that there would be no annuities that year because the federal government needed all its money to defeat the Confederacy. The rumor was false, of course, but it aroused the Indians who feared the worst.[63]

The Civil War had broken out in 1861, and the Sioux were well aware of the reverses suffered by the Union army during the first year of the war. As young men answered the call to arms, the able-bodied were taken away from the farms, and even many of the half-breeds had volunteered for service. The Sioux knew that there could be little organized resistance against an all-out Indian attack should things worsen.[64]

THE YEAR BEFORE, SOME MINNESOTA troops were sent to Texas to assist in quelling a rebellion led by Juan Cortina. Cortina was born at Camargo, Tamaupilas, Mexico, just south of the Rio Grande into a wealthy cattle-ranching family. In order to take over the management of some of his mother's many lands, sometime in the 1840s he moved north of the river into territory claimed by both Texas and Mexico. By the late 1850s, after the United States had annexed all lands north of the Rio Grande, Cortina had become an important political boss for the South Texas Democratic Party, and though the United States had invalidated many of his land claims, he still remained a large rancher.[65]

Cortina had developed a burning hatred for a clique of judges and unscrupulous Brownsville attorneys. He accused them of expropriating land from many Tejanos in the Lower Valley who were unfamiliar with the American judicial system. Families who had owned land during the Colonial and Mexican period were accused by the authorities of being in arrears on their taxes. In order to pay their "debt," some had to sell their land for a fraction of its worth.

Cortina, a veteran of the Mexican-American War, owned a ranch on the north bank of the river and also held a commission in the Mexican frontier army. For several years, he had been an inspirational leader to the Tejanos in the rough and tumble world of Cameron County politics.

The incident that ignited the violence occurred on July 13, 1859, when Cortina witnessed the Brownsville City marshal, an Anglo named Robert Shears, pistol whipping and arresting a Tejano who had once been employed by Cortina. Outraged, Cortina demanded that the marshal stop abusing the

142

Mexican, and when the marshal refused, Cortina shot him in the shoulder, took his former servant up onto his horse and fled with him to safety.

Two months later, on September 28, Cortina led an armed force back into Brownsville, released Mexicans whom he felt had been unfairly imprisoned, and executed four Anglos who had killed Mexicans but hadn't been punished. Here he proclaimed the Republic of the Rio Grande as his followers raised the Mexican flag and shouted, "Death to the gringos!" But Cortina did not pillage or terrorize the city. Instead, he soon withdrew to a nearby ranch, where he issued a proclamation invoking the "sacred right of self-preservation" and condemning the fact that so many were "prosecut[ed] and rob[bed] for no other cause than that of being of Mexican origin."

The six months following the Brownsville raid have been called "Cortina's War." The Texas rangers struck back furiously, often indiscriminately, punishing any Hispanic in the south Rio Grande Valley. Cortina, who soon had five or six hundred armed men under his command, resumed his raids when the rangers executed one of his lieutenants in Brownsville.

The Mexican government, fearing that Cortina's actions would embroil them in another war with the United States, sent a joint Mexican-Anglo force against Cortina, which he quickly defeated. Although some elite Mexican residents of Texas opposed Cortina and quietly aided his opponents, the bulk of the Tejano population supported him, often sending his troops supplies and refusing to help United States officials.

But this support proved to be no match for the U.S. Army, which dealt Cortina a sharp defeat in Rio Grande City on December 27, 1859. As Cortina was in retreat, Colonel Robert E. Lee

Robert E. Lee, 1863, Julian Vannerson, photographer. [Courtesy of the National Archives]

assumed command of the Military Department of Texas and set out for the Rio Grande. Leaving San Antonio with a small escort of the Second Cavalry, Lee rode to Eagle Pass and then turned downriver to Fort McIntosh at Laredo. Continuing through a rare South Texas snowstorm, he reached Ringgold Barracks during the first week of April 1860. Sporadic raiding and fighting continued for several months; observers reported settlements deserted, property destroyed and normal business activities cancelled along the 100-mile stretch of the border from Brownsville to Rio Grande City.

WHILE MINNESOTA SOLDIERS WERE ENGAGED elsewhere, a sense of insecurity prevailed at many of the state's frontier settlements. As fears mounted, the Sioux organized into what they called "Soldiers' Lodge" and, massing in considerable numbers, broke into the government warehouse, and in the presence of a company of soldiers, commenced carrying away flour, pork, bacon, and other provisions. Finally the soldiers took control, and the Indians were persuaded to disperse and return to their homes until the next pay period, which was already late. Although disgruntled, the Sioux complied.[66]

During the latter part of July, the Indian agent summoned the Sioux to Lower Sioux Agency to receive their pay. The agent, however, had promised to pay them in gold but insisted on paying them in currency. The Indians absolutely refused to accept the payment in paper money. Even the Sioux recognized that a swindle was being perpetrated upon them. On account of the stringency in gold coin caused by the war, gold commanded a very high premium, about twice the value of paper money. The government had, in fact, sent gold to the agent, who was accused of selling some of it for paper money, fully intending to grant the Indians dollar for dollar and pocket the profit for his own personal use.

No one fell for the ruse, and the agent had no recourse but to sell back the paper money for gold. This transaction would take time, of course, and again the Indians were told they would have to wait. The agent left for the East while the Indians again waited overtime, sadly in need of money.

On Sunday, August 17th, the Indians held an important council. Mounted messengers rode across the prairies spreading word to other bands of Sioux.

While many Sioux resented the white man's policy of manifest destiny, others embraced it. In 1852, less than a year after the treaty, a Christian Indian community was created in the Hazelwood-Yellow Medicine area near the Upper Sioux Agency. The community soon evolved into the Hazelwood Republic and could boast its own constitution and officers. The Indian agency recognized them as a separate band, although the separation was not to the liking of the missionaries or the non-Christian Sioux.[67]

But as early as 1849, the efforts to Christianize the Sioux at the Lac Qui Parle Mission were encouraging. "There has been more than ordinary attention to the religions of the Bible at this station, during the last four months," proclaimed a report in *The Missionary Herald*. "This has been manifested in various ways. The attendance on the Word preached has been greater than during any previous winter, for some years past; the average number present on the Sabbath, besides children, having been more than thirty. Some who have feared to come heretofore, are now regular attendants at the house of God. And at times there has appeared to be considerable interest in seeking the truth."[68]

Bishop Henry Whipple wrote President Lincoln on March 6, 1862:

TO THE PRESIDENT OF THE UNITED STATES:

The sad condition of the Indians of this State, who are my heathen wards, compels me to address you on their behalf. I ask only justice for a wronged and neglected race. I write the more cheerfully because I believe that the intentions of the Government have always been kind; but they have been thwarted by dishonest servants, ill-conceived plans, and defective instructions.

Before their treaty with the United States, the Indians of Minnesota were as favorably situated as an uncivilized race could well be. Their lakes, forests, and prairies furnished abundant game, and their hunts supplied them with valuable furs for the purchase of all articles of traffic. The great argument to secure the sale of their lands is the promise of their civilization. . . . The sale is made, and after the dishonesty which accompanies it there is usually enough money left, if honestly expended, to foster the Indians' desires for civilization. Remember, the parties to

President Abraham Lincoln. (Courtesy of the National Archives)

this contract are a great Christian Nation and a poor heathen people.

From the day of the treaty a rapid deterioration takes place. The Indian has sold the hunting-grounds necessary for his comfort as a wild man; His tribal relations are weakened; his chief's power and influence circumscribed; and he will soon be left a helpless man without a government, a protector, or a friend, unless treaty is observed.

The Indian agents who are placed in trust of the honor and faith of the Government are generally selected without any reference to their fitness for the place. The Congressional delegation desires to award John Doe for party work, and John Doe desires the place because there is a tradition on the border that an Indian agent with fifteen hundred dollars a year can retire upon an ample fortune in four years.

The Indian agent appoints his subordinates from the same motive, either to reward his friends' service, or to fulfill the bidding of his Congressional patron. They are often men without any fitness, sometimes a disgrace to a Christian nation; whiskey-sellers, bar-room loungers, debauchers, selected to guide a heathen people. Then follow all the evils of bad example, of inefficiency, and of dishonesty—the school a sham, the supplies wasted, the improvement fund curtailed by fraudulent contracts. The Indian, bewildered, conscious of wrong, but helpless, has no refuge but to sink into a depth of brutishness. There have been noble instances of men who have tried to do their duty; but they have generally been powerless for lack of hearty cooperation of others, or because no man could withstand the corruption which has pervaded every department of Indian affairs.

The United States has virtually left the Indian without protection. . . .
I can count up more than a dozen murders which have taken place in
the Chippewa County within two years. . . . There is no law to protect
the innocent or punish the guilty. The sale of whiskey, the open licen-
tiousness, the neglect and want are fast dooming this people to death,
and as sure as there is a God much of the guilt lies at the Nation's door.

The first question is, can these red men become civilized? I say, un-
hesitatingly, yes. The Indian is almost the only heathen man on earth
who is not an idolater. In his wild state he is braver, more honest, and
virtuous than most heathen races. He has warm home affections and
strong love of kindred and country. The Government of England has,
among Indians speaking the same language with our own, some marked
instances of their capability of civilization. In Canada you will find there
are hundreds of civilized and Christian Indians, while on this side of the
line there is only degradation.

The first thing needed is honesty. There has been a marked deterioration in Indian affairs since the office has become one of mere political
favoritism. Instructions are not worth the price of the ink with which
they are written if they are to be carried out by corrupt agents. Every
employee ought to be a man of purity, temperance, industry, and un-
questioned integrity. Those selected to teach in any department must
be men of peculiar fitness—patient, with quick perceptions, enlarged
ideas, and men who love their work. They must be something better
than so many drudges fed at the public crib.

The second step is to frame instructions so that the Indian shall be
the ward of the Government. They cannot live without law. We have
broken up, in part, their tribal relations, and they must have something
in their place.

Whenever the Indian desires to abandon his wild life, the
Government ought to aid him in building a house, in opening his farm,
in providing utensils and implements of labor. His home should be conveyed to him by a patent, and be inalienable. It is a bitter cause of com-
plaint that the Government has not fulfilled its pledges in this respect.
It robs the Indian of manhood and leaves him subject to the tyranny of
wild Indians, who destroy his crops, burn his fences, and appropriate the
rewards of his labor.

The schools should be ample to receive all children who desire to
attend. As it is, with six thousand dollars appropriated for the Lower
Sioux for some seven years past, I doubt whether there is a child at the
lower agency who can read who has not been taught by our missionary.
Our Mission School has fifty children, and the entire cost of the mission,
with three faithful teachers, every dollar of which passes through my
own hands, is less than seven hundred dollars a year.

In all future treaties it ought to be the object of the Government to
pay the Indians in kind, supplying their wants at such times as they

Biship Henry B. Whipple. (Author's collection)

may require help. This valuable reform would only be a curse in the hands of a dishonest agent. If wisely and justly expended, the Indian would not be as he now is—often on the verge of starvation. . . . It may be beyond my province to offer these suggestions; I have made them because my heart aches for this poor wronged people. The heads of the Department are too busy to visit the Indian country, and even if they did it would be to find the house swept and garnished for an official visitor. It seems to me that the surest plan to remedy these wrongs and to prevent them for the future, would be to appoint a commission of some three persons to examine the whole subject and to report to the Department a plan which should remedy the evils which have so long been a reproach to our nation. If such were appointed, it ought to be composed of men of inflexible integrity, of large heart, of clear head, of strong will, who fear God and love man. I should like to see it composed of men so high in character that they are above the reach of the political demagogues.

I have written to you freely with all the frankness with which a Christian bishop has the right to write to the Chief Ruler of a great Christian Nation. My design his not been to complain of individuals, nor to make accusations. Bad as I believe some of the appointments to be, they are the fault of a political system. When I came to Minnesota I was startled at the degradation at my door. I give these men missions; God has blessed me, and I would count every trial I have had as a way of roses if I could save this people. May God guide you and give you grace to order all things, so that the Government shall deal righteously with the Indian nations in its charge.

Your servant for Christ's sake,
H.B. WHIPPLE,
Bishop of Minnesota[69]

Reverend Stephen R. Riggs, however, wrote the following in a letter dated March 7, 1849: "It is gratifying to find that there is any increase of interest in the subject of religion among the Dakotas. But there do not seem to be any decisive indications that set time to favor this tribe of Indians is near at hand."[70]

Missionary work with the Cherokee, Choctaw, and other civilized tribes was phased out reluctantly by the American Board in the 1830s because of their removal to land west of the Mississippi and because of the general disarray of these tribes' existence. The mainstream of mission activities moved to Minnesota and focused on the Sioux. Thomas Williamson, a Presbyterian, was sent to the Dakotas by the American Board, in 1835. In these years the American Board was supported by Congregationalists and Presbyterians. Williamson was joined shortly by Stephen and Mary Riggs. Both these families were to collaborate in long careers with the Sioux. Riggs became an eminent scholar in the Sioux language, publishing a grammar and a dictionary in 1852. He and Williamson translated the Bible, which was published by the American Bible Society.[71]

The Riggses first worked in missions along the Minnesota River, where the Sioux were congregated after cession of large amounts of Minnesota land to the United States. They maintained that civilization and Christianization were "Siamese twins" in mission strategy and set out to reform Indian life.

Stephen Riggs, in his early life, had been desirous of

Reverend Stephen R. Riggs. [Author's collection]

149

becoming a missionary to China but yielded to what he considered the over-rulings of Providence, and, in 1837, he and his wife had moved to the frontier among the Sioux.[72] He reduced their language to writing and translated the Holy Scriptures and hymns. Ten well-ordered churches and many out-stations had been established in the region of his operations, reaching beyond the business line.[73]

While most Sioux men avoided the church, many women and children attended Christian worship on Sundays at Lac Qui Parle. The chiefs, however, attempted to prevent their attending the mission services by holding sacred feasts on the Sabbath and threatening to cut up the blankets of the women and children while they were at the mission. But, albeit slowly, more and more men began attending Christian worship services.

By August 1862, Dr. Thomas S. Williamson noted in his "Gospel Sermon," that about a hundred Dakota had been admitted to the church. Of the one hundred, sixty-five were members in good standing. One year earlier, Reverend Riggs had taken a party of his "civilized" Sioux to be examined by the District Court and admitted to citizenship.[74]

Initially most whites at the mission saw the Indians as "filthy savages, indecently clad . . . flattening their dirty noses on the window pane." When the Indians became more familiar with their white brethren, they resorted to their usual custom of walking in unannounced at any time of the day or night.[75]

Mrs. Huggins at the mission, however, enjoyed her "house full of chattering, unwashed Indians, smoking their dogwood and tobacco smoking mixture in the still air." She and her children were often alone with them, since her husband was working on the stable, but she felt comfortable around them. Only once was she given a good scare. She was combing her hair when a man sprang toward her with his tomahawk. He placed it against her head and pulled on her hair, but only to show his companions how long it was.

FLANDRAU WROTE ABOUT THE RESERVATION Indians and the government's call for half-breeds: "About the second week of August 1862, the agent [Thomas J. Galbraith] in charge of these Indians conceived the idea of forming a company of volunteers from the young half-breeds for the war, and succeeded in doing so, and about the 16th or 17th of August started from the agencies to have them mustered in at Fort Snelling. The Indians seized upon this fact as evidence that the government must be in desperate straits if it had to call upon these people for aid. . . ."[76]

On July 3rd, William J. Cullen, newly appointed superintendent of Indian affairs for the northern district, told the Sioux assembled at Yellow Medicine Agency that they must capture, kill, and bring in Inkpaduta and members of his band or face a suspension of annuity payments. Joseph R. Brown, a trader and later Indian agent, made light of Cullen's qualifications for the position and doubted that he could tell "the difference between . . . a Sioux Indian and a snapping turtle."[77]

Cullen and James W. Denver, new commissioner of Indian affairs, followed the ludicrous government policy of holding the entire band responsible for crimes committed by individuals, and threatened to withhold annuities until Inkpaduta's band was either captured or annihilated. The Indians objected strongly and threatened to tear down the agency's buildings and help themselves to their just dues. A confrontation between Indians and soldiers was finally averted when Little Crow offered to lead a band of warriors against Unkpaduta.[78]

Little Crow's party was gone for two weeks in pursuit of Inkpaduta. According to the Sioux, the soldiers had told them they would be paid one thousand dollars for each member of Inkpaduta's band that they killed. Little Crow had made a great effort to bring in Inkpaduta and his band. He chased them to Lake Champitizatanka and killed three of the marauders, wounded another, and took two women and a child prisoner. Little Crow showed the authorities a scar on his knee as proof of his fighting a battle.

The officials did not place any reliance in Little Crow's report, and told him had he accomplished what he claimed he would have brought back bodies as proof. An old chief asked what they wanted with the bodies—did they want to eat them? When the government was asked to meet their payment of annuities and pay the rewards promised Little Crow, he was told no rewards had been promised.[79]

Historian W.M. Wemett wrote in 1923: "The shameful treatment which the Indians received from the traders embittered them toward the white people and their government. They thought the government meant to be as dishonest with them as were the traders and some of the Indian agents whom they knew. The breaking of treaties later fanned their discontent into a flame of anger."[80]

Whites, however, who had rendered services in the hunt for Inkpaduta as far back as 1857, were paid by Superintendent Cullen. Volunteers who had participated in an expedition to Fort Slocum received $10.50 to $13.50 each to cover their individual expenses, leaving the "glory of the campaign to offset the items of lost time, hardships endured . . ."[81]

The money paid out was absorbed principally by bills for supplies, while the company under Captain Connor, who were on duty as long as any others were not paid at all. According to Major Cullen, only those men engaged in the actual pursuit of Inkpaduta deserved payment.

By the summer of 1862, the Santee Sioux were fed up with the white man. After two hundred years of resentment and frustration over contact with the government, they had had enough. Their culture had been assaulted, they had become dependent upon annuity payments, which were always late, they had fallen prey to the distribution of liquor from the traders, been pressured off of their lands, forced to accept Christianity, and faced with the unrealistic proposition of becoming farmers. They had ceded all of their remaining lands in Minnesota for $3,075,000, but they saw very little of the money. The debt-ridden Indians, victimized by corrupt and bungling government officials, watched their reservation turn into a powder keg.[82]

Whenever the Sioux left the reservation to hunt through the familiar lakes and swamps, they found the game depleted by the white man. Settlers from New Ulm were spreading out and moving onto the Sioux's remaining land. On April 3, 1861, thirty-two settlers sent a petition to President Abraham Lincoln asking for protection in their illegal occupation.[83]

Trouble began brewing at the Upper Sioux Agency at Yellow Medicine. Indian Agent Thomas J. Galbraith had charge of the food and clothing the government had promised the Dakota. Yellow Medicine was a small settlement, and its largest building was the storehouse where the provisions for the Indians were kept. Major Galbraith lived in a handsome brick house on the river, while the traders and merchants occupied log cabins at the agency.

In July 1862, both banks of the river were covered with Indian teepees as nearly five thousand Dakota had gathered there. They had come from all parts of the Dakota plains for their provisions and gold, which the government promised to pay them. Major Galbraith had their provisions but not their gold, and the Indians waited patiently once more. The hungry Indians began to grow impatient over the next few weeks, and once again asked about their payment.[84]

"We have no food," they told the soldiers. "Our wives and children are starving. We have eaten our dogs and some of the horses. We know there are provisions in the storehouse. They are for us. Why doesn't our agent give them to us? We will not go away until he gives us food."[85]

Word reached Major Galbraith, who informed the Indians to all come to the agency and be counted. By their cooperating with the count, he would know how many provisions to hands out to them. The jubilant Dakotas believed at last they were to be paid and rode back to the agency.

Dakota group shortly before the outbreak of hostilities. (Author's collection)

I was in the Indian country when the Sioux came and made bitter complaints about the non-payment for the land sold from their reservation [wrote Bishop Whipple]. Pay-Pay, an old Indian whom I had known at Faribault, came to me and asked, "How much money shall we receive at this payment?" "Twenty dollars per head," I answered, "the same as you have always received."

A few hours after, he brought Wa-cou-ta to me, saying, "Tell him what you said." I repeated my statement, feeling much anxiety, for it was evident that the Indians had heard that they were not to receive their payment. When I returned from the Upper Agency, where I found the Indians most turbulent. I said to a trader's clerk, "Major Galbraith, the agent, is coming down to enroll the Indians for payment." He replied: "Galbraith is a fool. Why does he lie to them? I have heard from Washington that most of the appropriation has been used to pay claims against the Indians. The payment will not be made. I have told the Indians this, and have refused to trust them."

I was astounded that a trader's clerk should claim to know more about the payment than the government agent. I had never seen the Indians so restless. Every day some heathen dance took place—a monkey dance, a begging dance, or a scalp dance. Occasionally one of the men would refuse to shake hands with me. I knew what it meant, that he wanted to boast that he would not take the hand of a white man, which was always a danger signal.[86]

But following the counting, Major Galbraith once more withheld their provisions. He informed them that he wanted to give them their gold and provisions at the same time, and the gold had not yet arrived. He expected no trouble as the Indians had always been peaceful.[87]

Lieutenant Timothy J. Sheehan, commander of the little squad of troops at the agency, did not feel so secure. He was angry with Galbraith for withholding their food and knew the Indians were very hungry and could not wait much longer. Sheehan discussed the Indians' plight with his men, who gave half their hardtack to the Indians.

Another week passed. There were no more dogs to eat, and although there were plenty of cattle in the pastures, they did not steal. Finally, on the morning of August 4th, they came to Lieutenant Sheehan and told him some of the Indians were coming to the agency to dance for the soldiers. They told him not to fear; there would be shooting, but no one would be hurt.

About nine o'clock, several warriors rode up to the agency whooping so loud that several whites came running out from their houses to see what the Indians were doing. One warrior stalked the storehouse yelling, "Wo-kay-zhu-zhu! Wo-kay-zhu-zhu! (The payment! The payment!) Then he raised his tomahawk and smashed in the door. Several Dakotas rushed into the open doorway and emerged carrying sacks of flour and fat strips of bacon.

Lieutenant Sheehan ordered his troops to fall in with guns in hand. Two cannons were aimed at the storehouse door as the Indians ran in and out gathering food supplies. The Indians were frightened by the cannons and fled into the woods, looking angrily back at their tormentors.

> There were several of us [who] went over to Yellow Medicine Agency because we had no food [recalled Robert Hakewaste (Good Fifth Son)]. Our agent [Galbraith] was up there at the time, and all at once we noticed that there was a disturbance up there among the people, evidently on account of something up there. There were some soldiers with an officer and a big gun or cannon up on the hill, and we noticed some men—Indians—coming along the river bottom, many on horseback and many of foot. Some of them had no garments on. We were told they were coming to fight. We went there because we wanted some food, and we understood they were in a starving condition, and they had no food among the Indians, and we heard we were going to receive some food and the soldiers had quieted the disturbance and, as the agent promised us to receive some food down there, we came away.[88]

Lieutenant Sheehan met with Galbraith the following day and convinced the reluctant major to hand out supplies. Over the next two days, supplies were given out, and when all were gone, the Indians packed their ponies and moved westward. The other Sioux bands dwelling over the rest of the state also headed westward, and daily the roads leading toward the Sioux Reservation were full of Indians all going toward the Lower Agency. But by the evening of the sixteenth all were gone. This strange movement, however, created not the slightest suspicion among the whites as the Indians had been in the habit of going to the reservation in great numbers to receive their annuities, which were then past due.

Sunday morning, August 17th, Little Crow, Inkpaduta, and Little Priest, chief of the Winnebagoes, attended religious service at the Episcopal

Church in the Lower Agency and listened attentively to the sermon preached by Rev. J.D. Hinman. That same afternoon, the three attended a large Indian council held again on Rice Creek, at which they were the principal spokesmen. The speakers dwelled upon how to rid their lands of the whites and redress their wrongs.[89]

Of course, the timing was right, as the whites were engaged in a great war among themselves. All the regular soldiers, who, heretofore, had been stationed in the frontier forts, had gone to the South, and their places were supplied by a mere handful of raw recruits. Fort Ridgely was occupied by Company B, Fifth Minnesota Volunteers, which comprised eighty men and four officers, who had enlisted only six months before, together with Ordinance Sergeant John Jones with six small pieces of artillery. With Post Surgeon Alfred Muller, Sutler B.H. Randall, and Indian Interpreter Peter Quinn, there were only eighty-eight men to guard hundreds of miles of frontier against 4,000 Sioux and 2,000 Winnebagoes. At the other frontier military posts, Forts Ripley and Abercrombie, only Companies C and A, of the same regiment, with about the same number of men, were stationed to keep in check the hordes of Chippewas and Sioux in the region of the north and west. Besides all this, four thousand of the best able-bodied men from the scattered homes of Minnesota had already gone to Southern battlefields, and five thousand more had recently enlisted and had just started for the great conflict until it seemed there were only women and children and old men left.

Company E., of the Ninth Regiment, was recruited in Blue Earth County and contained a large proportion of Welshmen. They had left Mankato only the previous Friday for Fort Snelling to be mustered in.

Ohiyesa later recalled:

> There were many mixed bloods among these Sioux, and some of the Indians held that these were accomplices of the white people in robbing them of their possessions; therefore, their lives should not be spared. My father, Many Lightnings, who was practically the leader of the Mankato band (for Mankato, the chief, was a weak man), fought desperately for the lives of the half-breeds and the missionaries. The chiefs had great confidence in my father, yet they would not commit themselves, since their braves were clamoring for blood. Little Crow had been accused of all the misfortunes of his tribe, and he now hoped by leading them

against the whites to regain his prestige with his people, and a part at least of their lost domain. There were moments when the pacifists were in grave peril. It was almost daybreak when my father saw them approaching.[90]

On the same day the Indian agent, Major Thos. J. Galbraith, having enlisted thirty men at the Upper Agency and twenty men at the Lower Agency, went with them to Fort Ridgely, and this very Sunday morning, being furnished transportation, they had left the fort accompanied by Lieutenant N.K. Culver, Sergeant McGraw, and four men of Company B for Fort Snelling, by way of New Ulm and St. Peter, to be sworn in and sent south with the thousands of able-bodied men there gathered from all parts of the state in answer to their country's call. At seven o' clock on the morning of this same Sunday, Lieutenant Sheehan, with fifty men of Company C, Fifth Regiment, who had been sent from Fort Ripley to aid Major Galbraith two months before in quelling certain disturbances that had broken out among the Indians of the Upper Agency, left Fort Ridgely to return to Fort Ripley, thinking the danger was all over. The watchful eye of the Indian had observed all this. Now, if ever, was the opportune time to avenge all their wrongs and recover all their lands from the hated paleface invader.

The Great Spirit had delivered the white people into their hands with all their rich spoil. It would be but a small pastime for the Indian warriors to kill the women and children and the few men—mostly old and decrepit—left in the country. These were the sentiments expressed with all the force of Indian oratory at this Sunday afternoon council. There were present, by special invitation, delegates from the Winnebagoes, Chippewas, and the tribes who dwelt on the great plains of Dakota, and all gave assurances of sympathy and aid in ridding the country of their common foe. It was thought prudent, however, to defer the attack until all the soldiers then mustering at St. Paul had left the state. To make sure of this, a delegation of Indians was to be sent to St. Paul to spy into affairs, under the pretext of seeking redress for their grievances. Little Crow and his associates planned well, and, undoubtedly, if these plans had been carried out to full maturity, the awful Indian massacre of 1862 would have been ten times more awful,

and the Indian prediction that all the whites in Minnesota, west of the
Mississippi, would be destroyed and corn planted on the sites of St. Peter,
Mankato, and Red Wing would have been fulfilled.

A merciful providence, however, hastened the massacre premature-
ly, and thus weakened the foe; and the gathering at Fort Snelling of so many
thousands of men enlisted ready for war turned out to be a very important
factor in saving the state from destruction by the savage tomahawk.

Big Eagle later talked of the causes of the uprising from a Sioux perspective in an 1894 interview:

> Of the causes that led to the outbreak of 1862, much has been said.
> Of course it was wrong, as we all know now, but there were not many
> Christians among the Indians then, and they did not understand as they
> should. There was great dissatisfaction among the Indians over many
> things the whites did. The whites would not let them go to war against
> their enemies. This was right, but the Indians did not then know it.
> Then the whites were always trying to make the Indians give up their life
> and live like white men—go to farming, work hard and do as they did—
> and the Indians did not know how to do that, and did not want to any-
> way. It seemed too sudden to make such a change. If the Indians had
> tried to make the whites live like them, the whites would have resisted,
> and it was the same way with many Indians. The Indians wanted to live
> as they did before the treaty of Traverse des Sioux—go where they
> pleased and when they pleased, hunt game wherever they could find it,
> sell their furs to the traders and live as they could.
>
> Then the Indians did not think the traders had done right. The
> Indians bought goods of them on credit, and when the government pay-
> ments came the traders were on hand with their books, which showed
> that the Indians owed so much and so much, and as the Indians kept no
> books they could not deny their accounts, but had to pay them, and
> sometimes the traders got all their money. I do not say that the traders
> always cheated and lied about their accounts. I know many of them were
> honest men and kind and accommodating, but since I have been a citi-
> zen, I know that many white men, when they go to pay their accounts,
> often think them too large and refuse to pay them, and they go to law
> about them, and there is much bad feeling. The Indians could not go to
> law, but there was always trouble over their credits. Under the treaty of
> Traverse des Sioux, the Indians had to pay a very large sum of money to
> the traders for old debts, some of which ran back fifteen years, and many
> of those who got the goods were dead and others were not present, and
> the traders' books had to be received as to the amounts, and the money
> was taken from the tribe to pay them. Of course the traders often were

of great service to the Indians in letting them have goods on credit, but the Indians seemed to think the traders ought not to be too hard on them about the payments, but do as the Indians did among one another, and put off the payment until they were better able to make it.

Then many of the white men often abused the Indians and treated them unkindly. Perhaps they had excuse, but the Indians did not think so. Many of the whites always seemed to say by their manner when they saw an Indian, "I am much better than you," and the Indians did not like this. There was excuse for this, but the Indians did not believe there were better men in the world than they. Then some of the white men abused the Indian women in a certain way and disgraced them, and surely there was no excuse for that.

All these things made many Indians dislike the whites. Then a little while before the outbreak there was trouble among the Indians themselves. Some of the Indians took a sensible course and began to live like white men. The government built them houses, furnished them tools, feed . . . and taught them to farm. At the two agencies, Yellow Medicine and Redwood, there were several hundred acres of land in cultivation that summer. Others staid [sic] in their tepees. There was a white man's party and an Indian party. We had politics among us and there was much feeling. A new chief speaker for the tribe was to be elected. There were three candidates—Little Crow, myself, and Wa-sui-hi-ya-ye-dan (Traveling Hail). After an exciting contest, Traveling Hail was elected. Little Crow felt sore over his defeat. Many of our tribe believed him responsible for the sale of the north ten-mile strip, and I think this was why he was defeated. I did not care much about it. Many whites think that Little Crow was the principal chief of the Dakotas at this time, but he was not. Wabasha was the principal chief, and he was of the white man's party; so was I; so was Old Shakopee, whose band was very large. Many think that if Old Shakopee would have lived there would have been no war, for he was for the white man and had great influence. But he died that summer, and was succeeded by his son, whose real name was Ea-to-ka (Another Language), but when he became chief he took his father's name and was afterwards called "Little Shakopee" or "Little Six," for in the Sioux language "Shakopee" means six. This Shakopee was against the white man. He took part in the outbreak, murdering women and children, but I never saw him in a battle, but he was caught in Manitoba and hanged in 1864. My brother, Medicine Bottle, was hanged with him.

As the summer advanced there was great trouble among the Sioux—troubles among themselves, troubles with whites, and one thing and another. The war with the South was going on then, and a great many men had left the state and gone down there to fight. A few weeks before the outbreak the president called for many more men, and a great many of the white men of Minnesota and some half-breeds enlisted and went to Fort Snelling to be sent South. We understood that the South was getting the best of the fight, and it was said the North would be whipped. The year before the new president had turned out Maj. Brown and Maj. Cullen, the Indian agents, and put in their places Maj. Galbraith and Mr. Clark Thompson, and they had turned out the men under them and put in others of their own party. There were a great many changes. An Indian named Shonk-sha (White Dog), who had been hired to teach the Indians to farm, was removed and another Indian named Ta-opi (The Wounded Man), a son of old Betsy, of St. Paul, put in his place. Nearly all of the men who were turned out were dissatisfied, and most of the Indians did not like the new men. At last Major Galbraith went to work about the agencies and recruited a company of soldiers to go South. His men were nearly all half-breeds. This was the company called the Renville Rangers, for they were mostly from Renville County. The Indians now thought the whites must be pretty hard up for men to fight the South, or they would not come so far out on the frontier and take half-breeds or anything to help them.

It began to be whispered about that now would be a good time to go to war with the whites and get back the lands. It was believed that the men who had enlisted last had left the state, and before help could be sent the Indians could clean out the country, and that the Winnebagoes, and even the Chippewas, would assist the Sioux. It was also thought that a war with the whites would cause the Sioux to forget the troubles among themselves and enable many of them to pay off some old scores. Though I took part in the war, I was against it. I knew there was no good cause for it, and I had been to Washington and knew the power of the whites and that they would finally conquer us. We might succeed for a time, but we would be overpowered and defeated at last.[91]

The Sioux treaties of the 1850s had marked the materialistic United States policy towards Indian lands, and the insensitive attitude toward the Indian way of life. No tactics of bullying, cheating or lying were neglected. When the whirlwind was reaped a decade later, the immediate victims were the comparatively innocent white settlers near the reservations, not the businessmen and politicians who were ultimately responsible.

160

Notes

[1]Mark Diedrich, *Dakota Oratory Great Moments in the Recorded Speech of the Eastern Sioux, 1695-1874*, Rochester, Coyote Books, 1989, p. 65.

[2]John Upton Terrell, *Sioux Trail*, New York, McGraw-Hill Book Company, 1974, p. 174.

[3]John Parker, editor, *The Journals of Jonathan Carver and Related Documents, 1766-1770*, St. Paul, Minnesota Historical Society Press, 1976, pp. 16-17.

[4]Dr. William Glenn Robertson, Dr. Jerold E. Brown, Major William M. Campsey, Major Scott R. McMeen, *Atlas of the Sioux Wars*, Combat Studies Institute, U. S. Army Command and General Staff College, Fort Leavenworth, Kansas.

[5]Jon Willand, *Lac Qui Parle and the Dakota Mission*, Madison, Minnesota, Lac Qui Parle County Historical Society, 1964, pp. 20-21.

[6]James L. Semsler, "The Dakota Indian: His Culture and his Religion," unpublished M.A. Thesis, Andover Newton Theological School, Newton Center, Massachusetts, 1955, p. 5.

[7]John Upton Terrell, *Sioux Trail*, p. 175.

[8]L.A. Rossman, *The Great White Father Gets the Land*, Grand Rapids, privately printed, 1950, pp. 1-2.

[9]Elliott Coues, *The Expeditions of Zebulon Montgomery Pike*, Volume I, Minneapolis, Ross & Haines, Inc., 1965, p. 231.

[10]Kern O. Pederson, *The Story of Fort Snelling*, St. Paul, Minnesota Historical Society Press, 1966, p. 8.

[11]Lucile M. Kane, June D. Holmquist, and Carolyn Gilman, editors, *The Northern Expeditions of Stephen H. Long: The Journals of 1817 and 1823 and Related Documents*, St. Paul, Minnesota Historical Society Press, 1978, pp. 9-10.

[12]Martha Coleman Bray, editor, *The Journals of Joseph N. Nicollet*, St. Paul, Minnesota Historical Society Press, 1970, p. 12.

[13]George W. Featherstonhaugh, *A Canoe Voyage up the Minnay Sotor*, Volume I, St. Paul, Minnesota Historical Society Press, pp. 299-300.

[14]*Old Mendota: A Proposal for Addition to Land to Fort Snelling State Historical Park*, St. Paul, Fort Snelling State Park Association and the Minnesota Historical Society, 1966, pp. 3-7.

[15]*Indian Affairs: Laws and Treaties*, Vol. II (Treaties), Compiled and edited by Charles J. Kappler, Washington: Government Printing Office, 1904; Oklahoma State University Library, Volume II, pp. 250-255.

[16]John J. Oyen, "The Lac Qui Parle Indian Mission," *The Watson Voice*, April 22, 1937, p. 5.

[17]Henry Has Holy interview with Henry Murphy, Shields, North Dakota, 1926-1928, Manuscript Collections, Microfilm Edition, North Dakota Historical Society.

[18]Mark Dietrich, "A 'Good Man' in a Changing World Cloud Man, the Dakota Leader, and His Life and Times," *Ramsey County History*, Volume 36, Number 1, Spring 2001, p. 10.

[19]Henry Has Holy interview with Henry Murphy, Shields, North Dakota, 1926-1928, Manuscript Collections, Microfilm Edition, North Dakota Historical Society.

[20]Marcus L. Hansen, *Old Fort Snelling 1819-1858*, Minneapolis, Ross & Haines, Inc, 1958, p. 184.

[21]Henry B. Whipple, *Light and Shadows of a Long Episcopate (1902) Being Reminiscences and Recollections of the Right Reverend Henry B. Whipple, Bishop of Minnesota.*

[22]Steve Kerns, *Winona Sunday News*, November 14, 1876.

[23]Edward J. Pluth, "The Failed Watab Treaty of 1853," *Minnesota History*, 57/1 Spring 2000, p. 4.

[24]Jane Lamm Carroll, "Native Americans and Criminal Justice on the Minnesota Frontier," *Minnesota History*, 55/2, Summer 1996, p. 48.

[25]Wayne E. Webb, *Redwood: The Story of a County*, St. Paul, Redwood Board of Commissioners, 1964, pp. 36-40; *Mankato Free Press*, July 20, 21, 23, 24, 1931.

[26]Thomas Sees the Bear Interview with Henry Murphy Shields, 1926-1928, Manuscript Collections, Microfilm Edition, North Dakota Historical Society.

[27]Thomas E. Mails, *The Mystic Warriors of the Plains*, New York, Marlowe & Company, 1996, pp. 20-21.

[28]*Old Mendota: A proposal for Addition to Land to Fort Snelling State Historical Park*, p. 9.

[29]Jon Willand, *Lac Qui Parle and the Dakota Mission*, p. 208.

[30]*History of Wabasha County*, Chapter 3, 1920.

[31]*Memorial of the Sioux Indian Outbreak 1862*, Fairfax, Fort Ridgely State Park and Historical Association, 1930, p. 5.

[32]"Little Crow as Remembered by Ohiyesa (Charles A. Eastman)," Internet.

[33]Alan Axelrod, *Chronicle of the Indian Wars from Colonial Times to Wounded Knee*, New York, Prentice Hall General Reference, 1993, p. 190.

[34]Jon Willand, *Lac Qui Parle and the Dakota Mission*, p. 208.

[35]*Mankato Free Press*, July 24, 1931.

[36]Ibid.

[37]"Minnesota: A State Guide," American Guide Series, Internet.

[38]Henry Lewis, (edited by Bertha L. Heilbron) *The Valley of the Mississippi Illustrated*, St. Paul, Minnesota Historical Society Press, 1967, p. 57.

[39]*The Redwood Gazette*, May 4, 1910.

[40]*Mankato Daily Free Press*, May 25, 1931.

[41]*Indian Affairs: Laws and Treaties*. Vol. II (Treaties). Compiled and edited by Charles J. Kappler. Washington: Government Printing Office, 1904.

[42]Annie D. Tallent, *The Black Hills: Or, The Last Hunting Ground of the Dakotahs*, Sioux Falls, Brevet Press, 1974, pp. 520-521.

[43]Charles E. Flandrau, "The Battle of New Ulm," Manuscript Collections, Brown County Historical Society.

[44]Wayne E. Webb, *Redwood: The Story of a County*, p. 49.

[45]*Mankato Independent*, July 10, 1858.

[46]*Mankato Independent*, June 26, 1858.

[47]*Mankato Independent*, July 3, 1858.

[48]*Mankato Independent*, December 23, 1858.

[49]*Mankato Independent*, January 20, 1859.

[50]*Mankato Record*, July 5, 1859.

[51]Charles E. Flandrau, "The Battle of New Ulm," Manuscript Collections, Brown County Historical Society.

[52]*Mankato Independent*, May 9, 1861.

[53]*Mankato Independent*, May 23, 1861.

[54]*Mankato Independent*, June 20, 1861.

[55]L.A. Fritsche, M.D., *History of Brown County Minnesota: Its People, Industries and Institutions*, Volume I, Indianapolis, B.F. Bowen & Company, Inc., 1916, pp. 184-185.

[56]Duane Schultz, *Over the Earth I Come: The Great Sioux Uprising of 1862*, New York, St. Martin's Press, 1992, pp. 8-9.

[57]George W. Crooks reminiscence, Dakota Conflict of 1862, Manuscripts Collections, Microfilm Edition, Reel 1, Minnesota Historical Society.

[58]L.A. Fritsche, M.D., *History of Brown County Minnesota*, pp. 185-186.

[59]Samuel W. Pond, *The Dakota or Sioux in Minnesota As They Were in 1834*, St. Paul, Minnesota Historical Society Press, 1986, pp. 62-63.

[60]Henry B. Whipple, *Light and Shadows of a Long Episcopate (1902) Being Reminiscences and Recollections of the Right Reverend Henry B. Whipple, Bishop of Minnesota*.

[61]Samuel W. Pond, *The Dakota or Sioux in Minnesota As They Were in 1834*, St. Paul, Minnesota Historical Society Press, 1986, pp. 62-63.

[62]L.A. Fritsche, M.D., *History of Brown County Minnesota*, p. 224.

[63]Ibid., p. 186.

[64]Hon. William G. Gresham, *History of Nicollet & LeSueur Counties, Minnesota Their People, Industries, & Institutions*, Indianapolis, B. F. Bowen & Company, Inc., 1916, p. 42.

[65]PBS, "New Perspectives of the West"; Ron Affolter letter to author dated September 5, 2003.

[66]L.A. Fritsche, M.D., *History of Brown County Minnesota*, pp. 186-187.

[67]Jon Willand, *Lac Qui Parle and the Dakota Mission*, p. 236.

[68]*The Missionary Herald*, June 1849.

[69]Henry B. Whipple, *Light and Shadows of a Long Episcopate (1902) Being Reminiscences and Recollections of the Right Reverend Henry B. Whipple, Bishop of Minnesota*.

[70]*The Missionary Herald*, June 1849.

[71]R. Pierce Beaver, *Pioneers in Mission*, Grand Rapids, Michigan: Wm. B. Eerdmans Publishing Co., 1966, p. 64.

[72]Reverend Stephen R. Riggs died at the age of seventy-one in Beloit, Wisconsin, in August 1883.

[73]*The American Missionary*, October 1883, Volume 37, Issue 10, pp. 290-291.

[74]*Mankato Independent*, June 17, 1861.

[75]Jon Willand, *Lac Qui Parle and the Dakota Mission*, p. 62.

[76]Charles E. Flandrau, "The Battle of New Ulm," Manuscript Collections, Brown County Historical Society.

[77]Peggy Rodina Larson, "A New Look at the Elusive Inkpaduta," *Minnesota History*, 48/1, Spring 1982, p. 32.

[78]Ibid; *Lakefield Standard*, February 1, 1896.

[79]Daniel Buck, *Indian Outbreaks*, pp. 38-39; *Lakefield Standard*, February 1, 1896.

[80]W.M. Wemett, *The Story of the Flickertail State*, Valley City, W.M. Wemett, 1923, p. 131.

[81]*Mankato Independent*, August 6, 1859.

[82]Raymond Wilson, "Forty Years to Judgment: The Santee Sioux Claims Case," *Minnesota History*, 47/7, Fall 1981, pp. 284-285.

[83]Angie Debo, A *History of the Indians of the United States*, Norman, University of Oklahoma Press, 1970, pp. 184-185.

[84]Raymond Wilson, "Forty Years to Judgment: The Santee Sioux Claims Case," Minnesota History, 47/7, Fall 1981, pp. 484-486.

[85]W.M. Wemett, *The Story of the Flickertail State*, p. 134.

[86]Henry B. Whipple, *Light and Shadows of a Long Episcopate (1902) Being Reminiscences and Recollections of the Right Reverend Henry B. Whipple, Bishop of Minnesota*.

[87]W.M. Wemett, *The Story of the Flickertail State*, p. 134; Gary Clayton Anderson, "Myrick's Insult: A Fresh Look at Myth and Reality," *Minnesota History*, 48/5, Spring 1983, pp. 199-200.

[88]Robert Hakewaste, "Evidence for the Defendants," *The Sisseton and Wahpeton Bands of Dakota or Sioux Indians v. the United States, 1901-1907*, U.S. Court of Claims no. 22524, part 2, pp. 358-359.

[89]Reverends Thomas E. Hughes and David Edwards, Hugh G. Roberts and Thomas Hughes, *Story of the Welsh in Minnesota*, Foreston and Lime Springs, Iowa. Gathered by the Old Settlers, 1895.

[90]"Little Crow as Remembered by Ohiyesa (Charles A. Eastman)," Internet.

[91]Henry H. Sibley Papers. Manuscript Collections and Government Records, Minnesota Historical Society.

Chapter Four

August 17, 1862
Acton

"Tonight the blood of the white man shall run like water in the rain."

—Lean Bear[1]

"We beg to assure our Eastern friends once again that there is not the slightest danger to the people of Minnesota from Indians. The three forts—Abercrombie, Ripley and Ridgely—in the Indian districts are well garrisoned and perfectly sufficient to prevent all disturbances of this kind, were any imminent."

—St. Cloud Democrat[2]

 CARCELY HAD THE YOUNG STATE begun to recover from the panic of 1857, when the summons to war drew thousands of young Minnesota men. Governor Alexander Ramsey was in the nation's capital, April 13th, the day on which the news of Fort Sumter's capture reached Washington. He immediately hastened to the War Department to see his old friend, Secretary of War Simon Cameron, and offered 1,000 men from Minnesota, "the first tender of troops from any quarter after the fall of the Charleston fortress."[3] Cameron was about to leave for a conference with President Abraham Lincoln and told Ramsey he would present the offer if

Ramsey would put it in writing. Ramsey did so at once, and Lincoln enthusiastically accepted the offer.[4]

Ramsey's message to President Lincoln read: "As the executive of the State of Minnesota, I hereby tender to the government of the United States, on the part of the state, 1,000 men to be ready for service as soon as the necessary information can be communicated to the people there." He also assured Lincoln that Minnesota's two senators were aware of—and approved of—his action.[5]

Before the attack on Fort Sumter, Governor Ramsey had arrived in Washington for a consultation with other governors and government officials, hoping to resolve the troubled situation between the North and South. Like other states, Minnesota was deeply interested in the national troubles and keenly aware of the critical condition of governmental affairs. The people of Minnesota were not planning for nor preparing for a war; they deprecated war and hoped for peace.

Within twenty-four hours, President Lincoln called for 75,000 volunteers from state militia groups and notified Ramsey that Minnesota's contribution would be the first regiment of infantry. Ramsey immediately telegraphed the message to Lieutenant Governor Ignatius Donnelly in St. Paul. Donnelly quickly published an order through the state adjutant general calling for ten companies of a hundred men each to prepare for active service. The local militia units responded immediately upon hearing the news.[6]

One day after the publication of Lincoln's war proclamation, Ignatius Donnelly, acting governor, issued a call for the First Regiment. It was assembled rapidly enough to replace almost immediately the regular army units at the frontier posts and to reach the Potomac in time for the first Battle of Bull Run.

THE FIRST CONTINGENT OF TROOPS had hardly reached the front before the families at home were confronted with one of the most serious Indian uprisings in the country's history.

Sioux problems had by no means been solved by the treaties. While various bands had moved to their reservations, it was not long before they showed an increasing tendency to roam, and so greatly did they annoy the settlers, that many wished to have them completely removed from the state.

Minnesota was still America's northwest frontier, and the territorial government sought to attract new settlers by every means possible. Advertisements were placed in European newspapers, a special exhibit was sponsored at the World's Fair in New York, and a commissioner of immigration was dispatched to New York to persuade settlers to move to Minnesota. In a single decade, the territory's population had increased twenty-fold, from fewer than 10,000 in 1850 to over 200,000 in 1861.[7]

The Indians, for their part, had many grievances: their leaders were alarmed by the weakening of tribal integrity and customs through contact with the white man's civilization; much resentment was felt against agency traders who charged them unfairly for supplies; often the government agents were charged with distributing food unfit for consumption. In the summer of 1862, the need for Civil War supplies superseded all other obligations, and neither money nor sufficient food was forthcoming for the Indians. Then there occurred the incident that fanned the long-smoldering bitterness into flames.[8]

By the outbreak of the Civil War in 1861, funding for promised annual rations to the tribes had been cut back substantially. At the same time, the government was building a network of forts on the Oregon and Santa Fe trails, as well as along southern routes from Kansas and Missouri to the Rio Grande. Everywhere the number of whites seemed to be multiplying. For years, supplies pledged to the tribe by treaty in exchange for prime hunting lands had been systematically diverted, then sold to their rightful recipients by local merchants at exorbitant prices. The training and equipment that would make them self-sufficient farmers never materialized. Complaints of illegal liquor sales and outrages against Indian women by whites were ignored by authorities. The fall harvest of 1861 had been blighted by an infestation of cutworms, and the bitterly cold winter that followed left the Santee impoverished, half-starved and desperate.[9]

Twenty Sioux left the Lower Sioux Agency on August, 10, 1862, to hunt deer in the Big Woods. The braves secured a wagon, which Chief Makpeyahwetah, one of their number, left with Captain Whitcomb as security for the purchase price of a sleigh.[10]

On August 13, 1862, the *St. Peter Tribune* published a brief article on "Indian Rumors." The article was printed because of Indian agitation over the failure of annuity payments at the Upper Sioux Agency. The newspaper was quick to note that most of the state's able-bodied men had gone to fight for the Union and suggested some troops should be stationed in the Minnesota Valley, just in case of a "sudden freak of the aborigines." The piece also suggested that women should be supplied with guns and that they had "spirit and courage enough to insure protection."[11]

But there was no serious anticipation of a Sioux outbreak by white settlers, and it is doubtful whether the Indians had laid any plans for an attack. The assault on white settlers was set off by an act of theft and another from a dare, and they came quickly and spontaneously.

About the time Little Crow was coming home from church, four Wahpeton Sioux braves, who had been with the hunting party—two dressed like Indians and two like white men—were returning from the hunt some forty miles northeast of their village of Rice Creek on the Lower Sioux. Brown Wing, Breaking Up, Killing Ghost, and Runs Against Something When Crawling—all in their twenties—were hunting Sunday morning, August 17, 1862.[12]

Near the tiny settlement of Acton Township in Meeker County, they stopped at the farmstead of Mr. and Mrs. Robinson Jones, who operated a combined general store and post office. The sudden appearance of the men did not frighten Jones as armed Indians were a common sight in frontier Minnesota. With Mr. Jones at the store were his two adopted children, Clara Wilson, fifteen, and her eighteen-month-old half-brother. Mrs. Jones was visiting her son by a previous marriage, Howard Baker and his wife and two children, who lived a scant half-mile away. Temporarily living in a covered wagon near the Baker home was a Wisconsin couple, Mr. and Mrs. Viranus Webster, who were seeking to purchase land in the area.

Next to Jones' split-rail fence was a hen's nest containing some eggs. One of the braves looked in the nest and scooped out the eggs. One of his companions cautioned him not to take the eggs because they belonged to a white man, and the act would get them all in trouble. The young man who had taken the eggs became angry and hurled the eggs to the ground. Looking his critic in the eye, he snapped: "You are a coward. You are afraid of the white man. You are afraid to take even an egg from him, though you are half starved. Yes, you are a coward, and I will tell everybody so."[13]

One of the eggs hurled to the ground had failed to break. The boy who had been addressed as a coward stomped on it with his foot, crushing it to pieces. "I am not a coward," he insisted. "I am not afraid of the white man. To show you that I am not, I will go to the house and shoot him. Are you brave enough to go with me?"

The young man who had initiated the dare said he would accompany him; he, too, wished to prove himself. All four walked to the Jones "public house," which also housed the post office, with Jones serving as postmaster. Jones exhibited a barrel of cheap whiskey, although he did not offer any of it to his Indian visitors who grew angry when they demanded a taste. One of the young men had allegedly borrowed a gun from Jones the previous winter and had not returned it, and Jones undoubtedly considered him untrustworthy.

A local newspaper, however, claimed Jones's wife was also in the store, which contradicts other accounts: "Mr. Jones soon discovered that their disposition was anything but friendly, and fearing for the safety of his family, he locked the door of his house, and with his wife, went to the house of Mr. Howard Baker, about a mile distant, and was followed by the Indians."[14]

When Jones left for the Baker house where his wife was visiting, he left his two young children to watch the store as the Indians milled about. The four Sioux men followed Jones and, at first, appeared to be friendly. They asked Baker for water and were given some. When they asked him for tobacco, he handed them some as well. They filled their pipes and sat down and smoked. They discussed with Jones the borrowed gun the Indian had used to shoot deer, but that young man denied it. Mrs. Baker asked Mrs. Jones if they had given the Indians any liquor, and she said they had not.[15]

As a token of their congeniality, the young hunters challenged the whites to a target shooting contest. Jones traded Mr. Baker's double-barreled shotgun for one of the Indian rifles and accepted the proposal. Webster owned a gun but did not go out with the party. One of the braves told Webster that the lock of his gun was defective and persuaded him to take the lock of his gun and loan it to him. After the Indians fired at a mark on a tree, they reloaded their rifles. Baker and Jones, however, did not.

One of the Sioux warriors began walking away in the direction of Forest City, his motive to ascertain whether there were any other whites nearby. He came back and spoke softly to his companions. Without warning, the Indians turned and shot Baker, Webster, and Mr. and Mrs. Jones to death. Jones had tried to run for the woods following the first volley but a second shot brought him down. Mrs. Webster remained inside her wagon and was not harmed, and Mrs. Baker took refuge in the cellar with her child. The Indians departed rather hastily, but soon returned and killed Clara Wilson, whom they saw watching them from a doorway. This was the point when Mrs. Baker, who was holding a child, ran into the cellar and hid.

After the Indians departed, Mrs. Barker came up from the cellar, and she and Mrs. Webster attempted to comfort the dying men by propping pillows under their heads. As Jones lay expiring, he kicked the earth with his heels and filled his mouth with dirt to keep from screaming. The woman watched their men die, fearful that the Sioux would return to slay them as well.[16]

A white man named Cox rode by the house on his horse, but when they called to him to halt, he laughed, waved, and continued on. The man believed the dying men were drunk and had fallen in a stupor and bloodied their noses. The man was a demented Irishman and presumed spy for the Sioux, who wandered aimlessly along the trails, unaware of the situation, which brought little hope to the hysterical women.

The women, with Mrs. Baker carrying an enfant who had survived the murders, dashed to the home of neighbor, John Blackwell, but they found no one at home. Continuing their flight, they made their way to the home of a Norwegian named Lars Olson, a blacksmith, a few miles away from the murder scene. Upon relating their terrible story to Olson, the farmer dispatched his twelve-year-old son on horseback to the town of Ripley, some twelve miles away. Few persons, however, believed the boy's ranting, and the few who did rationalized that the Indians had been drunk. No one was willing to ride to Acton, for they believed that, if the story was true, the Indians would be dealt with accordingly and swiftly by the town's citizens.[17]

Leaving the Blackwell place, Mrs. Baker and Mrs. Webster departed for Forest City (now Litchfield), some sixteen miles away from the massacre site. When they reached Forest City safely, they found that Ole Ingeman had arrived there about six o'clock and spread the alarm among the settlers.[18]

Daniel N. Danielson, who was nine years old and lived near the site at the time of the killings, later questioned the accuracy of the accepted accounts as to what transpired that fateful day:

> When Jones, accompanied by the Indians, reached the Baker home there was a trading of guns between the whites and the Indians previous to their shooting match. At the conclusion of this sport, the whites did not reload their guns, but the Indians recharged their firearms and without warning fired a bullet into the body of Howard Baker, who was seated beside his wife on a bench in the house. He arose from his seat and shouted, "Run!" which command they proceeded to obey. Mrs. Baker fell through a trap door into the cellar; Webster and Mrs. Ann Baker-Jones were the next victims and were shot in the doorway in their effort to escape. Jones had proceeded a short distance from the house and was killed near the corn crib. The Indians hurriedly left the premises and proceeded to the Jones cabin and killed Clara Davis Wilson. Mrs. Webster was seated in a covered wagon but for some unaccountable reason was not molested.[19]

In tracing the flight of Mrs. Webster and Mrs. Howard Baker and child to Forest City, Mr. Danielson contended that after leaving the blacksmith shop they hurried a half mile to Iver Jackson's home, and at that point, the alarm was given.

Dakota Indian George W. Crooks had a different assessment as to what transpired that fateful day:

At this time, four young Indian boys had gone hunting for some food to keep them from starving. They had gone some distance from the reservation. Having not much luck at hunting, the boys came to a farm house. They found some eggs, and being so hungry, one of the boys wanted to take the eggs. The other three, not wishing to be dishonest, appealed to the fourth to pay in some way for the eggs. The boy was becoming angry and told the others that he would show them how to deal with the white man, at the same time accusing his companions of being cowards.

Breaking the eggs with his foot, he drew his gun and shot down a cow that was grazing in the pasture. The farmer, seeing his property being destroyed, seized an axe and ran out to drive the intruders away. He was shot down by the crazed young Indian. His wife, running to the aid of her husband, was shot down in like manner.[20]

After murdering Clara Wilson, the Indians moved eastward toward Lake Elizabeth and stopped at the home of Peter Wicklund. While one of the braves held a gun on Wicklund, his wife, his daughter, and his son-in-law, A.M. Ecklund, the other three went out to the stable and took Ecklund's pair of horses. Riding two to a horse, they hurried toward their village at Rice Creek. They stole two more horses along the way and rode forty miles in about six hours, reaching the village about eight o'clock. According to a mixed-blood member of the village, they rode in shouting, "Get your guns! There is a war with the whites and we have commenced it!"[21]

Word of the Acton Massacre spread through the area the day after its occurrence, and families rallied to get what they needed and head eastward down the Crow River, to Manannah, then Forest City, which at this time was the county seat for Meeker County. The women and children were encouraged to go further eastward, to Monticello, or back to their families in states and provinces to the east.

Finally a messenger was sent to Forest City with the news of the killings, and Captain Whitcomb and twelve or fifteen horsemen rode to Acton, reaching the settlement at dusk. They placed a wagon box over Jones and left the bodies until an inquest was held the following morning. During the inquest, eleven Indians on horseback, who knew nothing of what had transpired, appeared, and several settlers jumped on their horses and gave chase. When the Indians crossed a slough, the whites checked their horses at the edge. One brave fellow from Forest City, however, pursued them alone and fired at them. One of the Sioux dismounted, returned the fire, and fled with his companions.[22]

John Blackwell came home in the afternoon on horseback and learned from Ole H. Ness, whom he met on the prairie, the tragic news about Acton. Blackwell had trouble believing the wild story, but Ness advised him to go to the Olson house where the women were and get the story first-hand from them.[23]

Blackwell immediately decided to search for the niece and child and rode back to where he had left Ness, whom he found with Henry Hulverson, A. Nelson Fosen, and several others who had gathered to discuss the situation. The men agreed to go together to the scene of the murders and look for the girl and the child.

They arrived at the Jones house after dark and found the eighteen-month-old grandson of Mary Anne Baker sitting on the floor and smiling at them. Blackwell brought the infant, who had been christened Robinson J. Cotton, with him to Forest City where he was cared for by T.C. Jewett and later adopted by Mr. and Mrs. Charles H. Ellis of Otsego, Wright County. The child, totally unaware of its tragic surroundings, had evidently been lying on the floor and had cried himself to sleep.[24]

On the morning of August 18, a party of men left Forest City and journeyed to Acton. The party was led by A.C. Smith, J.B. Atkinson, and Milton Gorton and included Mrs. Gorton and Mrs. Jewett. The party increased its numbers along the way, and, by the time it reached Acton, sixty persons constituted the rescuers.[25]

The next day, August 18, Judge Abner C. Smith of Meeker County held an inquest. Then, the five victims, who had not been mutilated, were buried in a single grave in Ness Norwegian Lutheran Cemetery, a few miles southwest of present-day Litchfield. Seventy-five persons attended the inquest as the entire community was terror-stricken, in fear of an all-out attack, which they felt was imminent. It was agreed that Jones had given the Dakota braves no liquor, and, during the inquest, all the liquor in the house was poured on the ground. A.C. Smith, judge of Probate and acting county attorney called upon Mrs. Howard Baker to give testimony.

About eleven o'clock a.m. four Indians came to our house [related Mrs. Baker], stayed about fifteen minutes, got up and looked out, had the men take down their guns and shoot them off at a mark, then bantered for a trade with Jones. About twelve o'clock two more Indians came and got some water; our guns were not reloaded; the Indians loaded their guns in the dooryard. I went back into the house, did not suspect anything at the time; supposed they were going away. Next I knew I heard the report of a gun and saw Webster fall; he stood and fell near the door; another Indian came to the door and aimed at Howard Baker and shot; did not kill him at that time; he shot the other barrel of gun at Howard and he fell.

My mother walked to the door and another Indian shot her; she turned to run and fell into the buttery; they shot at her twice as she fell. I tried to get out of the window, but fell down [the] cellar; saw Mrs. Webster pulling her husband into the house, don't know where she was prior to this; Indians immediately left the house; while I was in the cellar I heard firing out of doors.

Jones said they were Sioux Indians and that he was well acquainted with them. Two of the Indians had on white men's coats; one quite tall, one quite small, one thick and chubby and all middle-aged Indians, one had two feathers in his cap and one had three. Jones said, "They asked me for whisky but I would not give them any."[26]

Jones had run a frontier public house of sorts and was well acquainted with the Indians. He traded for their furs, and by some means the Dakota men had gotten into his debt for forty or fifty dollars, and he had made arrangements to be paid out of their annuities. Jones's traffic with the Dakota had been interfering with the successes of other traders, and had set a bad precedent. The Indians were dissatisfied with all the traders, Jones along with the rest.

The settlers discussed the week's "Indian sightings," which added fuel to their hysteria. Malpeyahwetak and his companions had been at Captain Whitcomb's house on Saturday and Sunday and had demanded the use of his wagon without paying the amount promised. The angry Sioux had threatened to chop his wagon to pieces and a couple of them held axes over his head. Thirteen braves had stopped at a house near Acton on Sunday and cleaned their guns and sharpened their knives; and fourteen of Little Crow's band had been seen in the adjacent county. Messengers were sent to St. Paul for aid.

The four Sioux hunters continued south until they reached the Eckland farmhouse, where a man, his daughter, and son-in-law were eating their dinner. The Indians crept up close to the house, stole two horses that were already harnessed, hitched them quietly to a wagon, and rode quickly away to their village on the reservation. They reached their village at Rice Creek just before dark and went directly to their chief, Red Middle Voice, and informed him and the other warriors what they had done.

The chief was mesmerized by how easily the whites had been slain, and he asked several questions as to how each of the men had been shot. Red Middle Voice, despite his fascination and excitement, cautioned the tribe that the whites would come, and their whole band would be in trouble. Not only had they killed men, but at least one woman. The soldiers would come after the killers, and the band's annuities would be withheld until the four young hunters were punished. If they did not turn over the killers, other tribes would seek to capture them and turn them over to the whites.

Chief Big Eagle later related:

> They told me they did not go out to kill white people. They said they went over into the Big Woods to hunt. That on Sunday, August 17th, they came to a settler's fence, and here they found a hen's nest, with some eggs in it. One of them took the eggs, when another said, "Don't take them, for they belong to a white man, and we may get into trouble." The other was angry, for he was very hungry, and wanted to eat the eggs, and he dashed them to the ground and replied: "You are a coward. You are afraid of the white man. You are afraid to take even an egg from him, though you are half starved. Yes, you are a coward, and I will tell everybody so." The other replied: "I am not a coward. I am not afraid of the white man, and to show you that I am not I will go to the house and shoot him. Are you brave enough to go with me?" The one who had called him a coward said: "Yes, I will go with you, and we will see who is the braver of us two." Their two companions then said: "We will go with you and we will be brave too." They all went to the house of the white man [Robinson Jones], but he got alarmed and went to another house [Howard Baker's], where were some other white men and women. The four Indians followed them and killed four men and two women. Then they hitched up a team belonging to another settler . . .[27]

Red Middle Voice had always been a militant. He reasoned that if he and his tribe were going to be punished anyway, they perhaps should go to war and drive the whites away once and for all. Of course, his band was not strong enough to attack the white settlements alone, so he led eight of his warriors downstream to Shakopee's village. But the news had preceded them, and when they reached Shakopee's village, they were greeted with chants and cheers from a people eager to go to war.

"The tale told by the young men created the greatest excitement," recalled Big Eagle. "Everybody was waked up and heard it."[28]

Shakopee told Red Middle Voice their two bands could not overthrow the whites, but they could perhaps do so by uniting all the Sioux bands in an all-out war. Shakopee suggested they needed a powerful chief to lead them, and they decided to visit Little Crow, who sat up in bed and listened to them. Big Eagle believed the war would reunite all the Mdewakantons and drive the whites from their lands. These Sioux had not been to Washington, and they believed the white man's army on the prairie included all the government's soldiers. They firmly believed a war could not be lost by the Dakota people since whites were so easy to kill.[29]

Little Crow, however, did not want to go to war against the whites. His father and grandfather had taught him to follow a policy of conciliation and compromise over confrontation. He had accepted many of the customs of the whites, and he advised his people to negotiate treaties with the government. He recognized, of course, the power of the federal government; he had visited Washington twice and was in awe of the splendor the white man's world offered. He told them that the Indians could not stop the white's westward expansion, that they would one day overrun all the Indian lands. He believed his people had no alternative but to work with the government and attempt to get the best possible terms for his people.[30]

He warned his followers: "We are only little herds of buffaloes left scattered; the great herds that once covered the prairies are no more. See! The white men are like locusts when they fly so thick that the whole sky is a snowstorm. You may kill one—two—ten; yes, as many as the leaves in the forest yonder, and their brothers will not miss them. Kill one—two—ten, and ten times ten will come to kill you. Count your fingers all day long and white men with guns in their hands will come faster than you can count. . . . Braves, you are little children—you are fools! You will die like the rabbits when the hungry wolves hunt them in the hard moon [January]. Ta-o-ya-te-du-ta is not a coward; he will die with you."[31]

George W. Crooks later recalled:

> The boys, returning home immediately, reported their crime to Chief Little Crow, who in turn tried to persuade the Indian people to turn the boys over to the soldiers at Fort Ridgely to receive their punishment. However, the seething anger that had been flaming in the hearts of the Indians who had been treated so cruelly by the whites burst into flame now.
>
> They refused to turn the boys over to the white men. They proceeded to get together and plan their revenge on the white people of the post. A few of them decided to go over to the post and kill the white people there.[32]

Although he was against a confrontation with the whites, Little Crow had no choice but to lead his people, since a war was already declared. The entire Sioux Nation of about 7,000 united in the uprising and 1,500 braves took the warpath. Said Big Eagle:

> Blood had been shed, the payment would be stopped, and the whites would take a dreadful vengeance because women had been killed. Wabasha, Wacouta, myself and others talked for peace, but nobody would listen to us, and soon the cry was, "Kill the whites, and kill all these cut-hairs who will not join us." A council was held, and war was declared. Parties formed, and dashed away in the darkness to kill settlers. The women began to run bullets and the men to clean their guns. Little Crow gave orders to attack

Big Eagle. (Author's collection)

177

the agency early the next morning, and to kill all the traders. When the Indians first came to him for counsel and advice he said to them tauntingly: "Why do you come to me for advice? Go to the man you elected speaker (Traveling Hail), and let him tell you what to do," but he soon came around all right, and somehow took the lead in everything, though he was not head chief, as I have said.

At this time my village was up on Crow Creek, near Little Crow's. I did not have a very large band, not more than thirty or forty fighting men. Most of them were not for the war at first, but nearly all got into it at last. A great many members of the other bands were like my men; they took no part in the first movements, but afterwards did.[33]

When the Sioux went on the warpath, a disgusted Bishop Henry Whipple was in northern Minnesota, having left the agency after witnessing Galbraith's refusal to pay the starving Indians.

I left the Sioux country, sad at heart, to pay a visit to the Chippewa Mission, and went as far as Red Lake, [wrote Bishop Whipple]. There I found the Chippewa much disturbed, showing that a storm was brewing. On my arrival at Crow Wing, Mr. Peake brought a letter from the post-office for Hole-in-the-Day, marked "immediate." I saw that the address had been written by Mr. Hinman. Hole-in-the-Day had gone to Leech Lake, and we asked one of his soldiers to read the letter which said: "Your young men have killed one of my people—a farmer Indian. I have tried to keep my soldiers at home. They have gone for scalps. Look out. (Signed) LITTLE CROW."

As the Sioux and Chippewas were bitter enemies it was evident that Little Crow had made some treaty of peace with Hole-in-the-Day. I at once inquired if there were any Indians away, and finding that a family were [sic] camped on Gull River, twenty miles distant, I sent for them that night and they were saved. On my return journey, a day from Gull Lake, my Indians saw tracks and told me that they belonged to the Sioux. I laughed at them and said, "There isn't a Sioux within a hundred miles." But they refused to go on. They stooped to the ground, and wherever they found traces of a footprint they carefully examined the crushed grass to see if the juices which had exuded were dry or fresh. Suddenly we came to a place where there had been a camp, and one of them picked up a moccasin, which he brought to me, saying, "Is that a Chippewa moccasin?" "No," I said, "it is a Sioux moccasin." The moccasins of the tribes are all made differently. The rest of the journey was of unceasing vigilance.

On Saturday I left Crow Wing for St. Cloud and heard of a party of Sioux back of Little Falls. I spent Sunday in St. Cloud, and that day these Indians committed a murder at Acton in order to precipitate a massacre. They reached Little Crow village before daybreak; a council of soldiers was called, and, against the advice of Little Crow, who afterward became their leader, they began their fearful warfare.

According to Big Eagle:

You know how the war started—by the killing of some white people near Acton, in Meeker County. I will tell you how this was done, as it was told me by all of the four young men who did the killing. These young fellows all belonged to Shakopee's band. Their names were Sungigidan ("Brown Wing"), Ka-om-de-i-ye-ye-dan ("Breaking Up"), Nagi-we-cak-te ("Killing Ghost"), and Pa-zo-i-yo-pa ("Runs Against Something When Crawling"). I do not think their names have ever before been printed. One of them is yet living. They told me they did not go out to kill white people. They said they went over to the Big Woods to hunt: that on Sunday, August 17, they came to a settler's fence, and here they found a hen's nest with some eggs in it. One of them took the eggs, when another said: "Don't take them, for they belong to a white man and we may get into trouble." The other was angry, for he was very hungry and wanted to eat the eggs, and he dashed them to the ground and replied: "You are a coward. You are afraid of the white man. You are afraid to take even an egg from him, though you are half-starved. Yes, you are a coward, and I will tell everybody so." The other replied. "I am not a coward. I am not afraid of the white man, and to show you that I am not I will go to the house and shoot him. Are you brave enough to go with me?" The one who had called him a coward said: "Yes, I will go with you, and we will see who is the braver of us two." Their companions then said: "We will go with you, and we will be brave, too." They all went to the house of the white man (Mr. Robinson Jones), but he got alarmed and went to another house (that of his son-in-law, Howard Baker where were some other white men and women—Jones, Baker, a Mr. Webster, Mrs. Jones and a girl of fourteen).

The four went into the Baker house, killed the occupants, took a wagon and team of horses, and went back to their village where they told what they had done. The tale told by the young men created the greatest excitement. Everybody was waked up and heard it. Shakopee took the young men to Little Crow's house (two miles above the agency), and he sat up in bed and listened to their story. He said war was now declared. Blood had been shed, the payment would be stopped, and the whites would take a dreadful vengeance because women had been killed. Wabasha, Wacouta, myself and others still talked for peace, but nobody would listen to us, and soon the cry was "Kill the whites and kill all these cut-hairs who will not join us." A council was held and war was declared. Parties formed and dashed away in the darkness to kill settlers. The women began to run bullets and the men to clean their guns.

News of the rebellion spread quickly through the settler and Indian communities. For the Sioux, this was a catharsis of violence; for the settlers, a nightmare had come true. Most settlers in the Minnesota River Valley had no experience with warring Indians. Those who did not flee to a fort or defended settlement fast enough were at the Indians' mercy. The Sioux killed most of the settlers they encountered but often made captives of the women and children.[34]

The state of Minnesota wasted little time in putting together a raw, makeshift army. Loren Webb wrote in his diary:

> Tuesday, 19th: Pleasant till noon, then rainy. I went to the Fort [Snelling] again to day. While there news came of Indian outrages. Gen. Sibley was chosen to go, and I was requested to go as Adjutant General of the expedition against them. We got [four] companies ready to go and remained till morn.
>
> Wednesday, 20th: Cool and damp. This morning early, we took boat for the scene of outrages. We went up the Minnesota River to Shakopee, then stopped and distributed the arms and ammunition to the troops, and went into quarters for the night.
>
> Thursday, 21st: Rainy. We went up the river today as far as Belle Plaine. There camped for the night. All is excitement to day. Hundreds of people are leaving their homes and rushing towards places of safety.[35]

The pictorial papers containing the Civil War scenes, which the traders kept on their counters, deeply interested the Indians, who plied questions about the battles and their results. Up to this time, August, 1862, the Union troops had been defeated. Major Galbraith had enlisted a company of Renville Rangers, largely made up of mixed bloods, and many of the Indians supposed that the government had sent for them to fight because so many of the white men had been killed. They said, "Now we can avenge our wrongs and get back to our country."[36]

Notes

[1]Mark Diedrich, *Dakota Oratory, Great Moments in the Recorded Speech of the Eastern Sioux*, Rochester, Coyote Books, 1989, Back Cover.

[2]Francis Paul Prucha, "The Army Post on the Minnesota Frontier," University of Minnesota, 1947, pp. 148-149. Thesis. Minnesota Historical Society.

[3]"Minnesota: A State Guide," American Guide Series, Internet.
[4]Kenneth Carley, Minnesota in the Civil War, Minneapolis, Ross & Haines, Inc., 1961, pp. 15-16.
[5]James A. Wright, edited by Steven J. Keillor, No More Gallant a Deed: A Civil War memoir of the First Minnesota Volunteers, St. Paul, Minnesota Historical Society Press, 2001, pp. 12-14.
[6]Kenneth Maitland Davies, To the Last Man: The Chronicle of the 135th Infantry Regiment of Minnesota, St. Paul, Ramsey County Historical Society, 1982, p. 2.
[7]Richard Moe, The Last Full Measure: The Life and Death of the First Minnesota Volunteers, New York, Avon Books, 1994, p. 6.
[8]"Minnesota A State Guide," American Guide Series, Internet.
[9]Dustyn Medicine Wolf, "Lakota History," Internet.
[10]Daniel Buck, Indian Outbreaks, p. 84.
[11]St. Peter Tribune, August 13, 1862.
[12]Albert Marrin, War Clouds in the West Indians & Cavalrymen 1860-1890, New York, Anthneum, 1984, pp. 79-80; Duane Schultz, Over the Land I Come: The Great Sioux Uprising of 1862, pp. 30-31.
[13]C.M. Oehler, The Great Sioux Uprising, New York, Oxford University Press, 1959, p. 4; W.M. Wemett, The Story of the Flickertail State, p. 138.
[14]The Pioneer & Democrat (St. Paul), August 20, 1862.
[15]Daniel Buck, Indian Outbreaks, p. 86.
[16]Duane Schultz, Over the Land I Come: The Great Sioux Uprising of 1862, pp. 32-34.
[17]C.A. Smith, A Random Historical Sketch of Meeker County, Minnesota from Its First Settlement, to July 4, 1876, Litchfield, Belfoy & Joubert, 1877, pp. 23-24.
[18]Frank B. Lamson, Condensed History of Meeker County 1855-1939, Brown Printing Company, p. 16.
[19]Ibid., pp. 17-18.
[20]George W. Crooks reminiscence. Dakota Conflict of 1862, Manuscripts Collections, Microfilm Edition, Reel 1, Minnesota Historical Society.
[21]Franklyn Curtiss-Wedge, History of McLeod County, Minnesota, Chicago & Winona, H.C. Cooper Jr. & Company, 1917, p. 143.
[22]Daniel Buck, Indian Outbreaks, pp. 88-89.
[23]C.A. Smith, A Random Historical Sketch of Meeker County, p. 24.
[24]Frank B. Lamson, Condensed History of Meeker County 1855-1939, Brown Printing Company, p. 17.
[25]C.A. Smith, A Random Historical Sketch of Meeker County, p. 24.
[26]Ibid., p. 25.
[27]Daniel Buck, Indian Outbreaks, p. 90.
[28]Ibid.
[29]Gary Clayton Anderson, Little Crow Spokesman for the Sioux, p. 131.
[30]Duane Schultz, Over the Land I Come: The Great Sioux Uprising of 1862, pp. 33-34.
[31]Gene Estensen, "War Comes to Norwegian Grove," Internet.
[32]George W. Crooks reminiscence. Dakota Conflict of 1862, Manuscripts Collections, Microfilm Edition, Reel 1, Minnesota Historical Society.
[33]Daniel Buck, Indian Outbreaks, pp. 90-91.

[34]Dr. William Glenn Robertson, Dr. Jerold E. Brown, Major William M. Campsey, Major Scott R. McMeen, *Atlas of the Sioux Wars*, Combat Studies Institute, U.S. Army Command and General Staff College, Fort Leavenworth, Kansas.

[35]Webb, Loren. *Diary of Captain Loren Webb, 1861-1863*, Firelands Historical Society. Norwalk, Ohio. 1995. Transcribed by Matthew L. Burr.

[36]Bishop Henry B. Whipple, *Light and Shadows of a Long Episcopate (1902) Being Reminiscences and Recollections of the Right Reverend Henry B. Whipple, Bishop of Minnesota.*

Chapter Five

August 18, 1862
Lower Sioux Agency

"Intelligence from Lower Sioux Agency, to the effect that Sioux had murdered several persons there, also...at Acton in Meeker County, several were killed. Drove up to Fort Snelling and appointed General Sibley commander of a force. . . ."
—Governor Alexander Ramsey[1]

"The white man is coming into this country, and your children may learn to read. But promise me that you will never leave the religion of your ancestors."
—Father of Artemas Ehnamane[2]

HE LOWER SIOUX AGENCY was located on the high bank of the Minnesota River about two miles below the present day town of Morton. The buildings at the agency were located around an open field called "Council Square." The traders were situated by the river—the Robert's post being the farthest away at a half-mile. A road from the ferry crossed the river bottoms and merged with the roads leading to Fort Ridgely, while another artery crossed the agency grounds and followed the river to New Ulm. One mile below this road were the villages of Wapa-sha (Red Leaf), Wa-kuta (Leaf Shooter), and Hu-sha-sha (Red Legs).[3]

No one understood better than Episcopal Bishop Whipple in 1862, the fallacy of the American treaty system with the Sioux. Disastrous

183

Lower Sioux Agency. (Photo courtesy of Diana Pierce)

consequences could not be averted because of the greedy white man and his dream of frontier expansion. The pauperizing effects of annuities, the political appointments of Indian agents, the establishment of reservations, and the slaughter of game on the Sioux hunting grounds, all contributed to the uprising that would terrorize Minnesota.

Bishop Whipple had been sending reports of the Sioux depredations for two years to Presidents James Buchanan and Abraham Lincoln. He warned there would be hell to pay unless there was reform in the treaty system, honest Indian agents appointed, and controls placed on the liquor situation. He denounced the Bureau of Indian Affairs and exclaimed to Lincoln that, "as sure as there is a God, much of the guilt lies at the nation's door."

The Sioux were restricted to land on both sides of the Minnesota River by the 1851 treaties, but they became angry over an 1853 pact placing them on a tiny tract along the south side of the river. Lincoln did not grant them permanency of occupation, and while Congress allocated nearly a hundred thousand dollars to the Lower Sioux and nearly twice that to the Upper, nearly the entire amount went to area traders.

The traders, with a nucleus consisting of Nathan and Andrew Myrick, Louis Robert, William H. Forbes, and Stuart B. Garvie, used the treaties for an opportunity to collect payment for Indian debts. Nearly all the traders had lived with the Sioux for only a year or two, surely not long enough to justify claims for enormous sums of money. These traders operated wholly on credit, providing goods and food for the Indians, and carrying the debts on their books until the annuity distribution arrived.

Acting Indian Commissioner Charles Mix met with Little Crow, (Tshe-ton Wa-ka-wa Ma-ni or The Hawk That Hunts Walking) and his chiefs in the spring, and the great chief related to Mix that the Mdewakantons and Wahpekutes had not received their annuities, tribal lands had been reduced by ninety percent, and the Sioux had lost their hunting privileges and were dependent on supplementary food. The threat of starvation was real.

"It takes plenty to enable a person to act like a man and not like a poor beggar," related Little Crow via an interpreter. "We went in pursuit of Inkpaduta (an outlaw chief) and neglected our cornfields. The government has also neglected to do its plowing."

"The Mdewakantons funds are safely kept in a strongbox of the National Treasury and will be sent when they can be applied properly to your tribe's benefits," stated Mix assuredly. "There is a time allotted for the food to be distributed. We must put this issue behind us and talk white man's talk. Our treaties are not being honored by either the white man or the Sioux. We must make more strong talk and strengthen our treaties with more agreement."

"There can be no more talk of treaty," answered the Sioux chief. "The Great Father has promised to deliver great amounts of money to my people and has failed in his promise. By the Treaty of 1854, we were promised $20,035 and it has never been paid. You started the money out from your house for I heard of that with my own ears, but, as I said before, it never reached us. If I were to give you an account of all the money that was spilled, it would take all night."

"The Great Father never gave you a paper to prove the government had promised you a reservation boundary line as far as the Big Cottonwood River," Mix insisted, badgering the chief on the boundary issue. "Do you recollect the provisions of the 1851 treaty?" Mix handed the chief a copy of the original treaty.

"I do not know how to read or write, and supposing the men sent by our Great Father to treat with us were honest, I signed the treaty."

"I do not wish to frighten or unnecessarily alarm you, but you and your people are now living on the land you occupy by the courtesy of the Great Father."

"You talk well and use fine language; but that's all. This is the way you do. But we never receive half what is promised or which we have to get. You then promised us that we should have this same land forever; and yet now, you want to take half of it away. It appears you are getting papers all around me, so after a while, I will have nothing left."

Newly appointed Indian agent, Thomas L. Galbraith, was unfamiliar with the problems of the Sioux. By June, both the upper and lower bands of Sioux were patiently awaiting annuity payments, which consisted of provisions and money, and many of the Indians were near starvation.

Mix, along with the traders, met again with Little Crow in June.

"You [Mix] gave me a paper and we had it explained, and from that, it would seem the Sioux Indians owe nothing. When I saw that paper it made me ashamed. We had, we supposed, made a complete treaty, and we were promised a great many things—horses, cattle, flour, plows, and farming utensils, but it now appears that the wind blows it all off. I want to do what is right."

"And you heathens owe us traders your lives and more," bellowed an angry Andrew Myrick. "Your annuities belong to me, to the other men in this room. You will walk with the dead before you get another cent from me."

"The dead walk because they are hungry for the souls of those that killed them. Beware, Myrick, not only of the dead, but of the living as well. We will wait once more but not many moons."

The aid from Washington did not come, and in July, five thousand hungry Sioux converged on the Yellow Medicine Agency. Galbraith did have the goods stored in the agency warehouse, but he said he would withhold the distribution until the annuity money was received from Washington. The angry Sioux broke into the warehouse and carted off more than a hundred sacks of flour before government troops stopped them. The Indians again watched and waited.

Little Crow arrived at the Lower Sioux Agency and met with Galbraith, Myrick and his fellow storekeepers, and a young missionary, John P. Wilson. A frightened Galbraith stared into the faces of the traders and said, "Well, boys, it is up to you now. What will you do?" The traders all looked to Myrick. Disgusted, he rose and walked out.

Galbraith also held back supplies at the Lower Sioux Agency, and the traders refused to extend credit. In mid-August, Chief Little Crow asked for food to feed his tribe and was refused. Galbraith was adamant over not releasing the goods until the annuities were received. Little Crow could not understand why, when their food supplies were in the warehouse, his people should have to go hungry.

Little Crow threatened Galbraith saying, "When men are hungry they help themselves."

Andrew Myrick, present at the confrontation, replied, "So far as I am concerned, if they are hungry, let them eat grass or their own dung."

The next day, signs appeared in all the stores reading, "No Credit for Indians."

The failed annuity payments were dispatched to Fort Ridgely too late and did not reach St. Paul until August 16. Some whites had been murdered in Acton the day before, and on the very day the payment arrived, the Sioux went on the warpath.

On the morning of August 18, 1862, the roads leading down to the Lower Agency were full of armed Sioux warriors, hideous with paint and feathers, and eager to begin the carnage. Within minutes, the startled inhabitants of the Lower Sioux Agency were aroused by a sudden barrage of gunfire. Although shocked, each and every person knew the meaning.

Wilhelmina Grose and her brother Michael had gone to the Redwood Agency that morning to trade butter and eggs for groceries. Upon hearing a gunshot, they asked a half-breed at the government store what was transpiring. The man, attempting to stay calm, conveyed that the Indians were only shooting the government's cattle because they were hungry, but the pair noticed that he was greatly excited. Wilhelmina and Michael immediately set off on an anxious two-mile ride home, continually plodding along the oxen and planning how they were to gather the four families to flee with them thirteen miles to Fort Ridgely.[4]

"When the inhabitants of the post saw the Indians coming, they tried to protect themselves, but they were outnumbered by the Indians," remembered George W. Crooks.[5]

Chief Big Eagle later recalled: "The next morning the force started down to attack the agency. I went along. I did not lead my band, and I took no part in the killing. I went to save the lives of two particular friends if I could. I think others went for the same reason, for nearly every Indian had a friend that he did not want killed; of course, he did not care about anybody else's friend."[6]

Reaching the agency about sunrise they began killing, plundering, and burning the government warehouse, private stores, and houses, and stealing the horses from the barns. So sudden and wholly unexpected was the attack that no resistance could be made, and in a few minutes about twenty persons were murdered.

James W. Lynd, who had lived on the reservation as a trader for five years and in 1861 had represented Brown County as a senator in the state legislature, was shot by a warrior named Plenty of Hail while standing in the doorway of Nathan Myrick's store. The rifle fire was the signal for the general onslaught, and almost simultaneously, attacks were launched on all four traders' stores along the Lac Qui Parle highway west of the agency. At the store of Captain Louis Robert, the most westerly of the four, Patrick McClellen, Antoine Young, and Joseph Belland were murdered.[7]

At Myrick's store, in addition to Lynd, George W. Divoll, the clerk, was killed, as was "Old Fritz," the cook. As the Sioux continued the slaughter, one particular angry warrior bellowed, "Now I will kill the dog who wouldn't give me credit." Another sought Myrick to avenge his sister. Myrick had fathered three children with the man's sister and then left her for a younger, more attractive woman.

Startled by the snarling warriors, Myrick tried to hide under a packing case upstairs of his store. When he heard one Indian scream he was setting the building on fire, Myrick jumped up, ran to a window, and slid down a lightning rod to a lean-to shed. He raced toward a clump of willows but was killed by a bullet before he reached his destination. Crazed warriors shot several arrows into Myrick and drove a scythe into his ribs.

Myrick was one of the first white men killed in the bloodbath, and when his brother Nathan found his body two weeks later, he found the Indians had stuffed his mouth with a tuft of green grass, caked with blood. "Myrick," the avenged red men boasted around their campfire, "is eating grass himself."

At the La Bathe store, which was nearest the agency, the Indians killed proprietor Francois La Bathe.

The superintendent of Indian Affairs at the agency, August H. Wagner, witnessed the Sioux entering the stables and taking the horses. Wagner and two of his assistants—John Lamb and Lathrop Dickinson—rushed outside to prevent the thievery and were immediately shot down. Wagner, from New Ulm, had earlier held the position of Brown County's first auditor.[8]

St. Peter resident, James Powell, who spent much of his time at the agency herding cattle for Wright, Clark & Dunning, government contractors, had just turned his cattle out of the yard and mounted his mule when the attack commenced. Seeing Lamb and Wagner shot down near him, he turned to flee when Lamb called to him for help. As he paused, two shots were fired at him, and he immediately spurred his mule and rode towards the bluff and down the hill to the ferry, reaching it just as the boat was leaving from shore. After safely crossing the river, Powell left the party of refugees fleeing to Fort Ridgely and rode boldly across the prairie to St. Peter without encountering a single Indian.

A few persons escaped by swimming the Minnesota River to Fort Ridgely, some twelve miles from the agency. But with more and more Sioux flooding the agency and surrounding area, escape for most was next to impossible.

George H. Spencer, a clerk in the William H. Forbes store, heard shots being fired outside and with several others ran to see what the excitement was all about. Spencer had learned to speak the Dakota tongue and had formed friendships with several members of the tribe. Many Dakotas had sought his advice and offered him their daughters for wives, which he rejected with a firmness they respected, but he also was aware that there were some in the tribe who were capable of doing him evil. Spencer was planning a trip to St. Paul to visit friends, where he was a member of the First Baptist Church, and had stopped off at the agency to spend the Sabbath. He was sure there was some mistake in what he saw transpiring until the Indians turned on his party.[9]

The Indians opened fire on them, killing four persons and severely wounding Spencer, who hid in the building. He later recalled:

When I reached the foot of the stairs I turned and beheld the store filling with Indians. One had followed me nearly to the stairs, when he took deliberate aim at my body, but providentially both barrels of his gun missed fire, and I succeeded in getting above without further injury. Not expecting to live a great while, I threw myself upon a bed, and while lying there could hear them opening cases of goods and carrying them out, and threatening to burn the building. I did not relish the idea of being burned to death very well, so I arose very quietly, and, taking a bedcord, I made fast one end to the bedpost, and carried the other to a window, which I raised. I intended in case they fired the building, to let myself down from the window, rather than to remain where I was and burn. The man who went upstairs with me, seeing a good opportunity to escape, rushed down through the crowd and rushed for life; he was fired upon, and two charges of buckshot struck him, but he succeeded in making his escape. I had been upstairs probably an hour when I heard the voice of an Indian inquiring for me. Upon being told that I was upstairs, he rushed up, followed by ten or a dozen others, and, approaching my bed, asked if I was mortally wounded. I told him I did not know, but that I was badly hurt. They then asked me where the guns were. I pointed to them, when my comrade assisted me in getting downstairs.
    The name of this Indian is Wakinyatawa, or, in English, "His Thunder." He was, up to the time of the outbreak, the head soldier of Little Crow, and some four or five years ago went to Washington with that chief to see their Great Father. He is a fine looking Indian, and has always been noted for his bravery in fighting the Chippewas. When we reached the foot of the stairs, some of the Indians cried out "Kill him! Spare no Americans! Show mercy to none!" My friend, who was unarmed, seized a hatchet that was lying nearby, and declared that he would cut down the first one that should attempt to do me any further

harm. Said he, "If you had killed him before I saw him it would have been all right; but we have been friends and comrades for ten years, and now that I have seen him, I will protect him or die with him." Then they made way for us, and we passed out. He procured a wagon, and gave me over to a couple of squaws to take me to his lodge. On the way we were stopped two or three times by armed Indians on horseback, who inquired of the squaws "What that meant?" Upon being answered that "This is Wakinyatawa's friend, and he has saved his life," they suffered us to pass on. His lodge was about four miles above the agency, at Little Crow's village. My friend soon came home, and washed me, and dressed my wounds with roots. Some few white men succeeded in making their escape to the fort. There were no other white men taken prisoners.[10]

According to William Bourat, who was a clerk in Forbes' store, about twenty-five to thirty Sioux assembled in front of the store. Four persons were in the store—George Spencer, George Thomas, the barber William Taylor, and himself. The Indians fired into the store, wounding Spencer in the arm and sides. The other three men rushed upstairs as the Indians took possession of the store. Bourat overheard one of them say, "Let us go up and kill them, and get them out of the way." Bourat decided to make a dash for his life, rushed down the stairs, slipped in and out of a shed at the rear of the building, and made about 200 yards when he was hit in the groin by buck shot. While lying on the ground, he was hit again, this time in the left leg. Believing him dead, the Indians threw a log across his body and left him lying where he fell. When they had gone, Bourat freed himself from the log and managed to escape from the agency to St. Cloud.[11]

"The killing was nearly all done when I got there," said Big Eagle. "Little Crow was on the ground directing operations."[12] He did, however, take credit for saving the life of Spencer:

"So many Indians have lied about their saving the lives of people that I dislike to speak of what I did, but I did save the life of George H. Spencer at the time of the massacre. I know that his friend Chaska has always had the credit of it, but Spencer would have been a dead man in spite of Chaska, if it had not been for me. I asked Spencer once about it, but he said he was wounded at the time, and so excited that he could not remember what he did."[13]

Chief Big Eagle said of Myrick: "I saw all the dead bodies at the agency. Andrew Myrick, a trader, with an Indian wife, had refused some hungry Indians credit a short time before when they asked him for some provisions. He said to them: 'Go and eat grass.' Now he was lying on the ground dead with his mouth stuffed full of grass, and the Indians were saying tauntingly: 'Myrick is eating grass himself.'"[14]

"When I returned to my village that day I found that many of my band had changed their minds about the war, and wanted to go into it," Big Eagle later related. "All the other villages were the same way. I was still of the belief that it was not best, but I thought I must go with my band and my nation, and I said to my men that I would lead them into the war, and we would all act like brave Dakotas and do the best we could. All my men were with me; none had gone off on raids, but we did not have guns for all at first."[15]

David Carruthers, an eye witness to the agency raid, stated in an interview:

> I do hereby certify on honor, that when I left Red Wood, on Monday morning at eight o'clock, the Indians were making war upon the whites at or near that place, and before I left had killed J. Widge; S.R. Henderson was wounded; Old man Earle, to the best of my belief was killed. They were still firing at him when I got out of hearing. His wife and children were captured. The wife and children of James Carruthers and the wife and children of David Carruthers were captured, and also the wife and children of S.R. Henderson.
> The settlers, who were my neighbors, had hitched up their teams to leave, but were surrounded by a body of Indians who were always considered the best and most civil Indians in the country. After compromising with them and giving them all we had, teams and all, we started and had got but a little way off, when they fired into us, and we returned the fire, and after a contest of near two hours, my comrades being killed, I made my way to Hutchinson, in Meeker County, a distance of forty-five miles, running nearly all the way, leaving my wife and family on the prairie, to the hands of the Indians.
> My place of residence was about four miles from the lower Sioux Agency. As I ran over the prairie, the Indians followed me nearly all day. One of my neighbors came direct from the Agency, and told me just before I started that the Indians had murdered nearly all the whites of that place. His name is Wrightman.[16]

Bishop Whipple later wrote:

The morning of this day of blood, Mr. Hinman was sitting on the steps of the Mission House at the Lower Agency, talking with a man who was building our church, when suddenly a rapid firing was heard at the trading-post a quarter of a mile away. Sun-ka-ska (White Dog) appeared on a run, and when asked what the firing meant, answered: "The Indians have bad hearts and are killing the whites. I am going to Wabasha to stop it." In a few minutes, running at full speed, Little Crow appeared, and the same question was asked him; but he made no answer and ran on to the government barn, where Mr. Wagner was trying to prevent the Indians from taking the horses. Little Crow cried, "Kill him!" and he was instantly shot.

Mr. Hinman hastened to Mr. [Philander] Prescott, the interpreter, who lived near by, to notify him of the outbreak. Mrs. Hinman was absent from the mission, but Miss West, the missionary, was advised to leave and cross the river, which she did, meeting on the way to the ferry a white woman and child whom he took under her protection. As they reached the bluff, after crossing the river, they met a party of Indians in war-paint and feather, who greeted them pleasantly with "He! Ho! Ho! You belong to the missionary. Washte! (Good!) Where are you going?" Miss West pointed to a house in the distance, and they said, "No, we are going to kill them," and motioned her to take the road leading to Fort Ripley. They threatened to kill the other woman, but to Miss West's statement that she had promised to take care of her they answered, "Ho! Ho!" and parted.[17]

Philander Prescott had come to Minnesota as an Indian trader in 1819, and as was the custom, he shortly after bought an Indian wife. He later became disgusted with his finances, deserted his family and went to Texas. While there, he went to a camp meeting and was converted. His first act of penitence was to return to his family, and he became one of the organizers of the Minnesota Agricultural Society. Later he became the interpreter at the Lower Sioux Agency.[18]

When Little Crow and the Sioux attacked the agency and began killing the traders, Prescott was ordered by the Indians to stay inside his house. While inside the house, he asked questions of everyone running by in an attempt to find out what was going on. Prescott knew that since his wife was an Indian woman, no serious harm would come to them if they remained

Little Crow. (Author's collection)

in the house. But after witnessing Little Crow bent on destruction, he became aware that all whites would be killed.

Realizing the seriousness of the situation, Prescott crept out his back door, moved unseen through the gardens, and reached the ferry. There he was seen by an Indian and fired upon, but the shot missed him and he successfully crossed the river. Farther on, he met a party of Indians who related to him that, "all white people must be killed," and shot him down.

According to captives whose stories came from the Indians, the warriors who had long been Prescott's friends listened to his plea for them to spare his life and did not kill him instantly. Prescott allegedly said: "I am an old man. I have lived with you now for forty-five years, almost half a century; my wife and children are among you, and are of your own blood; I have never done you any harm, and have ever been your friend in all your troubles; why should you wish to kill me now?" One of the Indians replied: "We would save your life if we could, but the white man must die. Our orders are to kill all white men, and you are a white man. We cannot save you." Seeing that all remonstrance was vain and hopeless, the old man said no more and was killed.[19]

The rest of the inhabitants taking advantage of the short respite the Indians spent in pillaging fled hurriedly toward Ft. Ridgely, thirteen miles distant. In order to reach the fort, the fugitives had to cross the Minnesota River. Their best hope was to do so by ferry boat.

Forty-one of them reached the fort in safety, but many were killed along the way. Among them were Dr. Philander Humphrey, the government physician of the Lower Agency, and his family, consisting of his wife and three children—a little girl and two boys, the oldest only twelve years old. Only one year earlier, Dr. Humphrey had replaced Dr. Daniels as the agency physician. The Humphreys left the agency during the slaughter at a very early hour. Upon reaching the ferry, they found the ferryman gone and the western flat-bottomed boat on the opposite shore.[20]

Mrs. Humphrey was sick and weak from a recent illness and after traveling three or four miles, she became so exhausted that they had to stop at the abandoned house of Edward Magner to rest. After arranging for their comfort, the doctor sent the oldest boy to a spring at the foot of the bluff close by after some water to drink. Dr. Humphrey meanwhile stationed himself at the front door with only an axe in his hand. As the boy was returning, he heard the report of the gun that killed his father, and hiding, watched the Indians chop off his father's head with an axe, set fire to the house, and burn his sick mother and little brother and sister in it.[21]

Sickened by what he had witnessed, the twelve-year-old boy returned to the ravine beneath the bluff where he had procured the water. After concealing himself in the brush for an hour or more, he started out through the timber along the highway towards Fort Ridgely. Traveling several miles, he finally reached the open road when he saw approaching him, Captain Marsh's company of soldiers on their way to quell the disturbances at the agency. He was given permission to accompany the expedition, and when they reached the Magner cabin, he saw the body of his father lying near the doorway. Behind him, the cabin was a mass of smoking ruins. His mother, brother, and sister had been burned alive.

Continuing with the company to the Redwood Ferry, he witnessed the death of Interpreter Quinn and the slaughter of half of Marsh's soldiers. He managed to escape through the thicket along the river with the survivors and reached the fort late that night.

Alexander Hunter, who had been crippled from frozen feet a few years earlier, fled with his young, mixed-blood wife, Marian Robertson, on the New Ulm Road. Since coming to the agency, young Hunter had resided with the family of his close personal friend, John Nairn, the government carpenter. Nairn's house was located at the east end of the agency, and when, early in the morning of the 18th he received news of unusual disturbances from Reverend Hinman, he readied his wife and four children for flight.

They set out on foot along the old Lac Qui Parle Trail towards Fort Ridgely with the Hunters. Nairn was aware that the first six or seven miles of the trail passed through the Indian villages of Wacouta, Wabasha, and Hushasha or Red Legs, but they had always been friends of the whites and he expected no trouble from them. A party of Indians dressed and armed as if for battle, met them on the road but did them no harm. The Indians suggested they keep to the timber, avoid the prairie and roads, and continue at all possible speed to the fort.

> Our escape from the agency was very Providential, [explained John Nairn years later]. Cut off from the river at the only place we could cross, our only course was to take a course and strike it twelve miles below, which we did. Our first intention was to try to get to New Ulm some thirty miles distant, being the nearest point of safety on the side of the river on which we were on, but Providence ordered it otherwise. When we were about eight miles from the agency at the road leading to the fort, a Mr. Reynolds overtook us in his wagon on his way to New Ulm. As the children were becoming tired, I proposed that he should take the two oldest with him, which he consented to do, and continued on his way. Shortly after he left us we suddenly changed our minds, and instead of following we concluded to make for the fort and attempt to cross the river. I am a good swimmer, you know, and I thought I could swim over and obtain assistance from the garrison. We turned off and made for the river, the crossing place

John Nairn. [Author's collection]

being about five miles distant. We had scarcely got out of sight in a low part of the country when two Indians rode over the very place where we had concluded to make for the fort. We finally got to the river, and a boat lay on the opposite side which I was not long having across and getting them all over, when you may imagine our feelings—but where were our children? I intended to go immediately after them but the road had become dangerous and I was prevented. [Mr. Nairn and his family reached the fort safely that same afternoon.][22]

The Hunters, however, were not as fortunate. Because Hunter walked with great difficulty, he and his wife had become separated from the Nairns. Along the way, they encountered some Indian friends who were aware of Hunter's handicap and induced them to stop at one of the villages overnight. One of the Indians suggested to them that they wait for him to return, promising he would secure for them a horse and buggy for their trip to the fort.[23]

The Hunters accepted the offer but, after waiting several hours, became suspicious and spent the night in the timber. Early Tuesday morning, they had progressed only a short distance when they encountered more Indians. One of them, Hinhan-shoon-koyag-mani (Walks Clothed in an Owl's Tail), without any greeting or warning, shot and killed Hunter. His wife was taken as his captive. Initially, she resisted, but gave in when her captor threatened to cut off her husband's head.

Two brothers named Martelle owned the Redwood Ferry, which was operated by a man eulogized with four different names—Jacob Mauley, Hubert Millier, Peter Martell, and Charlie Martell. He allegedly remained at the ferry all through the shootings and transported fleeing whites across the river. Among these was J.C. Dickinson, manager of the mess hall at the Lower Agency, who took a wagon across the river on the ferry and escaped to Fort Ridgely with his family, his "hired" girls, and others picked up at the landing. According to survivors such as Dickinson, the brave French-Canadian was killed at his post of duty while waiting for more persons, after saving thirty-seven lives.[24]

Not all the escapees, however, agreed with the alleged heroics of the ferryman. The slower fugitives found the ferry abandoned when they reached it. A few men, such as Joseph Schneider, swung themselves across on the ferry ropes when finding no one manning the ferry. The owners of the ferry certainly did not transport anyone across the Minnesota. Peter Martelle was killed near the stone mound at Morton, although Oliver and his wife reached Fort Ridgely safely.[25] Oliver Martelle later penned:

> Between seven and eight o'clock on the morning of August 18, 1862, I was standing in the door of my house by the ferry and Wacouta, a Sioux Indian chief's son appeared on the opposite side of the river, and [I] shouted something to him in the Indian language. Wacouta at once seemed excited and started quickly for the ferry, and my partner ferried him across. Then he and his son disappeared in the direction of the agency. During the crossing of the river, firing of small arms and guns began at the Agency, accompanied by the war whoops of the Indians. The firing was sometimes desultory, and again it sounded like a hundred or more being discharged simultaneously. As the ferry boat reached the other shore and the Indians left it, it was boarded by an Episcopal missionary, Rev. Hinman, and a party of ten or twelve men, women, and children, and immediately brought across.
>
> Mr. Hinman told me that an employee of the government, John Lamb, had been killed by the Indians, but they had let him and his family pass unharmed. There was no doubt that the Indians had broken out. He asked me if I had any horses. I replied that I had a team and a single horse in the stable. Mr. Hinman said, "Give me the team to take my family and these people to the fort and you saddle the single horse and go to Fort Ridgely and notify the commandant of the outbreak." I immediately started for the fort riding as fast as possible, and notifying all the settlers along the road of the trouble. On arriving at the fort I reported to Captain Marsh, the commandant who sent a man to St. Peter for reinforcements and prepared to go to the Agency at once.[26]

Charles Flandrau wrote of the agency murders: ". . . On the 18th of August there was a general uprising, and an indiscriminate Massacre of the whites commenced. They soon disposed of those about the agencies, and then sent out small marauding parties in all directions and butchered the whites without regard to sex or age. In about two days they killed nearly, if not quite one thousand people."[27]

The Grose family, warned of the attack by Wilhelmina and Michael, crowded together in a wagon and set off along the prairie road towards Fort Ridgely. As they approached their cornfield, they were attacked by a score of

Indians. The ox driver was killed immediately, and the family members attempted to flee on foot. The fastest runners were killed first.[28]

Michael's wife, Mary, soon to be a mother, and Wilhelmina, carrying her baby, stayed behind in the wagon. A Sioux warrior came forward and raised his gun to shoot Wilhelmina and her baby, but the cap snapped and the weapon did not go off. After three failed attempts to discharge the rifle, the brave lowered his weapon and decided they were protected by the Great Spirit.

Wilhelmina and her baby were taken captive and led away by three Indian women as she cried for Mary not to leave her. Told by the women that Mary would follow, Wilhelmina heard a shot behind her but was told it was only a dog that had been killed. As they marched along the river, Wilhelmina begged to be killed, but the Indian women only taunted her.

Her frightened baby cried incessantly. Once an Indian woman tried to drown the infant in a river while Wilhelmina swished their clothing in the water. On another occasion, they tried to choke her with a potato. Another time, while Wilhelmina was sewing dresses from cloth taken in plunder, a young Indian woman raised a sharp knife and went after the baby. Wilhelmina clasped her child to her breast and received a blow on her own head. Finally, the oldest Indian woman in the party intervened and personally guarded the baby from the others.

The band, fearing the pursuit of the soldiers, began fleeing westward. Wilhelmina was forced to march all day bare-headed in the hot sun, barefoot over the wild prairie grass, praying that the soldiers were not far away. When they reached the banks of the Redwood River, she tried to ride on an ox wagon, but the load was too heavy, and she had to wade through the water.[29]

Kearn Horan and his family lived on the Fort Ridgely Road in Renville County, four miles below the Lower Agency. On August 18th, his brother Patrick hurried from the agency and told them the Indians were murdering the whites. He and some Frenchmen had escaped, crossed the river by ferry, and were on their way to Fort Ridgely. Kearn, his brothers, and William and Thomas Smith immediately fled with Patrick.

We saw Indians in the road near Magner's, [Kearn later recalled].
Thomas Smith went to them, thinking they were white men, and I saw
them kill him. We then turned to flee, and saw men escaping with teams
along the road. All fled towards the fort together, the Indians firing upon
us as we ran. The teams were oxen, and the Indians were gaining upon
us, when one of the men in his excitement dropped his gun. The savages
came up to it and picked it up. All stopped to examine it, and the men
in the wagons whipped the oxen into a run. This delay enabled us to
elude them.[30]

As the Horan party passed the home of Ole Sampson, Mrs. Sampson
was standing at the door crying for help. Her three children were with her.
The Horans told her to go into the bushes and hide, for they could not help
her. The fleeing men ran into a ravine and hid in the grass. The Indians
approached the ravine hunting for them, calling out in good English, "Come
out, boys; what are you afraid of? We don't want to hurt you."

After the Sioux continued past them, the party made their way to
the fort, arriving there about four o'clock in the afternoon. The family of
Kearn Horan, who had left the farm earlier, was waiting for him at the fort.
Mrs. Sampson, too, had reached the fort in a prairie schooner covered with
cloth. The Indians had discovered her and the children hiding in the wagon,
grabbed one of the youngest, threw it on the ground, placed hay under the
wagon, set fire to it, and went away. Mrs. Sampson jumped down out of the
wagon, badly burned, and taking her infant from the ground, made her way
to the fort. Two of her children burned to death in the wagon. Her husband
had been killed previously about eighty rods from the house.

At Birch Coulee, in an area near La Croix Creek, people were massacred, driven away, or taken prisoners. Edward Magner, who lived eight
miles above the fort, was killed, although his wife and children made it safely to the fort. He had returned to look after his cattle and was shot. Patrick
Kelly and David O'Connor, both single men, were killed near Magner's
home. Peter Pereau, Frederick Clausen, a Mr. Piguar, Andrew Bahlke, Henry
Keartner, Charles Clausene, Mrs. William Vitt, and several others were also
killed. Mrs. Maria Frorip, an elderly German woman, was wounded four different times with small shot but escaped to the fort. Mrs. Henry Keartner

also escaped and reached Fort Ridgely. The wife and child of a Mr. Carenelle were taken prisoners, as were the wife and child of Frederick Clausen. Carl Witt made it to the fort but not until he had buried his murdered wife and also Mr. Piguar.

Mrs. Mary Hayden, who resided near Beaver Creek in Renville County, later recalled:

> On the morning of the 18th of August, Mr. [Patrick] Hayden started to go over to the house of Mr. J.B. Reynolds, at the Redwood River, on the reservation, and met Thomas Robinson, a half-breed, who told him to go home, get his family, and leave as soon as possible, for the Indians were coming over to kill all the whites. He came immediately home, and we commenced making preparations to leave, but in a few minutes we saw some three or four Indians coming on horseback. We then went over to the house of a neighbor, Benedict Eune, and found them all ready to leave. I started off with Eune's people, and my husband went back home, still thinking the Indians would not kill anyone, and intending to give them some provisions if they wanted them. I never saw him again.[31]

Mrs. Hayden and her party went about four miles when they saw a man lying dead in the road, his faithful dog watching by his side. They drove on until they came to the home of David Faribault, at the foot of a hill, about a mile and a half from the Agency ferry. Two Indians walked out of Faribault's house, stopped the teams, and shot Mr. Zimmerman, who was driving, and two of his boys. Mrs. Hayden grabbed her one-year-old child, jumped from the wagon, ran into the bushes and up a hill in the direction of Fort Ridgely. Approaching the home of Edward Magner, she saw Indians throwing furniture out the door. She raced back into the bushes and remained there until dark.

"While I lay here concealed, I saw the Indians taking the roof off the warehouse, and saw the buildings burning at the Agency," recollected Mrs. Hayden. "I also saw the firing during the battle at the ferry, where Marsh and his men were killed."[32]

Mrs. Hayden, carrying her child, started out for Fort Ridgely. She covered seventeen miles and arrived at the fort about one o'clock. On Tuesday morning she saw John Magner, who related that, when the soldiers went to the Agency the day before, they found her dead husband lying in the road near David Faribault's house. Patrick Hayden's brother, John, was found dead near La Croix Creek. His party had been taking Mrs. Eisenrich to the fort by oxen when they were overtaken by the Sioux. Eisenrich was murdered, his wife and children taken prisoner.

Mrs. Zimmerman, who was blind, and her remaining children, as well as Mrs. Eune and her five children, were taken prisoner and brought to the house of David Faribault. They were told by their captors that they would be tied up in the house and burned to death. During the night, the Indians let them go, and they made their way safely to the fort.[33]

Mrs. Zimmerman's daughter later recollected:

> Our family, that is, my father, blind mother, three brothers and a sister, were living on the banks of the Minnesota River near New Ulm. Life had been hard that first year in Minnesota, but we were having a fine crop and our new surroundings were pleasant. The morning . . . found my brother Bill and I digging potatoes not far from the house. We heard a galloping in the distance, and soon John Horton, our neighbor, rode up in a cloud of dust. Scarcely stopping, he informed us that the Sioux were on the warpath and were killing all the men and boys. I knew we must head for Fort Ridgely immediately. In terror, I told the family, while Bill hitched the oxen to the wagon. Leaving all worldly possessions behind in a mad race for life, we hurried to the ford a mile upstream. When we reached the halfway mark in the river, the crazed, half-naked warriors burst out of the woods behind us on their horses. With horrible yells they plunged into the river and in a short time they had shot my father and two older brothers right before our eyes. My youngest brother Sam was left alone because of his curly yellow hair and long dress-like garment. The leader, a tall mean-looking savage, shook his gun at my mother when leaving, taking with him our oxen and wagon. I believe my mother was thankful she was blind. Overcome with grief and fear, we staggered on to the protecting walls of Fort Ridgely.[34]

Six-year-old Fred Lammers had moved with his family from Cincinnati, after migrating from Germany, to Flora Township in Renville County. On August 18th, a neighbor boy rushed to his family's log hut screaming, "Hurry up, the Indians are killing the whites." Fred's father quickly loaded some of their belongings in a wagon, and as their neighbors came over, twelve ox teams started out for Fort Ridgely twenty-six miles distant.

After progressing only a couple of miles, they saw some Indians coming toward them. Within minutes, the Indians had encircled their caravan and asked them where they were going. They denied any knowledge of the outbreak and told the settlers to return to their "teepees."[35]

The grateful settlers concluded that the attacks were a hoax and started back to their homes with their Indian escorts riding in front of them. After going but a half mile, the Indians asked for money, and when the settlers, who had little, told them they had none to spare, the Sioux rode over to a small hill and dismounted. The band of settlers left their wagons and rushed into the tall grass and reeds of a slough to hide, but the children cried and the dogs howled.

As the Indians discussed their plans, the whites rushed back to the wagons, and Mr. Lammers told his family, "I'm afraid it's going to be hard with us."

> That was the last thing I heard him say, [recalled Fred Lammers], for the next second we were electrified by the horrible Indian war hoop. There was a second's wait before they descended on our little company. I was sitting at the front of our wagon with my feet dangling over the side, so I got a good view of the whole procedure. Having few guns, and almost no ammunition, our men decided not to put up a fight. Though the ox carts had been corralled, this was little protection. The Indians swooped down on the camp and killed every man. Four little boys about my age who were huddled together, frightened and crying, near our wagon, were killed outright. The Indians had to work fast because a thunderstorm was coming from the west, and rain would mean that shooting would be impossible since they used old muzzle-loaders that required dry powder. I was scared. I thought I would be killed next.[36]

The rain came down hard as a warrior went over to the Lammers wagon, aimed inside and shot, but there was only a flat click signifying that his powder was wet. The Indian circled the wagon three times firing his gun but with the same results. Mrs. Lammers could not believe her husband was dead as she lay in the wagon bleeding profusely from a cut she sustained by a scythe when scrambling into the wagon.

The captives were taken by canoe to the south side of the Minnesota River and to a site near Redwood Falls. The Indians began drinking whiskey and decided to kill their prisoners. The Indian women, however, took Mrs.

Lammers, her sons Fred and Charles, and several others into an abandoned building where they led them upstairs through a trap door. The drunken braves pounded on the door but could not get inside.

The captors with their captives, however, were on the move each day, and Little Crow, whom Fred Lammers called "not a bad looking man," continually rode out on his pony to scout the area. If he saw trouble ahead, he would give a danger signal by uttering a sharp cry and tapping his mouth with his fingers.

Agitated by the crying of Charles Lammers, who was only a baby, one of the Indian women grabbed him and threw him into the fire. Fred pulled him out by the foot in time to avoid serious injury or death, although his hands were severely burned, and rubbed scraped potatoes on his wounds, since there was nothing else to be found.

The shocking Indian attacks sent settlers scurrying over the Iowa border to relative safely, but Iowa, too, was gearing up for an attack. With only ninety-one soldiers of the Sioux City Cavalry available to protect the entire western and northern borders, Iowa Governor Samuel Kirkwood authorized the formation of the Northern Border Brigade and a chain of forts along Iowa's northern border with Minnesota.[37]

The new brigade was comprised of six troops of cavalry. Each company consisted of between forty and eighty men, all volunteers who had supplied their own horses and equipment. Two hundred and fifty men were mustered and organized into cavalry units in Sioux City, Denison, Crawford County, Fort Dodge, Webster County, and Spirit Lake, the scene of a massacre only five years earlier.

These citizen soldiers moved north to erect a fortified line along the border and to convince settlers to return to their abandoned farms. The farmers were needed to provide food for the Union army, which was battling the Confederacy. Confederate irregulars had already begun launching border raids on unsuspecting Iowans which led to the formation of the Southern Border Brigade.

But settlers in northern Iowa had Indians to fear, not Confederates, and blockhouses and stockades were quickly erected at Correctionville,

Cherokee, Peterson, Estherville, Chain Lake, and Spirit Lake. Most of these fortifications were constructed of wood or sod. At Spirit Lake the fort completely encircled a brick courthouse.

In Wisconsin, whites and Indians alike prepared for a Sioux massacre. Mrs. Florence Whitney later recalled:

> In the early spring of 1862 or 1863, I overheard John DuBay, who was a half-breed of French and Menominee parentage, and who had been an agent of the Hudson Bay Fur Company for many years, telling my father that the Indian runners from Northern Wisconsin had passed the night before and told him that the Sioux were on the warpath in northern Minnesota and were coming into Wisconsin to exterminate their ancient foes, the Chippewas, and also other Indians and the white people whom they claimed were occupying their hunting grounds. He said their message was, "that before the grass was four inches high the ground would run rivers of blood," and urged everyone to be on their guard.
>
> That the Indians believed this report was evidenced before the week was over by a flood of canoes of every kind and size from a birch bark canoe that would hold two with their worldly possessions, to big "dugouts" that would hold ten or twelve, all going in haste to Green Bay (Fort Howard) for the protection of the United States troops. These Indians of which there were many hundreds, came from the reservations in northern Wisconsin, Chippewas from LaPointe or Bad River, Court Oreilles and Lac du Flambeau. The Menominees from north of Wittenberg went on their ponies or afoot, and the roads were filled with them, as well as stages and wagons filled with white people who were looking for a safer place to stay.
>
> The people in Eau Pleine mostly decided to stay and protect themselves the best they could. Every night we went to bed expecting to be awakened by the war whoop of the Indians and probably tomahawked and scalped before morning. News traveled slowly in those days, so it was three weeks of terror before we heard that the government troops had been sent to Minnesota, the uprising put down and the Sioux driven back to their reservations. This was good news for us, and we dared draw a long breath again.[38]

Minnesotans began instituting defense measures immediately. On Friday morning, Major Galbraith left the agency with W.H. Shelly, Esq., and about fifty men, volunteers, for Fort Snelling, to be mustered into the service of the United States. On Monday afternoon they arrived at St. Peter and discussed the attack at the Lower Agency with a man who had been there.

According to a St. Paul newspaper, Galbraith was informed:

> that the Indians had commenced an attack on the people of Red Wood
> on Monday morning, at six o'clock, and that when he left, six men had
> been shot. Their names were James W. Lynde, formerly State Senator,
> John Lamb, teamster, _____ Wagner, the farmer, and three Germans,
> whose names were not given. Mr. Dickinson brought one of the wound-
> ed Germans to Fort Ridgely, twelve miles distant, and Dr. Muller pro-
> nounced him mortally wounded. When Mr. Dickinson got across the
> river from Red Wood, he saw the Indians firing into the traders' stores,
> and other buildings. About forty men fired into Merrick's store at once.
> Mr. Dickinson estimated the number of Indians engaged in the firing at
> about one hundred and fifty.[39]

When he learned what had taken place, Major Galbraith turned
back from St. Peter and started for Red Wood with his men, Shelly brought
dispatches from Lieutenants N.K. Culver and Thomas P. Gere. Galbraith
was astounded over the attacks. When he had left the agency, everything
was quiet and uneventful. He had believed the Indians had been satisfied
with his promise that he would send for them as soon as the money arrived
to pay off their annuities. Galbraith believed the Sioux had been induced to
commit the outrages by other Indians from Missouri.

"The command of the expedition was given to Ex-Governor Sibley,"
stated *The Pioneer & Democrat*. "The whole matter was confided to his discretion, and from his knowledge of the country and Indian character, there
can be little doubt of his success in preventing further outrages. We doubt,
however, whether he will be able to find a single Indian, when he arrives at
the reservation. If he had one or two companies of cavalry, they might possibly be overtaken. The miscreants deserve such a measure of vengeance, as
they have never yet received, and we hope it will be administered in the style
of Gen. Harney; if they are ever caught."[40]

Special Order Number 19 stated:

> I. Col. Smith, commanding the place of general rendezvous, at Fort
> Snelling, will forthwith detail four companies of his command to be
> placed under charge of Col. Sibley.
> II. Col. Sibley will proceed without delay with said four companies to
> our frontier, and will collect in addition on the way such forces of
> mounted infantry as he may deem advisable.

III. Col. Sibley is hereby authorized to provide all necessary subsistence and transportation for the troops under his command.
IV. Capt. Webb will be an adjutant to Col. Sibley.
V. Mr. Mills is hereby appointed quartermaster for this expedition."[41]

When news of the uprising reached President Abraham Lincoln in Washington, he was totally absorbed by Robert E. Lee's invasion of Maryland and had little time to devote to Indian affairs. He did, however, dispatch General John Pope to take charge of military operations against the Sioux. Pope accepted the post reluctantly, feeling that the president had been "feeble, cowardly, and shameful" in failing to defend him from his critics.

Once in Minnesota, however, Pope turned his animosity toward the Sioux. People all over Minnesota, Wisconsin, and Iowa were in a general panic and predicting "a general Indian war all along the frontier, unless immediate steps are taken to put a stop to it." Pope proclaimed that "it is my purpose utterly to exterminate the Sioux if I have the power to do so. . . . They are to be treated as maniacs or wild beasts."[42]

Bishop Whipple tried to talk sense to agitators like Pope:

> The system of trade was ruinous to honest traders and pernicious to the Indian. It prevented all efforts for personal independence and acquisition of property. The debts of shiftless and indolent were paid out of the sale of the patrimony of the tribe. . . . The Government has promised that the Indians' homes should be secured by a patent. . . . But no patent has ever been issued. Every influence which could add to the degradation of this hapless race seems to be its inheritance. . . . The voice of this whole nation has declared that the Indian Department is the most corrupt in the Government. Citizens, editors, legislators, heads of the departments, and President alike agree that it has been characterized by inefficiency and fraud.
> Four years ago the Sioux sold the Government part of their reservation, the plea for the sale being the need of funds to aid them in civilization. . . . Of ninety-six thousand dollars due to the Lower Sioux not one cent has ever been received. All has been absorbed in claims except eight hundred and eighty dollars and fifty-eight cents, which is to their credit on the books at Washington. Of the portion belonging to the other Sioux, eighty-eight thousand, three hundred and fifty one dollars and twelve cents were also taken for claims. . . . For two years the Indians had demanded to know what had become of their money, and had again and again threatened revenge unless they were satisfied.

Early last spring the traders informed the Indians that the next payment
would be only half the usual amount, because the Indian debts had been
paid at Washington. They were in some instances refused credit on this
account.

In June, at the time fixed by custom, they came together for the payment. The agent could give no satisfactory reason for the delay. There
was none to give. The Indians waited at the Agencies for two months,
dissatisfied, turbulent, hungry, and then came the outbreak.[43]

Notes

[1]Marion Ramsey Furness, *Governor Ramsey and Frontier Minnesota: Impressions from
His Diary and Letters*, St. Paul, Minnesota Historical Society Press, 1947, pp.
18-19.

[2]Stephen Riggs, *Mary and I: Forty Years with the Sioux* (Congregational Sunday
School and Publishing Society, 1880; reprint; Ross and Haines, Inc., 1969), p.
283.

[3]Marion P. Saterlee, *Outbreak and Massacre by the Dakota Indians in Minnesota in
1862*, Minneapolis, (Self-published), 1923, p. 14.

[4]Dorothy Kuske, "Account of Sioux Uprising Experiences." Dakota Conflict of 1862,
Manuscripts Collections, Microfilm Edition, Reel 1, Minnesota Historical
Society.

[5]George W. Crooks reminiscence. Dakota Conflict of 1862, Manuscripts Collections,
Microfilm Edition, Reel 1, Minnesota Historical Society.

[6]Daniel Buck, *Indian Outbreak*, p. 91.

[7]F.W. Johnson, "Outbreak at the Lower Agency," unpublished manuscript, Brown
County Historical Society, New Ulm.

[8]L.A. Fritsche, M. D., *History of Brown County Minnesota*, p. 188.

[9]Harriet E. Bishop McConkey, *Dakota War Whoop: Or Indian Massacres and War in
Minnesota, of 1862-3*, Minneapolis, Ross & Haines, 1970, Revised Edition, p.
52.

[10]Daniel Buck, *Indian Outbreaks*, pp. 94-95.

[11]*Pioneer & Democrat*, August 20, 1862; F.W. Johnson, "Outbreak at the Lower
Agency," unpublished manuscript, Brown County Historical Society, New
Ulm.

[12]Daniel Buck, *Indian Outbreaks*, p. 91.

[13]Ibid., pp. 95-96.

[14]Ibid., pp. 93-94.

[15]Ibid., p. 91.

[16]*The Pioneer & Democrat*, August 21, 1862.

[17]Bishop Henry B. Whipple, *Light and Shadows of a Long Episcopate* (1902) *Being
Reminiscences and Recollections of the Right Reverend Henry B. Whipple, Bishop of
Minnesota*.

[18]M.P. Satterlee, "Philander Prescott," unpublished manuscript, Brown County Historical Society, New Ulm.

[19]F.W. Johnson, "Outbreak at the Lower Agency," unpublished manuscript, Brown County Historical Society, New Ulm.

[20]Ibid; Joseph Connors, "The Elusive Hero of Redwood Ferry," *Minnesota History,* Summer 1955, p. 234.

[21]Reverends Thomas E. Hughes and David Edwards, Hugh G. Roberts and Thomas Hughes, *Story of the Welsh in Minnesota, Foreston and Lime Springs, Iowa. Gathered by the Old Settlers,* 1895; F.W. Johnson, "Outbreak at the Lower Agency," unpublished manuscript, Brown County Historical Society, New Ulm; Charles S. Bryant, *Indian Massacre in Minnesota: A History of the Indian Wars of the Far West,* pp. 94-95.

[22]John Nairn undated letter to Magdalene Nairn. Dakota Conflict of 1862, Manuscripts Collections, Microfilm Edition, Reel 3, Minnesota Historical Society.

[23]Reverends Thomas E. Hughes and David Edwards, Hugh G. Roberts and Thomas Hughes, *Story of the Welsh in Minnesota, Foreston and Lime Springs, Iowa. Gathered by the Old Settlers,* 1895; F.W. Johnson, "Outbreak at the Lower Agency," unpublished manuscript, Brown County Historical Society, New Ulm.

[24]Joseph Connors, "The Elusive Hero of Redwood Ferry," *Minnesota History,* Summer 1955, p. 234.

[25]*A Detailed Account of the Massacre by the Dakota Indians of Minnesota in 1862,* Minneapolis, Marion P. Satterlee, pp. 14-16.

[26]*Big Stone Headlight* (Big Stone City, South Dakota), December 29, 1904. Obituary of Oliver Martell.

[27]Charles Flandrau, *The Battle of New Ulm,* Manuscript Collections, Brown County Historical Society.

[28]Dorothy Kuske, "Account of Sioux Uprising Experiences." Dakota Conflict of 1862, Manuscripts Collections, Microfilm Edition, Reel 1, Minnesota Historical Society.

[29]Wilhelmina and her baby were set free at Camp Release.

[30]Franklyn Curtiss-Wedge, *The History of Renville County, Minnesota,* Volume II, Chicago, H.C. Cooper, Jr., & Company, 1916, p. 927.

[31]Charles S. Bryant, *A History of the Great Massacre by the Sioux Indians in Minnesota, Including the Personal Narratives of Many Who Escaped,* Cincinnati, Rickey & Carroll, p. 202.

[32]Ibid.

[33]Ibid.; Franklyn Curtiss-Wedge, *The History of Renville County, Minnesota,* Volume II, Chicago, H.C. Cooper, Jr., & Company, 1916, p. 927.

[34]"Elizabeth Zimmerman—My Grandmother—A Pioneer," unpublished manuscript in Fort Ridgely archives.

[35]1930 Interview with Fred Lammers, Fairfax, Minnesota. Brown County Historical Society, New Ulm.

[36]Ibid.

[37]Charles Flandrau, *The Battle of New Ulm*, Manuscript Collections, Brown County Historical Society.

[38]The above was written in 1927 and is taken from a collection of materials on the Story of Stevens Point, compiled by Marie Swallow in 1927-1928. Portage County Historical Society.

[39]*The Pioneer & Democrat*, August 20, 1862.

[40]Ibid.

[41]Ibid.

[42]David Herbert Donald, *Lincoln*, London, Jonathan Cape, 1995, pp. 392-393.

[43]Bishop Henry B. Whipple, *Light and Shadows of a Long Episcopate (1902) Being Reminiscences and Recollections of the Right Reverend Henry B. Whipple, Bishop of Minnesota.*

Chapter Six

August 18, 1862
Redwood Ferry

"Captain Marsh left this post at [ten] this morning to prevent Indian depredations at the Lower Agency. Some of the men have returned. I heard from them that Capt. Marsh is killed and only thirteen of his company are remaining.

"The Indians are killing the settlers and plundering the country. Send reinforcements without delay."   —Thomas P. Gere[1]

"The Indian Agent they have sent us is so mean that he carries around in his pocket a . . . rag into which he blows his nose, for fear that he will blow away something of value."   —Remark attributed to an anonymous Plains Indian leader.

 FEW PERSONS HAD ESCAPED THE SLAUGHTER at the Lower Agency via the Redwood Ferry. The Dakotas, knowing that these escapees would spread the word to the fort, captured the ferry boat, killed the ferryman, disemboweled him, chopped off his head, hands and feet, which they inserted into his body cavity, and then danced around their conquest. A boy attempting to escape, was chased down, stripped to the skin and pierced with sticks and knives as he was driven along. The warriors mimicked his agonies as they ran alongside him.[2]

Only seventy-six men were garrisoned at Fort Ridgely, located some twelve miles from the Redwood Agency. By nine o'clock the morning of the attack, the first refugees reached the fort with news of the murders. John F. Bishop recalled:

> The first indication of an Indian outbreak we saw at Fort Ridgely was a team from Lower Sioux Agency, bringing in a citizen badly wounded and pleading for help. This was about 8:30 a.m., August 18, 1862. Captain Marsh at once ordered the long row sounded, and the whole company fell in, about [eighty-five] men strong. He selected [fifty-four] men with [forty] rounds of ammunition and one day's rations, leaving the balance of the company, under command of Lieut. T.P. Gere, to guard the post.[3]

Captain Marsh believed the sight of the soldiers would frighten the Indians as it had so many times before.

Settlers fleeing down the Agency Road to the fort cautioned Captain Marsh and his men of the dangers facing them, but the soldiers paid them little heed. They also told Marsh that if he would not turn back, they should at least not enter the Minnesota River Valley, which meant almost certain death. But Marsh was determined to enter the valley three miles from the Lower Agency on his way to the Redwood Ferry.[4]

Marsh, with Peter Quinn as interpreter, moved toward the Lower Sioux Agency with his men. Marsh and Quinn rode mules while the soldiers rode in mule-drawn wagons. Along the way, they met several settlers also escaping from the Sioux onslaught, and only six miles from Fort Ridgely, they saw houses in flames and the mutilated but not yet cold corpses of men, women, and children lying at the roadside. Captain Marsh, forming his command on foot, hurried on. They reached the vicinity of the ferry at noon but all was quiet and uneventful.[5]

Oliver Martell and a settler named La Croix had also ridden out of the fort to see what the Indians were doing. After riding about ten miles, only three miles from the agency, they found three bodies lying alongside the road. The men had just been killed, for fresh blood still oozed from the wound in one dead man's neck. La Croix and Martell started back towards the fort.

> Five or six miles from the fort we met Captain Marsh with forty-five or forty-six soldiers, [recalled Oliver Martell]. He asked, "How do things look up there?" I answered, "We went as far as Mager's place and found

Ed Mager, Smith and another man dead, and we could see fire at the agency." I continued, "Captain, I don't know as how I have the right to give you advice, but if you will allow me, I will tell you what I would do in your place." The captain asked what I would do and I replied, "I wouldn't go up there at all. I have no doubt but that the Indians have broken out for good, and you haven't enough men to do any good." I described to him the position of the ferry, saying, "On one side is willow brush as thick as they can grow, and on the other side is an old field grown up to artichokes as high as a man's head. This is a splendid place for Indians to ambush, and whatever you do, don't try to cross the river there." We then returned to the fort and the troops went to the agency.[6]

The road was full of fugitives fleeing for their lives. Many of these pointed to the distant columns of smoke from burning homes at and near the agency. Marsh and his men also met a soldier named John Magill, who had been home on a furlough, at whose house Dr. Humphrey and family had stopped. He joined the command, making forty-seven soldiers besides Captain Marsh. Six miles out, they began to come across dead bodies of men, women and children, lying in the road, some horribly mutilated, while the smoke and flames of burning houses rose near and far all over the country before them, showing the appalling extent of the dreadful massacre. In spite of every warning, Captain Marsh and his little band of soldiers pressed resolutely on, past the body of Dr. Humphrey and the burning pile where his wife and his two children perished. Near this place the oldest boy came from his hiding place to join them.[7]

> We left the fort about [nine] o'clock A.M., taking a six-mule team along with extra ammunition, rations, blankets, etc., [penned Sergeant Bishop]. Citizens had already commenced arriving and lined the road, mostly panic-stricken women and children. We marched about six miles toward the agency and came to a small log house on fire. Dr. Humphrey, the agency physician, lay dead on the doorstep, tomahawked. Mrs. Humphrey lay in the center of the room on the floor, dead, tomahawked, and an infant two days old lay on her breast alive, but too far gone to be helped. We passed on half a mile further and found another citizen tomahawked and nearly dead; we laid him out on one side of the road, and Captain Marsh requested some citizens to help him to the fort.[8]

Captain Marsh, sensing danger, ordered his men to abandon the wagons and resume their march. At Faribault's Hill, only three miles from the Lower Agency, the wagon road descended from the high prairie, and crossed a small stream stretched across the wide bottom land of the Minnesota River. The column proceeded towards the ferry crossing. Halfway across this bottomland, Captain Marsh halted his command for a brief rest, before resuming their march towards the ferry.[9]

> Between the top of a hill (we used to call it Faribault Hill on account of a log house at the bottom, owned by a half-breed named Faribault) and the bottom we found [four] citizens dead; at the bottom, in a small creek, we found [four] men; out of Faribault's house came about [twenty-five] women and children, and they fled toward the fort as we passed by. Faribault's house was about nine miles from the fort on the road to the agency. Between the creek and ferry, we found we found [two] more citizens dead in the road—one was the ferryman. These citizens all appeared to have been overtaken and murdered within a few minutes of our arrival. The ferry at that time was located about one mile down the river from the Lower Sioux Agency, and I think about eleven miles above Fort Ridgely. The Minnesota River at this point keeps close to the bluffs on the southwest side. These bluffs at that time were covered with a thick growth of hazel-brush and small trees, while on the east side was a wide bottom, covered with heavy, high grass.[10]

They hurried on across the wide valley of the Minnesota with the tall grass on each side until they drew close to the ferry at the agency crossing. The brave French ferryman had stood by his post like a hero that morning and had crossed over all the fleeing fugitives from the agency until at last he fell doing his duty. His body disembowelled, with head and hands chopped off and inserted into the cavity, lay by the road-side, a horrible sight.

Reaching a point about a mile from the ferry, the soldiers again began marching single file along the river until they reached the crossing. The ferry lay unfastened on the fort side of the river. The water at the ford was very riley as though recently disturbed, and a troop of Indian ponies was noticed standing a little way off in the grass. There were bushes and tall grass merging with scattered thickets of hazel and willow, interspersed with open sand patches left by the overflowing of the river. A larger thicket extended southward along the riverbank some two miles in width from twenty to 200 feet. Across the river near the west bank, stood the high bluffs upon which the Lower Agency was situated, their steep face smothered by a thick growth of young trees and underbrush.

Across the river on a high bluff stood the Redwood Agency where Captain Marsh planned to meet with Sioux chiefs and restore order through peaceful means. The slope leading from the river to the lip of the hill was covered with a thick growth of brush and timber.

The soldiers formed in line facing the river, and Corporal Ezekiel Rose and another soldier went a few feet above the ford for water. They returned saying they had seen the heads of many Indians peering over the logs by the agency saw mill just across the river. Up to this time, only a few Indians had been spotted, those being on the high prairie west of the river, south of the agency, on their horses. Suddenly Indian women and children stood on the bluff west of the river.

To Marsh's dismay, the ferry boat was on the other side of the river, and because there was no effective means of crossing the stream, he consulted his men. Standing on the opposite side of the river, they saw White Dog, a Dakota brave who had been hired by the government to teach farming to his people. Quinn conveyed to Marsh that White Dog asked in his native tongue to speak with Marsh, but the captain balked at the request.[11]

When Captain Marsh finally addressed him through his interpreter, White Dog said, "Come across; everything is right over here. We do not want to fight and there will be no trouble. Come over to the agency and we will hold a council."[12]

Captain Marsh was suspicious and ordered his men to remain in their places and not move onto the boat until he could ascertain whether the Sioux were waiting in ambush in the ravines on the opposite shore. The soldiers were in the act of drinking water when confronted by the lone Indian.

Wrote Sergeant Bishop:

> We arrived at the ferry on the east side about twelve o'clock noon, and found the ferry boat on the east side, apparently ready to take us over, but Captain Marsh and probably the ferryman, whom we had just passed, was the last man over and had left it on this side. One lone

Indian, "White Dog," chief, I believe of a small band of Upper Sioux tribe, stood on the opposite side of the river. Captain Marsh commenced talking to him through Interpreter Quinn. In a few minutes Quinn said, "I don't know this Indian, he don't belong here." I told Captain Marsh I had seen this same Indian among the Upper Sioux at Yellow Medicine, under Chief Standing Buffalo. Captain Marsh then asked him what he was at Little Crow Agency for. He said, "On a visit for a few days." He, the chief, urged Captain Marsh to cross over and go up to the agency and hold a council. He said the Indians were all up there waiting for us, and all would be right. He said they had had some troubles with the traders, but the captain could fix it up with the Indians, and all would be right. In the meantime I had stepped down to the edge of the river to dip up a cup of water to drink; I found the water riley and twigs and leaves floating down. I think the captain was about to order his men onto the boat, when I said to him, "Captain Marsh, I believe we are being surrounded by Indians crossing the river above us," and gave him my reasons.[13]

The Sioux, had in fact, crept through bushes and grass to a bend above the soldiers, and crossed the river in canoes as White Dog conversed with Interpreter Quinn. While the two men talked, the approaching Sioux crept silently up on the party of soldiers.[14] Two soldiers went to the river to collect water for the men and discovered the heads of many Indians concealed behind logs in the brush on the opposite side. A drunken man at the ferry house conveyed to the soldiers, "You are all gone up; the Indians are all around you; the side hill is covered with Indians."[15]

Captain Marsh ordered his men to move forward slowly towards the ferry crossing. The posts to which the ferry ropes were attached had obviously been loosened. Having noticed the ropes, the soldiers formed in line facing the river. Sergeant Bishop stepped to the riverbank to fill his cup, and returning, whispered to Captain Marsh that he believed the Indians were crossing the river above to the east to surround the soldiers.

Sergeant Bishop recalled:

I then ran up on a pile of sand caused by grading the approach to the ferry, and looked over the river; in a small ravine between the ferry and the agency on the west side of the river, I saw a lot of ponies switching their tails in the bush, and at once reported this to Captain Marsh. He then ordered Quinn to ask White Dog what the ponies were there, just above him, for, if the Indians were all up at the agency. The Indian, who had been talking to us, then raised his gun. Quinn exclaimed, "Look out!!!" the Indians fired, an in an instant afterward a volley of shot came from the brush on the opposite side of the river; about one-half of our men dropped dead where they had been standing, Quinn with about ten or twelve balls through him.[16]

The Indians had planned to launch their attack once the soldiers were on the ferryboat. They opened fire from both sides of the river.

A fearful yell, right behind us, followed the volley from the opposite side of the river, [continued Bishop]. I heard Captain Marsh call out, "Steady men!" I was standing on the sand pile at this time, about twenty feet to the right

Redwood Ferry marker. [Photo courtesy of Diana Pierce]

of the company, who were facing the river. Indians rushed in upon us from behind, firing mostly double-barrel shotguns, when Captain Marsh and his surrounding comrades turned about, advanced to the top of the river bank and fired a volley at them. Then a hand to hand encounter took place, every man fighting the best he knew how to cut his way out of the terrible looking mob around us. They were all painted and naked, except breech clouts. Sergeant Trescott of Chatfield, two others and myself tried to cut our way through, in order to get into the ferryman's log house or barn, which stood on opposite sides of the road leading to the ferry on our side of the river. Trescott fell about two hundred feet from the house; the others fell before they reached it, shot by Indians inside the house or barn. Both were full of Indians. I could not stop to argue right of passage, but darted through between the buildings. I don't think they were over one hundred feet apart. The charge on Hood at Nashville, December 16, 1864, was a quiet promenade for me in comparison to this dash; a large sized ball shivered the stock of my musket and cut a flesh wound in the thigh, but not a very serious one. A little beyond the ferry house, I met an Indian with a double shotgun; he gave me the contents of both barrels, which struck the sand in the road at my feet; he was excited, I suppose, as well as myself. We both commenced loading; he had both barrels loaded as I rammed my cartridge home. A gun barrel then came up under my left arm. Supposing it to be an Indian in my rear about to use his hatchet, I did not turn to see how it was to be done; the gun went off and the Indian fell and the road was clear once more. Young James Dunn of Chatfield, afterward killed at Nashville, spoke up and said, "Is your gun loaded?" "Yes, as soon as I can cap it." He said, "You lead, my gun is empty." We went about three hundred feet further, and five Indians jumped into the road from the grass. We then turned off to the south, in hopes to find an opening, but they bore down on us, and others joined them, and we were pressed or crowded to the south and went in kind of a circle, until we reached the thicket just below the ferry. This thicket, at that time, varied from one rod to ten in width, and ran along the edge of the river about one mile to nearly opposite the Faribault house, where it ended in an open bottom beyond. When we entered it we found Captain Marsh and [eleven] men had reached it before us.[17]

Marsh had concluded that he and his men could not defend themselves and ordered his men to follow a thicket downriver. He and fifteen of his men managed to get into the thicket, which lay down the river a few rods.

Lieutenant Gere wrote in his report: "Captain Marsh now only hoped to reach Fort Ridgely with the remnant of his command. The Indians riddled the thicket with buckshot and ball, but had the troops no longer at such a serious disadvantage; and deterred too, by their own heavy losses, they fired at longer range.[18]

From their shelter, the soldiers kept the Indians at bay all that afternoon until four o' clock when the lower end of the strip of wood was reached. Here the Indians had concentrated their force to receive the soldiers as they emerged from the timber. Many of the soldiers panicked and ran; twenty-six of them were killed. Marsh met Bishop where the underbrush ended.

After the Indians closed in on us, it became utterly impossible for a soldier to rejoin his command if he had become in any way separated from it, [recollected Bishop]. The Indians seemed determined to cut our men off from the command one or two at a time, as in that manner they were more easily disposed of. Most of our loss after the first volley occurred by the men being thus crowded out of their ranks by the Indians.

The Indians surrounded the thicket, yelling, and shooting shot and ball in thick and fast, and here we commenced to use our ammunition carefully under cover of brush and grass, to stand the devils off. This was kept up until about [four] o'clock P.M., when, our ammunition being reduced to not more than four rounds to a man, Captain Marsh ordered his men to swim the river and try and work our way down the west side.[19]

Taking his sword and revolver in hand, he led his men into the river which was at this point about ten rods wide. He waded out perhaps two-third of the distance, when he found the water beyond his depth, and dropping his hands, he attempted to swim the river. The dazed captain made it only a short way when he began shouting loudly for help. Privates Brennan, Dunn, and Van Buren swam to his assistance, Brennan reaching him the second time he was sinking. Brennan pulled him to the surface by grasping his shoulder, but he lost his grip, and Captain Marsh sank below the water. The three men quickly joined their command on the shore.[20]

According to Sergeant Bishop, "[Marsh] entered the river first, and swam to about the center, and there went down with a cramp. I ordered two of the best swimmers to try and help him; one reached him when he came to a surface a second time, only to be drawn under. I will never forget the look that brave officer gave us just before he sank for the last time—will never forget how dark the next hour seemed to us, as we crouched underneath the bank of the Minnesota River, and talked over and decided what next best to do."[21]

While likely not hit by an enemy's ball, Captain Marsh drowned after experiencing a leg cramp. His body was recovered a month later among some driftwood about a mile downstream. Sergeant Bishop, only nineteen years old, took charge of the survivors.[22]

The command then devolved on Sergeant Bishop, who took charge of three corporals and eleven privates. Bishop had been wounded and Private Svendson was so badly shot, he had to be carried. Bishop concluded that they must continue southward on the east side of the river.

Sergeant Bishop related: "While we were holding this council all became quiet outside the thicket, and upon further examination we found the Indians had all left us, crossed the river near, and were lying in ambush, they having supposed we were crossing when they saw Captain Marsh and his helpers floundering in the water."[23]

219

The Indians believed the soldiers had made their way to the west side, and many of the Sioux crossed at an adjacent ford and waited in ambush in a thicket. An overhanging bank of the river, however, afforded the soldiers concealment, and, carrying the wounded man, they passed unseen by the Sioux. When they were only five miles from Fort Ridgely, Bishop dispatched Privates Dunn and Hutchinson to move ahead and tell the soldiers at the fort where they were.[24]

Mrs. Margaret Hern, who was at the fort, later remembered:

> We knew nothing of what was happening to this little handful of soldiers, but as more and more refugees came in with the terribly mutilated, our fears increased. We knew a small group of the savages could finish us. Just at dusk, Jim Dunn, a soldier of nineteen who always helped us about our work, came reeling in, with blood and sweat. I said, "For God's sake, what is the news, Jim?" He only panted, "Give me something to eat quick." After he had swallowed a few mouthfuls, he told us that nearly all of the boys had been killed by the Indians. He said, "The devils got us in the marsh by the river. Quinn told the captain not to go down there, but he held his sword above his head and said, 'All but cowards will follow me.' The Indians on the other side of the river were challenging us to come by throwing up their blankets way above their heads." Only three more of the boys came in that night.[25]

The main party of fleeing soldiers under Sergeant Bishop followed soon after. "We then worked our way toward the fort," recalled Bishop. "Our progress was slow on account of two wounded, including myself, the other having to be carried for ten miles. After dark, when about five miles out, I dispatched two of our best men to warn the post commander of what had happened, that he might prepare for what was likely to follow. In an instant after his arrival a man was mounted upon the swiftest horse to be found and started out for St. Paul with dispatches to the Governor for help, and to warn St. Peter, Henderson, LeSueur, and Shakopee, and all settlers."[26]

Bishop led fourteen men safely back to Fort Ridgely by various circuitous routes. Eight other soldiers who had become separated from the others later reached the fort on their own. By the time they returned, as many as 500 refugees had come into the fort.[27]

We reached the fort about [ten] o'clock P.M., [wrote Bishop]. Some things we saw that day are too revolting to relate; it chills my blood now to think of them. Just after dark, when five or six miles from the fort, we discovered something moving in the grass near the road. I thought we had run upon our enemy again, but demanded who was there, when a lone woman arose, and approaching us, exclaimed, "Have I found help at last? Am I saved?" She then asked us to help her sister, lying in the grass near by, with a new-born child not an hour old. We helped them in with our wounded, which made our progress very slow.[28]

One of the party, Dennis O'Shey, managed to kill one of the Indians while making his getaway alone through the brush to thee river, staying out of sight of the Indians. He stayed under cover of the bushes until after dark when he waded into the Minnesota River and floated downstream for several miles. Keeping out of sight by day, he reached Fort Ridgely safely at one o'clock on the morning of August 20th without having had a morsel of food for two days. Upon his arrival at the fort, he was placed in charge of a cannon because of his previous artillery experience.[29]

The Pioneer & Democrat reported: "Letters from members of the party give the same accounts of the killing of a portion of Capt. Marsh's company, as were embraced in the dispatch of Lieut. Gere to the governor." A letter written by A.J. Vorhks from Fort Ridgely on August 20th, stated:

Knowing the intense excitement that must prevail throughout the state in consequence of the Indian outbreaks and massacres of the past two days, and with the hope that a full knowledge of the facts will stimulate the government and citizens to prompt and decisive action, I hasten to communicate such items as the excitement of the hour, and the exigencies of affairs as they appear to one on the ground, will suggest.

It is well known that dissatisfaction has existed in the various tribes for some weeks past in consequence of the delay of the government in making its annual payment; but no one dreamed of a well organized and systematically outbreak, embracing tribes which have ever been hostile to each other. This fact, in connection with circumstances which have come to my knowledge within the past few days, convince me that it is a part of the plan of the great rebellion. The government will be convinced of this fact, should it prove that this is a systemized raid all along the border, from Pembina to the Missouri River.

The party attending Mr. Wycoff, acting superintendent who was on his way to the Upper Sioux Agency to the annual payment, met a messenger about six miles from this place, on Monday morning, announcing an out-break at the Lower Sioux Agency, and the murder of all the whites in the vicinity, except the few who had made their escape. Upon our arrival here, we found the statement confirmed. Upon learning the facts Captain Marsh immediately set out for the agency with forty-five men of his command—leaving some twenty at the garrison. In the evening, seventeen of his men returned. At the ferry opposite the agency, Captain Marsh encountered a large body of warriors, who opened fire on him. After a few volleys a large body of Indians ambushed in his rear, also opened upon him, immediately killing a number of his men. A retreat was attempted in which it was thought expedient to make a crossing of the river. While in the water a vol-ley was fired upon Capt. Marsh, who immediately went down. Beside the captain, three sergeants and four corporals are known to be killed, and a large number of his command. Up to this time but four additional soldiers have returned—three of them mortally wounded.

Monday night was a night of anxiety and peril to the little band at the garrison. Every man became a soldier, and every precaution was taken to protect the fort. Lieut. Gere of Company B, did all in his power, whose efforts were seconded by every civilian. The lights of burning buildings and grain stacks lighted the entire horizon. Escaped citizens came in during the night, giving accounts of horror too terrible for the imagination to conceive or appreciate.[30]

Sergeant Bishop explained that Captain Marsh had been the only com-missioned officer on their ill-fated expedition. Under Marsh had been three sergeants and four corporals. Two of the sergeants—Findley and Trescott—had been killed. Bishop, in his report, described how difficult it had been for his men to find him in the thicket and that Tom Parsley of Chatfield and four others were cut off in another thicket. Three of them were killed before dark although Parsley crawled out during the night and found his way back to the fort.

William A. Sutherland had been shot through the breast, the ball passing through his right lung and exiting near the back of his shoulder blade. He lay unconscious for some time while the Sioux took his gun, car-tridge belt and box, his cap, coat, and shoes, leaving him with only his shirt and trousers. Returning to consciousness, he lifted his head only to hear the voices of Indians nearby. Thirsty, he crawled towards the river through the high grass and weeds.[31]

After drinking his fill, he waited until nightfall before attempting an escape. While the Sioux conducted their scalp-dance on the agency side of

Redwood Falls. (Photo courtesy of Diana Pierce)

the river, he found an old boat on the bank partially filled with water. He bailed as much water as he could, climbed in, and moved down the sluggish river under cover of darkness. For two nights and a day he glided along the river until his body became so stiffened, he was forced to abandon the water-logged boat and crawl through the underbrush. Half-naked and racked with pain, he reached Fort Ridgely on the morning of August 20th. An hour later, Sioux warriors swarmed over the road by which he had made his escape.

William A. Sutherland and William Blodgett of Chatfield, related Bishop, "were both shot through the body, and remained where they fell until in the night, when they arrived, and I believe they found an old canoe and with it floated down the river and arrived at the fort the next day. E. Rose of Chatfield, shot through the arm, cut his way through alone and started for the fort on the night, got lost, and was picked up on the prairie between Fort Ridgely and Hutchinson, nearly dead from loss of blood. Corp. W.B. Hutchinson and Private M.H. Wilson were survivors in the party with me and are still living; other names have passed from my memory. . . ."[32]

When the people of Mankato heard of the murders at the Lower Agency and of the fate of Captain Marsh, three men—Porter, Dukes, and Tate—were sent to New Ulm to learn if there was any truth in the stories being circulated. Mr. Porter arrived in the city on Tuesday and found the local citizens making preparations to bury five persons who had been killed between the agency and New Ulm. Other bodies, all horribly mutilated, were also being brought into the city for burial.[33]

Mr. Porter was led into a building where he discovered four more dying persons, all of them bleeding profusely from hatchet wounds in the head and arms. One little girl was cut across the face, breast, and side as was a little boy and middle-aged woman. In an adjoining room, Porter saw a child with his head cut off and eleven other persons severely mutilated. He was informed that forty persons had been murdered in the area, although it was believed that another two hundred settlers had been killed, their bodies not yet found.

When Porter left New Ulm, its citizens had resolved to defend their lives and property. The women were busy caring for the wounded while the men drilled in the streets with fowling pieces and rifles, learning bayonet tactics with pitchforks.

> There can be no exaggeration as to the alarm which prevails in the neighborhood where the murders were committed. We are informed that hundreds of settlers, with their families, came into Carver on Tuesday, and were constantly arriving during the night, having left their homes on the instant they received the intelligence of the Indian raid. Some of these people were perfectly terror-stricken, although they had not seen an Indian for a month. They brought reports of the burning of Glencoe, and of horrors indescribable, which had been imparted to them by others, or which their own fears had conjured up. Many even came down to St. Paul on the steamer, while others arrived last evening with their own teams, in a state of complete exhaustion from excitement and want of sleep. Men, women and children, some of them half-clothed, barefooted and hungry, have arrived here, who were actually stampeded from their homes by terror.[34]

Settlers continued to pour into Carver, Shakopee, and Chaska, but the alarm was gradually subsiding, and many of them returned to their homes. The reports of the burning of Glencoe turned out to be false. General

Sibley divided his force, sending a portion up to the agency, and the balance into the interior beyond Carver. "They have very little expectation of finding hostile Indians," conjectured *The Pioneer & Democrat*.

On August 21st, Governor Alexander Ramsey issued the following proclamation:

> The Sioux Indians upon our western frontier have risen in large numbers, attacked the settlements, and are murdering men, women and children. The rising appears concerted, and extends from Fort Ripley to the southern boundary of the state.
>
> In this extremity, I call upon the Militia of the Valley of Minnesota, and the counties adjoining the frontier to take horses, and arm and equip themselves, taking with them subsistence for a few days, at once report separately or in squads, to the officer commanding the expedition now moving up the Minnesota River to the scene of hostilities. The officer commanding the expedition has been clothed with full power to provide for all exigencies that may arise.
>
> Measures will be taken to subsist the forces so raised.
>
> This outbreak must be suppressed, and in such manner as will ever prevent its repetition.
>
> I earnestly urge upon the settlers of the frontier that while taking all proper precautions for the safety of their families and homes, they will not give way to any unnecessary alarm. A regiment of infantry, together with 300 cavalry, have all been ordered to their defence [sic], and with the voluntary troops now being raised, the frontier settlements will speedily be placed beyond danger.[35]

Bishop, however, knew that the regiment of infantry and cavalry could not stop the Sioux, not with their superior numbers:

> A young Indian whom I had often befriended and who was captured by General Sibley, told me one night while in camp near Henderson while on route for Fort Snelling under charge of General Marshall, that he was in the fight at the ferry, and that Little Crow had about 325 or 350 armed warriors, about fifty warriors from the upper band, and about [twenty or twenty-five] Winnebagoes, besides some boys with bows and arrows, whom they did not consider fighters. He said their trick was to entice us onto the ferry-boat, then cut the rope and let us drift down the stream and shoot us at their leisure. After we were all disposed of, they were to cross their ponies and ride to the fort, and capture them, then take their squaws and children along in the rear and attack Mankato, St. Peter and other towns, as far as possible.[36]

Bishop believed the great mistake made by Captain Marsh was in not deploying two or three of his men to each side of the road on their way to the ferry once they began finding the bodies of victims. Had this been carried out, the skirmishers may have discovered Indians hiding in the grass as they approached the ferry. The burning buildings of the agency were a pretty clear indication that hostiles were in the immediate area. He explained:

> Many have censured Captain Marsh because he did not turn back when he commenced finding the dead along the road about four miles from the ferry. I will say in explanation for him, that no brave officer could have turned back and left those defenseless women and children between that band of Indians and ourselves. They were continuously swarming by us in groups of a dozen, more or less, at the time; not less than 200 to 300 of them passed us between Fort Ridgely and the ferry when we found the Indians in ambush. An officer who would order his men back in the face of these facts would deserve to be shot without a trial, and dishonor would certainly have followed him, and there would have resulted the murder of many women and children who escaped while we were pressing forward. Moreover, if we had returned to the fort at once, the band of Indians would certainly have followed us in hot pursuit, and would have undoubtedly captured the fort that night, and there would then have been nothing to stop them until they reached Fort Snelling.[37]

Following the killings at Redwood Ferry, Judge Josiah F. Marsh, brother of Captain Marsh, journeyed up the Minnesota River to investigate the death of his brother and others in the area. Accompanying Marsh was an escort of thirty mounted men, his old neighbors from Fillmore County. They failed to find the body of Captain Marsh despite conducting a thorough search of the river. On the day before and after this fruitless search, 200 Indians were scouting the river on the very ground the search party was exploring.[38]

Upon Judge Marsh's return, he reported that the number of whites killed was close to 500, based upon the number of bodies he and his party had discovered along the roads and trails, as well as those found at the agency. Marsh stated that it was his firm belief that all the missionaries had been killed. According to a St. Paul newspaper, "The civilized Indians, or those who have discarded the blanket and leggins [sic], are said to have exceeded their savage brethren in atrocities."[39]

226

Two weeks after Judge Marsh's unsuccessful trip, another search was made in boats along the river, and this time, they were successful. His body was discovered a mile and a half below where he was killed, under the roots of a tree standing at the water's edge, from beneath which the earth had been washed by the action of the river current. One of his arms appeared above the surface of the water. His remains were brought back to Fort Ridgely for burial in the post cemetery.[40]

The Captain Marsh Monument at Fort Ridgely reads: "In Memory of Capt. John Marsh, First Sergeant Russell H. Findley, Serg't Joseph S. Besse; Privates Charles R. Bell, Edwin F. Cole, Charles E. French, John Gardner, Jacob A. Gehring, John Holmes, Christian Joerger, Durs Kanzing, James H. Kerr, Wenzel Kusda, Henry McAllister, Wenzel Norton, Moses P. Parks, John W. Parks, John Parsley, Harrison Phillips, Nathaniel Pitcher, Henry A. Shepherd, Nathan Stewart, Charles W. Smith of Co. B, died Aug. 18, 1862. Private Mark M. Greer, Co. C, died Aug. 22, 1862. Fifth Regiment Minnesota Volunteer Infantry. Peter Quinn, U.S. Interpreter, Killed at Redwood Ferry, Aug. 18, 1862." The face of the monument reads: "Erected by the State of Minnesota 1873."[41]

These men are buried in two trenches. The bodies of Wenzel Kusda, Henry McAllister, and Henry A. Shepherd were never found, but there names are inscribed on the monument.

Notes

[1]*The Pioneer & Democrat*, August 20, 1862.
[2]Harriet B. McConkey, *Dakota War-Whoop*, p. 46.
[3]Sioux Uprising—The Encounter at Redwood Ferry. Sergeant [John F.] Bishop's Story of the Disaster, Manuscripts Collections, Brown County Historical Society.
[4]L.A. Fritsche, *History of Brown County*, p. 265.
[5]Harriet B. McConkey, *Dakota War-Whoop*, pp. 61-62; "Sioux Uprising—The Attacks Upon Fort Ridgely. Lieutenant Gere's Account," Manuscripts Collections, Brown County Historical Society. New Ulm.
[6]*Big Stone Headlight* (Big Stone City, South Dakota), December 29, 1904. Obituary of Oliver Martell.

[7]Reverends Thomas E. Hughes and David Edwards, Hugh G. Roberts and Thomas Hughes, *Story of the Welsh in Minnesota*, Foreston and Lime Springs, Iowa. Gathered by the Old Settlers, 1895.

[8]Sioux Uprising—The Encounter at Redwood Ferry, Sergeant [John F.] Bishop's Story of the Disaster, Manuscripts Collections, Brown County Historical Society.

[9]Sioux Uprising—The Attacks Upon Fort Ridgely. Lieutenant Gere's Account, Manuscripts Collections, Brown County Historical Society, New Ulm.

[10]Sioux Uprising—The Encounter at Redwood Ferry. Sergeant [John F.] Bishop's Story of the Disaster, Manuscripts Collections, Brown County Historical Society.

[11]Harriet B. McConkey, *Dakota War-Whoop*, pp. 61-62.

[12]Sioux Uprising—The Attacks Upon Fort Ridgely, Lieutenant Gere's Account, Manuscripts Collections, Brown County Historical Society. New Ulm.

[13]Sioux Uprising—The Encounter at Redwood Ferry. Sergeant [John F.] Bishop's Story of the Disaster, Manuscripts Collections, Brown County Historical Society.

[14]Harriet B. McConkey, *Dakota War-Whoop*, pp. 61-62.

[15]Sioux Uprising—The Attacks Upon Fort Ridgely, Lieutenant Gere's Account, Manuscripts Collections, Brown County Historical Society. New Ulm.

[16]Sioux Uprising—The Encounter at Redwood Ferry. Sergeant [John F.] Bishop's Story of the Disaster, Manuscripts Collections, Brown County Historical Society.

[17]Ibid.

[18]Sioux Uprising—The Attacks Upon Fort Ridgely, Lieutenant Gere's Account, Manuscripts Collections, Brown County Historical Society. New Ulm.

[19]Sioux Uprising—The Encounter at Redwood Ferry. Sergeant [John F.] Bishop's Story of the Disaster, Manuscripts Collections, Brown County Historical Society.

[20]Sioux Uprising—The Attacks Upon Fort Ridgely, Lieutenant Gere's Account, Manuscripts Collections, Brown County Historical Society. New Ulm.

[21]Sioux Uprising—The Encounter at Redwood Ferry. Sergeant [John F.] Bishop's Story of the Disaster, Manuscripts Collections, Brown County Historical Society.

[22]Harriet B. McConkey, *Dakota War-Whoop*, pp. 61-62.

[23]Sioux Uprising—The Encounter at Redwood Ferry, Sergeant [John F.] Bishop's Story of the Disaster, Manuscripts Collections, Brown County Historical Society.

[24]Sioux Uprising—The Attacks Upon Fort Ridgely, Lieutenant Gere's Account, Manuscripts Collections, Brown County Historical Society. New Ulm.

[25]Lucy Leavenworth Wilder Morris, editor, *Old Rail Fence Corners: Frontier Tales Told by Minnesota Pioneers*, St. Paul, Minnesota Historical Society Press, 1976, p. 146.

[26]Sioux Uprising—The Encounter at Redwood Ferry, Sergeant [John F.] Bishop's Story of the Disaster, Manuscripts Collections, Brown County Historical Society.

[27]Harriet B. McConkey, *Dakota War-Whoop*, pp. 61-62.

[28]Sioux Uprising—The Encounter at Redwood Ferry. Sergeant [John F.] Bishop's Story of the Disaster, Manuscripts Collections, Brown County Historical Society.

[29]*Fairfax Standard*, 1912.

[30]*The Pioneer & Democrat*, August 21, 1862.

[31]L.A. Fritsche, *History of Brown County*, pp. 274-278.

[32]Sioux Uprising—The Encounter at Redwood Ferry. Sergeant [John F.] Bishop's Story of the Disaster, Manuscripts Collections, Brown County Historical Society.

[33]*The Pioneer & Democrat*, August 22, 1862.

[34]*The Pioneer & Democrat*, August 21, 1862.

[35]*The Pioneer & Democrat*, August 22, 1862.

[36]Sioux Uprising—The Encounter at Redwood Ferry, Sergeant [John F.] Bishop's Story of the Disaster, Manuscripts Collections, Brown County Historical Society.

[37]Ibid.

[38]Charles S. Bryant & Abel B. Murch, *A History of the Great Massacre by the Sioux Indians, in Minnesota, Including the Personal Narratives of Many Who Escaped*, St. Peter, E. Wainwright & Son, Publishers, 1872, p. 185.

[39]*Pioneer & Democrat*, August 23, 1862.

[40]Charles S. Bryant & Abel B. Murch, *A History of the Great Massacre by the Sioux Indians, in Minnesota, Including the Personal Narratives of Many Who Escaped*, p. 186.

[41]Franklyn Curtis-Wedge, *The History of Renville County*, Volume II, Chicago, H.C. Cooper, Jr., & Company, 1916, p. 1346.

Chapter Seven

August 18, 1862
Upper Sioux Agency

"We are the braves. We have sold our land to the Great Father. The traders are allowed to sit at their pay table, and they take all our money. We wish you to keep the traders away from the pay table, and we desire you to make us a present of a beef."
—Unidentified Sioux Chief[1]

"The Indians' enormities increase, with each successive Courier from the Indian border. Five hundred whites, it is feared, have been killed."
—Governor Alexander Ramsey[2]

N JUNE 1861, DR. JOHN L. WAKEFIELD was appointed physician for the Upper Sioux Indians at Pajutazee, or Yellow Medicine Agency. After receiving their annuities, the Indians, with the exception of those who remained to farm the land, returned to their homes many miles away. Sarah F. Wakefield, wife of Dr. Wakefield, later wrote:

> And I will state in the beginning that I found them very kind, good people. The women sewed for me, and I employed them in various ways around my house, and began to love and respect them as well as if they were whites. I became so much accustomed to them and their ways. . . .[3]

During the spring of 1862, Major Thomas Galbraith, Dr. Wakefield, and others visited the Sioux living near Big Stone Lake. The whites found

Minnesota River near Granite Falls. [Author's collection]

Upper Sioux Agency marker. [Photo courtesy of Diana Pierce]

them quiet, content, and pleased with what the government was doing for them. In leaving, Major Galbraith instructed them not to come to the agency until he sent for them as he was unsure as to the time of payment. The Indians began coming in within a few weeks, however, because many of them were frightened of the Chippewas, who had murdered some Sioux. Soon the entire tribe camped around the agency buildings, where they stayed for several weeks, hungry and in despair over not receiving their annuities.

Early rumblings of trouble with the Indians at the Upper Agency were echoed as much as two months before the assault on the government warehouses, although most of the settlers were in fear of an attack by Inkpaduta or other Indians from outside the state. Dr. Thomas S. Williamson had written Agent Galbraith on June 2, 1862, hinting of Indian unrest:

> I am requested by your Dakota children to write to you. Marpiya (Cloud Man) requests me to say to you through Wammidupiduta (Scarlet Feather), who returned from the buffalo region in the northwest last Friday, and also in other ways, he is informed that five parties of Ehanktowan, one of them headed by a son of Inkpaduta (Scarlet Point), have started to steal horses. Some of these parties, he thinks, will come to this neighborhood, some to the Medawakantan and some to the white settlements. He says further, that the Ehanktowan, to the number of 300 or 400 tents, are killing buffalo on the Peh (or Elm) River, a branch of James River, due west of Lac Travers and the head of the Coteau of the Prairie, and are expecting large accessions to their numbers from the Sioux beyond the Missouri, and talk of coming here to demand of the Wahpehtonwan and Sissetonwan, pay for their lands, sold at the treaty in 1851, and say if they do not get it, they will kill the Indians dressed like white people, and the white people, and burn the houses, and on this account he wishes you to have a large number of soldiers here. This is the report told to me by the Cloud Man. It is a new edition of the tale which we have had every year, except one, sine 1857. But for the fact that many men from Minnesota have gone to the war, and these distant Indians hear very exaggerated reports of this, which may lead them to think the frontiers wholly unprotected, these reports might merit very little attention. As circumstances are, I think they should not be wholly neglected. I think it probable from [fifty] to 100 Ehanktowan warriors, and possibly two or three times that number, may come here in two or three weeks. They will probably not come intending to fight, but prepared to do so, and as their presence is likely to cause alarm, when they see the people here are afraid of them, this may encourage them to do mischief, especially if they think they can do so with impunity. As it seems very desirable you should be here when the Ehanktowans arrive, I would suggest that you return as soon as you dispose of your business in St. Paul.
>
> The Indians here say there are willing to arm and defend themselves, but many of them are destitute of guns and ammunition. They say also

that the Mdewakantowan are willing to come to their assistance, which is no doubt true in regard to many. I do not think it would be proper to ask Indians to go away from their country to fight white men, but under present circumstances I think it would be right and proper to require those who are receiving so much aid from our government, to arm and organize themselves as home guard for the defense of their own homes against other Indians. If properly armed and organized, I have no doubt they are able to defend the reservation against all other Indians who can come to it. You can do more toward arming and organizing them than anyone else. Some of the civilized Indians may need to be furnished with guns, which probably can be obtained of the traders. That the Ehanktowan may know that the reports which they have heard, that all the white men and soldiers from Minnesota have gone to war, I think it desirable when they come here, they should see as many soldiers here as they have seen in past years in time of payment. Perhaps by seeing Governor Ramsey you can make some arrangement to send other soldiers to Fort Ridgely, so that the entire company which is there may come up here and remain while the Ehanktowan may be here.

I hope you will not suffer anything which I have written in this letter to be divulged in such a way as to cause a panic or alarm in the white settlements. We are not alarmed here, and I think there is no occasion for anything of the kind, and I write this that there may be none in the future.[4]

On June 14th, Galbraith penned a letter to Clark W. Thompson, superintendent of Indian Affairs in St. Paul and warned him that the Yanktonais Indians were coming to the agency with every intention of remaining through the annuity payments. According to Galbraith, the Indians planned to demand a share of the annuities and certain goods the government had bought for them that they had earlier refused.

"They make threats which I deem wise to provide against," wrote Galbraith in requesting 150 troops be sent to Yellow Medicine to "preserve order, protect life and property, and prevent the usual panic incident to the payments at that place." He went on to clarify that the troops sent should have tents, transportation, and rations for at least fifteen days, and should report to him by June 25th.[5]

Thompson wrote Governor Ramsey that same day: "I have to request that you order 150 troops, or as near that number that is practicable, to report themselves to Major Galbraith at Yellow Medicine, by the 25th of this month, or as soon thereafter as possible, for the purpose of preserving

Upper Sioux Agency. (Photo courtesy of Diana Pierce)

order and protecting United States property during the time of payment to the Upper and Lower Sioux. The troops should be provided with transportation, and at least [fifteen] days' rations."[6]

Lieutenant Timothy J. Sheehan's command marched from Fort Ridgely on June 30th with their fifteen days' rations, and in addition to small arms, one twelve-pounder mountain howitzer. They camped that evening at the Lower Sioux Agency after crossing the Minnesota River on the Redwood Ferry. They continued their march on the following day and arrived at the Upper Sioux Agency on July 2nd, fifty-two miles from Fort Ridgely, and went into camp 150 yards from the government buildings.[7]

The Indians had already arrived at the agency in great numbers to wait for their annuities, and each day following their numbers increased. The payment of annuities was the sole purpose of their being present, and as early as July 8th, a party of warriors sent word through Interpreter Quinn to Lieutenants Sheehan and Gere that they desired a council with them. In expressing their needs to the officers, the Indians were told that the regulations concerning the payments were in the hands of the Indian agent appointed by the Great Father. The Sioux were also told that the soldiers had no provisions except their own rations, but that their request would be communicated to the agent.

As more Sioux arrived, Indian dances and demonstrations were conducted regularly, and there was some dissatisfaction expressed over the non-payment of annuities. A large number of Yanktonais and Cut-heads, not entitled to any payment, were encamped near the annuity Indians. On July 14th, Lieutenant Sheehan visited their camp and discovered 659 lodges of annuity Indians, seventy-eight lodges of Yanktonais, thirty-seven of Cut-heads, and five of Winnebagoes.

Major Galbraith expected the annuities to arrive between the 18th and 20th. The Indians reported on the 18th that they were starving and the whites anticipated trouble unless the Sioux could get something to eat. Major Galbraith felt no alarm was necessary as the hungry Indians had issued no threats. Lieutenant Sheehan, however, sent a detail to Fort Ridgely for a second mountain howitzer, and the party returned on the 21st. On that day, Lieutenants Sheehan and Gere met with Major Galbraith, who promised he would count the Indians, issue the provisions, and send them away to await their money.

On the morning of the 24th, a war party of 1,200 Sioux, stripped and painted, passed close by the agency buildings and camp of the soldiers in pursuit of a band of Chippewas who had a day earlier killed two Sioux about

Annuity Center site, Upper Sioux Agency. (Photo courtesy of Diana Pierce)

eighteen miles from the agency. The party returned in the afternoon without overtaking their enemies.

On July 26th, Major Galbraith commenced the counting of Indians. All the Indians were congregated in an area adjacent to the government building, and encircling it by a continuous chain of sentinels. The various chiefs called their bands forward, and once the number in each family was recorded, each passed outside the line of guards homeward. The counting took twelve and one-half hours. Crackers were issued and scattered by the soldiers to appease the hungry Indians.

Galbraith wrote Lieutenant Timothy J. Sheehan on July 27th:

> I have to request that you detail a small detachment of your com-
> mand, and with it proceed forthwith in the direction of Yellow Medicine
> River, in search of Inkpaduta and his followers, who are said to be
> camped somewhere in the region, having in their possession stolen hors-
> es, etc. You will take said Inkpaduta and all Indian soldiers with him,
> prisoners, alive if possible, and deliver them to me at the agency. If they
> resist, I advise that they be shot. Take all horses found in their posses-
> sion and deliver them to me. A party of reliable citizens will accompany
> you; they will report to you and be subject to your orders. Ten or twelve
> men in my opinion will be sufficient. They should by all means be
> mounted on horses or mules. You should stay at least nine days' rations,
> and should start a sufficient time before daylight to get away without the
> knowledge of the Indians. While I recommend prompt and vigorous
> action to bring these murderers, thieves, and villains to justice, dead or
> alive, yet I advise prudence and extreme caution.[8]

Lieutenant Sheehan and his men left about midnight, leaving Lieutenant Gere in charge of the camp. In spite of the secrecy of the mission, the Indian camp learned promptly of the departure of the party, and warned Inkapaduta. Lieutenant Sheehan returned on August 3rd, having been unsuccessful in his search.

Early on the morning of August 4th, the Sioux sent two messengers to the camp, relating they were coming down to fire a salute and conduct one of their demonstrations. They said they wanted to inform the soldiers in advance, so they would understand it was all right. The proposition was not unusual and no remonstrance was made.[9]

Soon, 800 warriors, mounted and on foot, startled the soldiers with wild yells, rifle fire, and within minutes completely surrounded the detachment. The soldiers were aware that something beyond their normal demonstration was transpiring. Suddenly the leader of the party that had ridden past the camp rushed to the door of the government warehouse and struck it with his hatchet.

The soldiers were outnumbered eight to one as they watched in shock the Indians cocking their guns on all sides at a distance of less than 100 feet. But none of the soldiers panicked and the command quickly stepped into line. Lieutenant Gere promptly removed the tarpaulin covering the mountain howitzer, and his soldiers leveled their rifles at the government warehouse door where the Indians had broken in and were removing sacks of flour.

The Indians immediately moved back to either side of the line covered by the howitzer. Sixteen soldiers led by Sergeant S.A. Trescott and Lieutenant Sheehan, marched straight through the opening to the govern-

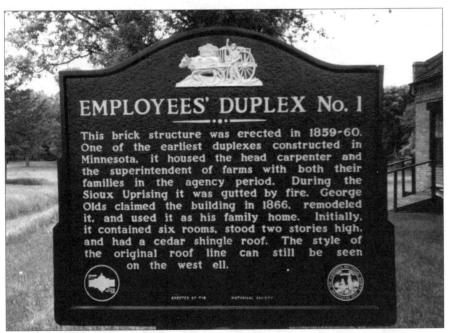

Employees' duplex No. 1 site, Upper Sioux Agency. (Photo courtesy of Diana Pierce)

ment building. Sheehan went directly to Galbraith's office to seek his advice, while Trescott and his men drove the Indians from the warehouse. By this time, twenty sacks of flour had been removed.

The Indians surrounding the camp moved toward the warehouse, and forming in groups, were addressed by the chiefs and leading braves. The Sioux leaders told them that the much-needed provisions had been sent by the Great Father in Washington, that the agent refused to give them their food while their wives and children starved, that the provisions were theirs, and that they had a right to take them. Lieutenant Sheehan was in favor of giving them their provisions, but Major Galbraith feared any concession would only lead to loss of control over the Indians in the future. He also demanded that the Sioux return to the warehouse all the flour that had been removed.

Galbraith finally decided to give the Sioux some pork and flour if they would leave at once and send their chiefs for a council on the following day. Although given the provisions, the Indians became insolent and refused to leave the agency. The entire detachment of troops moved to the warehouse and formed a battle line, with both howitzers in position. The Indians then decided to return to their camps and immediately withdrew.

The settlement at Yellow Medicine was a farming community constituting eighty-acre farms owned by the "farmer" Indians. Here at Hazelwood was the mission of Reverend Riggs, built of wooden logs, clapboarded on the exterior; a large, commodious house sufficient for a school for the young children who boarded there. A small wooden church with a steeple housing a bell stood there as well.[10] One mile below this point was the mission house of Dr. Williamson. Three miles below that stood the agency with all its government buildings and homes of private citizens. The "Upper Indians" came to the agency for their annual payment.

On August 5th, the command stationed at the warehouse with armed citizens heard a rumor that the Indians had proposed a general attack on the agency. No attack, however, took place. Major Galbraith penned a letter that same day to Lieutenants Gere and Sheehan.

> Your interpreter, Quinn, is a man whom I cannot trust to communicate or correspond with my Indians. I have therefore to respectfully

request that said Quinn be at once ordered to hold no communication, direct or indirect, with any Sioux Indian under my jurisdiction. And I further request that he be ordered off the reservation and placed in the charge of Captain Marsh, commanding at Fort Ridgely, with a copy of this request.[11]

After receiving this letter, Lieutenant Gere departed at five o'clock in the morning of August 6th with Interpreter Quinn for Fort Ridgely to advise Captain Marsh of the situation of affairs at the agency and ask him to go there in person. Marsh responded and reached the agency where he and Major Galbraith held a council with the Sioux. An agreement was reached calling for Galbraith to issue all the annuity goods immediately, whereupon the Indians would leave and not return until they were notified that the money to which they were entitled had arrived.

The delivery of provisions commenced at once and continued on the eighth and ninth. The Indian camp had disappeared on the 10th, and on the 11th, the detachment marched to Fort Ridgely, arriving on the evening of the 12th. With the flour incident settlement solved peacefully, Captain Marsh ordered Lieutenant Sheehan to report to Fort Ripley on the 17th. That same day, Lieutenant Culver and six men of Company B were detached to St. Peter, with transportation for a company of fifty recruits, who had just enlisted at the agencies en route to Fort Snelling for mustering. This action left only two officers and seventy-six men at Fort Ridgely.

Another council of the entire Sioux nation with as many Winnebagoes and other Indians as wished to come met on Sunday the 17th of August, at Rice Creek, sixteen miles above the Lower Agency.[12]

John Otherday was seated at the council. Four years earlier, he had been a drunk, but following conversion to Christianity, he fought against evil and wholeheartedly argued against any confrontation with the whites. Otherday dressed as a white man, and seated beside him by the fire was a white woman he had brought from Washington to be his wife. Having once lived in a crude bark lodge, he now lived in a comfortable brick home. He urged the Indians who advocated war to avoid hostilities and told them they should listen to the good spirit.[13]

Early in the morning, the Indians had sent couriers on swift horses to inform the Sioux of the Upper Agency of the outbreak and to urge their co-operation in the war against the whites. Couriers were also dispatched in haste to all the various bands scattered through the length and breadth of the reservation, and within six hours after the first gun had been fired at the Lower Agency there was not an Indian between the Little Rock River and Lake Traverse that did not know the massacre of the whites had begun and had been invited to participate in the glory and booty it would bring. The news reached Yellow Medicine about noon and was so unexpected to the Indians themselves that at first they hesitated to believe it. Later couriers soon followed confirming the report and showing how wonderfully successful the Indians had been.[14]

They had captured the Lower Agency and utterly destroyed it without the loss of a single Indian. They had met, defeated and would soon annihilate the soldiers from Ft. Ridgely. A council was summoned at once and met that afternoon to determine what action they, the Upper Sioux, would take. The council was divided in opinion. The heathen party were enthusiastic to join in the massacre, while the Christian Indians and some of the others were opposed to it. As fresh reports came continually of the success of the Lower Indians, it became evident to the friendly Christian Indians that they could not stem the rising tide of war. So, toward evening, on Monday the 18th, John Otherday, full-blooded Indian and an influential member of Dr. Williamson's church, with a number of his Christian companions at once notified the whites of the Upper Agency and gathered them into a brick warehouse, and with their guns stood guard outside all night determined to die in defense of their white friends.

The *St. Paul Pioneer Press* reported on August 28, 1862: "On Monday, the 18th, about eight o'clock A.M., word came to the Upper Agency at Yellow Medicine that all the white people at the Lower or Red Wood Agency had been murdered by the M'dewakanton Sioux. . . . Other-Day himself addressed them. He told them that they might easily enough kill a few whites—five, ten, or a hundred. But the consequence would be that their whole country would be filled with soldiers of the United States, and all of them killed or driven away."[15]

Sarah Wakefield was preparing dinner when her husband, John, came home. He held her in is arms and told her that she must leave immediately because there were growing tensions between the whites and the Dakota. He thought that war was very possible.

> Monday, soon after dinner, my husband came in and said that I had better get ready to go down to Fort Ridgely that afternoon, instead of waiting for the stage, [wrote Sarah Wakefield]. Mr. Gleason had come up on Saturday and wished to return and had no conveyance, and had offered to drive me and my children to the fort if my husband would let him take our horse and wagon. At two o'clock we started. I felt unusually sad. I remember going from room to room taking a final look. My husband grew impatient and asked me what I was doing, and I made some excuse. As we were starting, he said, "Gleason, drive fast, so as to get to the fort early."[16]

Mrs. Wakefield climbed into the wagon, and they started for the fort. After fifteen minutes of traveling, they discerned smoke rising over the horizon. The children could not see the smoke because the wagon cover was blocking their view. Sarah urged George to go faster just to be safe.

> As we got to the mound which is halfway between the two Agencies, we could see distinctly the smoke of the burning buildings, [recalled Sarah]. I said to him that the Indians were destroying the Agency. "Oh, no, it is the saw mill or the prairie on fire." I became frightened, and tried again to persuade him to return. I was so excited I could not sit still, and endeavored to jump out of the wagon. Then he really scolded me, saying it was very unpleasant for him to have me act that way. "Very well," said I.[17]

After another ten minutes of traveling through the woodland near the Redwood River, they came upon a farm house with two Dakota braves standing outside. George slowed down. Sarah urged Gleason to draw his pistol, but he told her he wasn't carrying one. After a brief parley with the Indians, they resumed their journey. Sarah turned to watch the Indians go in the opposite direction. Instead she saw one man—Happa, and the other Chaska—not move at all. She remembered them from when they had come to the Lower Agency and how kind they had been.

Suddenly Happa or Chaska raised his shotgun and shot Gleason through the shoulder. Gleason screamed and let go of the reigns of the horses. The horses, spooked by the gunfire, galloped off. Happa fired again and Gleason was knocked from the wagon to the ground. Chaska rushed to the wagon and grabbed Sarah and asked her if she was the wife of the doctor. She told him she was as he dragged her from the wagon and removed the children too.

"I saw the other Indian loading his gun, and I expected every instant to be launched into eternity," related Sarah. ". . . I begged him to spare me for my children's sake, and promised to sew, wash, cook, cut wood, anything than rather die and leave my children. But he would not speak, only scowl hideously."[18]

Happa reloaded and glanced at Gleason writhing on the ground in pain and screaming. He walked up to Gleason as the wounded man shouted Mrs. Wakefield's name. Happa silenced him with a bullet to the head, reloaded his shotgun and raised it to Sarah. Chaska stood in the line of fire to protect Sarah, knowing that Happa would not shoot him. Happa and Chaska argued briefly, with Happa saying that she must die; all whites were bad, and better off dead. Chaska, on the other hand, argued that she was a good white. Happa agreed to take her back to their home camp. When Sarah and her children entered the Dakota camp, the Indian women cried and laid out blankets for her, recognizing her as the doctor's wife.

The situation at the Upper Agency had caught many of the settlers and traders by surprise. At sunset the settlers were surprised to see a large body of Indians gathered on a hill west of the settlement. A half-breed was sent to go up and talk with them, but he learned nothing definite. In a little while, John Otherday came in with news of the terrible massacre which had been raging thirty miles away.[19]

The people of the settlement were hastily gathered into the government warehouse, and resolved to defend themselves to the last extremity. Sixty-two men, women, and children remained awake and distressed through the night. About two o'clock in the morning, a trader named Garvie knocked for admittance. He had been guarding his store and was shot in the bowels, but managed to escape through his garden to the warehouse. Two men, Kennedy and Boardman, were asleep in another store. A man ran and told them to run for their lives. One took to the warehouse, and the other started for Fort Ridgley.

In a short time the Indians had killed or driven off all the storekeepers of the place, and instantly began the work of plunder. Peter Patoile was shot through the breast and left for dead. He crawled to some bushes on the river bank, and remained there all the following day. At nightfall he dragged himself to the shores of the Minnesota River, and forded the stream. Finding a deserted settler's house, he passed the night there, but in the morning, discovering Indians about, seized a blanket and hid in a neighboring ravine. He wandered about through an uninhabited country and finally struck a settlement far up the Sauk Valley, where his wound was dressed for the first time.

At the Yellow Medicine warehouse, John Otherday remained on watch all night. The shouts of the Indians could be heard in the darkness as they proceeded in their work of plunder and destruction at the trading post, half a mile away. As the Sioux broke into the stores and houses of the Upper Agency, they shot two or three persons, who had failed to heed the warning. It was evident that to remain where they were meant certain death. The seriousness of the situation was appalling. Slender as were the chances of escape, the resolve was taken to attempt it. Teams were hastily harnessed to such wagons as could be had, and into them climbed the women and children. While the attention of the Sioux was absorbed, Otherday seized the opportunity to load the white people into the wagons, and well-knowing the terrible chances he ran, placed himself at the head of the caravan, which comprised twenty men and forty-two women and children, and piloted them across the trackless prairie to Hutchinson and thence by St. Cloud to Shakopee, where they all arrived safely the following Friday.[20]

A small supply of provisions was thrown together, and just at dawn the terrified procession of which the male members were on foot, crossed the Minnesota River, and, guided by John Otherday, struck across the prairie in

John Otherday. (Author's collection)

the direction of the settlements of the Kandiyohi Lakes and Glencoe. Mr. Goodell, the superintendent of farms at the Yellow Medicine Agency had proposed a different escape route, but he was informed by Otherday that if he persisted, he would have to part from them.

A turbulent storm overtook the party, during which Garvie died. But because of the unflinching devotion of John Otherday, a pure full-blooded Indian, who only three years before, had been considered one of the wildest savages, the lives of sixty-two persons were rescued from the massacre—forty-two of these were women and children. Yielding to his advice to not attempt flight in the direction of Fort Ridgley, where they would be certainly destroyed, the party placed their lives in his hands, and struck into a trackless wilderness, with which he alone was acquainted. They had a few carriages for the women and children, and the men walked. They kept on the move all through the night, and the following evening, stayed with an old Swede whose family had run away.

They went to Hutchinson and on to Glencoe and Carver. During the trip, Mrs. Galbraith and two children and a Miss Charles rode in a carriage. Miss Charles, Goodell later wrote, was the bravest girl he had ever seen and enlivened the party by her cheerful demeanor. On Friday, the 22nd, he guided them safely into Shakopee, Scott County.

Other Christian Indians went the same Monday evening and warned Dr. Williamson and Dr. Riggs at their respective mission stations. With them were a number of young ladies teaching in the mission schools. Through the protection and aid of the faithful Christian converts, all were saved. Dr. Riggs and his company were taken at midnight to an island in the Minnesota River, three miles away. At the island, Reverend Riggs was informed by friendly Indians that his home had been broken into and everything destroyed. He was also told that Amos W. Huggins and his family had been murdered at the Lac Qui Parle Mission.[21]

The following morning being supplied with some food and Mr. Cunningham's wagon, they started for Ft. Ridgely. Cunningham had slipped back into the Indian village and procured the wagon for their escape. The friendly Indians seemed very concerned about their safety.[22]

All of the Indians belonging to the Hazelwood Republic were in great fear for their own lives, and as soon as they learned of the outrages at the agencies, put on their blankets and prepared to flee. These Indians had met at Mr. Cunningham's house and made their plans to escape.

Andrew Hunter and his family and a part of Dr. Williamson's party hid further down the river with their team and cattle. They commenced their dangerous journey on Tuesday. On the way they were joined by a few settlers, making in all forty-two souls. A thunderstorm obliterated their tracks so the Indians could not follow them. They started out across the prairie in a northeasterly direction, and on Wednesday morning turned southeast, until they reached the Lac Qui Parle Road. From there, they headed directly for Fort Ridgely.

On Friday afternoon, they passed quite near the Beaver Creek settlement. When within six miles of the fort, they saw two Indians on horseback, who gazed at them for a few minutes, then rode off. The party soon discovered that the fort was surrounded by Indians.

Andrew Hunter managed to crawl through the underbrush and make his way into the fort about eleven o'clock Friday night. Once inside the garrison, Lieutenant Sheehan told him that it was certain death for his company of more than forty people to attempt to make their way through the lines of the Indians into the fort.

He returned at midnight to his party and found that they had advanced to within a mile and a half of the fort. He reported that Lieutenant Sheehan had related to him that it would be unsafe to try to reach the fort and proposed that they attempt to reach Henderson instead. The officer had also told him that he and his men had fought a continual fight for days, were exhausted, and could not hold out much longer. He had also explained that there were about 500 women and children in the fort and finding water had become difficult. Heart-sick, the fugitives resumed their weary march across the prairie. All around the horizon they could see the reflected red light from burning dwellings.

Unable to enter the fort because of the siege, they passed around it, and, in hearing the Indian guns and in sight of the burning houses, they journeyed all day through Nicollet County on the road that lay next to and parallel with the one on which the Indians were massacring the people. On some farms, they saw oxen yoked and standing in the yards. Cattle grazed in the grain fields, while others stood in the yards with no food or water. Desolation was everywhere.

As they passed within five miles of the Norwegian Grove settlement, they could see high, rising flames from the burning buildings, leaving no doubt that the entire village was destroyed and the Indians nearby. They saw only one body on the road, and that was about six miles from Fort Ridgely.

Reverend Dr. Williamson and his family parted company with the party about eighteen miles south of Henderson and proceeded to St. Peter where he had left other family members. He planned to go back to the agency with the soldiers. Hunter and the main party finally reached Henderson in safety. Reverend Riggs concluded that their escape was successful only because the Indians were preoccupied with stealing goods from the stores.[23]

A few days after the attack on the Upper Sioux Agency, Antoine Frenier, who had spent most of his life among the Sioux, volunteered to go alone to the Indian country, trusting to his knowledge of their customs, disguised as one of them, complete with Indian dress and paint. Frenier traveled forty-five miles to the Upper Sioux Agency, arrived there at night, and found the agency a "habitation of death." Frenier went inside all the houses and discovered their former occupants dead, some on doorsteps, others inside, and others scattered in their yards.[24]

After ascertaining that there were no Indians about, Frenier entered the home of Joseph R. Brown, and recognized every member of the family, eighteen in all, murdered, including Brown's son-in-law, Charles Blair, and his wife. At a house one mile below the agency he found five frightened children in a room still alive but nearly dead from hunger. Frenier went to another house and procured some crackers for the children. He told them to stay in the room and that he would return for them in a few days.

Frenier visited Beaver Creek, where he discovered that fifty families had been killed. He entered several homes and found that he recognized most of the bodies. Among those recognized at the agency were N. Givens and family, Mrs. Galbraith and children, Dr. Wakefield and family, Dr. Humphrey and family, John Fadden's family, the missionaries Reverend Dr. Williamson and Reverend Mr. Riggs, and John and Edward Mayner. He also learned that when the attack was made, George Gleason and Philander Prescott were captured, but a promise was made to spare them if they would deliver up the stores. Frenier, however, found no trace of either man.

Bishop Whipple later wrote:

> For weeks we had no tidings from the Sioux or Chippewa missions. They were dark days. When news came, we found that both missions had been destroyed; but our hearts were made glad when we learned that the only lives saved during that holocaust of death were by the Christian Indians, or friendly Indians, who had been influenced by the missionaries.
> The wily chief, Hole-in-the-Day, had planned for a massacre at the same time on the northern border. But Enmegahbowh had sent a faithful messenger to Mille Lacs, to urge the Indians to be true to the whites and to send men to protect the fort. More than a hundred Mille Lacs warriors went at once to the fort, but meantime Emmegahbowh himself walked all night down Gull River, dragging a canoe containing his wife and children, that he might give warning to the fort. Two of his children died from the exposure. Messages were also sent to the white settlers, and before Hole-in-the-Day could begin war the massacre was averted.
> The commissioner of Indian Affairs, who was at the fort, was so filled with gratitude at the Mille Lacs Indians for their protection that he

promised them that they should not only be rewarded by the government, but should not be removed from their reservation. Pledges to that effect were incorporated in a treaty made shortly after, but the pledges were broken.

It would be too long a story to tell of the heroism of Taopi, Good Thunder, Wabasha, Wa-ha-can-ka-ma-za (Iron Shield), Simon A-nag-ma-ni, Lorenzo Laurence, Otherday, Thomas Robertson, Paul Maza-kute, Wa-kin-yan-ta-wa, and others who, at the risk of life, saved help-less women and children.[25]

A frantic Governor Ramsey dispatched a telegram requesting military aid: "Saint Paul, Minn., August 21, 1862—4 p.m. Hon. E.M. Stanton, Secretary of War: The Sioux Indians on our western border have risen, and are murdering men, women, and children. I have ordered a party of men out, under Col. H.H. Sibley, and given the command of the Sixth Regiment, also ordered up, to Capt. A.D. Nelson, U.S. Army. I must have Nelson. Telegraph at once.—Alex Ramsey."

Secretary of State J.H. Baker also penned an urgent message that same day: "St. Paul, Minn., August 21, 1862. Hon C.P. Wolcott, Assistant Secretary of War: A most frightful insurrection of Indians has broken out along our whole frontier. Men, women, and children are indiscriminately murdered; evidently the result of a deep-laid plan, the attacks being simultaneous along our whole border. The governor has ordered out infantry. It is useless. Cannot you authorize me to raise 1,000 mounted men for the special service? –J.H. Baker, Secretary of State."

General-in-Chief Henry W. Halleck responded the following day: "War Department, Washington, August 22, 1862. Brigadier-General Schofield, St. Louis, Mo.: Send the Third Regiment Minnesota Volunteers against the Indians on the frontier of Minnesota.—H.W. Halleck, General-in-Chief."[26]

On August 27th, D.W. Moore of New Jersey, with his wife, arrived in St. Paul from Henderson. The Moores had been part of the group of missionaries who had escaped from the Upper Agency during the attack. They had boarded with Reverend Riggs at Hazelwood for six weeks, some six miles from the Upper Agency.[27]

After saving the lives of many persons at the Upper Agency, John Otherday was invited to St. Paul where he was "quite a lion" in the streets.

He received congratulations from many St. Paulites, and in the evening, was introduced to a large audience assembled for the organization of a home guard at Ingersoll's Hall. Otherday addressed the group with a speech he had prepared and was well received.[28]

But there was only one John Otherday and thousands of Sioux roaming the Minnesota prairies. Settlers in nearly every county in the state began making preparations for defense in case of an Indian attack. Although the Sioux had killed only one family in Wright County, the citizens were swept by a panic of fear which lasted for several years. On August 20, 1862, just after Company E, Eighth Minnesota Volunteer Infantry, left for Fort Snelling, word came that the Sioux had committed atrocities at Acton, Lower and Upper Agencies, and other places. In addition to the reports of grisly killings came rumors of widespread pillage, rapine, and massacre.[29]

Every settler believed that the area just west of him was swarming with painted-faced, tomahawk-toting Indians. Settlers living along the Mississippi and Crow Rivers had been told that Waverly had been burned and Buffalo was running red with blood. People living in the center of the county believed that the western part had been reduced to carnage and ruin, while those in the west were told every family in Meeker County had been slaughtered.

Facing possible horrible death, the pioneer families left their crops and livestock behind and journeyed to St. Paul, Minneapolis, St. Anthony, and Fort Snelling. The Indian scare was as great in Wright County as in any other part of the state. Panic in the Big Woods ran rampant because the clearings around the cabins were small. Unlike the people on the prairie, the settlers in the Big Woods could command a view of the landscape for only a short distance from the house. They were easy prey for any Indians who chose to attack them.

During the initial exodus, plans were made to hold the fleeing settlers at Buffalo, but after this failed, stands were made at Monticello, Clearwater, and Rockford. Stockades were quickly erected in several towns, and an attempt was made to accommodate all those who desired protection.

The men of Rockford thought it wise to build a stockade. They hurriedly used whatever materials were available, part of which happened to be the planks which had recently been sawed at the mill for John Batdorf's barn.

Holes were cut in the planks for the men's rifles. The Indians did not attack. After about two months, the stockade was torn down and John built his barn. The rifle holes were reminders of early days as long as the barn stood.[30]

About eight o' clock on the morning of August 19th, messengers rushed into Carver from Walker's Landing and erroneously reported that Indians had slaughtered all the troops at Fort Ridgely, burned the fort and the Upper and Lower agencies, killing all the inhabitants, burned New Ulm and St. Peter and attacked Henderson. The messengers related that they had heard heavy firing at Henderson before they left, and that the village was burning at the time of their departure. They also reported that there were between five and ten thousand Indians on the warpath, and it was their intent to lay waste to all the country from Fort Ridgely to Fort Snelling.[31]

Soon after their arrival, a great panic erupted with men, women, and children coming into the settlement screaming in fear. Some were barefoot, some shirtless, others wearing little clothing at all, and the majority unarmed.

There was a big Indian scare in Fillmore County. There were no hostile Indians for 140 miles, but the village of Preston was jammed full of people and teams of horses. All houses, shops, mills, and every available shelter were crowded with people. Not one shot was fired during this panic.

But in August 1862 the fear of an Indian attack caused several measures to be taken. Every house, shop, store, shed, and barn was filled with families from the western part of the county. Military law was established, and men and boys took their turns as guards. The state sent muskets and ammunitions but their clumsy proportions were later little more than a source of amusement.[32]

But there was little amusement for captives such as the Wakefields. Minnie Buce Carrigan, another captive, later recalled:

> The next morning . . . I heard a great commotion again. On investigation I saw a most disgusting spectacle. Side by side, with their throats cut and their feet in the air, lay a number of dogs. I returned to the tent sickened by the sight, but in a little while my curiosity got the better of my sensations, and I went out again. By this time the Indians were singeing the hair off the dogs with burning hay. I recognized our little white

poodle among the carcasses. The Indians had eight or ten kettles on the fire and as soon as a dog was singed it was thrown into the boiling water. Perhaps they were only scalding them preparatory to cooking. I concluded they were cooking without preparation and resolved not to eat any of the meat if I had to starve. The men were about the kettles for several hours, the squaws not daring to come near. At last the women and children were driven out of the tent and only the men partook of the dog feast. Even the boys, to their great dissatisfaction, were not allowed to participate. We had to stay out until after midnight. For three nights they kept up their dog feast in adjoining tents. I have heard since that they were religious feasts and indulged in only by warriors who on this occasion were preparing for battle. After the feasts were over, all the warriors left camp on another murdering expedition.[33]

Sarah Wakefield and her children were led into the camp with a large group of white women and children. She recognized many people she had known at the Lower Agency. Chaska broke through the huddled women and children and sternly ordered Sarah and her son James to follow him. He was accompanied by three older Indian women. These Dakota women took up positions all around Nellie and James. Sarah followed Chaska to a tepee. Chaska opened the flap and departed, speaking briefly with the women to make sure that they had understood that Sarah was not to be harmed.[34]

Sarah recalled that when Chaska spoke with her, he said: "As long as I was with them (the Dakota women) I must try to be pleased and not to mistrust them; make them think that I had confidence in them, and they would learn to love and respect me, that doing this would prolong the life of my children as well as my own." She added: "Soon, I was changed from a white woman to a squaw . . . how humiliating it was to adapt to such a dress, even under such circumstances." Dakota women grabbed fistfuls of dirt and rubbed the dirt into her skin to make her blend in. During that day they moved from one tepee lodge to another. There were rumors that all the whites were to be killed. There was also another rumor that the Sisseton tribe would come and take the whites and make them their slaves.

The squaws also tried to disguise James and Nellie, but James had blond hair although such was not the case with Nellie. Another rumor reached the tent, the children were to be kept and ransomed off to the

"Great Father" and the parents killed. Sarah stole a knife and was prepared to kill her children before she died. She had the knife close to James when a Dakota woman verified that all the rumors were false.

The following afternoon, Chaska's mother burst into the lodge speaking rapidly in broken English. A drunken warrior was coming to kill all the whites residing there. Acting on instinct, Chaska's mother took some crackers and some water in a deerskin flask. She gave them to Sarah. She led the Wakefields down to a ravine behind the lodge. Sarah then realized that she had had Nellie taken from her arms by one of the Dakota women. Chaska's mother explained that it was better off to have Nellie with the squaws because she could pass for a Sioux.

Throughout the night, mud slide after mud slide threatened their lives, sometimes burying them up to their necks. They had to dig out before the next one hit. The rain let up after five hours. Chaska's mother came down the sides of the ravine and took the two where they could get food. Sarah and James were famished. Then they were led on a three-mile hike to another Dakota encampment. Once there Sarah and James bathed and put on new clothes.

Sarah and her children were later rescued by Colonel Sibley and his soldiers. She went back to what remained of her home and discovered that her husband was still alive.

Notes

[1]"Sioux Uprising—Early Rumblings at the Upper Agency. Lieut. Gere's Account of the Disturbances," Brown County Historical Society, New Ulm.

[2]Marion Ramsey Furness, *Governor Ramsey and Frontier Minnesota: Impressions from His Diary and Letters*, p. 19.

[3]Sarah F. Wakefield, *Six Weeks in the Indian Tepees*, Ye Galleon Press, 1985, p. 7.

[4]Thomas S. Williamson letter to T.J. Galbraith dated June 2, 1862, "Sioux Uprising—Early Rumblings at the Upper Agency Letter of Dr. Thomas Williamson." Brown County Historical Society, New Ulm.

[5]Thomas J. Galbraith letter to Clark W. Thompson dated June 14, 1862, "Sioux Uprising—Early Rumblings at the Upper Agency. Official Requests for Troops." Brown County Historical Society, New Ulm.

[6]Clark W. Thompson letter to Governor Alexander Ramsey dated June 14, 1862. "Sioux Uprising—Early Rumblings at the Upper Agency," Official Requests for Troops." Brown County Historical Society, New Ulm.

[7]"Sioux Uprising—Early Rumblings at the Upper Agency. Lieut. Gere's Account of the Disturbances," Brown County Historical Society, New Ulm.

[8]Thomas J. Galbraith letter to Lieutenant Timothy J. Sheehan dated July 27, 1862, "Sioux Uprising—Early Rumblings at the Upper Agency. Agent Galbraith's Instructions to Lt. Sheehan." Brown County Historical Society, New Ulm.

[9]"Sioux Uprising—Early Rumblings at the Upper Agency. Lieut. Gere's Account of the Disturbances." Brown County Historical Society, New Ulm.

[10]Charles Eugene Flandrau letter to E.M. Tebbets dated September 20, 1897, Dakota Conflict of 1862. Manuscripts Collections, Microfilm Edition, Reel 1, Minnesota Historical Society.

[11]"Sioux Uprising—Early Rumblings at the Upper Agency. Lieut. Gere's Account of the Disturbances," Brown County Historical Society, New Ulm.

[12]Reverends Thomas E. Hughes and David Edwards, Hugh G. Roberts and Thomas Hughes, Story of the Welsh in Minnesota, Foreston and Lime Springs, Iowa. Gathered by the Old Settlers, 1895.

[13]Harriet E. Bishop McConky, Dakota War Whoop, pp. 48-52.

[14]Reverends Thomas E. Hughes and David Edwards, Hugh G. Roberts and Thomas Hughes, Story of the Welsh in Minnesota, Foreston and Lime Springs, Iowa. Gathered by the Old Settlers, 1895.

[15]St. Paul Pioneer Press, August 28, 1862.

[16]Sarah F. Wakefield, Six Weeks in the Indian Tepees, p. 14.

[17]Ibid., p. 15.

[18]Ibid., p. 17.

[19]St. Paul Pioneer Press, August 28, 1862.

[20]St. Paul Pioneer Press, August 28, 1862; Pioneer & Democrat, August 24, 1862.

[21]Ibid.

[22]Pioneer & Democrat, August 28, 1862.

[23]St. Paul Pioneer Press, August 28, 1862; Pioneer & Democrat, August 24, 1862; Pioneer & Democrat, August 28, 1862.

[24]Pioneer & Democrat, August 23, 1862.

[25]Bishop Henry B. Whipple, Light and Shadows of a Long Episcopate (1902) Being Reminiscences and Recollections of the Right Reverend Henry B. Whipple, Bishop of Minnesota.

[26]War of the Rebellion, a Compilation of the Official Records of the Union and Confederate Armies, Government Printing Office, Washington, D.C., 1880. Courtesy of Cornell University Digital Library Project.

[27]Pioneer & Democrat, August 28, 1862.

[28]Pioneer & Democrat, August 27, 1862.

[29]Franklyn Curtiss-Wedge, History of Wright County, Minnesota, Chicago, H. C. Cooper, Jr., & Company, 1915, pp. 141-158.

[30]"1868–1968 Maple Plain & Independence Past–Present," published by the Maple Plain Garden Club.

[31]*Pioneer & Democrat*, August 29, 1862.

[32]Franklyn Curtiss-Wedge, *History of Wright County, Minnesota*, Chicago, H. C. Cooper, Jr., & Company, 1915, pp. 141-158.

[33]Minnie Buce Carrigan, *Captured by the Indians: Reminiscences of Pioneer Life in Minnesota*, Forest City, South Dakota, Forest City Press, 1907.

[34]Sarah F. Wakefield, *Six Weeks in the Indian Tepees*, Ye Galleon Press, 1985, p. 7.

Chapter Eight

August 18, 1862
Sacred Heart and Beaver Creek

"I am a Dakota Indian, born and reared in the midst of evil. I grew up without the knowledge of any good thing. I have been instructed by Americans, and taught to read and write. This I found to be good. I became acquainted with the Sacred Writings, and there learned my vileness. At the present time I have fallen into great evil and affliction, but have escaped from it; and with fifty-four men, women, and children, and no moccasins, without food, and without a blanket, I have arrived in the midst of a great people, and now my heart is glad. I attribute it to the mercy of the Great Spirit." —John Otherday[1]

"During the last night was called up half a dozen times by couriers from the seat of war or by parties concerned about the panic, which is driving out the people. Whole counties, North and West of the Minnesota River being depopulated." —Governor Alexander Ramsey[2]

ACRED HEART, A FLOURISHING GERMAN SETTLEMENT, had sprung up on the Sacred Heart River near Patterson's Rapids, twelve miles below the Upper Agency at Yellow Medicine. Nearly all the early settlements in this part of Renville Country were started along rivers and streams, where the pioneers could find plenty of water, timber, and hay for their needs. True to this custom, the first band of settlers in Sacred Heart selected this site in the Minnesota River Valley and on the prairie along the natural groves of timber.[3]

The daily sighting of Indians in the Sacred Heart-Beaver Creek area was not uncommon, for the Sioux roamed the prairie hunting a bulbous root they called *teepson* (wild turnip), which they used for food. The plant was but a few inches high and possessed one slender, straight stem which extended into the ground three or four inches. Here, the bulb was formed, and below was a taproot.[4]

On August 12th, a Renville County Republican Convention was held at the James Carruthers' home, and Carruthers was chosen delegate to the Congressional Convention to be held at Owatonna on the 19th. He left home for the convention on the 17th. Mrs. Carruthers was at the home of a neighbor, S.R. Henderson, taking care of his wife, who was suffering from inflammation of the bowels or appendicitis. She had been treated by the agency physician, Dr. Philander P. Humphrey, who had given up all hope of Mrs. Henderson's recovery.[5]

On the evening of the 17th, the settlers heard very plainly the sound of Indian drums. According to Mrs. Carruthers, the Hendersons were strongly prejudiced against the old Indian medicine man and never missed a chance to abuse or ridicule him. But with Mrs. Henderson failing, her husband suddenly begged for the medicine man's help. The medicine man agreed on the condition that only Mrs. Carruthers would assist with the nursing. Unfortunately for Mrs. Henderson, fate intervened when, on the 18th, about six o'clock in the morning, four Indians appeared at the Henderson home.

> They shook hands with us, but somehow did not seem quite as friendly as usual, [recalled Mrs. Carruthers years later]. I gave them something to eat, and they went away to the other settlers' houses in the neighborhood and looked into them, doubtless to see how many men were about. They went to the house of Mr. Jonathan W. Earle, where they were quite saucy and overbearing. One of them took down Mr. Earle's gun and was going off with it, when Mr. Earle took it away from him. The Indian said they were going to kill Chippewas and would return the gun, but Mr. Earle refused to let them have it, and they then went to the back of the house and sat down on a woodpile, as if for consultation.[6]

E.W. Earle later recalled:

Monday, the 18th, father rose very early, and it excited no fear. When called to breakfast, father came down from the roof and, out of curiosity, went to the Indians and asked them why they were there. They told him something about Chippewa Indians, but he learned but little from them, so came in, and we sat down to breakfast. While we were eating, one of the Indians, a magnificent specimen over six feet tall, came in dressed in a breech cloth and covered with war paint. He asked father for our two rifles, which of course, [father] refused. They hung by straps to the joists overhead and a bed stood directly below them. The Indian seemed determined to have them and stepped on the bed as though he were going to reach [for] the rifles. At that father rose and said, "No," with a decided shake of the head and a look in his eyes which convinced the Indian father meant all he said. The Indian turned about and left the house, apparently much excited and angry.[7]

Ezmon W. Earle. (Courtesy of the Brown County Historical Society)

Earle's sons were preparing the teams to haul hay when they saw a party of Indians a mile across the prairie attempting to catch some horses belonging to the settlers. Earle and two other men tried to stop them, but the Indians insisted they needed the horses to kill Chippewas. Jonathan Earle instructed his boys to go find the horses and bring them home. Chalon and Radnor went east, believing they would locate them on the prairie, while Ezmon followed the creek.

Ezmon located several horses the Indians had driven into a corner between two fences at the Hunter farm. Young Earle saw immediately that his family's horses were not in the enclosure, but when sighted by the

Indians, he was told to go in and capture the horses. Ezmon insisted the horses were not his, so he could not help catch them. When ordered to help form a line to trap them, he realized that when the horses broke, they would come directly at him. When they charged, he pretended to try to stop them. The Sioux fell for his ruse and chased after the fleeing animals.

While Ezmon watched the chase, an old Indian woman appeared, and in a low voice told him to go far away. He, however, hesitated and the same warrior who had come to his house and demanded rifles, grabbed him around the neck, threatened to scalp him, and struck him over the head with his lariat. During the struggle, Ezmon punched his attacker in the ribs and the Indian released his grip, grunted, and walked off.

"I had caught a glimpse of old Beaver Creek, who was the only one that I knew," recalled Ezmon Earle years later. "I thought that surely he would explain the strange doings, but he refused to say a word to me. When I approached him, he hastily turned away and seemed greatly excited. Still my suspicions were not aroused for I thought all these strange acts were because of the Chippewa raid. I did not dream of any danger to the whites."[8]

Earle started home. Rather than follow the prairie road, he rushed into the bushes and lost himself in the timber along the bluffs. Reaching home safely, he discovered that Chalon and Radnor had brought back the horses. Ezmon and Chalon quickly led the seven horses out towards the prairie where the Indians could not get them.

As they rode eastward on the prairie, they encountered Mr. Wichman, a neighbor, running in his shirt sleeves towards the settlement from the agency. Wichman was greatly excited and told them to flee the area as the Sioux were killing all the whites at the agency. The boys started for home, stopping along the way to warn David Carruthers, the Hendersons, and others. All were told to meet at the Earle home.

Meanwhile, Jonathan Earle had given in and returned to the house, when a rider rushed in and related that the Indians had broken out and were killing the settlers at the Lower Agency. He told Earle he had witnessed several persons murdered during his escape to Beaver Creek, where he hoped to get his wife and children safely to Fort Ridgely.[9]

At Beaver Creek, twenty-eight men, women, and children gathered in the home of Jonathan W. Earle. The settlement was located three miles west of Birch Coulie Creek and about eighteen miles from Fort Ridgely. A Swedish settlement was located three miles west of Beaver Creek on another stream which emptied into the Minnesota River. The Redwood Agency, six miles distant, could be seen from the village of Beaver Creek. Like many other water courses in the state, Beaver Creek entered a valley much lower than the prairie land between thickly timbered bluffs. The creek ran north and south and emptied into the Minnesota River about two miles from the village.[10]

After hitching up several teams, the party started for Fort Ridgely, carrying with them the ill wife of S.R. Henderson, her children, the family of N.D. White, the wife and two children of James Carruthers, David Carruthers and family, Earle and family, Henderson, and a German named Wedge.[11]

"We carried poor Mrs. Henderson, then almost in a dying condition, on a feather bed from her house to Mr. Earle's and laid her in a wagon," recalled Mrs. Carruthers. "Our party had three wagons, the one containing Mrs. Henderson and her two children in the rear. The other women and children rode in the other two; the men walked alongside. The road to Fort Ridgely ran over the prairie."[12]

Having traveled a short distance, they were surrounded by Indians who told them, "We are going to kill you." Following some negotiations, the Sioux agreed to allow them to go, but the Indians appropriated all the wagons but one and the buggy that Mrs. Henderson rode in. They were stopped again a short distance up the road and the remaining wagon was taken. The men pulled Mrs. Henderson in her buggy by hand.[13]

When Mr. Henderson protested the appropriation of his colts, he was told by the Indians that he could keep a yoke of oxen. He explained to them that they could not use the oxen because the iron neck yoke was bolted to the end of the buggy pole so that the pole could not enter the yoke ring. His plea fell upon deaf ears.[14]

> We had not gone more than half a mile when, to our horror, a considerable number of Indians—perhaps [seventy-five] in all—rose up out of the

tall prairie grass and surrounded us, [remembered Mrs. Carruthers]. I was the only one in the company who could speak their language. I stood up in the wagon and asked the leader of the band what they meant to do. He replied: "We are going to kill you all." I knew he expressed their real purpose. I pleaded for our lives. I reminded them how I had always been their good friend, how I had lived among them for four years, that my children had been born among them and had often been carried to their teepees on the backs of their women, that I and my children loved the Indian people as our own.[15] [They were permitted to continue].

We had just reached the foot of a little descent and the Indians were at the top of it, when they fired the firsts shot, a single one which passed over our heads and landed a short distance ahead, [wrote Ezmon Earle]. Dave Carruthers, much excited, dodged and shouted, "Look out." No one else uttered a sound, but hurried on. Of course we soon found out that we could never take the buggy out of reach of the Indians and that an attempt to do it meant death. We could not possibly do Mrs. Henderson any good either by remaining, for we could not defend her, nor by trying to take her along, which was impossible. And hard as it was we were forced to abandon her and her two little girls. . . . Mr. Henderson said that he could not leave his wife, and for this we all honored him. Wedge said that Mrs. Henderson had nursed him in his sickness, and he would not leave her. By this time the Indians were firing quite rapidly and every instant someone had a narrow escape. So we left them, uncertain as to their fate, hoping yet fearful.[16]

Mrs. Carruthers penned: "We had gone but little over a mile. I was ahead of the company some thirty rods, when I was startled by hearing the Indian death song. Looking back I saw the whole band we had left coming after us, and heard the reports of three guns. The dreadful truth flashed upon me; the Indians were killing us! Several bullets struck the wagon. Mrs. David Carruthers, my sister-in-law, who was holding an umbrella over poor Mrs. Henderson, jumped from the wagon, two bullets passing through her dress before she reached the ground."

While the Indians fired on the men pulling the buggy, the women, children, and David Carruthers had gone on ahead. Knowing they could not save Mrs. Henderson, Mr. Earle raced ahead and caught up with the fleeing women and children. S.R. Henderson waved a white flag of truce, but the Sioux shot off his fingers and killed Wedge. Henderson realized he could not save his wife and children and ran away.[17] Ezmon Earle related:

. . . We saw firing from the rear of the buggy, and very shortly I saw Mr. Henderson emerge from the middle of the line of Indians and run rapidly toward us. We slackened our pace and waited for him. Every one of the [sixteen] Indians discharged both barrels of his gun at Mr. Henderson, and I do not doubt that some reloaded and fired bullets. . . . He was not entirely unhurt. They had shot the hat off his head, and his shirt was riddled on both sides of his body. The fore finger of the right hand was shot off at the first joint, and the second finger had a slit from the middle joint to the end.

He also said that Wedge was dead and that he thought his wife and children had also been killed, but he was not certain. He afterwards told me his story in detail. It seems that nearly all of the Indians passed the wagon without giving them any attention, but the last two, who were at a short distance behind, fired upon them. He shouted at them, but Mrs. Henderson told him to take off a pillow case and hold it up as a flag of truce. This he did but they fired again and shot off the finger [of the hand] that held it. Then they stopped and made a sign which he and Wedge understood to take hold of the buggy and take it back. So each one took an end of the neck yoke and started to turn when the Indians fired again and Wedge fell. He then ran back to the wagon, but as the Indians continued to fire, he suddenly resolved to leave his wife and try to save himself. So he started to come to us.[18]

The Indians approached the buggy, removed the helpless woman and children, threw them on the ground, placed a blanket over them, set it on fire, and raced after the fleeing fugitives.[19]

Mrs. Carruthers later recalled:

Some of the Indians made a big fire and when it was burning fiercely they lifted the featherbed on which Mrs. Henderson lay, and tossed bed and woman and the mangled portions of her children into the flames. O, the horror of this scene! The dense smoke of the feathers of the bed and the burning human flesh, the yells of the Indians, the shrieks of anguish of those who witnessed the horror, and the groans of the poor woman.

[The burned and blackened remains of the woman and her children were later found by a burial party and buried.]

Another red fiend caught up the nine-month-old baby girl, and holding her by one foot, head downwards, deliberately hacked the body, limb from limb, with his tomahawk, throwing the pieces of the head [onto] Mrs. Henderson.

An Indian seized . . . a sweet pretty little girl of but about two and a half years, and beat her savagely over the face and head with a violin box, mashing her head horribly out of its natural shape. Then he took

261

the poor little thing by her feet and swinging the body around dashed her against the wheel of the wagon, the blood and brains splattering over the dying mother. Several times the wretch swung the body against the wheel and at last threw the crushed and mutilated remains into the wagon upon the body of the wretched mother.[20]

As the Indians busied themselves with Mrs. Henderson and the two children at the wagon, Mrs. Carruthers and her two children fled. "With my children I was rushing on, when I stumbled into a slough," stated Mrs. Carruthers. "Realizing that escape was impossible, I turned, and with my arm around each of my darlings, I stood awaiting my doom and witnessing horrors which even now, forty-two years afterward, fairly appall me."[21]

An Indian approached them, and Mrs. Carruthers expected to be killed. The brave, however, spoke to her in friendly tones and shook hands, removing her rings as he did so. He told her the medicine man had demanded that she and her children not be killed, and to save them, he was taking the trio to his teepee where she would become his squaw.

The pursuing Indians caught up with the fleeing women and children and all were taken prisoner except for the two children of David Carruthers, who had been shot in the chase after Carruthers, Earle, and the sons of Earle and White. Both White and Earle lost a son during the chase.[22]

Wrote Earle: "We were fleeing from the Indians yet we were not going as fast as we might, and we maintained a show of defense although not a gun had been discharged on our side. We had no ammunition to spare and really our guns were only useful as they kept the Indians at a little distance. For knowing probably that three of our guns only carried shot, while theirs carried ounce bullets, they kept beyond the range of our guns, while keeping us still within the range of theirs."[23]

The Indians kept a distance of fifteen to twenty rods between them and the fleeing whites. The settlers formed a line several feet apart from one another for defensive purposes. An Indian leveled his rifle and hit Eugene White on the inside of his right knee. He fell, but immediately rose to a sitting position and grasped his wounded knee with his hands. Earle ran over and asked where he had been hit, and White told him that his leg was broken. The wound, however, did not keep White from jumping up and running with his companions.

White soon turned to his left and ran a bit to one side where he lay down and concealed himself in the tall grass. By this time, the firing had become heavy, and White had to be left behind to fen for himself. Earle watched as an Indian ran a short distance to where he lay and fired both barrels of his gun at him. "Of course I knew what happened," wrote Earle years later.

The Sioux came close to their quarry and began crowding them in an attempt to get around their right flank. Jonathan Earle stepped atop a small mound, took aim and fired. As an Indian went down, the others opened fire on the elder Earle, who had run out of ammunition. In a foolish move, Earle threw away his gun, and the Sioux moved in for the kill. Radnor rushed to his side and threw himself on the ground to face two of the enemy.

As he fired, so did the two Indians, and the brave fifteen-year old gave his own life to save that of his father.

Carruthers escaped to the Crow River and on to St. Paul while Earle, two of his sons, and a son of Mr. White, made their way safely to Cedar City before reaching St. Peter and Fort Ridgely.[24]

The Indians returned to the homes of the settlers with the captive women and children and plundered and destroyed everything in each dwelling. They gathered the stock and drove them to their village, taking their captives with them. The Indian warriors and their women poured into Little Crow's camp from every direction, the women laden with plunder, the men brandishing the bloody scalps of their victims on their belts.

Mrs. Carruthers, Mrs. Earle, and Mrs. White were kept together, and while walking past Little Crow's house, they saw a white man walking in the distance. Rushing to him, they learned he was George H. Spencer, a clerk at one of the agency stores. Wounded in seven places, he was the only white man in the camp at that time, and the women dressed his wounds.[25]

After Mrs. White was taken away, Mrs. Carruthers learned that the Indians planned to kill her and, with her two children, escaped during a storm. After a harrowing journey, they were rescued by Lieutenant N.K.

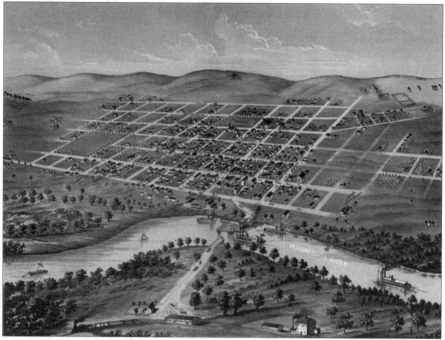

St. Peter, Minnesota, 1870. (Author's collection)

Culver of Company B, Fifth Minnesota, three soldiers, and J.W. De Camp half a mile from Fort Rodgely. Her tattered skirt given her by an Indian woman in the cornfield did little to cover her body, and the three soldiers went back to the fort to procure clothes for her before her entrance into the enclosure.

On the 18th, word came to Mrs. Justina Krieger at the settlement that the Sioux were murdering the whites. Mrs. Krieger, the youngest daughter of Andrew Kitzman of Posen, Prussia, had married Frederick Krieger in 1857, and, with six children (three from a previous marriage), they had settled on a homestead on the Minnesota River near Sacred Heart, twenty-seven miles above Fort Ridgely and eleven miles above the mouth of Beaver Creek.

The news of the killings was conveyed by two Sacred Heart settlers, August Frass and Emil Grundmann, who had been on their way to the Lower Agency, "and had seen the lifeless and mutilated remains of the murdered victims lying upon the road and in their plundered dwellings towards Beaver Creek."[26]

About six miles below the Krieger home, they had come upon the bodies of a woman and two children who had been murdered while attempting to get to Fort Ridgely. A broken box, a stove, some scattered bedding, and the absence of the team and its driver all indicated that a tragedy of unusual character had taken place. Hoping for some answers to the mystery, one of the men remained at the scene with their team while the other walked to the farm of Gottfried Buce, only a mile away. Upon reaching the farm, he found that Buce, his wife, and three of their children had been ruthlessly murdered. Stopping at a neighboring farm, he found all the doors and windows broken and all valuables purloined. The body of Gottlieb Mannweiler, who had been shot through the chest, was discovered about fifteen yards from the house. He then moved on to John Roessler's place and found the farmer and his wife lying dead near the doorway at a grindstone, where they apparently had been sharpening a scythe. Two children, with their heads split open, were lying on the ground near their mother.[27]

Minnie Buce Carrigan later recalled the atrocities committed on her family by the Indians:

> That dreadful Monday—Aug. 18, 1862—my father was putting up hay a mile east of our house. I remember that dinner was a little late and father complained. He was in a hurry to finish his haying that he might go to work again at Yellow Medicine to put up hay for the government cattle where he could get good wages. When he had started for his work, my brother climbed on the roof to see where our cattle were. We had to keep watch of them as they ran at large on the prairie. Sometimes the Indians would stampede them, and we would have to hunt for days to find them again. When my brother came down, he told mother that he heard shooting and someone scream at Roessler's and that father was looking toward Mr. Roessler's house as far as he could see him. Mother thought maybe the Indians were shooting at a mark and wanted August to go to Mr. Roessler's and borrow some sowing needles. We did all our trading at New Ulm and often had to borrow such articles. When he returned he said, "O mother, they are all asleep. Mrs. Roessler and the little boy were lying on the floor and the boy's ear was bleeding. The big boy was lying in the clay pit and was all covered with clay." My mother was standing by the table cutting a dream for my little sister when my

brother returned. "O, my God," she exclaimed, "the Indians have killed them. We must fly for our lives. You children stay here and I will go and call father." But my brother and I refusing to remain in the house, were then told to hide in the cornfield on the south side where she and father would meet us. She then ran to tell father. My brother took the baby Bertha, aged three months, and I took little Caroline while Augusta, aged five years and three months, and Amelia, aged four, walked along with us. We had hardly reached the cornfield when the Indians came whooping and yelling around the west side of the field from Mr. Boelter's. We sat down, and they passed us so closely that it was strange they did not see us. They rushed into our house and we went on. Looking back we saw them throwing out the feather beds and other articles. We reached the south side of the field safely, and father and mother were already there. I think we would have been safe there at least for a time, but father taking the baby from Augusta, started out on the open prairie. Mother took Caroline from me and tried to stop father, but it was useless. The terrible circumstances must have unbalanced his mind, naturally being very nervous.

The Indians had cleared out of our house and were returning to Mr. Boelter's. As they were passing a little corner of the timber one of them saw father and uttered a wicked piercing yell. It was but a moment when the whole band, about [twenty] men and some squaws, were upon us. My father began talking to the foremost Indians. My brother has told me that father asked them to take all his property but to let him and his family go. But the Indian replied in the Sioux language, "*Sioux cheche,*" (the Sioux are bad.) He then leveled his double barreled shot gun and fired both barrels at him. He dropped the baby—she was killed—and running a few yards down the hill, fell on his face, dead. The same Indian then went to where my mother had sat down beside a stone with little Caroline in her lap, reloaded his gun and deliberately fired upon them both. She did not speak or utter a sound, but fell over dead. Caroline gave one little scream and a gasp or two and all was over with her. The cry rang in my ears for years afterward. My father was thirty-three and my mother thirty years of age when they were so cruelly murdered by the Indians. How painfully distinct are all the memories of the scenes of this dreadful afternoon. While my mother was being murdered I stood about ten feet away from her paralyzed with fear and horror, unable to move. The Indian began loading his gun again and was looking significantly at me and my sister Amelia, who sat by my side. Suddenly I regained my self-control and, believing that I would be the next victim, I started up and ran wildly in an indefinite direction. Accidentally I came to where my father lay. He had on a checked shirt the back of which was covered with blood, the shot having passed clear through his body. That was the last thing I knew. The next thing I remember was an Indian holding me in his arms, looking at my face. I screamed, and he put me down. My brother then told me not to be afraid as they would not kill us but were going to take us with them.[28]

She added that, when they arrived at the Boelter house, they discovered that the Indians had already murdered most of the family. They found three of the children lying among some logs between the house and the well. The right cheek of the oldest girl had been shot away clear to the bone. The Indians had thrown some clothes over the body of the second girl. Minnie's brother went to remove them, but the Indians called him back. They had taken the youngest child by the feet and beaten her over a log, as her dress was unfastened, and her back bare black and blue. After glimpsing the children, the Indians took them to the house.

"I started to go into the house, but my brother, who was standing at the door, stopped me," she recalled. "I waited a few minutes until he went away and then looked in. There lay Grandma Boelter on the floor with every joint in her body chopped to pieces."

The entire community, with the exception of Johann Schwandt, assembled at the home of Paul Kitzman, with their oxen and wagons, and prepared to escape to Fort Ridgely.[29] A messenger was dispatched to the Schwandt home but most members of the family had been murdered by means of Indian rifles and tomahawks. Two family members survived, including a boy, August, "who witnessed the awful scene of butchery," before making his way safely to Fort Ridgely. A seventeen-year-old girl, then residing at Redwood, was captured and taken prisoner.

Mrs. Krieger later recalled:

It was about eight o'clock in the evening when we all determined to flee to Fort Ridgely. However, one of our neighbors, Johann Schwandt, had not been informed of the raid, as far as we knew, and some delay was occasioned by the sending of messengers to his house to notify him of our intentions. Upon the return of these messengers, we were told that when they arrived at the house they found the body of John Walz, a son-in-law of Mr. Schwandt, lying in the doorway, shot through the body with three balls, which had undoubtedly caused instant death. It was dark by that time, and they made no attempt to make further investigation. Later, we learned that Mr. Schwandt had been shot while shingling the roof of his house, and that his wife had been dragged some distance into a newly ploughed field where her head was severed from her body; that two small children, aged five and seven years, were also killed; that John Frass, a hired man, was found dead near the remains of Mrs. Schwandt; and that Mrs. Walz, the oldest Schwandt daughter, who was with child, had been brutally murdered and mutilated, her unborn infant being taken from her body and nailed to a nearby tree. Her brother August, a lad of [thirteen] years, witnessed the horrible tragedy, and was then beaten so badly by the Indians that they left him on the ground for dead. He survived, however, and after the departure of the savages managed to crawl to the adjacent timber. A few hours of recuperation gave him strength to walk, and as soon as it became dark he started along the prairie road in the direction of Fort Ridgely. Traveling only at night, and remaining in hiding during the daytime, he reached the posts on the 22nd.[30]

Kitzman's party of thirteen families with eleven teams started out for the fort in the evening, striking across country towards the head of Beaver Creek and avoiding the settlements and traveled roads. They moved first toward the Chippewa on the prairie, considering it safer to take a longer, roundabout route than taking a more direct path along the traveled roads. They traveled in wagons at night, slowly adjusting their course towards Fort Ridgely and covered fourteen miles by daybreak. About two hours later, they encountered eight painted Sioux braves on horseback, who put down their guns to show they were friendly Indians and meant them no harm. The braves told them the Chippewas, and not the Sioux were committing the murders, and that they had come over to protect them and punish the murderers. Kitzman knew some of the braves; one, in fact, had gone fishing with him and dined at his house.[31]

Only half the whites in the wagon were armed, and while some wanted to fire upon the Indians immediately, the others talked them out of it. The Indian who knew Kitzman climbed down from his horse and embraced him, advising him and the others to return to their homes since the Chippewas had already left the area. To Kitzman he related, "You are a good man. It is too bad that you should be killed." The other Sioux dismounted and shook hands with the whites, and when the Sioux put their guns away into their cases, the whites stacked their own in one of the wagons. Everyone sat down to a meal of bread and milk and nearly all the white adults gave the Indians some money.

The settlers turned their teams and started back towards their homes with the Indians accompanying them. All the shotguns belonging to the whites were in one wagon, placed there while the wagons were being turned. Each Indian, however, carried a loaded and cocked double-barreled shotgun. Both Kitzman and Frederick Krieger were apprehensive over the situation.

Mrs. Krieger recalled:

After we had gone this distance some of the men asked the Indians if they thought there would be any risk in unyoking the oxen for a time in order to give them a chance to feed. To this they offered no objections, the suggestion, instead, seeming to meet with their approval. During the halt, they again asked for something to eat, and we gave them bread and butter and watermelon. Taking this, they withdrew from the caravan a quarter of a mile or so and ate their meal alone. When they had finished they signaled us to move on, and to Paul Kitzman, who went to see them, they said that they would follow directly and would not leave until we had safely reached our homes. As the caravan started, they drew up, some of them taking a position alongside the train and the others in front and rear. This unexpected behavior could not help but arouse our suspicions. Most of the men could see in it nothing but the traditional Indian treachery, and, after talking it over among themselves in German, they were almost unanimous in their desire to fight it out with the savages at once. Kitzman, alone, held out against such a rash undertaking, and succeeded, for the second time, in dissuading them. He still had faith, he said, in the word of his old Indian friend. "Besides," he continued, "our guns are all in the wagons. The Indians no longer have theirs in their cases, as we supposed, but in their hands, ready to use them in an instant. At the first move on your part to reach your weapons, everyone of you would be killed at the first shot."[32]

By mid-afternoon, the caravan reached a point where corpses lay in the road. The Indians suddenly became insolent and impatient and drew up a line in the rear of the train as if they were going into battle. All of them but one possessed double-barreled shotguns and were capable of firing fifteen shots without reloading. They leveled their guns and demanded money; one of them came forward to collect it while the others sat on their horses prepared to fire should there be a refusal. Justina Krieger handed her husband five dollars to give to the Sioux. The Sioux took the money and rode away and the wagons continued homeward.[33]

Cut Nose. (Author's collection)

Not far from the Krieger house, the fleeing settlers discovered the bodies of two white men, a good indication their adversaries were still in the area. The men retrieved their shotguns and headed for the Krieger house to make a stand. About a hundred yards from the house, fourteen Indians emerged and commenced firing on them. The attackers were part of the Rice Creek and Shakopee bands led by Shakopee and Cut Nose. All but three of the white men were slain; Frederick Krieger survived by hiding behind the oxen. "It all happened so quickly that I could not see whether any of our men fired or not, although I believe some of them did," Mrs. Krieger recollected.

The women went into a state of panic when the Indians cried out that any women that came with them would be spared and those who refused would be killed. When some of the women walked out from behind the wagons, Justina Krieger refused, conveying to the Sioux that she would die with her husband and children. While Frederick pleaded with her to go, another woman stepped forward, hesitated, and called out to Justina. She was immediately shot to death, as were six other women and two men, leaving Frederick Krieger the only surviving male.[34]

The enraged Indians began beating the children with the butts of their guns. Justina Krieger recollected, "Some [children] soon after rose up from the ground with the blood streaming down their faces, when they were beaten again and killed. This was the most horrible scene I had yet witnessed."[35]

Minutes later, Frederick Krieger was shot to death. When the first shot failed to finish the task, two more were fired, one of the balls entering his head, the other his shoulder. As Justina started to jump from her wagon, she was shot in the back, dragged to the ground, and a brave shoved the wagon over her body. She recalled:

> I suppose the savages then left me for dead, as I must have been there for some time. When I was shot, the sun was still shining brightly, but when I recovered consciousness it was dark. My baby, as my children told me afterwards, was, when they found it, lying about five yards from me, crying. The oldest of my stepchildren, a girl of [thirteen] years, found it there, and supposing me to be dead, carried it off the field of slaughter to a hiding place in the nearby timber. Three of the other children, all girls, also managed to get to the woods, and soon found the retreat of their elder sister. The two oldest boys, aged seven and eight years, likewise succeeded in reaching the timber, and remained there in hiding, along with a neighbor boy, August Gest, for three days, during which time they witnessed the burning of our homes.[36]

With most of the infants murdered, a woman and some surviving children took refuge in the Krieger house. The woman had been shot twice so was of little assistance to the children, the oldest of which was thirteen years old. One four-year old, the daughter of Eckmel Groundman, had had her hand shot off. The following day, the woman took her baby and two older children and left the house. While hiding in the thicket, she saw Indian warriors plunder the house and set it afire with seven children inside.

Justina Krieger regained consciousness only to discover two Indians removing valuables from the dead. She feigned death and was kicked by one of the Indians, who then felt her pulse. Mrs. Krieger remained silent, kept her eyes shut, and held her breath.

> They conversed in Sioux for a moment, [she later recalled]. I shut my eyes and awaited what else was to befall me with a shudder. The next moment a sharp-pointed knife was felt at my throat, then passing downward, to the lower portion of the abdomen, cut not only the clothing entirely from my body, but actually penetrating the flesh, making but a slight wound on the chest, but at the pit of the stomach entering the body and laying it open to the intestines themselves. My arms were then taken separately out of the clothing. I was seized rudely by the hair and hurled headlong to the ground, completely naked.[37]

Mrs. Krieger lost consciousness once more, but when she came to, she saw an Indian had picked up her niece, Wilhelmina Krieger, and was holding her upside down by one foot. He then produced a knife "with which he hastily cut the flesh around one of the legs, close to the body, and then, by twisting and wrenching, broke the ligaments and bone, until the limb was entirely severed from the body, the child screaming frantically, 'Oh God! Oh God!' When the limb was off, the child, thus mutilated, was thrown down on the ground, stripped of her clothing, and left to die."

Justina passed out once more, and when she came to, she found that the right side of her body was paralyzed. She pulled herself up on her left side and wrapped her shredded clothing around her as best she could. Then ever so slowly she began sliding along the road in the direction of what she hoped was Fort Ridgely some forty miles away.

> I made my way, first, to a creek, [she later remembered], some five hundred yards from the house, and there washed the blood from my body, and drank some water. Thus refreshed and strengthened, I renewed my journey, and during the rest of the night, must have traveled at least six miles. Towards daylight I came to a small settlement in the timber, now deserted, which I could not recall ever having seen before. I knew, however, that the creek on which it was located emptied into the Minnesota, and here I remained, weak, sick, wounded and faint from the loss of blood, for three long days, my only nourishment during all that time being the water which I obtained from the creek. At the end of three days, I heard Indians in the neighborhood, and, being afraid that I might receive still other injuries, I made my way to the left and out onto the prairie. It was on Saturday, the 23rd, I think, that I lay down and thought I should die of hunger. It was then that I began to eat grass and drink water from the sloughs. Sunday night, I came to a creek, far out on the prairie, where I saw great quantities of bedding and furniture scattered about, and likewise many dead bodies. One of these was that of a woman lying on her back, with a child nearby, pulled asunder by the legs.[38]

Mrs. Krieger crossed the stream, water up to her armpits, and then wandered aimlessly across the prairie without food or drink. After three days, she came upon a road and followed it to some water standing in puddles in the mud. She attempted to dip some of the muddy water up to her mouth with her clothes but the puddles were too shallow. She then fell upon her knees and sucked it up from the mud.

The road brought her to Beaver Creek on the twelfth day where she managed to get her bearings. Upon ascending a hill, she saw an Indian in the distance, with his back towards her and his gun raised to his shoulder in taking aim at some particular object she could not see. The brave did not fire, and when he went away, Mrs. Krieger retraced her steps into the timber. In an abandoned house, she found the remnants of a buffalo robe and cuddled up in it on the riverbank.

On the morning of September 1st, she raised herself despite a nagging fever to survey her surroundings. "To my surprise, I saw two persons with guns, but could not tell whether they were white men or Indians," wrote Mrs. Krieger. "I rejoiced, however, because I thought that here, at last, would be an end to all my misery. As they came nearer I saw the bayonets on their guns, and knew that they were soldiers from the fort. I beckoned them to come to me, which they did after some hesitation, and I recognized in one of them a former neighbor of ours, Lewis Daily."[39]

The soldiers, part of a burial expedition sent out from Fort Ridgeley that morning, gave her water to drink, bathed her head and face, and carried her to a vacant house. At another abandoned homestead, one of the men found a badly torn dress and helped Mrs. Krieger put it on. Dr. Daniels, traveling with the burial party, caught up with them, and after examining her wounds, gave her water and wine, requisitioned a wagon, prepared a bed in the wagon box and helped Mrs. Krieger into it.

The little party continued on up the bottom road onto the prairie where they found the remains of a woman and her two children cut to pieces. After burying the victims, they moved on to the Henderson place, turned back into the valley, and joined the rest of the burial party on its way to a designated camp at Birch Coulee. Upon reaching the camp, Dr. Daniels dressed her wounds and did everything he could to make her comfortable.

Mary Jane Hill Anderson, who was living near the Minnesota River during the outbreak, later recalled a woman, who was engaged in her morning chores, saw several Indians surround a neighbor's house just down the hill. When they started shooting through the windows, she frantically dragged a feather bed down into the cellar, carried her daughter and baby down, and locked the trap door.[40]

Before she did so, however, she put strychnine, which they used to kill rats, in a bottle of whiskey that she left sit out to be found. She could hear them rattling dishes and moving around above her and, finally, the sound of groaning, kicking, and writhing, a true sign the poison had done its work. She could not lift the trap door, however, for a dead Indian was lying across it. When her son-in-law came home, they found eleven dead Indians on the floor.

The Reyff family had moved from Helenville, Jefferson County, Wisconsin, in the spring of 1862 and settled in Middle Creek, Minnesota, after residing briefly in Forest City. On Monday, August 18th, Emannuel Reyff was driving rafting logs down the Minnesota River to New Ulm for a saw mill. The river, however, was quite low, so the boss paid them off and sent his workers home.

Reyff and a friend, Bill Laur, left together and went as far as the hill at Beaver Creek. Here they split up, with Laur going to New Ulm, and Reyff going to the home of a brother.

> Just as I was coming to the cow yard the Indians were coming from the opposite direction to the house, [recalled Reyff]. My brother and his son, Ben, a boy [ten] years of age, were stacking hay near the house. One of the Indians shot at my brother with an arrow. It struck him under the jaw bone near the ear. As he fell from the load, the Indians grabbed him, cut off both his hands and scalped him before he was dead. Ben jumped off the stack and tried to escape, but there were about [forty] Indians and poor little Ben had no [chance]. One of the Indians grabbed him by the hair while the other Indians jumped off the hayrack, which was nearly empty, turned up the wagon tongue and tied Ben's feet together with a rope and hung him to the wagon tongue by his heels. Then they cut his pants off with a butcher knife and slashed up his body as only an Indian knows how. Then they poured powder over his body and set it on fire. He died quickly. I thanked God when he was dead. They scalped him, also. He was such a fat little fellow, and they seemed to like the job. My sister-in-law came out of the house and begged on her knees for her life. An Indian rudely seized her by the hair and held her while the other Indians drove four stakes into the ground and tied her to them: then they mutilated her body with butcher knives. After she was dead, they scalped her, too. Little Annie rushed out of the house

screaming with fright. Two squaws grabbed her by the arms and cut her to pieces with butcher knives on the door step.[41]

Twice Reyff drew his weapon to fire at the Indians but changed his mind knowing it would be him against forty of the Sioux. The Indians passed directly under the tree he was hiding in and went to the Kochendurfer place while Reyff rushed to the Smith house.

"Here I saw one of the most horrible sights I ever witnessed in my life," continued Reyff. "Mrs. Smith's head was lying on the table with a knife and fork stuck in it. They had cut off one of her breasts and laid it on the table beside the head and put her baby nursing her other breast. The child was still alive. The dog they had killed on the doorstep."[42]

Reyff ran out of the house towards the Minnesota River pursued by several Indians who had come over the bluff. He swam the river and started for Fort Ridgely, but there were so many Indians surrounding the fort, that he changed course and went to New Ulm.

On August 18th, seventeen-year-old Samuel J. Brown, back from Shattuck College to spend his vacation at home, and his sister Ellen, crossed the Minnesota River at their ferry and rode towards Hazelwood, the Williamson and Riggs mission, to deliver the family washing to an Indian woman. En route, they met a Sioux Indian named Little Dog, who warned them that the Indians were killing everyone at the Lower Agency and intended to slaughter settlers all the way to St. Paul. He also related that he was passing along this warning at the risk of his own life.[43]

The two young riders, children of Joseph R. Brown, paid the warning little heed and rode on, and as they passed the agency, they met George Gleason, the government clerk. Gleason imparted that he was going to the settlement that day with James W. Lynd and Mrs. Sarah Wakefield, but upon their return, he promised they would stop at the Brown house for a little hunting and fishing. Gleason and Lynd were killed by Indians later that same day and Mrs. Wakefield taken prisoner.

As the Browns were returning from Hazelwood, they were warned again of danger by a Sioux woman, who told them to convey the message to their mother. That evening a family meeting was held between Mrs. Brown,

Ellen, Samuel, Lydia and her husband, Charles Blair, and their two children; Angus Brown and his wife; twins Emily and Amanda, Augusta, Joseph R., Jr., Sibley, and little Susie. Joseph R. Brown, Sr., was in New York perfecting a tractor.

After the family had gone to bed, they were awakened by a desperate pounding on the door by Peter Roulliard yelling, "For God's sake, hurry, the Yanktonnais have broken out and are burning the stores and killing everybody at the agency." A hired man was sent to bring the horses in from the prairie, but after being unable to catch them, he yoked up three pair of oxen to three lumber wagons.

The family set out with six others families in the wagons while Angus Brown and Charles Blair caught a couple horses and followed the party. Shortly after their departure, John Otherday came to the house intending to deliver them to safely with the other sixty-two whites he had already rescued. Soon after the Brown house was destroyed by the Indians.

But Roulliard had made a mistake—the Mdewakantons, not the Yanktonnais, had perpetrated the attack, and the route to Fort Ridgely that the settlers followed brought them into the heart of hostile country. After progressing only a few miles, the party was surrounded by Indians who hid in the tall grass with tufts tied about their heads as camouflage. Mrs. Brown stood up in the wagon and shouted that she was a Sisseton and relative of Wannatan, Scarlet Plume, Sweet Corn, Ah-Kee-Pah, and friend of Standing Buffalo. Cut Nose, Shakopee, and Dewanniye were about to have them killed, when a brave leaped into the wagon and told the others how Mrs. Brown had kept him from freezing to death. This act of gratitude undoubtedly saved their lives. The white men were ordered to leave on foot, while Mrs. Brown and her children were escorted by the Indians.

While in the custody of the Sioux, Mrs. Brown was impressed by the kindness shown her from Little Crow, who told her of the trouble that had come upon his people.

> He appeared very sad, [wrote G. G. Allanson, granddaughter of Mrs. Brown]. He said some of his young men had murdered some whites, that they, with a large number of relatives and friends had come to him before daybreak the next morning while he was still in bed and wanted

him to push the movement of a war against the whites, saying it had always been the policy of the government to punish the entire tribe and not the individuals in a case of this kind and they would all suffer anyway. That he strongly opposed it at first but when he saw he could not stop it, he entered into the project and was bending all his energies to its success. He said it was bound to come anyway as the Indians had no redress for injuries done them, but were made to pay dearly for any injury real imaginary, mostly the latter, done by any Indian against the whites. He expected to involve all the Indians including the Winnebagos and Chippewas and clear all their ancient grounds of the whites.[44]

Major Brown was intercepted by telegram at Chicago and hurried home to learn of the outbreak, the destruction of his home, and capture of his family. Henry Sibley persuaded him to accept an appointment as major in the Sioux campaign. His wife and children were released at Camp Release.

Notes

[1]*Pioneer & Democrat*, August 27, 1862.
[2]Marion Ramsey Furness, *Governor Ramsey and Frontier Minnesota: Impressions from His Diary and Letters*, p. 19.
[3]Franklyn Curtiss-Wedge, *The History of Renville County*, Vol II, Sacred Heart Township, Chicago, H.C. Cooper, Jr., & Co.,1916, pp. 1329-1333.
[4]E.W. Earle reminiscence. Dakota Conflict of 1862, Manuscripts Collections, Microfilm Edition, Reel 1, Minnesota Historical Society.
[5]Helen M. Tarble, *The Story of My Capture and Escape During the Minnesota Indian Massacre of 1862*, St. Paul, The Abbott Printing Company, 1904, pp. 23-24.
[6]Ibid.
[7]E.W. Earle reminiscence, Dakota Conflict of 1862, Manuscripts Collections, Microfilm Edition, Reel 1, Minnesota Historical Society.
[8]Ibid.
[9]Helen M. Tarble, *The Story of My Capture and Escape During the Minnesota Indian Massacre of 1862*, St. Paul, The Abbott Printing Company, 1904, pp. 23-24.
[10]E.W. Earle reminiscence. Dakota Conflict of 1862, Manuscripts Collections, Microfilm Edition, Reel 1, Minnesota Historical Society.
[11]Franklyn Curtiss-Wedge, *The History of Renville County, Minnesota*, Volume II, p. 928.
[12]Helen M. Tarble, *The Story of My Capture and Escape During the Minnesota Indian Massacre of 1862*, p. 25.
[13]Franklyn Curtiss-Wedge, *The History of Renville County, Minnesota*, Volume II, p. 928.

[14]E.W. Earle reminiscence, Dakota Conflict of 1862, Manuscripts Collections, Microfilm Edition, Reel 1, Minnesota Historical Society.

[15]Helen M. Tarble, *The Story of My Capture and Escape During the Minnesota Indian Massacre of 1862,* p. 27.

[16]E.W. Earle reminiscence, Dakota Conflict of 1862, Manuscripts Collections, Microfilm Edition, Reel 1, Minnesota Historical Society.

[17]Franklyn Curtiss-Wedge, *The History of Renville County, Minnesota,* Volume II, p. 928.

[18]E.W. Earle reminiscence, Dakota Conflict of 1862, Manuscripts Collections, Microfilm Edition, Reel 1, Minnesota Historical Society.

[19]Franklyn Curtiss-Wedge, *The History of Renville County, Minnesota,* Volume II, p. 928.

[20]Helen M. Tarble, *The Story of My Capture and Escape During the Minnesota Indian Massacre of 1862,* pp. 28-29.

[21]Ibid.

[22]Franklyn Curtiss-Wedge, *The History of Renville County, Minnesota,* Volume II, p. 928.

[23]E.W. Earle reminiscence, Dakota Conflict of 1862, Manuscripts Collections, Microfilm Edition, Reel 1, Minnesota Historical Society.

[24]Franklyn Curtiss-Wedge, *The History of Renville County, Minnesota,* Volume II, p. 928.

[25]Helen M. Tarble, *The Story of My Capture and Escape During the Minnesota Indian Massacre of 1862,* pp. 32-42.

[26]Franklyn Curtiss-Wedge, *The History of Renville County, Minnesota,* Volume II, p. 928.

[27]"Story of Justina Krieger," Fort Ridgely Archives.

[28]Minnie Buce Carrigan, *Captured by the Indians: Reminiscences of a Pioneer Life in Minnesota,* Forest City, South Dakota, Forest City Press, 1907.

[29]Franklyn Curtiss-Wedge, *The History of Renville County, Minnesota,* Volume II, p. 928; Marion P. Satterlee, "The Massacre at Sacred Heart," Dakota Conflict of 1862, Manuscripts Collections, Microfilm Edition, Reel 2, Minnesota Historical Society.

[30]"The Narrative of Justina Krieger," Fort Ridgely Archives.

[31]Franklyn Curtiss-Wedge, *The History of Renville County, Minnesota,* Volume II, p. 928; Marion P. Satterlee, "The Massacre at Sacred Heart," Dakota Conflict of 1862, Manuscripts Collections, Microfilm Edition, Reel 2, Minnesota Historical Society.

[32]"The Narrative of Justina Krieger," Fort Ridgely Archives.

[33]Franklyn Curtiss-Wedge, *The History of Renville County, Minnesota,* Volume II, p. 928; Duane Schultz, *Over the Earth I Come: The Great Sioux Uprising of 1862,* pp. 80-83.

[34]A.A. Davidson, "Narrative from the Indian Outbreak of 1862," Dakota Conflict of 1862, Manuscripts Collections, Microfilm Edition, Reel 2, Minnesota Historical Society.

[35]"The Narrative of Justina Krieger," Fort Ridgely Archives.

[36]Ibid.
[37]Ibid.
[38]Ibid.
[39]Ibid.
[40]Mary Jane Hill Anderson, *Autobiography of Mary Jane Hill Anderson, Wife of Robert Anderson 1827-1924*, Minneapolis, Agnes Anderson Twichell, 1934, p. 28.
[41]Minnie Buce Carrigan, *Captured by the Indians: Reminiscences of a Pioneer Life in Minnesota*.
[42]Ibid.
[43]G.G. Allanson, *Stirring Adventures of the Jos. R. Brown Family*, Sacred Heart, *Sacred Heart News*, Dakota Conflict of 1862, Manuscripts Collections, Microfilm Edition, Reel 1, Minnesota Historical Society.
[44]Ibid.

Chapter Nine

August 18, 1862
Milford and Leavenworth Townships

"*After a pleasant visit I started back to the Stocker home Monday morning and when about half way I met several Indians. Having always been afraid of Indians I ran as fast as I could into a wheat field. The Indians called to me but in words I could not understand. They did not follow me but continued on their way. This incident caused me to turn off the regular road to Stocker's and in doing so I had to pass close to the John Martin Fink house. Mrs. Fink gave me a melon and I went rapidly on because there was still a mile to my destination. I arrived just at noon and found Stocker had prepared the noon meal.*"
— Cecilia Ochs[1]

 UNDAY, AUGUST 17TH, BEGAN as a beautiful day. The sun shone bright over New Ulm, and nearly all of its citizens were out in the open.

While they were thus occupied several wagons came in filled with recruits, men who were willing, if necessary, to sacrifice their lives in behalf of their country, [recalled Brown County Sheriff Charles Roos]. Wherever recruits appeared the desire to get one's self at the command of the fatherland which was in trouble, manifested itself, and so it was here. Major [Thomas J.] Galbraith, the Indian agent, was the leader of the party. After the customary greetings he was asked to deliver a speech which he agreed to do. The people assembled in large numbers in Gross's hotel in the afternoon where Major Galbraith was received with cheers. After he had given it as his firm conviction that there was absolutely no danger to be feared from the Indians because he had complied with their every wish, he called upon the young men of New Ulm to enlist in the volunteer army for the purpose of putting down the rebels of the South, while those whose conditions would not permit them to take active part in the campaign could indirectly assist in getting up a volunteer company. After the speaker had closed his address and had been roundly applauded, as is usual under such circumstances, several of the New Ulm people began to collect money and to secure men for a company. Among these were Schneider, Dietrich, and Fenscke. These three were not able to go personally but were willing to do all in their power to recruit a company in Brown and adjoining counties. On the same day a committee consisting of the above three and Jacobs and Rudolph commenced to circulate a subscription list for money and by night had also secured [eighteen] signatures for a company. In the evening Major Galbraith delivered another speech at the Gross hotel. The committee decided to send a recruiting party into Milford the next day with wagons, music and flags, a regular German recruiting party. Monday morning Major Galbraith left with his recruits.[2]

Early the next morning, the Milford recruiting party, consisting of about fifteen persons, started out for Milford with wagons, music, and flags. As they moved towards Milford, the band played patriotic tunes that could be heard well in advance of their party.

Meanwhile, most of the Sioux warriors who sought revenge against the whites had just struck the Beaver Creek settlements across the Minnesota River from Redwood or at Milford Township, northwest of New Ulm in Brown County. Many of these warriors, including Little Crow, believed the farmers in these areas had stolen land from them. The Sioux did not discriminate between men, women, and children as their victims—the killing of an enemy of any age or sex would lead to the wearing of an eagle feather.[3]

Between nine and ten o'clock in the morning on August 18th, a party of six to eight Indians appeared at the home of Johann Massapust and asked for water, which was given to them. Milford's western line bordered the reservation, and because of its proximity to Sioux lands, Indians were frequently seen in the area. The people of Milford knew the Indians well and had often fed them.[4]

The Massapusts—Johann, Sr., (a widower), his two daughters Maria, twenty, and Julia, eighteen, and fifteen-year-old son John, Jr., were home when the visitors arrived. Absent were two older boys.[5] The father was seated near his two daughters who were washing dishes, with John, Jr., standing by the door when the Indians suddenly leveled their guns and fired. The girls and their father fell mortally wounded, while young John, who was standing near the Indians, was struck by a blow from a hatchet or tomahawk. Only slightly injured, he rushed up the stairs for lack of a better place to run.

Just then two teams hauling goods from New Ulm to the Indian agency came up the road a short distance from the house. Witnessing their arrival, the Sioux quickly dashed outside to kill the teamsters. This timely incident provided young John with a means of flight, and he dashed outside and hid in a slough. The Sioux did not see him escape because their vision was blocked by a hill which stood between the house and the slough.

As he dashed outside, his dying sister Julia managed to crawl after him, begging him to take her with him, but the crazed boy was compelled to leave her to the mercy of the Indians. Some of the returning Sioux detected the boy and chased him through the swamp. Hindered by his wet clothing, John discarded his trousers and ran like a hunted animal. Out-distancing his pursuers, he was able to warn the settlers of the impending doom and thereby saved the lives of many persons in the more remote parts of town.

A neighbor boy, L.A. Fritsche, recalled seeing young Massapust in flight:

> . . . A man with nothing but a shirt on had crossed the land west of us, running as fast as he could to Zagrotzky's and the Indians soon after him, but not running so fast, yet we did not think of any serious trouble or disturbance, and about two o'clock P.M. went for another load of wheat; we had not reached our part of the field, when Conrad Zeller, living on the southeast end on the ridge aforesaid, came running to meet us, telling us that the Indians had been killing all the neighbors and that he had carried Martin Henle (one of the party that left at the same time that we did), whom the Indians had left for dead, had shown signs of life, into his house, after the Indians had left; the signs of which he bore plainly, as he was covered with blood by carrying the wounded boy. As Mr. Zeller talked very excited and in a great hurry, father thought that some drunken Indians had perhaps committed the outrage, and so made for the house, saying to me, "Take your fork and come along!" When we entered the house, nobody but what seemed to be a bloody corpse was

lying on a cot in the room, the family of Zeller having been in the cellar were coming out. Martin Henle was, to all appearances, dead.[6]

Meanwhile, the Sioux warriors had murdered the teamsters. While a few Indians returned to the Massapust house, the others went to the house of a Mr. Stocker, whose place bordered the timber on the opposite side of the road. Stocker had witnessed the killing of the teamsters, and although he saw Indians approaching his house, he merely locked his door and awaited his fate.

Just as we sat down to the table, Stocker noticed that the Fink house was on fire, [recollected Cecilia Ochs, who took care of Mrs. Stocker who was ill and confined to bed]. Mrs. Stocker begged her husband to go over and help them, which he did and, when he returned he had a great many things to tell us. Fink's house had burned down and he had been unable to discover anyone except a small child, a grandchild of the Finks who was lying in front of the door. It had been shot through the breast with an arrow, but was still alive. The child died, and he left it in the home of Max Zeller, a relative. Because of the fact [that] the Indians had occasionally caused trouble, Stocker thought this was the case again. We were discussing this, quite excitedly, when we saw a wagon approaching with several men in it. They had an Americana flag, and Stocker thought they were white men from New Ulm come to help us, but I saw two Indians in their native costumes running across the field towards our house.

We then saw that the others were Indians also and learned later that they ambushed a party of New Ulm people and robbed them of their clothes. These men, who were ambushed and robbed had started out with a band and a flag on the way to the Henle home to secure recruits for the Union Army in the Civil War.

When Mrs. Stocker learned the Indians were coming, she begged us to carry her into the woods, but this was impossible. In order to create the impression that we were unafraid, we sat down to our noon meal. In the meantime one of the Indians had picked up some washing which had been left on the grass to dry. Mrs. Stocker, who was familiar with the artifices practiced by the redskins, said to her husband, "Don't take the washing from him because he wants to entice you outside."[7]

Finding the door locked, one of the braves smashed a window and tried to induce Stocker to come outside. When he saw he could not lure the settler out, he dropped the washing, and leveled his rifle at Mrs. Stocker. She cried out, "Stand aside, he will do nothing to me, only pray." Her husband quickly grabbed the barrel of the gun and attempted to wrestle it free, but when he could not, he ran into a corner. Mrs. Stocker begged the brave to spare her life and told him she would give him everything she owned, but the brave shot and killed Mrs. Stocker.

> I distinctly heard when the rifle was cocked, a retort quickly followed and, the shawl covering her face was rent in twain, [recalled Cecilia Ochs]. Stocker, who was near the stairway, rapidly turned around and ran upstairs. I, in my fright, ran past the Indian, who stood at the window and also mounted upstairs. Stocker, however, had dropped the trapdoor and stood on it. He wanted to get out of the upstairs window. There I stood, and before I could gather my thoughts the trapdoor opened and Stocker sprang rapidly down the steps. He told me later that there was an Indian on the roof keeping guard, and that is why he came down.
>
> He ran into the cellar and I followed him. We listened intently to hear what was going on above and heard the Indians shove the bed out of the way and sing the death dance. By that Mrs. Stocker was dead.[8]

The Indians immediately set fire to the house knowing Stocker would have to emerge or stay behind and be burned alive. He quickly began digging and lay down, covering himself with dirt as protection from the flames. Little Cecilia tried emulating him but could only get loose a few handfuls of dirt. They tried digging a hole in the front section of the house but noticed an Indian standing guard there.

At the opposite end of the house was another cellar filled with straw used for storing potatoes. This cellar was not connected to the one they were in. Stocker began digging, discovered a small opening under the sill leading outside, and tried to enlarge it. He found some shingles, used to cover milk pans, and he dug a passage large enough for him and the girl to crawl through. The pair emerged on the north side of the house and escaped unseen into the timber. They ran three miles in the direction of New Ulm until they reached the home of the John B. Zettel family. Inside, they found Zettel lying dead on the floor with a loaf of bread in his arms saturated with blood. In the next room lay the corpses of three children.

Hearing someone call out, they found Mrs. Zettel hiding in a shock of wheat. She was bleeding from several head wounds and asked to be conveyed to bed. She related that the Indians had attacked just as they were sitting down to their noon meal. Mr. Zettel had attempted to give the Indians the loaf of bread but was shot down and killed. Stocker found the body of the fourth Zettel child behind the house.

Stocker and Cecilia returned to the woods and came to the John Fischerbauer place. Thinking they were Indians, Fischerbauer was about to shoot them when he suddenly recognized Cecilia and invited them inside the house. Mrs. Adolph Schilling was inside with her son. Her husband had been killed on the way, she had been wounded by a tomahawk, and her son had had a knife thrust into his back.

Stocker sent Cecilia alone to her parents' place to see if they were alive, but she found no one home. Christian Haag, a neighbor boy, came running over to her and related that his father had had been killed but his mother and four siblings were home. Cecilia and the Haags started out for New Ulm, and when they were only five miles from their destination, they met Stocker, Henle, and others. Two of the men helped the fatigued girl walk the remainder of the way by taking her hands and holding her up. Upon reaching the Dacotah House in New Ulm, Cecilia found her parents, who could hardly believe she was still alive.

L.A. Fritsche recalled the terrifying moments of his own experience with the Sioux:

> The next few minutes were the most exciting of my life, and I shall not forget them to my last day. Father had gone but a short distance, when suddenly, out of the timber, not far to the northeast of us, about a dozen Indians, all mounted, came galloping along the road. As soon as I saw them I recalled father, and, as he was hard of hearing, I had to call rather loud. The Indians, hearing me before father did, all halted and looked our way. Father, now seeing the Indians, and now being convinced that something serious was going on, told me to stay where I was and watch the Indians, and should they come our way, hide in the slough nearby or in the cellar, so that at least one of us might be saved. He would try and reach home and help mother and the little ones, but, should the Indians come our way, he would have no [hope] in reaching home. My protest did no good.[9]

The roving bands of Indians went from one house to another. The family of M. Fink was wiped out before they realized what was happening. Another settler, Christian Haag, spotted Mr. Fink's house burning and possessing no knowledge of the marauding Indians, mounted his horse and rode to help them extinguish the blaze. He was met on the road by several braves and was shot down.

Florian Hartman was working in the fields when his wife appeared with refreshments. She arrived just in time to see her husband shot down by two Indians from a short distance away. Her husband was not dead, although he was unable to move. She rushed to him and attempted to drag him into a nearby cornfield, which she was unable to do. Leaving him to his terrible fate, she dashed off to safety. John Rohner, who assisted Hartman with the harvest, was also murdered. Mrs. Hartman later recalled her terrifying experience:

Milford monument. (Photo courtesy of Diana Pierce)

My husband, Florian Hartman, was on the 18th of August engaged with another man, John Rohner, in binding wheat near our house. When I had their dinners ready for them, I heard some noise, and on looking out I could see houses on fire, and also thought I could see them at work trying to save the buildings. At the same moment I heard a cry "*Nippo!*" (kill) and the reports of several rifles. Thinking the Indians were killing some cattle, I ran out to see what was going on. An Indian came close up to the house, stared at me then ran away. Full of fear I hurried toward my husband who was about forty rods from the house, and on crossing the road I noticed a man lying on the ground and thought he was asleep. It was Hartman's hired man, Rhoner, and he was covered with blood. Looking for my husband I found him about thirty steps from Rhoner, lying on the ground. He motioned to me to keep quiet and to drag him into the cornfield, because he was shot. Stricken with fear, I was powerless to do it. I cast myself down beside my husband, and in my excessive grief knew not what to do. Soon after, two Indians came up to the dying Rhoner and fired two more shots at him. My poor husband then begged me to hide in the cornfield, because I could not do him any good where I was. I ran and hid as he told me, digging a hole in the ground with my hands to creep into. I remained there till toward evening. Two Indians passed close by me, but did not notice me.

About eight o'clock I heard someone weeping bitterly, but did not dare to leave my place, thinking it might be an Indian. After a while I crept toward my husband, and found him cold and stiff in death. I took some hair from his head as a remembrance, and fled into the woods. Even the animals seemed to know what was going on. Under a large oak, in the vicinity of a spring, I remained all night, and toward four o'clock in the morning I hurried to the Minnesota in order to escape across the ferry into Nicollet County. But the boat was on the other side of the river. I tried in vain to get across on the rope, and so I had to hide all day in the woods, and suffered greatly from the mosquitoes. About eight o'clock in the evening I went back to our house and passed five Indian teepees on my way. I went into the house to take some clothing, and in picking up some of the bedding that was lying on the floor I noticed a wounded Indian lying thereon, and immediately ran away. When I passed the barn in my flight an Indian fired at me, but missed me on account of the darkness of the night. During the whole of that night and the following day I remained in concealment. On the fourth day it rained heavily. I was very tired and completely worn out. Such sadness overcame me that I was almost sorry for not having found death at the hands of the Indians. The rain continued on the fifth day, and being completely drenched, I ventured back to the house; but on going in I found everything gone. However, I felt happy to find some dry underclothing to put on. The hogs were in the pen and screaming from hunger. I had compassion on them and gave them some corn. I was lucky enough to find a loaf of bread, and with this I went back to my hiding place. But I was sorry to have betrayed my presence through my compassion for hungry animals. On the sixth day I wanted to go to the house, but noticing some Indians near the place I hurried back. During this and the next day I heard continual shooting. On the evening of the eighth day my dog came to me and was overjoyed to see me. I, too, rejoiced as if I had met with a friend in my terrible loneliness. I shared the remainder of my bread with him. He seemed to be very hungry. But at the same moment the thought struck me that he might betray my hiding place and in order to remove that danger I took my apron and strangled him with it. But he fought so fiercely, that it was with the greatest exertion that I succeeded in killing him.

On the morning of the ninth day I heard a great noise which seemed to come nearer and nearer; but I soon felt relieved when I found it to be only a few hogs. I remained two more days in my concealment, and hardly dared to go a hundred steps farther. In my terrible condition, living on a little bread and wild berries, life seemed to have new charms. I enjoyed the singing of the birds, and thanked my Creator and prayed for the preservation of my life.[10]

The Sioux proceeded to the house of John Zettel, killed Zettel and his four children, and left Mrs. Zettel for dead. A rescue party from New Ulm found her later in the day and revived her. A small child, who was home alone, was killed at the Franz Massapust home. When his mother returned, she found his body near the house. She and the rest of her children escaped into the timber and made their way to New Ulm, where she was joined by her husband. Mr. and Mrs. Petzl, who lived near the timber, were also killed.

> A strange presentment made me leave my hiding place on the twelfth day, [related Mrs. Hartman]. I went to the homes of my brothers, and to that of Cassimir, but found them all empty. A terrible sight presented itself to me in Zettels' house. There I found the bodies of the father and his four children, and between them a loaf of bread. I was very hungry and greatly desired to take the bread, but the odor of the corpses was so repulsive that I could not eat it. In Pelzyls' house I found the dead bodies of his father and of a woman. A short distance from the house I found the bodies of old Messmer and of a girl.[11]

The Indians entered the house of Anton Henle and killed the four little children they found in inside. A little baby boy asleep in his cradle, was struck a glancing blow with a hatchet, but the child survived. Mrs. Hartman entered the house and said the "air was everywhere filled with the stench of the corpses."

Theresa Henle later related her story:

> My husband, Anton Henle, went to New Ulm on the 18th of August, intending to return soon to haul in some wheat, because it was a very fine day. Besides running a farm we kept a sort of stopping-place for travelers. A Frenchman who had remained at our house overnight left our house at nine o'clock, intending to go to the Lower Agency, a distance of about twenty miles. Several men who were hauling freight for him to that place had left our house earlier. Nothing extraordinary happened except that at [ten] o'clock the Frenchman returned and drove toward New Ulm as fast as he could go. It was very strange to see him thus pass our place without even a simple look toward it, since he was never known to pass without calling in. Toward noon I went to my mother who lived near us, to get some lettuce. [The Henle home was situated only fifteen to twenty rods from that of his father-in-law, Mr. Messmer, the homes separated by a grove.] On returning home, I saw three naked Indians, and went back to warn mother. I found her in the garden. As soon as I approached her she was shot, and falling down, she cried aloud: "O, Theresa!" Seized

with terror I ran toward my house, fearing for my children. I found three Indians in the house. One of them jumped at me, but I ran down the incline into the woods which was only a little way off. There I stood for a while not knowing what to do. I understand now why the Frenchman had returned in such great haste. Filled with a desire to at least save my baby, I went back toward the house, but noticed too many Indians around to do anything. I then went to a neighbor, Benedict Drexler, whose house was about fifty rods from ours. I went in through the window, and found no one at home. Later on, Drexler was found beheaded in the field. His wife and children were in the cornfield. The Indians shot at her but she fled. When I heard the shooting I ran into the woods in order to get back to mother, but saw a large number of Indians who were putting up a red and white flag. I turned back again into the woods and remained in the dry bed of a creek, from which place I could hear the rattling of the wagons coming from New Ulm, and also the shots that were fired at them by the Indians, because I was hardly five hundred steps from the place where the Indians were lying in ambush. I remained there, tortured with the most terrifying thoughts about my husband and children, which troubled me more than my own misery. While sitting there, neglected and forlorn, my two dogs came up to me trembling. Toward evening I heard the voice of my husband in the direction of the house calling me, and I came forth from my hiding place.[12]

With her husband was the party of men who were canvassing the area in search of volunteers to fight in the Union Army against Confederate forces in the South. The wagons continued on along the road and were about to cross a creek in a ravine, which drained part of the lowlands.

As the first wagon bridged the creek, it was fired upon by Indians hiding in the ravine, and three men—Detrich, Sneider, and Fenske, were killed in the first volley. The wagons turned back, and after picking up some wounded white settlers, returned hastily to New Ulm.

When the party came to a point about one mile this side of Henle's they found the mutilated remains of a man named Messmer, lying near the roadside, [recalled Charles Roos. Joe Messmer was already dead and another man, A. Schilling, whom they found by the roadside, died along the way.]

They immediately stopped and as the man was still alive it was assumed that the Indians must have committed this act just a few minutes previously, [related Roos]. It was decided forthwith, as it was generally believed that this was the work of a few drunken Indians, to give chase and capture them. The teams started out on this mission at full speed but only a few rods away was a thicket and a creek over which there was a bridge. Schneider passed the bridge when firing was opened up upon them from the thicket and Schneider and Dietrich were immediately killed. On the second wagon was Fenscke who was also killed and Haupt and Steimie, who were wounded. Haupt managed to save himself by making for the third wagon which was still held by the wounded man along the road. When the survivors saw that the Indians were there in such large numbers and well armed they saw the futility of having a further encounter with the savages especially as they were all unarmed. They, therefore, gathered up the wounded in the wagons and drove full gallop to New Ulm. On the way they warned the people living near the road and filled up their wagons with women and children. A part of the party had, when the firing commenced, figured out that the wagons were not safe places and jumped out and escaped into the woods and returned to New Ulm afoot. About noon a man galloped into the city calling, "The Indians are coming. They are massacring everything on the way and are only a few miles off. They have already killed the recruiting party."[13]

One of the Milford settlers recalled having seen Joe Messmer shortly before his death:

> Shortly before noon, while we were about ready with our load of wheat to take home, Mr. Messmer, father-in-law of Anton Henle, Martin, a son of Henle, and about twelve years old, and a young girl whose name I do not now remember, crossed with a load of barley close in front of our team in going home in a northern direction. Now, immediately north of where we were a range or continuation of hills (northwest to southeast), obliterated the view to the north, and Mr. Messmer and his companions had to cross this hill in going home, so, when passing us, he remarked: "I guess this will be the last load." Of course he meant the last load before noon, but it was the last load in his life, for scarcely had they crossed said hill, when they were met by Indians and killed. We had perhaps gone ten or twelve rods in the home direction when I heard two or three shots in quick succession, and when I told father (whose hearing was impaired), he remarked there might be some drunken Indians about, wasting their powder, so we went home, not thinking of any danger, and had our dinner.[14]

The Indians had been acting strangely and had visited the home of a neighbor, Victor Zagrotzky, and had stayed a long time. When they left, they emitted a terrifying howl. Upon a hill, an Indian sitting on a horse all morning, looking more like a statue than a human being, watched the jubilation of his companions.

The families of Casimer Herman and Athanasius Henle had witnessed some of the slayings and rushed off into the timber, warning Alois Palmer along the way. They crossed the Minnesota River on Palmer's ferry and made it safely to New Ulm where they spread the word of the Milford slaughter.

Still hiding in the woods near Milford was Mrs. Hartman who was determined to get to New Ulm, some six miles distant.

> In the cemetery, [she said], I noticed a white flag, which filled me with courage and hope. But when I came near town and noticed that many buildings had been burned down and the town was deserted, new fear and anxiety came over me. I did not go farther, but returned immediately to my hiding place because I was afraid I might meet Indians in town. At seven o'clock in the evening I was again at my brother Anton's house, from which I could hear a great noise. I went in because I thought I would have to die anyhow. The noise, however, was caused by all kinds of animals that had gathered in the house.
>
> From there I went to my own house, and to bed, and reproached myself for having gone so far. On the following day I searched for some potatoes; but it was only with great difficulty, and after going to two other houses, that I could find a match. As soon as I had found some matches I returned to my house, feeling rich and happy, and prepared a soup. I had two matches left, and for fear that I might lose them I kept up a fire at a stump nearby.
>
> On the fourteenth day I found some eggs and a sack of flour, but could not make use of the flour. After that I remained indoors most of the time. An ox came up to the house with an ugly wound. I washed the wound, and the animal got well. A calf had one of its eyes shot out but it got well. I then began to gather plums and nuts and dig potatoes, because I had lost all hope of being rescued, and wanted to provide for the winter. I was under the impression that all the settlers had been put to death.
>
> On the seventeenth day I went to look for the body of my husband, and, on my way thither, I heard some shooting and the barking of dogs. I almost fainted on looking up and seeing eight men coming toward me. One of them leveled his gun, and now I thought I would after all have to die. But the cry, "Oh, sister!" roused me again, and in a moment I was in the arms of my brother, Athanasius, who had taken me for a squaw on account of the changes made by my sufferings and anxieties. Fortunately, I knew of an old wagon nearby which had been left by the Indians. My brother had only a sled for his horse. The wagon was fixed up and we went to town in it, where I again enjoyed the society of human beings, of which I had been deprived for more than a fortnight.[15]

Sheriff Roos was convinced the atrocities were being carried out by a party of drunken Indians, but as a matter of precaution, he assembled a posse to capture the drunkards and place them in the county jail. The thirty-man posse was armed with rifles, double-barrel shotguns, and other weapons hurriedly taken. While the posse was being formed and ammunition being given them, more refugees came into New Ulm, insisting the party of Indians committing the murders was a large band.[16]

Roos ordered the militia to arms and barricaded a portion of the city before leaving with his little army for Milford. On the outskirts of town, the party met the wagon carrying the wounded Haupt. Proceeding another three miles, they came upon the wagon carrying Steimle. Unable to speak because his wound to the throat, Steimle wrote upon a piece of paper that Fenscke, Dietrich, and Schneider had been murdered and where their bodies were lying. He also wrote that there were many Indians involved in the slaughters.

Roos' party deployed as skirmishers and moved rapidly toward the scene of the killings. A few wagons caught up with the posse for the purpose of picking up any dead or wounded upon reaching Milford.

Arriving safely upon the scene, the left flank marched forward in double quick time, while the right, which had to traverse a creek and thicket, marched a little slower. The plan called for the men to catch the Indians between the two forces. The left wing moved onto the opening of the creek where the men could control the bridge without placing their lives in danger, while the right hid in the thicket. The center party moved first across the bridge and found the body of Fenscke. The bodies of Dietrich and Schneider were discovered about 100 yards on the other side, the latter's body stripped of all clothing but a shirt.

> The party had to continue its way close to the woods, [wrote Roos]. The left wing was, therefore, sent into the fields, the center moved forward on the highway and two men were sent into the woods. The houses along the road were examined and a live child was found in the first. When they reached Henle's, Mrs. Henle, who had hidden herself in the woods, appeared. After a few minutes rest most of the men moved on while the wagons and a few armed men remained to load up the wounded and to arrange the wagons for such other wounded as they might find. About one mile further on the party saw a man driving an ox team

across the prairie. At first they thought they had before them a farmer and they called to him to come with them because it was too dangerous to go on alone but it was only a short time before they recognized in him an Indian and the Indian also noticing them made a signal to the woods with a cloth and gave the war whoop. John Hauenstein leveled his rifle and sent the savage a greeting which struck him in the back. The Indian fell but jumped up again and the chase began. A slough was passed as rapidly as possible, the Indian receiving a second shot from Hauenstein's trusty rifle, which to judge by the actions of the Indian who again fell to the ground, must have struck him like the first in the left side. He had great advantage over his pursuers because he was on dry ground while they were in the slough. The slough was, nevertheless, passed in double quick order and then chase was given up to the woods, a distance of about one mile. The quarry escaped, but blood spots were found on the route he had taken. Up to now the party had seen but one Indian, but were of the opinion that the savages were in the timber close by. The timber was part of the "Reserve." Not knowing how many might be hidden in there and night coming on, the posse concluded that it would be better to desist from following them any farther and that it would be more sensible to take the wounded and the women and children who had been found in the city and to attack the Reserve later with a larger force. The party after they had seen in the distance the ruins of a burning house returned home. A number of them went along through the timber and in German called as loudly as they could for all to come out and place themselves under their protection.[17]

Returning to Henle's cabin, they found several wagons filled with people. One woman hiding in the timber was rescued by the party, as was a wounded boy. Sheriff Roos' party made it safely back to New Ulm about 10:00 P.M. with the wounded they had rescued, among them Mrs. Zettel and Martin Henle. Both died about two weeks later.

Twelve-year-old August Gluth, who lived on a farm in Milford with his parents, was herding cattle forty miles up the Minnesota Valley near Beaver Falls when the Sioux attacked the family home and burned it to the ground. While watching the herd, the Sioux took the cattle by storm and captured young Gluth. Brought to Little Crow's camp, he was forced to hand over the ox teams the Sioux had appropriated.[18]

During his captivity, Gluth stayed alive by eating wild berries. He attempted to escape on three separate occasions. The first time, he received a warning, the second time a scalp wound. Finally, after five weeks of maltreatment, he and two other boys took flight, with two Indians on ponies in close pursuit. While hiding in a slough, they were rescued by a small party of soldiers.

Murders in Leavenworth Township, southwest of New Ulm, occurred between August 18th and 25th, and there were few survivors who lived to tell about the atrocities they witnessed and suffered. John Bluem, his wife, and five children were driving to New Ulm for safety. Both parents and four of the children—Margaret, Elizabeth, Charles, and Adam were murdered, but the fifth child, John, Jr., escaped.[19]

William Carroll, whose long friendship with the local Indians, inclined him to scoff at rumors of a Sioux attack. To prove that he was right, he mounted his horse, leaving his wife and child at home, and started for New Ulm promising to return. Upon arriving in the city, he learned that the rumors were, indeed, true and decided to return immediately to Leavenworth for his family. Pickets surrounding New Ulm, however, refused to allow him to leave.[20]

Seth Henshaw attempted to drive to New Ulm with a Mrs. Harrington and two children, and a Mrs. Hill. Ambushed by Indians, Henshaw was killed, and Mrs. Harrington and the younger child were slightly wounded. They were all thrown from the wagon, but while the Indians were occupied catching the team, the women escaped into the brush. Mrs. Hill and one child made it safely to New Ulm, while Mrs. Harrington and her wounded child wandered for eight days, finally reaching Colonel Flandreau's camp at Crisp's Farm, between New Ulm and Mankato.[21]

The atrocities, it was discovered, had been committed by about fifty Indians from the Lower Sioux Agency. Described as "very noisy and perfectly naked," they had slaughtered about forty German settlers in Milford and Leavenworth, two small communities on the Cottonwood and Minnesota rivers. The fifty Indians included Tazoo, Hapan, Mazabomdoo, Wyatahtowa, and also Godfrey, who later claimed to have been an unwilling participant.[22]

Similar attacks, precipitated by Shakopee's warriors, were launched north and south of the Beaver Creek region, where perhaps as many as several thousand white settlers lived. While several families made it safely to New Ulm or Fort Ridgely, hundreds of others were slaughtered. Acts of brutality

Cottonwood River near New Ulm. (Author's collection)

committed by the Sioux included the mutilation of bodies, heads, and limbs, all of which were in keeping with traditional Sioux warfare. Dakota warriors believed their enemies should not be left intact because they would have to fight them again in the next world.

But the action was not at an end. Ahead was the bulk of the Indian Uprising, and the fortification of New Ulm and Fort Ridgely had begun.[23]

Notes

[1]*New Ulm Journal*, June 26, 1962.
[2]"Sioux Uprising," The Battles of New Ulm, An Account written by Sheriff (Charles) Roos. Manuscript Collections, Brown County Historical Society.
[3]Gary Clayton Anderson, *Little Crow Spokesman for the Sioux*, p. 139.
[4]Daniel Buck, *Indian Outbreaks*, p. 114.
[5]L.A. Fritsche, M.D., *History of Brown County, Minnesota*, pp. 189-194.
[6]Ibid., pp. 195-196.
[7]*New Ulm Journal*, June 26, 1962.
[8]Ibid.
[9]L.A. Fritsche, M.D., *History of Brown County, Minnesota*, p. 196.
[10]Ibid., pp. 201-204.
[11]Ibid., p. 204.
[12]Ibid., pp. 199-200.
[13]"Sioux Uprising," The Battles of New Ulm, An Account written by Sheriff (Charles) Roos. Manuscript Collections, Brown County Historical Society.
[14]L.A. Fritsche, M.D., *History of Brown County, Minnesota*, pp. 194-195.
[15]Ibid., pp. 204-205.
[16]"Sioux Uprising," The Battles of New Ulm, An Account written by Sheriff (Charles) Roos. Manuscript Collections, Brown County Historical Society.
[17]Ibid.
[18]Harry B. West letter to Minnesota Tourism Bureau dated July 29, 1933. Dakota Conflict of 1862, Manuscripts Collection, Minnesota Historical Society.
[19]"Sioux Uprising," The Battles of New Ulm, An Account written by Sheriff (Charles) Roos. Manuscript Collections, Brown County Historical Society.
[20]"The Ill-Fated Leavenworth Expedition and Marker," unpublished manuscript, Brown County Historical Society, New Ulm.
[21]"Sioux Uprising," The Battles of New Ulm, An Account written by Sheriff (Charles) Roos. Manuscripts Collections, Brown County Historical Society.
[22]C.M. Oehler, *The Great Sioux Uprising*, pp. 44-45.
[23]Gary Clayton Anderson, *Little Crow Spokesman for the Sioux*, p. 139.

Bibliography

Books and Pamphlets

Adams, Alexander B., *Sunlight and Storm: The Great American Plains*, New York, G.P. Putnam's Sons, 1977.

Aleshire, Peter, *The Fox and the Whirlwind: General George Crook and Geronimo, a Paired Biography*, New York, John Wiley & Sons, Inc., 2000.

Allen, Arthur Francis, *Northwestern Iowa, Its History and Traditions 1804-1926*, Chicago, S. J. Clarke Publishing Company, 1927.

Ambrose, Stephen E., *Crazy Horse and Custer: The Parallel Lives of Two American Warriors*, Garden City, New York, Doubleday & Company, Inc., 1975.

Anderson, Daniel Clayton, *Little Crow Spokesman for the Sioux*, St. Paul, Minnesota Historical Society Press, 1986.

Anderson, Mary Jane Hill, *Autobiography of Mary Jane Hill Anderson Wife of Robert Anderson 1827-1924*, Minneapolis, Agnes Anderson Twichell, 1934.

Andreas' History of the State of Nebraska, 1882

Annals of Iowa, Vol. XVIII, No. 5, October 1932, F.I. Herriott, "The Aftermath of the Spirit Lake Massacre March 8-15, 1857."

Annals of Iowa, Vol. XVIII, No. 5, Des Moines, Iowa, July 1932, Third Series, F.L. Herriott, "The Origins of the Indian Massacre Between the Okobojis, March 8, 1857."

Annals of Iowa, 3rd Series, Charles Aldrich, Volume III, Number 7.

Armstrong, Benjamin G., *Early Life Among the Indians*.

Atlas of Winneshiek County, 1905, Sec. II.

Axelrod, Alan, *Chronicle of the Indian Wars from Colonial Times to Wounded Knee*, New York, Prentice Hall General Reference, 1993.

Bakeman, Mary Hawker, *Legends, Letters and Lies: Readings about Inkpaduta and the Spirit Lake Massacre*, Roseville, Park Genealogical Books, 2001.

Ballou, Robert, "The Indian War in the Klickitat Valley," *Early Klickitat Valley Days*, Goldendale: The Goldendale Sentinel, 1938.

Basler, Roy P., editor, *The Collected Works of Abraham Lincoln*, Volume VI, New Brunswick, New Jersey, Rutgers University Press, 1953

Beard, Reed, *The Battle of Tippecanoe: Historical Sketches of the Famous Field upon Which General William Henry Harrison Won Renown That Aided Him in Reaching the Presidency Lives of the Prophet and Tecumseh with Many Interesting Incidents of their Rise and Overthrow, The Campaign of 1888 and the Election of General Benjamin Harrison*, Chicago, Hammond Press, W.B. Conkey Company, 1911.

Beaver, R. Pierce, *Pioneers in Mission*, Grand Rapids, Michigan: Wm. B. Eerdmans Publishing Co., 1966.

Beck, Paul N., *Soldier, Settler, and Sioux: Fort Ridgely and the Minnesota River Valley 1853-1867*, Sioux.Falls, The Center for Western Studies, Augustana College, 2000.

Berg, Lillie Clara, *Early Pioneers and Indians of Minnesota and Rice County*, San Leandro, Calaifornia, published by author, 1959.

Berghold, Alexander, *The Indians' Revenge*, San Francisco, P.J. Thomas Printing, 1891.

Berthong, Donald J., *The Southern Cheyennes*, Norman, 1963.

Blegen, Theodore C., *Minnesota: A History of the State*, Minneapolis, University of Minnesota Press, 1963.

Bourke, John G., *On the Border with Crook*, Lincoln & London, University of Nebraska Press, 1971. Reproduced from the 1891 original published by Charles Scribner's Sons.

Bowen, Richard D., editor, *The Second Nebraska's Campaign Against the Sioux*, reprinted from Nebraska History, Volume 44, Number 1, March 1963.

Boyd, Robert K, *Two Indian Battles*, Grand Rapids, Michigan, Custer Ephemera Society, 1972 reprint of 1928 original.

Brady, Cyrus Townsend, *Indian Fights and Fighters*, Lincoln & London, University of Nebraska Press, 1971.

Bray, Edmund C. and Bray, Martha Coleman, *Joseph N. Nicollet on the Plains and Prairies*, St. Paul, Minnesota Historical Society Press, 1976.

Bray, Martha Coleman, editor, *The Journals of Joseph N. Nicollet*, St. Paul, Minnesota Historical Society Press, 1970.

Brininstool, E.A., *Troopers with Custer: Historic Incidents of the Battle of the Little Big Horn*, Lincoln & London, University of Nebraska Press, 1952.

Brown, Bob, *Northwest Iowa's Greatest Tragedy: The Spirit Lake Massacre* (Reprint of a Series of Six Articles on the March, 1857, Spirit Lake Massacre,

Written by Bob Brown and Published in the *Fort Dodge*, Iowa, *Messenger* February 18-25, 1957.

Brown, Dee, *Bury My Heart at Wounded Knee*, New York, Henry Holt and Company, 1970, p. 440.

Brown, Dee, *The Fetterman Massacre*, Lincoln & London, University of Nebraska Press, 1971.

Brown, Mark H., *The Plainsmen of the Yellowstone: A History of the Yellowstone Basin*, Toronto, Longmans, Green & Company, 1961.

Brown, Mark H. and Felton, W.R., *The Frontier Years*, New York, Bramhall House, 1955.

Bryant, Charles S. Bryant, *A History of the Great Massacre by the Sioux Indians in Minnesota, Including the Personal Narratives of Many Who Escaped*, St. Peter, E. Wainwright & Son, Publishers, 1872.

Bryant, Charles S. and Murch, Abel, *Indian Massacre in Minnesota: A History of the Indian Wars of the Far West*.

Buck, Daniel, *Indian Outbreaks*, Minneapolis, Ross & Haines, Inc., 1965.

Bunnell, Lafayette Houghton, *Discovery of the Yosemite and the Indian War of 1851, Which Led to that Event*.

Capps, Benjamin, *The Old West: The Indians*, New York, Time-Life Books, 1973.

Carley, Kenneth, *Minnesota in the Civil War*, Minneapolis, Ross & Haines, Inc., 1961.

Carrigan, Minnie Buce, *Captured by the Indians: Reminiscences of Pioneer Life in Minnesota*, Forest City, South Dakota, Forest City Press, 1907.

Carruth, Gorton, *The Encyclopedia of American Facts and Dates*, 10th Ed. New York: Harper Collins Publishers, 1997.

Catlin, George Catlin, *Letters and Notes on the Manners, Customs, and Conditions of North American Indians*, 2 volumes, 1844. Reprinted by Dover Publications, New York, 1973.

Childs, James, *A History of Waseca County, 1854-1904*, Waseca, 1904.

Coffin, Charles Carleton, *The Seat of Empire*, 1890.

Cohen, M.M., *Notices of Florida and the Campaign*, Gainesville, University of Florida Press, 1964, Reprint of 1836 Edition.

Connell, Evan S, Connell, *Son of the Morning Star*, New York, North Point Press, 1984.

Connolly, A.P., *A Thrilling Narrative of the Minnesota Massacre and the Sioux War of 1862-63*, Chicago, A.P. Connolly Publisher.

Coues, Elliott, *The Expeditions of Zebulon Montgomery Pike*, Volume I, Minneapolis, Ross & Haines, Inc., 1965.

Coues, Elliott, editor, *Forty Years a Fur Trader: The Personal Narrative of Charles Larpenteur*, Minneapolis, Ross & Haines, Inc., 1962.

Crawford, Lewis F., *The Exploits of Ben Arnold, Indian Fighter, Gold Miner, Cowboy, Hunter, & Army Scout*, Norman, University of Oklahoma Press, 1926.

Crook, George Crook, Schmitt, Martin F, editor, *General George Crook, His Autobiography*, Norman & London, University of Oklahoma Press, 1986.

Curtiss-Wedge, Franklyn, *History of McLeod County, Minnesota*, Chicago & Winona, H.C. Cooper Jr. & Company, 1917.

Curtiss-Wedge, Franklyn, *The History of Renville County, Minnesota*, Volume II, Chicago, H.C. Cooper, Jr., & Company, 1916.

Curtiss-Wedge, Franklyn, *History of Wright County, Minnesota*, Chicago, H.C. Cooper, Jr., & Company, 1915.

Custer, General George A., *My Life on the Plains*, Lincoln, University of Nebraska Press, 1966.

D.R. Farnum's *History of Rice County*, 1880.

Dally, Captain Nate, *Tracks and Trails Or Incidents in the Life of a Minnesota Territorial Pioneer*, Cass County Pioneer, Walker, 1931.

Davies, Kenneth Maitland, *To the Last Man: The Chronicle of the 135th Infantry Regiment of Minnesota*, St. Paul, Ramsey County Historical Society, 1982.

Debo, Angie, *A History of the Indians of the United States*, Norman, University of Oklahoma Press, 1970.

Dick, Everett, *Vanguards of the Frontier*, New York & London, D. Appleton-Century Company, Inc., 1941.

Diedrich, Mark, *Dakota Oratory: Great Moments in the Recorded Speech of the Eastern Sioux, 1695-1874*, Rochester, Coyote Books, 1989.

Donald, David Herbert, *Lincoln*, London, Jonathan Cape, 1995.

Eastlick, Mrs. L., *A Personal Narrative of Indian Massacres 1862*, published 1864.

Eastman, Charles A., *Indian Heroes and Great Chieftains*, Seattle, The World Wide School, 1998.

"1868–1968 Maple Plain & Independence Past–Present," published by the Maple Plain Garden Club.

Faust, Patricia L., editor, *Historical Times Illustrated Encyclopedia of the Civil War*, New York, Harper & Row Publishers, 1986.

Featherstonhaugh, George W., *A Canoe Voyage up the Minnay Sotor*, Volume I, St. Paul, Minnesota Historical Society Press.

Folwell, William Watts, *A History of Minnesota*, Vol. II, St. Paul, Minnesota Historical Society Press, 1956.

Forrest, Robert B, *A History of Western Murray County*, Murray Co., Minnesota, 1947.

Forsyth, General George A., *Thrilling Days in Army Life*, Lincoln & London, University of Nebraska Press, 1994. Reprinted from the original 1900 edition published by Harper & Brothers.

Fridley, Russell W., *Charles E. Flandrau and the Defense of New Ulm*, New Ulm, Brown County Historical Society, 1962.

Fritsche, L.A., M.D., *History of Brown County Minnesota: Its People, Industries and Institutions*, Volume I, Indianapolis, B.F. Bowen & Company, Inc., 1916.

Fuller,George W., *A History of the Pacific Northwest* (New York: Alfred A. Knopf, 1948.

Furness, Marion Ramsey, *Governor Ramsey and Frontier Minnesota: Impressions from His Diary and Letters*, St. Paul, Minnesota Historical Society Press, 1947.

Gardner, Abigail, *History of the Spirit Lake Massacre! 8th March 1857, and of Miss Abigail Gardiner's Three Months Captivity among the Indians*, New Britain, CT., L.P. Lee, Publisher, 1857.

Grafe, Ernest & Horsted, Paul, *Exploring with Custer, the 1874 Black Hills Expedition*, Custer, South Dakota, Golden Valley Press, 1995.

Gresham, Hon. William G., *History of Nicollet & LeSueur Counties, Minnesota: Their People, Industries, & Institutions*, Indianapolis, B.F. Bowen & Company, Inc., 1916.

Grinnell, George Bird, *The Fighting Cheyennes*, New York, 1915.

Hafen, LeRoy R and Young, Francis Marion, *Fort Laramie and the Pageant of the West*, Lincoln and London, University of Nebraska Press, 1938.

Hagan, William T., *Quanah Parker, Comanche Chief*, Norman, University of Oklahoma Press, 1993.

Hage, George S., *Newspapers on the Minnesota Frontier 1849-1860*, St. Paul, Minnesota Historical Society Press, 1967.

Hansen, Marcus L., *Old Fort Snelling 1819-1858*, Minneapolis, Ross & Haines, Inc, 1958.

Hardin, Terri, editor, *Legends & Lore of the American Indians*, New York, Barnes & Noble, 1993.

Heard, Isaac V.D., *History of the Sioux War and Massacres of 1862 and 1863*. New York, Harper & Brothers, 1863.

Heitman, Francis B., *Historical Register and Dictionary of the United States Army, from Its Organization, September 29, 1789, to March 2, 1903*, Washington, Government Printing Office, 1903.

History of Franklin County, Pennsylvania, Early settlers and Indian Wars, 1887.

History of Wabasha County, 1920.

A History of Waukesha County, Wisconsin, (Exact Date & author unknown) 1880s.

Hoffman, Arnie, Extracted from the *Eau Claire Leader Telegram*, Special Publication, *Our Story: The Chippewa Valley and Beyond*, Eau Claire, 1976.

Hoig, Stan, *The Battle of the Washita*, Lincoln & London, University of Nebraska Press, 1976.

Houlette, Dr. William, *Iowa: The Pioneer Heritage*, Des Moines, Wallace-Homestead Book Company, 1970.

Howard, Helen Addison, *Saga of Chief Joseph*, Lincoln & London, University of Nebraska Press, 1978,

Hughes, Daisy Ellen, *Builders of Pope County*, Issued in connection with the homecoming, historical pageant and dedicatory ceremonies celebrating the completion of Pope County's new courthouse in Glenwood, Minnesota, June 19-20-21, 1930.

Hughes, Thomas, *History of Blue Earth County and Biographies of Its Leading Citizens*, Chicago, Middle West Publishing Company.

Hughes, Reverends Thomas E. and Edwards, David, Roberts, Hugh G. and Hughes, Thomas Hughes, *Story of the Welsh in Minnesota, Foreston and Lime Springs, Iowa. Gathered by the Old Settlers*, 1895.

In Commemoration of the Sioux Uprising, Tracy, Murray County Historical Society, 1982.

Jackson, Donald, Gold, *The United States Cavalry Expedition of 1874*, Lincoln & London, University of Nebraska Press, 1972.

Jennewein, Leonard D., *Dakota Panorama*, Midwest Beach, Sioux Falls, 1961.

Johnson, Clint, *In the Footsteps of J.E.B. Stuart*, Winston-Salem, John F. Blair, Publisher, Inc., 2003. (The third volume of the trilogy of *In The Footsteps of Robert E. Lee* [2001] and *In The Footsteps of Stonewall Jackson* [2002].)

Juni, Benedict, *Held in Captivity, Experiences Related by Benedict Juni of New Ulm, Minn., as an Indian Captive During the Indian Outbreak in 1862*, New Ulm, Liesch Walter Printing Company, 1926.

Kane, Lucile M., Holmquist, June D., and Gilman, Carolyn, editors, *The Northern Expeditions of Stephen H. Long: The Journals of 1817 and 1823 and Related Documents*, St. Paul, Minnesota Historical Society Press, 1978.

Kappler, Charles J., editor, *Indian Affairs: Laws and Treaties*, Vol. II (Treaties), Washington: Government Printing Office, 1904; Oklahoma State University Library, Volume II.

Kelly, Fanny, *Narrative of My Captivity Among the Sioux Indians*, Stanford, Connecticut., Longmeadow Press, 1990.

Kelsey, D.M., *History of our Wild West and Stories of Pioneer Life*, Chicago, Charles C. Thompson Company, 1901.

Kennedy, Roger G., *Men on the Moving Frontier from Wilderness to Civilization: The Romance, Realism, and Life-Styles of One Part of the American West*, Palo Alto, California, American West Publishing Co., 1969.

Kingsbury, George W., *History of Dakota Territory*, Vol. I., 1915.

Lake, Herb, *Iowa Inside Out*, Ames, Iowa State University Press, 1968.

Lamson, Frank B., *Condensed History of Meeker County 1855-1939*, Brown Printing Company.

Lamson, Frank, *West Tier of Towns*, United States Geological Survey.

Lass, William E., "Mississippi River Steamboating," in Janet Daily Lysengen and Ann M. Rathke, *The Centennial Anthology of North Dakota: History Journal of the Northern Plains*, Bismarck, State Historical Society of North Dakota, 1996.

Laumer, Frank, *Dade's Last Command*, Gainesville, University Press of Florida, 1995.

Lewis, Henry (edited by Bertha L. Heilbron), *The Valley of the Mississippi Illustrated*, St. Paul, Minnesota Historical Society Press, 1967.

Lounsberry, Colonel Clement A., *Early History of North Dakota: Essential Outlines of American History*, Washington, D.C., Liberty Press, 1919.

Mails, Thomas E., *The Mystic Warriors of the Plains*, New York, Marlowe & Company, 1996.

Marrin, Albert, *War Clouds in the West Indians & Cavalrymen 1860-1890*, New York, Anthneum, 1984.

McConkey, Harriet E. Bishop, *Dakota War Whoop: Or Indian Massacres and War in Minnesota, of 1862-3*, Minneapolis, Ross & Haines, 1970, Revised Edition.

McNamara, Bea, *The Okoboji and Spirit Lake Massacre and Kidnapping Story*, Arnolds Park, Iowa, 1957.

Memorial of the Sioux Indian Outbreak 1862, Fairfax, Fort Ridgely State Park and Historical Association, 1930.

Merington, Marguerite, editor, *The Custer Story: The Life and Letters of George A. Custer and His Wife Elizabeth*, New York, Barnes & Noble, 1994.

Mitchell, William Bell, *History of Stearns County*, Chicago, H.C. Cooper, Jr., 1915.

Moe, Richard, *The Last Full Measure: The Life and Death of the First Minnesota Volunteers*, New York, Avon Books, 1994.

Monaghan, Jay, editor-in-chief, *The Book of the American West*, New York, Julian Messner, Inc., 1963.

Morris, Lucy Leavenworth Wilder, editor, *Old Rail Fence Corners: Frontier Tales Told by Minnesota Pioneers*, St. Paul, Minnesota Historical Society Press, 1976.

Murray, Robert A., *The Army Moves West Supplying the Western Indian Wars Campaigns*, Fort Collins, Colorado, The Old Arm Press, 1981.

Neihardt, John F., *Black Elk Speaks*, Lincoln & London: University of Nebraska Press, 1932.

Neill, Rev. Edward D., *History of the Upper Minnesota Valley Minnesota*, 1881.

Oehler, C.M., *The Great Sioux Uprising*, New York, Oxford University Press, 1959

Old Mendota: A Proposal for Addition to Land to Fort Snelling State Historical Park, St. Paul, Fort Snelling State Park Association and the Minnesota Historical Society, 1966.

Parker, John, editor, *The Journals of Jonathan Carver and Related Documents, 1766-1770*, St. Paul, Minnesota Historical Society Press, 1976.

Pate, O'Nell L., *Ranald Slidell Mackenzie, Brave Cavalry Colonel*, Austin, Texas, Eakin Press, 1994.

Pederson, Kern O., *The Story of Fort Snelling*, St. Paul, Minnesota, Historical Society Press, 1966.

SMOKE

Peirce, Parker I., *Antelope Bill*, Minneapolis, Ross & Haines, Inc., 1962.

Pierce, Michael D., *The Most Promising Young Officer: A Life of Ranald Slidell Mackenzie*, Norman & London, University of Oklahoma Press, 1993.

Peithmann, Irvin M., *The Unconquered Seminole Indians*, St. Petersburg, Great Outdoors Association, 1957.

Petersen, William J., *The Story of Iowa: The Progress of an American State*, Volume I, New York, Lewis Historical Publishing Company, Inc., 1952.

Pond, Samuel W, *The Dakota or Sioux in Minnesota as They Were in 1834*, St. Paul, Minnesota Historical Society Press, 1986.

Potter, Woodburne, *The War in Florida*, Baltimore, Lewis & Coleman, 1836.

Quelle, R.A., Garden County, *Who's Who in Nebraska*, 1940.

Reese, M. Lisle, *South Dakota: A Guide to the State Compiled by the Federal Writers' Project of the Works Progress Administration*, New York, Hastings House Publishers, 1976.

Richmond, Minnesota Centennial History 1856 to 1956.

Riggs, Stephen, *Mary and I: Forty Years with the Sioux*, Congregational Sunday School and Publishing Society, 1880; reprint; Ross and Haines, Inc., 1969.

Robertson, Dr. William Glenn, Brown, Dr. Jerold E, Campsey, Major William M., McMeen, Major Scott R., *Atlas of the Sioux Wars*, Combat Studies Institute, U.S. Army Command and General Staff College, Fort Leavenworth, Kansas.

Robinson III, Charles M., *A Good Year to Die: The Story of the Great Sioux War*, Norman & London, University of Oklahoma Press, 1995.

Robinson III, Charles M., *Bad Hand: A Biography of General Ranald S. Mackenzie*, Austin, Texas, State House Press, 1993.

Robinson, Elwyn B., *History of North Dakota*, Lincoln, University of Nebraska Press, 1966.

Rose, Arthur P., *An Illustrated History of Jackson County, Minnesota*, Jackson, Northern Historical Publishing Company, 1910.

Rose, Arthur P., *An Illustrated History of Yellow Medicine County*, Marshall, Northern Historical Publishing Company, 1914.

Rossman, L.A., *The Great White Father Gets the Land*, Grand Rapids, Privately printed, 1950.

Sage, Leland L., *A History of Iowa*, Ames, The Iowa State University Press, 1974.

Satterlee, Marion P., *A Detailed Account of the Massacre by the Dakota Indians of Minnesota in 1862*, Self-published, Minneapolis.

Saterlee, Marion P., *Outbreak and Massacre by the Dakota Indians in Minnesota in 1862*, Minneapolis, (Self-published), 1923.

Schrader, Julie Hiller, *The Heritage of Blue Earth County, MN*, 1990.

Schultz, Duane, *Over the Earth I Come: The Great Sioux Uprising of 1862*, New York, St. Martin's Press, 1992.

304

Smart, A.B., *Outlines of Pioneer History*, Tamblyn Printing Wessington Springs 1970.

Smith, C.A., *A Random Historical Sketch of Meeker County, Minnesota from Its First Settlement, to July 4, 1876*, Litchfield, Belfoy & Joubert, 1877.

Smith, W.W., *Sketch of the Seminole War, and Sketches During a Campaign*, Charleston, South Carolina, Dan J. Dowling, 1836.

Smythe, William E., *History of San Diego 1542-1908, An Account of the Rise and Progress of the Pioneer Settlement on the Pacific Coast of the United States*, San Diego, San Diego Historical Society, 1907.

A Soldier in Company "H," 6th Regiment, A Journal of Sibley's Indian Expedition During the Summer of 1863 and Record of the Troops Employed, Minneapolis, James D. Thueson, Publisher, 1980.

Sprague, John T. Sprague, *The Origin, Progress, and Conclusion of the Florida War*, New York, Appleton, 1948.

Stanley, Henry M., *My Early Travels and Adventures in America and Asia*, London, 1895, v. 1.

Sully, Langdon Sully, *No Tears for the General: The Life of Alfred Sully, 1821-1879*, Palo Alto, California, American West Publishing Co., 1974.

Thomas, David and Ronnefeldt, Karin, editors, *People of the First Man: Life Among the Plains Indians in Their Final Days of Glory*, New York, Promontory Press, 1982.

Tallent, Annie D., *The Black Hills: Or, The Last Hunting Ground of the Dakotahs*, Sioux Falls, Brevet Press, 1974.

Tarble, Helen M., *The Story of My Capture and Escape During the Minnesota Indian Massacre of 1862*, St. Paul, The Abbott Printing Company, 1904.

Terrell, John Upton, *Sioux Trail*, New York, McGraw-Hill Book Company, 1974.

Thrapp, Dan L., *Encyclopedia of Frontier Biography*, Volume II of III, Lincoln & London, University of Nebraska Press, 1988.

Tinkham, George H, *California Men and Events*, Panama-Pacific Exposition Edition, 1915.

Tolzmann, Don Heinrich, editor, *The Sioux Uprising in Minnesota, 1862: Jacob Nix's Eyewitness History*, Indianapolis, Max Kade German-American Center and Indiana German Heritage Society, Inc., 1994.

Twichell, Lois Clarinda, *The Life of Lois Clarinda Twichell, Beloved Wife of George Blackwell*, 1908.

Utley, Robert M., *Cavalier in Buckskin: George Armstrong Custer and the Western Frontier*, 1988.

Utter, Jack, *Wounded Knee and the Ghost Dance Tragedy*, Lake Ann, Michigan, National Woodlands Publishing Company, 2000.

Wakefield, Sarah F., *Six Weeks in the Indian Tepees*, Ye Galleon Press, 1985.

Wall, Joseph Frazier, *Iowa: A Bicentennial History*, 1978.

Wall, Joseph Frazier, *Iowa: A History*, New York, W.W. Norton & Company, Inc., 1978.

Ware, Captain Eugene F., *The Indian War of 1864*, Lincoln, University of Nebraska Press, 1965.

Waterbury, Jean Parker, *The Oldest City: St. Augustine Saga of Survival*, St. Augustine, St. Augustine Historical Society, 1983.

Webb, Loren, *Diary of Captain Loren Webb, 1861–1863*, Firelands Historical Society. Norwalk, Ohio, 1995, Transcribed by Matthew L. Burr.

Webb, Wayne E., *Redwood: The Story of a County*, St. Paul, Redwood Board of Commissioners, 1964.

Wemett, W.M., *The Story of the Flickertail State*, Valley City, W.M. Wemett, 1923.

West, Elliott, *Contested Plains, Indians, Goldseekers, and the Rush to Colorado*, Lawrence, University Press of Kansas, 1996.

Whipple, Henry B., *Light and Shadows of a Long Episcopate (1902) Being Reminiscences and Recollections of the Right Reverend Henry B. Whipple, Bishop of Minnesota*.

White, Helen McCann, editor, *Ho for the Gold Fields: Northern Overland Wagon Trains of the 1860s*, St. Paul, Minnesota Historical Society Press, 1966.

Willand, Jon, *Lac Qui Parle and the Dakota Mission*, Madison, Minnesota, Lac Qui Parle County Historical Society, 1964.

Williams, J. Fletcher Williams, *A History of the City of St. Paul and of the County of Ramsey, Minnesota*, St. Paul, 1876.

Williams, John Lee, *The Territory of Florida*, New York, Goodrich, 1837.

Wilson, Captain Eugene M., "Narrative of the First Regiment of Mounted Rangers," in *Minnesota in the Civil and Indian Wars, 1861-1865*, St. Paul, St. Paul Pioneer Press Co., 1891.

Wright, James A., edited by Steven J. Keillor, *No More Gallant a Deed: A Civil War memoir of the First Minnesota Volunteers*, St..Paul, Minnesota Historical Society Press, 2001.

Ziebarth, Marilyn and Ominsky, Alan, *Fort Snelling: Anchor Post of the Northwest*, St. Paul, Minnesota Historical Society Press, 1979.

Magazines, Articles and Presentations

"The Abercrombie Siege and Massacre at Breckenridge," Fort Abercrombie 1862, Supplement of *Richland County Farmer-Globe*, Wahpeton, North Dakota, September 22, 1936.

"An Early Picture of Fort Abercrombie," Fort Abercrombie 1862, Supplement of *Richland County Farmer-Globe*, Wahpeton, North Dakota, September 22, 1936.

Anderson, Gary Clayton, "Myrick's Insult: A Fresh Look at Myth and Reality," *Minnesota History*, 48/5, Spring 1983.

"The Beauties of Abercrombie," Supplement Fort Abercrombie 1862, of *Richland County Farmer-Globe*, Wahpeton, North Dakota, September 22, 1936.

Bergland, Betty Ann, "The Guri Endreson Rosseland Story." Brief Extracts from a paper presented at the Seventh International Interdisciplinary Women's Congress: Women'sWorlds held in Tromsø, Norway, June 20-26, 1999, at Session: VII, Gendering the Past: "Women Pioneers and Activists" on Friday, June 25, 1999. The title was "Norwegian Immigrants and Indigenous Peoples: Gendered Perspectives on Interethnic Relations in Nineteenth Century Midwestern United States."

Bowen, Richard D., "The Second Nebraska's Campaign against the Sioux," *Nebraska History*, Volume 44, Number 1, March 1963.

Boyd, Mark F., "The Complete Story of Osceola," Reprinted in *Florida Historical Quarterly*, 33, Numbers 3 & 4, January-April 1955.

Bristow, David L., "Inkpaduta's Revenge: The True Story of the Spirit Lake Massacre," *The Iowan Magazine*, January-February 1999.

Carr, S.V. letter to "Brother McBride" dated November 16, 1862, "Soldier Writes of March to Relieve Fort Abercrombie," Fort Abercrombie 1862, Supplement of *Richland County Farmer-Globe*, Wahpeton, North Dakota, September 22, 1936.

Carroll, Jane Lamm, "Native Americans and Criminal Justice on the Minnesota Frontier," *Minnesota History*, 55/2, Summer 1996.

Clark, Dan Elbert, "Border Defense in Iowa During the Civil War," in Benjamin F. Shambaugh, editor, *Iowa and War*, The State Historical Society of Iowa, Number 10, April 1918.

Connors, Joseph, "The Elusive Hero of Redwood Ferry," *Minnesota History*, Summer 1955.

Daffodil Valley Times, Internet.

"Dakota Conflict at . . . Shetek, 1862-1987, Year of Reconciliation," Supplement to the *Tracy Headlight-Herald*, Shetek Captives Taken to Dakotas.

Davis, Theodore R., "A Summer on the Plains," *Harper's New Monthly Magazine*, New York, v. 36, February, 1868.

Dietrich, Mark, "A 'Good Man' in a Changing World: Cloud Man, the Dakota Leader, and His Life and Times," *Ramsey County History*, Volume 36, Number 1, Spring 2001.

Dixon, Bvt. Captain James W., "Across the Plains with General Hancock," *Journal of the Military Service Institute*, US7, 1886.

Estensen, Gene, "War Comes to Norwegian Grove," Internet.

Estherville, Iowa Chamber of Commerce, "A Brief History of Fort Defiance."

"The Battle of the Little Bighorn, 1876," Eye Witness to History, www.eyewitnesstohistory.com, 1997.

Ferch, David L., "Fighting the Smallpox Epidemic of 1837-38," *Museum of the Fur Trade Quarterly*, Volume 20 Number 1, Spring 1984.

Foot, Jamie Lee, "Foot and the Dakota Conflict," Internet;

Fort Ridgely: A Journal of the Past, Minnesota Historical Society newspaper.

Garfield, Marvin M., "Defense of the Kansas Frontier, 1866-67," *Kansas Historical Quarterly*, v. 1, August, 1932.

Gewalt, C.A., "The Building of Fort Abercrombie," Supplement Fort Abercrombie 1862, of *Richland County Farmer-Globe*, Wahpeton, North Dakota, September 22, 1936.

Gewalt, C.A., "The Impending Indian Uprising and Beginning of Fortifications," Fort Abercrombie 1862, Supplement of *Richland County Farmer-Globe*, Wahpeton, North Dakota, September 22, 1936.

Gimmestad, Dennis, "Territorial Space Platting New Ulm," *Minnesota History*, 56/6 Summer 1999.

Gorman, James H. letter to Samuel Brown dated July 25, 1863. Joseph R. Brown Heritage Society, *JRB/News*, Volume 2 Number 1 / March 1997.

Guenter, Levy, "Were American Indians the Victims of Genocide?" *George Mason University's History News Network*, Commentary, November 22, 2004.

Henson, C.L., "From War to Self Determination: A History of the Bureau of Indian Affairs," American Studies Today Online.

"History of Minnehaha County," Internet.

Johns, Larry H., "If They are Hungry, Let Them Eat Grass," *True West*, May-June 2003.

Kip, Lt. Lawrence, "The Indian Council at Walla Walla, May and June of 1855," *Army Life on the Pacific: a Journal*.

Lancaster (Pennsylvania) County Historical Society, Volume 57.

Larson, Peggy Rodina, "A New Look at the Elusive Inkpaduta," *Minnesota History*, 48/1, Spring 1982.

Laut, Agnes C., "The Story of Guri Endreson: The Heroine of Kandiyohi," 1908.

Leonard, Steven M., "Frederick W. Benteen: Custer's Nemesis," *Wild West*, June 2001.

Ligman, Alison, Dickey County, North Dakota, "Whitestone Hill," Internet.

"Little Crow as Remembered by Ohivesa (Charles A. Eastman)," Internet.

McCann, Lloyd E., "The Grattan Massacre," *Nebraska History*, Volume XXXVII, Number 1, March 1956.

Medicine Wolf, Dustyn, "Lakota History," Internet.

"Minnesota A State Guide," American Guide Series, Internet.

"Old Frontiersman Tells of Massacre." Fort Abercrombie 1862, Supplement of *Richland County Farmer-Globe*, Wahpeton, North Dakota, September 22, 1936.

Oregon Blue Book, Internet.

Oyen, John J., "The Lac Qui Parle Indian Mission," *The Watson Voice*, April 22, 1937.

PBS, "New Perspectives of the West."

Pluth, Edward J., "The Failed Watab Treaty of 1853," *Minnesota History*, 57/1 Spring 2000.

Schiller, Judi, "Whitestone Hill: A Place in History," *Crooked Creek Observer*.

Sheldon, Addison Erwin., "History and Stories of Nebraska," Internet.

Shellum, Bernie, "A Rude Birth and Other Lake Hanska Tales," Internet.

Shonley, Tom, "Jerauld County before 1650-1866," Internet.

South Dakota History, the *Journal of the South Dakota State Historical Society*, Volume 18, Number 4.

Stachurski, Richard J. "Harney's Fight at Blue Water Creek," *Wild West*, April 2003.

Sultzman, Lee, "Winnebago History," Internet

Treuer, Anton and Treuer, David, "Ojibwe," *Minnesota History*, 56/4, Winter 1998-99.

Wilson, Bonnie, "Secretary Nicolay's Souvenir Album, 1862," *Minnesota History*, 58/7, Fall 2003.

Wilson, Raymond, "Forty Years to Judgment, The Santee Sioux Claims Case," *Minnesota History*, 47/7, Fall 1981.

Manuscripts, Letters, and Theses

Ron Affolter letter to author dated September 5, 2003.

G.G. Allanson, Stirring Adventures of the Jos. R. Brown Family, Sacred Heart, Sacred Heart News. Dakota Conflict of 1862, Manuscripts Collections, Microfilm Edition, Reel 1, Minnesota Historical Society.

Captain Joseph Anderson letter to Dr. J.W. Daniels dated August 9, 1894. Dakota Conflict of 1862, Manuscripts Collections, Microfilm Edition, Roll 1, Minnesota Historical Society.

Captain Joseph Anderson's report of the actions of his men, Company A of the "Cullen Frontier Guards" at the Battle of Birch Coulee dated September 4, 1862. Dakota Conflict of 1862, Manuscripts Collections, Microfilm Edition, Roll 1, Minnesota Historical Society.

Anonymous, "Notes by the Way Side on the Indian Expedition," Dakota Conflict of 1862, Manuscripts Collections, Microfilm Edition, Roll 1, Minnesota Historical Society.

Julia Ann (Peters) Arledge Papers, 1892. Jerry Smalley Website, Internet.

Dick E. Blanchard Account, Dakota Conflict of 1862, Manuscripts Collections, Minnesota Historical Society.

Christiana Hudson Brack Account, Dakota Conflict of 1862, Manuscripts Collections, Microfilm Edition, Reel 1, Minnesota Historical Society.

"Brown County and the Sioux Massacre," document origin unknown, Brown County Historical Society, New Ulm.

Brown County Journal, date unknown. "Fort Ridgely—The Indian Uprising of 1862: How a Broken Oath Prevented a Surprise Attack." Fort Ridgely Archives.

Major Benjamin Wetherill Brunson Reminiscence, Dakota Conflict of 1862, Manuscripts Collections, Microfilm Edition, Reel 1, Minnesota Historical Society.

Henry Ladd Carver letter to his wife dated July 19, 1863. Dakota Conflict of 1862, Manuscripts Collections, Microfilm Edition, Reel 1, Minnesota Historical Society.

Fred Ceser, Howard Lake Herald, Early 1900s, exact date unknown.

Ezra T. Champlin reminiscence, Dakota Conflict of 1862, Manuscripts Collections, Microfilm Edition, Reel 1, Minnesota Historical Society.

L.W. Collins, E.T. Champlin, and Mathias Holl, Report on the Battle of Wood Lake, Manuscript Collections, Brown County Historical Society.

Lieutenant Loren Warren Collins Memorandum of Sibley's Expedition 1863. Dakota Conflict of 1862, Manuscripts Collections, Microfilm Edition, Reel 1, Minnesota Historical Society.

Thomas D. Christie letter to his father dated September 25, 1862. Dakota Conflict of 1862, Manuscripts Collections and Government Records, Minnesota Historical Society.

Thomas D. Christie letter to his father dated September 26, 1862. Dakota Conflict of 1862, Manuscripts Collections and Government Records, Minnesota Historical Society.

Christopher Columbus: Extracts from a Journal, 1492, A Treasury of Primary Documents.

A.P. Connolly, "Another Reminiscence," Brown County Historical Society, New Ulm.

George W. Crooks reminiscence, Dakota Conflict of 1862, Manuscripts Collections, Microfilm Edition, Reel 1, Minnesota Historical Society.

Mary Crowell letter to a friend dated September 14, 1862, Dakota Conflict of 1862, Manuscripts Collections, Microfilm Edition, Reel 1, Minnesota Historical Society.

Electa Currier letter to Henry Currier dated September 12, 1862, Dakota Conflict of 1862. Manuscripts Collections, Microfilm Edition, Reel 1, Minnesota Historical Society.

A.A. Davidson, "Narrative from the Indian Outbreak of 1862," Dakota Conflict of 1862, Manuscripts Collections, Microfilm Edition, Reel 2, Minnesota Historical Society.

Statement of David J. Davis. Dakota Conflict of 1862, Manuscripts Collections, Microfilm Edition, Reel 2, Minnesota Historical Society.

Statement of Thomas Y. Davis. Dakota Conflict of 1862, Manuscripts Collections, Microfilm Edition, Reel 2, Minnesota Historical Society.

William J. Duley letter to Neil Currie dated August 24, 1885, Dakota Conflict of 1862. Manuscripts Collections, Microfilm Edition, Reel 1, Minnesota Historical Society.

E.W. Earle reminiscence. Dakota Conflict of 1862, Manuscripts Collections, Microfilm Edition, Reel 1, Minnesota Historical Society.

Ezmon Earle reminiscence. Dakota Conflict of 1862, Manuscripts Collections, Microfilm Edition, Reel 1, Minnesota Historical Society.

Paul H. Elmen, "Tomahawks are Red," Dakota Conflict of 1862, Manuscripts Collections, Microfilm Edition, Reel 1, Minnesota Historical Society.

Captain James Fisk letter, Minnesota pioneer sketches; from the personal recollections and observations of a pioneer resident with the Indians in the Badlands, Library of Congress.

Charles E. Flandrau, "The Battle of New Ulm," Manuscript Collections, Brown County Historical Society.

Charles Eugene Flandrau letter to E.M. Tebbets dated September 20, 1897, Dakota Conflict of 1862, Manuscripts Collections, Microfilm Edition, Reel 1, Minnesota Historical Society.

C.W. Fogg letter to the *St. Paul Pioneer Press* dated December 7, 1883, Dakota Conflict of 1862, Manuscripts Collections, Microfilm Edition, Reel 1, Minnesota Historical Society.

Jamie Lee Foot, "Foot and the Dakota Conflict," Internet;

Jamie Lee Foot letter to author dated May 4, 2003.

"Fort Abercrombie—Captain Vander Horck's Account," Manuscripts Collections, Brown County Historical Society, New Ulm.

Andrew Friend statement taken by Thomas J. Hughes. Dakota Conflict of 1862, Manuscripts Collections, Microfilm Edition, Reel 2, Minnesota Historical Society.

Provost-Marshal-General James B. Fry letter to the governor of Minnesota dated July 27, 1864, Military letters, Military District of Minnesota, 1863–1866, from the Division of Archives & Manuscripts, Minnesota Historical Society.

Edwin L. Fryer reminiscence, Dakota Conflict of 1862, Manuscripts Collections, Microfilm Edition, Reel 1, Minnesota Historical Society.

Thomas J. Galbraith letter to Clark W. Thompson dated June 14, 1862, "Sioux Uprising—Early Rumblings at the Upper Agency, Official Requests for Troops," Brown County Historical Society, New Ulm.

Thomas J. Galbraith letter to Lieutenant Timothy J. Sheehan dated July 27, 1862, "Sioux Uprising—Early Rumblings at the Upper Agency, Agent Galbraith's Instructions to Lt. Sheehan," Brown County Historical Society, New Ulm.

Harry L. Gervais letter to Walter E. Spokesfield dated April 1, 1927, Dakota Conflict of 1862, Manuscripts Collections, Microfilm Edition, Reel 1, Minnesota Historical Society.

James H. Gorman letter to Samuel Brown dated July 25, 1863, Joseph R. Brown Heritage Society, *JRB/News*, Volume 2 Number 1, March 1997.

Franklin Clinton Griswold letter to his parents dated August 25, 1862, Dakota Conflict of 1862, Manuscripts Collections, Microfilm Edition, Reel 1, Minnesota Historical Society.

Franklin Clinton Griswold letter to his parents dated August 28, 1862, Dakota Conflict of 1862, Manuscripts Collections, Microfilm Edition, Reel 1, Minnesota Historical Society.

Franklin Clinton Griswold letter to his parents dated September 7, 1862, Dakota Conflict of 1862, Manuscripts Collections, Microfilm Edition, Reel 1, Minnesota Historical Society.

Charles D. Hatch, "In Re: Indian Massacre in Minn., 1862," Dakota Conflict of 1862, Manuscript Collections, Microfilm Editions, Reel 2, Minnesota Historical Society.

"Narrative of Charles D. Hatch's Experiences in the Indian War in Minnesota in 1862," Dakota Conflict of 1862, Manuscripts Collections, Microfilm Edition, Reel 2, Minnesota Historical Society.

"The Ordeal of Hinhankaga as told to Floyd J. Patten by Clem Felix, Hinhankaga's Grandson," Dakota Conflict of 1862, Manuscripts Collections, Microfilm Edition, Reel 2, Minnesota Historical Society.

Joseph Holt letter to President Abraham Lincoln dated December 1, 1862, Abraham Lincoln Papers, A Collaborative Project Library of Congress Manuscript Division and Lincoln Studies Center, Knox College.

Ingar Johnson Holmquist Reminiscence, Dakota Conflict of 1862, Manuscripts Collections, Microfilm Edition, Reel 2, Minnesota Historical Society.

"The Ill-Fated Leavenworth Expedition and Marker," unpublished manuscript, Brown County Historical Society, New Ulm.

"Indian Raid in Cambria, September 10, 1862, Statement of William P. Jones," Dakota Conflict of 1862, Manuscripts Collections, Microfilm Edition, Reel 2, Minnesota Historical Society.

Narrative of Thomas Ireland. Dakota Conflict of 1862, Manuscripts Collections, Microfilm Edition, Reel 1, Minnesota Historical Society.

Calvin Ives File, Brown County Historical Society, New Ulm.

"Story of "William J. Jones," Dakota Conflict of 1862, Manuscripts Collections, Microfilm Edition, Reel 2, Minnesota Historical Society.

F.W. Johnson, "Outbreak at the Lower Agency," unpublished manuscript, Brown County Historical Society, New Ulm.

Lillian Everett Keeney reminiscence, Dakota Conflict of 1862, Manuscripts Collections, Microfilm Edition, Reel 1, Minnesota Historical Society.

Second Letter of Fanny Kelley, Minnesota pioneer sketches; from the personal recollections and observations of a pioneer resident with the Indians in the Badlands, Library of Congress.

Maria Koch reminiscence, Dakota Conflict of 1862, Manuscripts Collections, Microfilm Edition, Reel 1, Minnesota Historical Society.

"The Narrative of Justina Krieger," Fort Ridgely Archives.

Dorothy Kuske, "Account of Sioux Uprising Experiences,." Dakota Conflict of 1862, Manuscripts Collections, Microfilm Edition, Reel 1, Minnesota Historical Society.

Ralph Lane report entitled 'The Colony at Roanoke" sent to Sir Walter Raleigh in 1586, The American Colonist's Library, A Treasury of Primary Documents.

Rebecca MacAlmond Diary (August 18–September 24, 1862), Dakota Conflict of 1862, Manuscripts Collections, Microfilm Edition, Reel 2, Minnesota Historical Society.

"The Manannah Massacre" by Dr. A.C. Nelson, son of James Nelson and grandson of Carlos Caswell, pioneer residents of Union Grove and Manannah townships at the time of the tragedy. Internet.

Rachel A .Maservey Linn, "Account of building a block house at Maine Prairie, Minn., During the Uprising," Dakota Conflict of 1862, Manuscripts Collection, Microfilm Edition, Reel 2, Minnesota Historical Society.

Diary of Richard McConnell, General Sully's Fisk Expedition, Actions in 1864, Manuscripts Collections, Microfilm Edition, North Dakota Historical Society.

John Ford Meagher letter to J. Fletcher Williams dated December 26, 1887, Dakota Conflict of 1862, Manuscripts Collections, Microfilm Edition, Minnesota Historical Society.

Governor Stephen Miller letter to Brigadier General Henry Sibley dated August 31, 1864, Military letters, Military District of Minnesota, 1863–1866, from the Division of Archives & Manuscripts, Minnesota Historical Society.

Sarah Purnell Montgomery, "Some Recollections of the Sioux Outbreak of 1862," Dakota Conflict of 1862, Manuscripts Collections, Microfilm Edition, Reel 2, Minnesota Historical Society.

James Morgan. Dakota Conflict of 1862, Manuscripts Collections, Microfilm Edition, Reel 2, Minnesota Historical Society.

Morton Enterprise, July 8, 1926, Robert K. Boyd, "The Battle of Birch Cooley," Brown County Historical Society, New Ulm.

Morton Enterprise, July 15, 1926, Robert K. Boyd, "The Day Before the Battle," Brown County Historical Society, New Ulm.

Morton Enterprise, July 29, 1926, Robert K. Boyd, "The Battle of Birch Cooley," Brown County Historical Society, New Ulm.

Morton Enterprise, August 5, 1926, Robert K. Boyd, "How the Indians Fought," Brown County Historical Society, New Ulm.

Morton Enterprise, August 19, 1926, Robert K. Boyd, "The Battle of Birch Cooley," Brown County Historical Society, New Ulm.

Morton Enterprise, October 9, 1930, Robert K. Boyd, "Survivor Tells of Indian Massacre," Brown County Historical Society.

Aaron Myers letter to Neil Currie dated November 20, 1894, Dakota Conflict of 1862, Manuscripts Collections, Microfilm Edition, Reel 1, Minnesota Historical Society.

John Nairn undated letter to Magdalene Nairn, Dakota Conflict of 1862, Manuscripts Collections, Microfilm Edition, Reel 3, Minnesota Historical Society.

Charles Ness, "The Ness Church," Internet.

Assistant Adjutant-General R.C. Olin, via orders issued by General Sibley, letter to Major C.P. Adams, commanding Hatch's Battalion in St. Paul, July 20, 1864, Military letters, Military District of Minnesota, 1863–1866, from the Division of Archives & Manuscripts, Minnesota Historical Society.

Assistant Adjutant-General R.C. Olin letter to Colonel M.T. Thomas, Commanding First Sub-District, Saint Cloud, April 27, 1864, Military letters, Military District of Minnesota, 1863–1866, from the Division of Archives & Manuscripts, Minnesota Historical Society.

Assistant Adjutant-General R.C. Olin, by command of Brigadier-General Sibley, letter to Colonel M.T. Thomas dated May 27, 1864, Military letters, Military District of Minnesota, 1863–1866, from the Division of Archives & Manuscripts, Minnesota Historical Society.

Diary of Ole N. Orland, a soldier with Company A, First Regiment, Dakota Cavalry, with Sully's Expedition to Dakota Territory in 1864, Manuscripts Collections, Microfilm Edition, North Dakota Historical Society.

Julius Owen, "The Hanging of Thirty-Eight Sioux Indians at Mankato." Dakota Conflict of 1862, Manuscripts Collections, Microfilm Edition, Reel 3, Minnesota Historical Society.

Edward Patch Diary for July 16, 1853, Dakota Conflict of 1862, Manuscript Collections, Microfilm Edition, Reel 1, Minnesota Historical Society.

Edward Patch Diary for July 24, 1863, Dakota Conflict of 1862, Manuscripts Collections, Microfilm Edition, Reel 1, Minnesota Historical Society.

Edward Patch Diary for July 26, 1863, Dakota Conflict of 1862, Manuscripts Collections, Microfilm Edition, Reel 1, Minnesota Historical Society.

Edward Patch Diary for July 28, 1863, Dakota Conflict of 1862, Manuscript Collections, Microfilm Edition, Reel 1, Minnesota Historical Society.

Ole Paulson reminiscence, Dakota Conflict of 1862, Manuscripts Collections, Microfilm Edition, Reel 3, Minnesota Historical Society.

John Nelson Pettibone reminiscence, Dakota Conflict of 1862, Manuscripts Collections,
Microfilm Edition, Reel 3, Minnesota Historical Society.

Eli K. Pickett letter to his wife dated July 25, 1863, Dakota Conflict of 1862, Manuscript Collections, Microfilm Edition, Reel 1, Minnesota Historical Society.

General John Pope letter to President Abraham Lincoln dated November 24, 1862, Abraham Lincoln Papers, A Collaborative Project Library of Congress Manuscript Division and Lincoln Studies Center, Knox College.

General John Pope letter to Headquarters, Department of the Northwest, Milwaukee, Wisconsin, dated August 29, 1863, Military letters, Military District of Minnesota, 1863–1866, from the Division of Archives & Manuscripts, Minnesota Historical Society.

Major General John Pope letter to Major-General Henry W. Halleck dated September 16, 1863, Military letters, Military District of Minnesota, 1863–1866, from the Division of Archives & Manuscripts, Minnesota Historical Society.

Major-General John Pope letter to Major-General Henry W. Halleck dated December 3, 1863, Military letters, Military District of Minnesota, 1863–1866, from the Division of Archives & Manuscripts, Minnesota Historical Society.

Major-General John Pope letter to Henry Sibley dated September 28, 1862, Dakota Conflict of 1862, Manuscripts Collections, Minnesota Historical Society.

Major-General John Pope letter to Brigadier-General Henry Sibley dated April 30, 1864, Military letters, Military District of Minnesota, 1863–1866, from the Division of Archives & Manuscripts, Minnesota Historical Society.

Major-General John Pope letter to Brigadier-General Henry Sibley dated May 26, 1864, Military letters, Military District of Minnesota, 1863–1866, from the Division of Archives & Manuscripts, Minnesota Historical Society.

Major-General John Pope letter to Brigadier-General Henry Sibley dated September 2, 1864, Military letters, Military District of Minnesota, 1863–1866, from the Division of Archives & Manuscripts, Minnesota Historical Society.

Ellen Parks Porter, "Early Days in Minnesota [Blue Earth County]," Dictated to her daughter, Stella Porter Clague at Washington, D.C., 1924.

Statement of David Price, Dakota Conflict of 1862, Manuscripts Collections, Microfilm Edition, Reel 2, Minnesota Historical Society.

Francis Paul Prucha, "The Army Post on the Minnesota Frontier," University of Minnesota, 1947, Thesis, Minnesota Historical Society.

Alexander Ramsey letter to President Abraham Lincoln dated November 28, 1862, Abraham Lincoln Papers, A Collaborative Project Library of Congress Manuscript Division and Lincoln Studies Center, Knox College.

Stephen R. Riggs letter to President Abraham Lincoln dated November 17, 1862, Abraham Lincoln Papers, A Collaborative Project Library of Congress Manuscript Division and Lincoln Studies Center, Knox College.

Stephen R. Riggs letter to President Abraham Lincoln dated November 21, 1862, Abraham Lincoln Papers, A Collaborative Project Library of Congress Manuscript Division and Lincoln Studies Center, Knox College.

Reverend Stephen Riggs undated letter to the editor of the *St. Paul Pioneer*.

Thomas A. Robertson reminiscence, Dakota Conflict of 1862, Manuscripts Collections, Microfilm Edition, Reel 3, Minnesota Historical Society.

Mrs. Peter Rodange, "A Midnight Ride and a Battle with Sioux Indians in Meeker County," Dakota Conflict of 1862, Manuscripts Collections, Microfilm Edition, Reel 1, Minnesota Historical Society.

Paul Rosendahl Diaries, Dakota Conflict of 1862, Manuscripts Collections, Microfilm Edition, Reel 1, Minnesota Historical Society.

M.P. Satterlee, "Philander Prescott," unpublished manuscript, Brown County Historical Society, New Ulm.

Satterlee, Marion P., "The Massacre at Sacred Heart," Dakota Conflict of 1862, Manuscripts Collections, Microfilm Edition, Reel 2, Minnesota Historical Society.

W.E. Seelye reminiscence, Dakota Conflict of 1862, Manuscripts Collections, Microfilm Edition, Reel 3, Minnesota Historical Society.

James L. Semsler, "The Dakota Indian: His Culture and his Religion," unpublished M.A. Thesis, Andover Newton Theological School, Newton Center, Massachusetts, 1955.

Henry H. Sibley Papers, Manuscript Collections and Government Records, Minnesota Historical Society.

Colonel Henry Sibley letter to Assistant Secretary of the Interior dated December 19, 1862, Dakota Conflict of 1862, Manuscripts Collections, Minnesota Historical Society.

General Henry Sibley letter to Headquarters, District of Minnesota, Department of the Northwest, dated September 2, 1863, Military letters, Military District of Minnesota, 1863–1866, from the Division of Archives & Manuscripts, Minnesota Historical Society.

Colonel Henry Sibley letter to his wife dated October 17, 1862, Dakota Conflict of 1862, Manuscripts Collections, Minnesota Historical Society.

General Henry Sibley letter to Major-General John Pope dated January 25, 1864, Military letters, Military District of Minnesota, 1863–1866, from the Division of Archives & Manuscripts, Minnesota Historical Society.

Brigadier-General Henry Sibley letter to Major-General John Pope dated February 11, 1864, Military letters, Military District of Minnesota, 1863–1866, from the Division of Archives & Manuscripts, Minnesota Historical Society.

Brigadier-General Henry Sibley letter to Major-General John Pope dated February 16, 1864, Military letters, Military District of Minnesota, 1863–1866, from the Division of Archives & Manuscripts, Minnesota Historical Society.

Brigadier-General Henry Sibley letter to Major-General John Pope dated March 21, 1864, Military letters, Military District of Minnesota, 1863–1866, from the Division of Archives & Manuscripts, Minnesota Historical Society.

Brigadier-General Henry Sibley letter to Major-General John Pope dated April 9, 1864, Military letters, Military District of Minnesota, 1863–1866, from the Division of Archives & Manuscripts, Minnesota Historical Society.

Brigadier-General Henry Sibley letter to Major-General John Pope dated May 18, 1864, Military letters, Military District of Minnesota, 1863–1866, from the Division of Archives & Manuscripts, Minnesota Historical Society.

Brigadier-General Henry Sibley letter to Major-General John Pope dated May 23, 1864, Military letters, Military District of Minnesota, 1863–1866, from the Division of Archives & Manuscripts, Minnesota Historical Society.

Brigadier-General Henry Sibley letter to Major-General John Pope dated September 9, 1864, Military letters, Military District of Minnesota, 1863–1866, from the Division of Archives & Manuscripts, Minnesota Historical Society.

Charles F. Sims, November 1864, Minnesota pioneer sketches; from the personal recollections and observations of a pioneer resident with the Indians in the Badlands, Library of Congress.

"Sioux Uprising—The Attacks Upon Fort Ridgely, Lieutenant Gere's Account," Manuscripts Collections, Brown County Historical Society, New Ulm.

"Sioux Uprising—The Battle of Birch Coulie, *The St. Paul Pioneer-Democrat* Account," Brown County Historical Society, New Ulm.

"Sioux Uprising—The Battle of Birch Coulie, Brilliant Narrative of Judge [James J.] Egan," Brown County Historical Society, New Ulm.

"Sioux Uprising—The Battle of Birch Coulie, Captain H.P. Grant's Version," Brown County Historical Society, New Ulm.

"Sioux Uprising—The Battle of Birch Coulie, Official Report of Col. McPhail," Brown County Historical Society, New Ulm.

"Sioux Uprising—The Battle of Wood Lake, Report of Lt. Col. [William] Marshall," Manuscript Collections, Brown County Historical Society.

"Sioux Uprising—The Battle of Wood Lake, Official Report of Colonel [Henry] Sibley," Manuscript Collections, Brown County Historical Society.

"Sioux Uprising—Early Rumblings at the Upper Agency. Lieut. Gere's Account of the Disturbances," Brown County Historical Society, New Ulm

"Sioux Uprising—The Encounter at Redwood Ferry, Sergeant [John F.] Bishop's Story of the Disaster," Manuscripts Collections, Brown County Historical Society.

"Sioux Uprising—The Battles of New Ulm, An Account written by Sheriff (Charles) Roos," Manuscript Collections, Brown County Historical Society.

L.D. Smith letter to Messrs. Burbank dated August 25, 1862, *Pioneer & Democrat*, August 28, 1862.

"Snana's Story," Dakota Uprising of 1862, Minnesota Historical Society, Collected Manuscripts and Government Records, Microfilm Edition.

St. Paul Pioneer Press, August 1887, "Sioux Uprising—The Battle of Birch Coulie, First Publication of the Grant Account," Brown County Historical Society, New Ulm.

St. Paul Pioneer Press, September 1, 1887, "Sioux Uprising—The Battle of Birch Coulie Recollections of Survivors," Brown County Historical Society, New Ulm.

Thomas R. Stewart Papers, Manuscripts Collections, Minnesota Historical Society.

John Henry Strong, "A Journal of the Northwestern Indian Expedition under General Sully," Dakota Conflict of 1862, Manuscripts Collections, Microfilm Edition, Reel 3, Minnesota Historical Society.

Roger Avery Stubbs, Milton and Elizabeth Turnham Stubbs.

Rosanna Sturgis letter to her husband William Sturgis dated October 8, 1862, Dakota Conflict of 1862, Manuscripts Collections, Microfilm Edition, Reel 1, Minnesota Historical Society.

Marie Swallow, editor, A collection of materials on the Story of Stevens Point, compiled in 1927-1928. Portage County Historical Society.

J.H. Swan, "Sioux Uprising—The Battle of Birch Coulie: Dispute over Who was in Command," Brown County Historical Society, New Ulm.

Solomon Taylor statement taken by Thomas J. Hughes, Dakota Conflict of 1862, Manuscripts Collections, Microfilm Edition, Reel 2, Minnesota Historical Society.

Statement of David Thomas, Dakota Conflict of 1862, Manuscripts Collections, Microfilm Edition, Reel 2, Minnesota Historical Society.

Clark W. Thompson letter to Governor Alexander Ramsey dated June 14, 1862, "Sioux Uprising—Early Rumblings at the Upper Agency: Official Requests for Troops," Brown County Historical Society, New Ulm.

U.S. Army Mounted Rangers Orders issued July 5, 1863 by R.C. Olin by Command of General Henry Sibley, Manuscripts Collections, Minnesota Historical Society.

J. Vander Horck letter dated August 25, 1862, *Pioneer & Democrat*, August 28, 1862.

Oscar G. Wall, "A Woman in Battle," Fort Ridgely—Tributes to Dr. and Eliza Muller, Fort Ridgely Archives.

Oscar Garret Wall Diary for July 20, 1863, Manuscript Collections, North Dakota Historical Society.

Oscar Garret Wall Diary for July 24, 1863, Manuscript Collections, North Dakota Historical Society.

Oscar Garrett Wall Diary for July 28, 1863, Manuscript Collections, North Dakota Historical Society.

Oscar Garrett Wall Diary for July 29, 1863, Manuscript Collections, North Dakota Historical Society.

Statement of Mrs. Stephen Walters. Dakota Conflict of 1862, Manuscripts Collections, Microfilm Edition, Reel 2, Minnesota Historical Society.

Edward A. Washburn letter to his father dated April 21, 1857, Edward and William Washburn Papers, Minnesota Historical Society.

Amos B. Watson, "Reminiscences of the Sioux Outbreak," Dakota Conflict of 1862, Manuscripts Collections, Microfilm Edition, Reel 3, Minnesota Historical Society.

JOHN KOBLAS

Letter, or diary entry of Loren Webb—August 1862, Minnesota (found among loose-leafed papers of the Platonian Literary Society "Old Plato," McKendree College [Archives], Lebanon, Illinois), from McKendree College Archives McKendree College Lebanon, Illinois, Transcribed by Jonathan Webb Deiss, archival assistance provided by Dr. Mark Young, Historian and Archivist at McKendree, 28 September 2001.

Harry B. West letter to Minnesota Tourism Bureau dated July 29, 1933, Dakota Conflict of 1862, Manuscripts Collection, Minnesota Historical Society.

Bishop Henry B. Whipple letter to Editor of *Republican Pioneer*, November 1862.

George F. Whitcomb letter to George Bradley dated July 18, 1933, Dakota Conflict of 1862, Manuscripts Collections, Microfilm Edition, Reel 3, Minnesota Historical Society

Wilkes Family Papers, Special Collections, Duke University.

G.E. Williams Diary for July 15, 1863, Manuscript Collections, North Dakota Historical Society.

G.E. Williams Diary for July 21, 1863, Manuscript Collections, North Dakota Historical Society.

G.E. William Diary for July 22, 1863, Manuscript Collections, North Dakota Historical Society.

G.E. Williams Diary for July 24, 1863, Manuscript Collections, North Dakota Historical Society.

G.E. Williams Diary for July 25, 1863, Manuscript Collections, North Dakota Historical Society.

G.E. Williams Diary for July 26, 1863, Manuscript Collections, North Dakota Historical Society.

G.E. Williams Diary for July 28, 1863, Manuscript Collections, North Dakota Historical Society.

G.E. Williams Diary for July 29, 1863, Manuscript Collections, North Dakota Historical Society.

G.E. Williams Diary for July 30, 1863, Manuscript Collections, North Dakota Historical Society.

G.E. Williams Diary for July 31, 1863, Manuscript Collections, North Dakota Historical Society.

Jane L. Williamson letter to Stephen R. Riggs dated November 14, 1862, Abraham Lincoln Papers, A Collaborative Project Library of Congress Manuscript Division and Lincoln Studies Center, Knox College.

Thomas S. Williamson letter to T.J. Galbraith dated June 2, 1862, "Sioux Uprising—Early Rumblings at the Upper Agency Letter of Dr. Thomas Williamson," Brown County Historical Society, New Ulm.

Dr. Thomas S. Williamson letter to Reverend Stephen Riggs dated November 24, 1862.

Sally Wood letter to her brother dated August 26, 1862, Dakota Conflict of 1862, Manuscripts Collections, Microfilm Edition, Reel 3, Minnesota Historical Society.

"Elizabeth Zimmerman—My Grandmother—A Pioneer," unpublished manuscript in Fort Ridgely archives.

Newspapers

The American Missionary, October 1883, Volume 37, Issue 10, pp. 290-291.

Big Stone Headlight (Big Stone City, South Dakota), December 29, 1904.

Rogers, Ken, "When Custer Fell," Voices from the Little Bighorn Special Edition, Bismarck, *Bismarck Tribune*, 1996.

Bismarck Tribune, November 21, 1877.

Black Hills Visitor, Spring 2005.

Boston Daily Courier, August 15, 1863

Columbus (Georgia) *Inquirer*, February 10, 1835.

Davenport Daily Gazette, September 17, 1862.

Decorah Journal, 1882.

Detroit Lakes Tribune, June 25, 1925.

Eau Claire Leader, August 15, 1925.

Fairfax Standard, 1912.

Fort Dodge, Iowa, *Messenger* February 18-25, 1957.

Fort Dodge Sentinel, September 10, 1857.

Henderson Democrat, April 16, 1857; May 7, 1857.

White, Lonnie J., "The Hancock and Custer Expeditions of 1867," *Journal of the West*, Los Angeles, v. 5, No. 3, July, 1966.

Junction City Weekly Union, March 30, June 1, 1867.

Lakefield Standard, December 7, 1895; December 14, 1895; January 4, 1896; January 11, 1896; January 18, 1896; February 1, 1896; February 8, 1896; February 15, 1896.

Mankato Independent, October 27, 1857; June 26, 1858; July 3, 1858; July 10, 1858; October 21, 1858; December 23, 1858; January 20, 1859; April 7, 1859; August 6, 1859; May 9, 1861; May 23, 1861; June 17, 1861; June 20, 1861.

Mankato Free Press, January 28, 1931; February 10, 1931; March 27, 1931; May 25, 1931; July 20, 1931; July 21, 1931; July 23, 1931; July 24, 1931; August 20, 1931; August 21, 1931; September 25, 1931; September 28, 1931; April 21, 1961.

Mankato Record, July 5, 1859.

Mankato Review, October 18, 1862; July 25, 1894; August 1, 1894; March 12, 1919.

Minneapolis Journal, 1924 (exact date unknown); October 14, 1927.

Minneapolis Star, April 13, 1956.

Minneapolis Times, April 13, 1857.

Minneapolis Tribune, April 26, 1888.

Minnesota Pioneer & Democrat, March 26, 1857; April 11, 1857; April 18, 1857; April 21, 1857; April 24, 1857; May 16, 1857; February 17, 1859; December 6, 1859; August 20, 1862; August 21, 1862; August 22, 1862; August 23, 1862; August 24, 1862; August 26, 1862; August 27, 1862; August 28, 1862; August 29, 1862, August 30, 1862; August 31, 1862; September 5, 1862; September 6, 1862.

The Missionary Herald, June 1849.

Morton Enterprise, January 29, 1909; July 8, 1926; July 15, 1926; July 29, 1926; August 5, 1926; August 19, 1926; October 9, 1930.

New Ulm Journal, September 6, 1938; June 30, 1940; June 26, 1962.

New York Herald, Date unknown.

New York Herald, July 1876.

Pipestone County Star, April 10, 1997.

Redwood Gazette, May 4, 1910.

Rochester Post-Bulletin, January 29, 1985.

Rogers, Ken, "Custer Considered Victory a Certainty," *Voices from the Little Bighorn* Special Edition.

Sauk Centre Herald, April 22, 2003.

St. Cloud Democrat, August 21, 1862.

St. Paul Daily Press, August 24, 1862.

St. Paul Minnesotan, October 14, 1862;

St. Paul Pioneer Press, June 25, 1857; August 28, 1862; July 4, 1893; August 20, 1902.

St. Peter Tribune, August 13, 1862.

Tracy Headlight-Herald, Lake Shetek Massacre Edition, 2nd section, Vol. 80, Aug. 16, 1962

Winona Sunday News, November 14, 1876.

The Wright County Eagle (Delano), February 17, 1881.

Interviews

Henry Has Holy interview with Henry Murphy, Shields, North Dakota, 1926-1928, Manuscript Collections, Microfilm Edition, North Dakota Historical Society.

Fred Lammers, 1930 Interview, Fairfax, Minnesota, Brown County Historical Society, New Ulm.

Elizabeth Whitcomb interview with Irene Persons, Friday, June 11, 1937 at the Home for Aged Women, 3201 First Avenue South, Minneapolis, Dakota Conflict of 1862, Manuscripts Collections, Microfilm Editions, Reel 3, Minnesota Historical Society.

Public Documents and Records

The Association for the Preservation of Virginia Antiquities, Internet.

The Civil War Archive, Union Regimental Histories, Minnesota First Regiment Cavalry "Mounted Rangers."

Great Lakes Indian Fish and Wildlife Commission, 1995, A Guide to Understanding Chippewa Treaty Rights: Minnesota Edition, July, Odanah, Wisconsin.

Hadley, James A., "The Death of Lieutenant Kidder," Indian Depredations and Battles, Clippings, Volume I.

Robert Hakewaste, "Evidence for the Defendants," The Sisseton and Wahpeton Bands of Dakota or Sioux Indians v. the United States, 1901-1907, U.S. Court of Claims No. 22524, Part 2.

Indian Affairs: Laws and Treaties. Vol. II (Treaties), Compiled and edited by Charles J. Kappler, Washington: Government Printing Office, 1904.

Josephine County (Oregon) Historical Society Archives.

Kansas State Historical Society; Report of the Secretary of War, 1867, 40 Cong., 2 sess., Ser. No. 1324.

Mallery, Garrick, Picture Writing of the American Indians, 10th Annual Report of the Bureau of American Ethnology (1893).

Meeker County Historical Society.

Minnesota Department of Transportation.

Mormon Trails Association.

National Archives, accessioned in the Department of the West, February 13, 1855; Washington, D.C., Roll 11, No FM 95, Record Group 48, General Services Administration.

Ohio Historical Society Archives.

Paynesville Historical Society.

Reports of Major General W. S. Hancock Upon Indian Affairs, With Accompanying Exhibits; Difficulties With Indian Tribes, 41st Cong., 2d Sess., House-Exec. Doc. No. 240 (Serial 1425).

South Dakota State Historical Society Historical Collections Vol. 27.

Teachers Manual (K-6) which were developed for the American Indian Curriculum Development Program of United Tribes Technical College.

War of the Rebellion, a Compilation of the Official Records of the Union and Confederate Armies, Government Printing Office, Washington, D.C., 1880, Courtesy of Cornell University Digital Library Project.

Washington University Library Archives.

Index